METHODIST
SECONDARY EDUCATION

METHODIST
SECONDARY EDUCATION

*A History of the Contribution of Methodism
to Secondary Education in the United Kingdom*

By

F. C. PRITCHARD
M.A., Ph.D.

LONDON : THE EPWORTH PRESS

PUBLISHED BY

THE EPWORTH PRESS
(FRANK H. CUMBERS)

25-35 CITY ROAD, LONDON, E.C.

| New York | . | Toronto |
| Melbourne | . | Cape Town |

★

PRINTED AND BOUND IN ENGLAND BY
HAZELL WATSON & VINEY LTD
AYLESBURY LONDON

TO THE
MEMORY OF
MY FATHER
TO WHOM I OWE
SO MUCH

Preface

EDUCATION is a vital part of Methodist work, but only one book has so far been published on the subject—*John Wesley and Education*, by Alfred H. Body, M.A.—and though there is in that book a concluding chapter on the educational legacy of Wesley, the story is carried only as far as the close of the eighteenth century. Henry Cloke, M.A., too, dealt with the contribution of Methodism to national education, but his work, though it can be seen in the University of London Library of Theses, has not been published. There is, in fact, a gap in Methodist history, and I have tried to fill that gap as far as secondary education is concerned. After completing my own work, I learned that the Rev. H. F. Mathews, M.A., B.D., was preparing a book on Methodist elementary education. To some extent, therefore, his book and mine are complementary.

I am indebted to the late Rev. A. W. Harrison, M.C., B.A., B.Sc., D.D., for his help and encouragement when I began this work. It was he who first interested me in historical research, and to him and to many other ministers and laymen I am grateful for guidance and for the introductions they have given me to the by-ways of Methodist history by the loan of letters, diaries, and papers.

The extracts from Wesley's *Works* are taken from the Third Edition, 1829.

Not least, I am indebted to my wife for her patience, interest, and encouragement, which made it possible for me to complete a work which war interrupted.

F. C. P.

CHESTERFIELD
May 1949

Note

Throughout this work reference to John Wesley's own works are shown under three headings, as follows:

JOURNAL   Page references are those of the Standard Edition, edited by Nehemiah Curnock and published by The Epworth Press (1938—Bicentenary Issue).

LETTERS   Page references are those of the Standard Edition, edited by John Telford and published by The Epworth Press (1931).

WORKS   References to sermons and matters other than the *Journal* and *Letters* are those of the Third Edition of *John Wesley's Works,* published by the Methodist Bookroom (John Mason, 1829)—the earliest edition with the final corrections of the author.

References to the writers of other works are made in full, giving author and title. A list of the works consulted and quoted is appended at the end of this work.

Contents

Appendices

CONTENTS

CHAPTER ONE

John Wesley's Educational Theory

ALFRED H. BODY, in his *John Wesley and Education*, has pointed out the importance of realizing what is owed to John Wesley's own theories of education if a true estimate is to be made of the work done by Methodist schools during the past hundred and fifty years.

Methodism owes its inspiration and its fundamental organization entirely to John Wesley. His conversion—the incident of the warmed heart as a result of what he heard in a room in Aldersgate Street—is a household story in Methodist circles; but to understand Wesley's work for education, a work on which the future structure of Methodist education was built, it is necessary to know, not only the facts of his conversion, but something, too, of the events which led up to it. We know that from that time onward he taught a doctrine of 'justification by faith', but such a phrase means little in a study of education. It is necessary to translate the phrase into terms of everyday life and to appreciate what it meant in the first half of the eighteenth century. Briefly stated, justification by faith means the formation of a link between God and man through spiritual realization or awakening. It emphasizes the fact that God is a Father who sent His Son to this world to save humanity. Christ's death brought release from the punishment of sin to all peoples. Even the most hardened criminal, once he had become convinced of his sin and convinced of what Christ's death meant to him personally, was saved. He became happy. It was this which was repugnant to the clergy of the eighteenth century, for they felt that righteousness could only be attained by long service and by 'much painful exercise'. Righteousness to them was a treasure which could be amassed slowly, but could not be obtained, as it were, by a sudden gift from God. The gold-standard of religion was being debased by over-production when the lowliest and most depraved character in the country could attain to righteousness by sudden revelation. These were the views which caused the vehement attacks made on Wesley and his preachers at the birth of Methodism. Wesley taught that righteousness was a treasure not laboriously stored up on earth,

11

scious that Christ had died for him—not for the world and for society in general, but for him personally, and therein lies the keynote of Methodist doctrine. It is a personal religion, and it was just that personal touch between God and man which was so needed to revive the dulled spirits of the working classes in the eighteenth century. Wesley and his preachers went about the country telling people of this new outlook on religion in a way that brought that religion into their everyday life. It was not something to be understood only by saints and martyrs standing aloof from the world, nor was it a hope of salvation to be eagerly grasped only by those lying on their death-beds. It gave joy and a sense of kinship with God to the most depraved character who was conscious of his sin and sincerely repented of his wrong-doing. Wesley taught people of all ages, educated them, but he did so primarily only in one subject—religion. Gradually, as an appreciation of what this religion meant spread from the poorer classes to the middle classes, there came a demand for a wider form of education. In the first days of Methodism, the Connexion was fully occupied in teaching the Gospel, and in educating adults in religion as it affected them personally. When schools were established by the Connexion, they were Sunday- and day-schools for young children, and all the emphasis was placed on religious instruction. The three R's were taught only in so far as they were needed to assist that teaching of religion. That was the pivot round which all early Methodist education centred. But later, when shopkeepers and small employers began to be drawn into Methodism, difficulties arose. It had been possible to instil by emotional appeal the personal message of Methodism into minds practically devoid of the intellectual power to reason. It was not so possible to give the simple personal message to people who had learned to think, still less was it possible to give it to those who had received a fair education and who had read the classics and become interested in politics and social problems. Wesley's followers did not always appreciate this. They had been educated as preachers by Wesley himself, and he had been educated at Charterhouse and Oxford. There was a crying need for men with academic qualifications similar to those of Wesley, but there was nowhere to obtain the training. The Methodists and dissenters were barred from Oxford and Cambridge and the great public schools.[6] The standard of scholarship amongst the leaders

[6] *Wesley: the Man, his Teaching, and his Work*, p. 251. This work is

of the Methodist Connexion fell off for a time after Wesley's
death, and, until Jabez Bunting reached the peak of his reputation, Adam Clarke was the only man whose name was known
for scholarship outside Methodism. During Wesley's lifetime
he was assisted by fellow priests of the Established Church—
men of good education like himself; but after his death, these
friends tended to revert to the Established Church as leaders of
the Evangelical party, and the Methodist preachers failed, for
lack of opportunity, to reach a cultural standard equal to theirs.
The preaching of the early Methodist ministers showed an
evangelical spirit of emotional appeal rather than a spirit of
logical argument. Quite apart from the needs of the laity, the
preachers themselves needed schools where they could receive
higher education.

It is necessary, however, to return to Wesley and what his
conversion meant to him. After the experience in Aldersgate
Street, he had no clear idea of what he ought to do or what
changes were necessary in his outward life. Praying, thinking,
conversing, he was unable to obtain that joy of which the
Moravians had so often spoken. It was natural that he should
turn to them for further help in finding that joy, and he determined to visit Germany. 'I hoped the conversing with those
holy men who were themselves living witnesses of the full power
of faith, and yet able to bear with those that are weak, would
be a means, under God, of so establishing my soul, that
I might go on from faith to faith and "from strength to
strength".' [7]

He went to Germany. He joined in their services and prayers.
He conversed privately with leaders and students of the Moravian community, and it is an interesting and significant fact that
the first mention of the words 'brethren' and 'sisters' occurring
in Wesley's *Journal* is found in that section which deals with this
visit to Germany. The custom of addressing each other as
'brother' and 'sister' is dying out today, but it has been a feature
of Methodism, and it is one of the outward signs of that family
attitude toward religion by which Wesley was first influenced
in his relationships with the Moravians. If God is a Father,
then all men are brothers. What that meant to the social life
of the eighteenth century can be imagined. It explains, too, the

frequently referred to in the following pages. It is a collection of Sermons
and Addresses given at City Road Chapel during the Centenary Commemoration of Wesley's death, published by Charles H. Kelly (London, 1891).
[7] *Journal*, Vol. I, p. 483.

Christ; that all men are members of one family of whom God is the Father.

It would be wrong to suppose that Wesley worked out and drew up a carefully organized scheme of education. He did not even work out the constitution of Methodism in detail. He could not, for Methodism was a growing organism. Such details could only be the outcome of years of experience, each development issuing from the previous step, not envisaged as an ideal and finished whole from the beginning. The only ideal scheme of organization which Wesley did possess was his picture of the relation between God and man. That was the underlying theme on which the development of Methodism was based. Quintillian, Plato, Comenius, and other educational theorists developed their theories of education, and left them clear-cut for succeeding generations. Wesley did not do that, and because of this the educational side of his work has tended to be neglected. 'The evangelistic side of the history of Methodism is properly so prominent and so truly marvellous that it eclipses in some measure its educational spirit.' [11] But the spirit was there and, as will be noticed later, John Wesley was interested in education before he had the experience in Aldersgate Street. Before his conversion he was interested in the education of the young; afterwards, the whole world became his parish, and the whole of humanity was a potential school. His conversion gave him that idea of universality, and he came to realize that a revival of religion and an awakening of religious conscience can only be complete if special efforts are made to train children. It has been said that Wesley was utterly unsuited to train children. This statement is belied by an incident that occurred in Georgia —an incident which suggests a very real insight into the child mind.

When Delamotte, Wesley's companion in Georgia, founded a boys' school in that country, there was an outbreak of juvenile snobbery such as is not infrequently seen in schools. The pupils who were too poor to wear stockings or shoes became the butts of the more fortunate. Delamotte tried and failed to put an end to this undesirable social distinction, and at last consulted Wesley, who agreed to do what he could. The following Monday, to the surprise of the boys in Delamotte's school, Wesley entered the classroom in bare feet and proceeded to teach in the usual manner. Before a week had passed, not only had criticism of

[11] J. T. Slugg, *Woodhouse Grove School*, p. 10.

the barefooted ceased, but some of the erstwhile stockinged feet had taken to bare feet! [12]

That example of practical education was delivered by one who has been accused of not understanding the first thing about the working of the child mind. The truth is that Wesley, had he been a schoolmaster, would have been a good one, for he combined the common sense so necessary for dealing with children with the careful study of theory. We have evidence of Wesley's popularity with children and of his realization of their place in society when at Raithby, Oldham, Yeadon, Bolton, and Stockton-on-Tees they flocked around him and sat on the pulpit steps. Speaking of them, Wesley wrote: 'The fire kindled and ran from heart to heart, till few, if any, were unaffected. Is not this a new thing in the earth? God begins His work in children. Thus it has been also in Cornwall, Manchester, and Epworth.' [13] These words explain his attitude to the strange 'revivals' which took place at Kingswood and elsewhere amongst the pupils, and which will be dealt with later.

Though Wesley was not primarily a child educationist, during the course of his work it was borne in upon him that it was of no avail merely to educate the adult members of the spiritual family. In one of his sermons he said:

'You should particularly endeavour to instruct your children, early, plainly, frequently, and patiently. Instruct them *early,* from the first hour that you perceive reason begins to dawn. Truth may then begin to shine upon the mind far earlier than we are apt to suppose. And whoever watches the first openings of the understanding may, by little and little, supply fit matter for it to work upon, and may turn the eye of the soul toward good things, as well as toward bad or trifling ones. Whenever a child begins to speak, you may be assured reason begins to work. I know no cause why a parent should not just then begin to speak of the best things, the things of God. And from that time no opportunity should be lost of instilling all truths as they are capable of receiving.' [14]

During the greater part of the eighteenth century John Locke was the greatest formative factor in educational theory, and this quotation from the *Works,* in addition to much of the actual organization of Kingswood School, is evidence that Wesley

---

[12] *Methodist Magazine* (1808), Vol. XXXI, p. 490.
[13] *Journal*, Vol. VI, p. 514. See also ibid., p. 124.
[14] *Works*, Vol. VII, p. 81.

found much that was good in Locke's teaching, even though he never acknowledged any debt to that philosopher.[15]

Wesley believed that the foundation of a good education could only be laid in the home long before a child was old enough to attend any sort of school. We do not know exactly when the theory of education first began to interest Wesley, but in his *Plain Account of Kingswood School,*[16] which he published in 1781, he recalled how, about forty years before, one or two tracts upon education came into his hands, and how these led him to consider educational methods, especially those at Charterhouse where he himself had been educated. When Wesley visited the Moravian community at Herrnhut, he had some hours of talk with Christian David and others of the brethren there, and this talk made so great an impression upon him that he immediately afterwards wrote down its substance.[17] The name of John Amos Comenius (1592–1670) was mentioned. Comenius was the last bishop of the Moravians, but is best remembered today as an educationist. In the course of the conversations at Herrnhut the organization of education in the Moravian community was discussed. It is impossible to believe that Wesley did not later, if not at that time, consider the writings of Comenius on education. This is supposition, but we do know that among the educational works with which Wesley was conversant were Milton's *Tractate on Education* and John Locke's *Essay concerning Human Understanding.*[18] But mere theory did not satisfy him. All too clearly, by considering the schools of his day, did he see the difference between theory and practice.

He turned therefore to one whom he knew to be a practical educationist—his own mother; and, because it was from her more than from any other single source that we believe Wesley drew his educational theory and practice, the letter which Susanna Wesley wrote at her son's request is printed here in full.

July 24, 1732.

'DEAR SON,

'According to your desire, I have collected the principal rules I observed in educating my family; which I now send you as they occurred to my mind, and you may (if you think they

---

[15] For a careful examination of this matter, see A. H. Body's *John Wesley and Education,* pp. 56–61.
[16] *Works,* Vol. XIII, pp. 255–67.
[17] *Journal,* Vol. II, pp. 28–36.
[18] See *Works,* Vol. XIII, pp. 262, 416–25.

can be of use to any) dispose of them in what order you please.

'The children were always put into a regular method of living, in such things as they were capable of, from their birth: as in dressing, undressing, changing their linen, etc. The first quarter commonly passes in sleep. After that they were, if possible, laid into their cradles awake, and rocked to sleep; and so they were kept rocking till it was time for them to awake. This was done to bring them to a regular course of sleeping; which at first was three hours in the morning and three in the afternoon; afterwards two hours, till they needed none at all.

'When turned a year old (and some before), they were taught to fear the rod, and to cry softly; by which means they escaped abundance of correction they might otherwise have had, and that most odious noise of the crying of children was rarely heard in the house, but the family usually lived in as much quietness as if there had not been a child among them.

'As soon as they were grown pretty strong, they were confined to three meals a day. At dinner their little table and chairs were set by ours, where they could be overlooked; and they were suffered to eat and drink (small beer) as much as they would; but not to call for anything. If they wanted aught they used to whisper to the maid which attended them, who came and spake to me; and as soon as they could handle a knife and fork, they were set to our table. They were never suffered to choose their meat, but always made eat such things as were provided for the family.

'Mornings they had always spoon-meat; sometimes at nights. But whatever they had, they were never permitted to eat at those meals of more than one thing; and of that sparingly enough. Drinking or eating between meals was never allowed, unless in case of sickness; which seldom happened. Nor were they suffered to go into the kitchen to ask anything of the servants when they were at meat; if it was known they did, they were certainly beat, and the servants severely reprimanded.

'At six, as soon as family prayers were over, they had their supper; at seven the maid washed them; and, beginning at the youngest, she undressed and got them all to bed by eight; at which time she left them in their several rooms awake—for there was no such thing allowed of in our house as sitting by a child till it fell asleep.

'They were so constantly used to eat and drink what was given them that, when any of them was ill, there was no difficulty in making them take the most unpleasant medicine; for they durst not refuse it, though some of them would presently throw it up. This I mention to show that a person may be taught to take anything, though it be never so much against his stomach.

'In order to form the minds of children, the first thing to be done is to conquer their will, and bring them to an obedient temper. To inform the understanding is a work of time, and must with children proceed by slow degrees as they are able to bear it; but the subjecting the will is a thing that must be done at once, and the sooner the better. For, by neglecting timely correction, they will contract a stubbornness and obstinacy which is hardly ever after conquered; and never, without using such severity as would be as painful to me as to the child. In the esteem of the world they pass for kind and indulgent whom I call cruel parents, who permit their children to get habits which they know must be afterwards broken. Nay, some are so stupidly fond as in sport to teach their children to do things which in a while after they have severely beaten them for doing. Whenever a child is corrected, it must be conquered; and this will be no hard matter to do if it be not grown headstrong by too much indulgence. And when the will of a child is totally subdued, and it is brought to revere and stand in awe of the parents, then a great many childish follies and inadvertences may be passed by. Some should be overlooked and taken no notice of, and others mildly reproved; but no wilful transgression ought ever to be forgiven children without chastisement, less or more, as the nature and circumstances of the offence require.

'I insist upon conquering the will of children betimes, because this is the only strong and rational foundation of a religious education, without which both precept and example will be ineffectual. But when this is thoroughly done, then a child is capable of being governed by the reason and piety of its parents, till its own understanding comes to maturity, and the principles of religion have taken root in the mind.

'I cannot yet dismiss this subject. As self-will is the root of all sin and misery, so whatever cherishes this in children ensures their after-wretchedness and irreligion; whatever checks and mortifies it promotes their future happiness and piety. This is still more evident if we farther consider that religion is nothing else than the doing the will of God, and not our own; that, the one grand impediment to our temporal and eternal happiness being this self-will, no indulgences of it can be trivial, no denial

22

unprofitable. Heaven or hell depends on this alone. So that the parent who studies to subdue it in his child works together with God in the renewing and saving a soul. The parent who indulges it does the devil's work, makes religion impracticable, salvation unattainable; and does all that in him lies to damn his child, soul and body, for ever.

'The children of this family were taught, as soon as they could speak, the Lord's Prayer, which they were made to say at rising and bed-time constantly; to which, as they grew bigger, were added a short prayer for their parents, and some collects; a short catechism, and some portions of Scripture, as their memories could bear.

'They were very early made to distinguish the Sabbath from other days, before they could well speak or go. They were as soon taught to be still at family prayers, and to ask a blessing immediately after, which they used to do by signs, before they could kneel or speak.

'They were quickly made to understand they might have nothing they cried for, and instructed to speak handsomely for what they wanted. They were not suffered to ask even the lowest servant for aught without saying, "Pray give me such a thing"; and the servant was chid if she ever let them omit that word. Taking God's name in vain, cursing and swearing, profaneness, obscenity, rude, ill-bred names, were never heard among them. Nor were they ever permitted to call each other by their proper names without the addition of Brother or Sister.

'None of them were taught to read till five years old, except Kezzy, in whose case I was overruled; and she was more years learning than any of the rest had been months. The way of teaching was this: the day before a child began to learn, the house was set in order, every one's work appointed them, and a charge given that none should come into the room from nine till twelve, or from two till five; which, you know, were our school hours. One day was allowed the child wherein to learn its letters; and each of them did in that time know all its letters, great and small, except Molly and Nancy, who were a day and a half before they knew them perfectly; for which I then thought them very dull; but since I have observed how long many children are learning the horn-book, I have changed my opinion. But the reason why I thought them so then was because the rest learned so readily; and your brother Samuel, who was the first child I ever taught, learned the alphabet in a few hours. He was five years old on the 10th of February; the next day he began to learn; and, as soon as he knew the letters, began at the first chapter of Genesis. He was taught to spell the first verse, then to read it over and over, till he could read it off-hand without any hesitation; so on to the second, etc., till he took ten verses for a lesson, which he quickly did. Easter fell low that year; and by Whitsuntide he could read a chapter very well; for he read continually, and had such a prodigious memory that I cannot remember ever to have told him the same word twice.

'What was yet stranger, any word he had learned in his lesson he knew wherever he saw it, either in his Bible or any other book; by which means he learned very soon to read an English author well.

'The same method was observed with them all. As soon as they knew the letters, they were put first to spell, and read one line, then a verse; never leaving till perfect in their lesson, were it shorter or longer. So one or other continued reading at school-time, without any intermission; and before we left school each child read what he had learned that morning; and, ere we parted in the afternoon, what they had learned that day.

'There was no such thing as loud talking or playing allowed of, but every one was kept close to their business, for the six hours of school: and it is almost incredible what a child may be taught in a quarter of a year, by a vigorous application, if it have but a tolerable capacity and good health. Every one of these, Kezzy excepted, could read better in that time than the most of women can do as long as they live.

'Rising out of their places, or going out of the room, was not permitted unless for good cause; and running into the yard, garden, or street, without leave was always esteemed a capital offence.

'For some years we went on very well. Never were children in better order. Never were children better disposed to piety or in more subjection to their parents, till that fatal dispersion of them, after the fire, into several families. In these they were left at full liberty to converse with servants, which before they had always been restrained from; and to run abroad, and play with any children, good or bad. They soon learned to neglect a strict observation of the Sabbath, and got knowledge of several songs and bad things, which before they had no notion of. That civil behaviour which made them admired when at home by all which saw them was, in great measure, lost; and a clownish accent and many rude ways were learned, which were not reformed without some difficulty.

'When the house was rebuilt, and the children all brought home, we entered upon a strict reform; and then was begun the custom of singing psalms at beginning and leaving school, morning and evening. Then also that of a general retirement at five o'clock was entered upon, when the oldest took the youngest that could speak, and the second the next, to whom they read the Psalms for the day, and a chapter in the New Testament; as, in the morning, they were directed to read the Psalms and a chapter in the Old; after which they went to their private prayers, before they got their breakfast or came in to the family. And, I thank God, this custom is still preserved among us.

'There were several by-laws observed among us, which slipped my memory, or else they had been inserted in their proper place; but I mention them here, because I think them useful.

'1. It had been observed that cowardice and fear of punishment often led children into lying, till they get a custom of it, which they cannot leave. To prevent this, a law was made, That whoever was charged with a fault, of which they were guilty, if they would ingenuously confess it, and promise to amend, should not be beaten. This rule prevented a great deal of lying, and would have done more, if one in the family would have observed it. But he could not be prevailed on, and therefore was often, imposed on by false colours and equivocations; which none would have used (except one), had they been kindly dealt with. And some, in spite of all, would always speak truth plainly.

'2. That no sinful action, as lying, pilfering, playing at church, or on the Lord's Day, disobedience, quarrelling, etc., should ever pass unpunished.

'3. That no child should ever be chid or beat twice for the same fault; and that, if they amended, they should never be upbraided with it afterwards.

'4. That every signal act of obedience, especially when it crossed upon their own inclinations, should be always commended, and frequently rewarded, according to the merits of the cause.

'5. That if ever any child performed an act of obedience, or did anything with an intention to please, though the performance was not well, yet the obedience and intention should be kindly accepted; and the child with sweetness directed how to do better for the future.

25

'6. That propriety be inviolably, preserved, and none suffered to invade the property of another in the smallest matter, though it were but of the value of a farthing or a pin; which they might not take from the owner without, much less against, his consent. This rule can never be too much inculcated on the minds of children; and from the want of parents or governors doing it as they ought proceeds that shameful neglect of justice which we may observe in the world.

'7. That promises be strictly observed; and a gift, once bestowed, and so the right passed away from the donor, be not resumed, but left to the disposal of him to whom it was given; unless it were conditional, and the condition of the obligation not performed.

'8. That no girl be taught to work till she can read very well; and then that she be kept to her work with the same application, and for the same time, that she was held to in reading. This rule also is much to be observed; for the putting children to learn sewing before they can read perfectly is the very reason why so few women can read fit to be heard, and never to be well understood.' [19]

John Wesley may have based much of his educational theory on what he saw at Herrnhut or Jena; he may have been influenced by Milton and John Locke; but in the above lengthy letter can be seen the fundamental principles of his views on education, later to be expressed in some measure at the London Foundery and at Kingswood. The fundamental principle of education on which he is totally at variance with modern educationists, and on account of which he has been severely criticized, is expressed in the following statements: 'In order to form the minds of children, the first thing to be done is, to conquer their will.' [20] And again, a little later: 'I insist upon conquering the wills of children betimes; because this is the only foundation for a religious education.' [21] Here he is unquestionably following the principles of his mother. Elsewhere he reminds parents, however, that whatever has to be done in the conquering of children's wills should be done with mildness, indeed with kindness too. [22] Whatever may appear harsh and lacking in understanding of child nature is due entirely to Wesley's own philosophy, which made him submit without question to the

---

[19] *Journal*, Vol. III, pp. 34–9. See also G. Elsie Harrison's *Son to Susanna*, Chapter 3.
[20] *Works*, Vol. VII, p. 103.   [21] ibid.   [22] ibid., p. 80.

will of God. Throughout his life that was one of the lessons which he attempted to teach to all people. In the case of children, the earthly father, or the professional educator *in loco parentis,* acts as the instrument of God. 'The will of a parent is to a little child in the place of the will of God.' [23] It was right, then, in Wesley's view that children should submit without question to that will. Wesley was no utilitarian in the usual sense of the word. He was a practical man, but he was preparing for a spiritual life after death and not for the earning of a living upon earth. Life on earth was regarded by all Methodists in the early days of the Connexion as a journey, sometimes across 'a desert drear'. The education of children was merely the start of the training for that future life. There would be hardships when the child grew to manhood. Wesley saw nothing strange in the fact that there should be hardships in childhood too. In speaking of the upbringing of children, he says: 'Let it be remembered, that I do not speak to the wild, giddy, thoughtless world, but to those that fear God. I ask, then, for what end do you send your children to school? "Why, that they may be fit to live in the world." In which world do you mean—this, or the next?' [24] It is this far-seeing outlook of Wesley's which explains the attacks made on him as an educationist. The fact that he himself recognized that this overcoming of a child's will entailed strictness and, perhaps, harshness is shown by a chance entry in his *Journal,*[25] where, speaking of Kingswood School, he wrote: 'The Rules were printed; and, notwithstanding the strictness of them, in two or three months we had twenty-eight scholars.' Instead of sublimating childish instincts, as modern educationists try to do, Wesley attempted to suppress them. Herein he is condemned by modern educationists, but that different outlook of his does not come from any abstruse psychological theory, but from his philosophy of life—a philosophy which included in its scope the life beyond death. It is neither the body nor the mind which is all-important, but the soul. 'As self-will is the root of all sin and misery, so whatever cherishes this in children, insures their after-wretchedness and irreligion; and whatever checks and mortifies it, promotes their future happiness and piety. This is still more evident, if we consider that religion is nothing else but the doing the will of God, and not our own. . . . So that the parent who

[23] *Works,* Vol. VII, p. 92.   [24] ibid., p. 83.
[25] *Journal,* Vol. III, p. 530.

studies to subdue it in his children, works together with God in the saving of a soul.' [26] In the sermon in which Wesley writes these words he is quoting almost word for word from that letter which his mother had sent him years before.

In Wesley's opinion, one of the most damaging things an educator could do was to allow the child to follow the dictates of its own will. Again and again he insists that the child's will must be conquered by the adult. That was the only safe foundation for a religious education, he believed. And it was a religious education that Wesley demanded and tried to supply. He looked in vain, however, for evidence of it in the schools of his day.[27]

All that has been said so far applies equally to primary and secondary education as we know it today, but Methodist education, simply because it insists upon preparation for an after-life, and on the training of spirit rather than body or mind, requires a more advanced education than that given in any primary school. That Kingswood School was not merely primary in its scope is proved by the curriculum laid down for it and by the books in use there. Wesley himself wrote English, Latin, Greek, Hebrew, and French Grammar textbooks.[28]

This work deals primarily with the direct working-out of Methodist traditions and principles through schools founded by Methodists, but a short digression is necessary to show how Methodism exerted also an indirect influence on secondary education. 'In the vast work of social organization which is one of the dominant characteristics of nineteenth-century England, it would be difficult to over-estimate the part played by the Wesleyan revival,' writes Elie Halévy in his *History of the English People in 1815*.[29] It influenced, not only the outcast poor among whom were found the majority of the first Methodists, but also the Established Church and, through it, the middle and upper classes. Wesley was driven out of the Church in which he was an ordained priest, but throughout his life he had many friends in that Church—Walker, the Cornish revivalist, James Hervey, author of *Meditations among the Tombs,* Grimshaw, the 'mad' Yorkshireman, John Newton who befriended the poet Cowper, Venn, Romaine, and many more beside. The alliance between Methodism and the Evangelical party in the Established Church was spiritual rather than practical, however. Wesley wrote to his clergymen friends, and was

[26] *Works,* Vol. VII, p. 103.
[27] ibid., p. 83.
[28] ibid., Vol. XIV, pp. 1–160.
[29] p. 372.

allowed to preach in their churches; but only a few of the clergy actively helped him in the missionary work of Methodism, as did William Grimshaw of Haworth, who took charge of two Methodist circuits in addition to his own parish work and conducted love-feasts and class-meetings; or John Fletcher, who refused a good living to help a rough Methodist mining community in Madeley, Shropshire. As time went on and Methodism became separated from the Established Church, the co-operation between Methodism and the Evangelicals became less close and intimate, but by that time a new religious conscience had been awakened, and the seeds were already sown which were to produce a harvest of social reformation. There were many among the Evangelicals too who had never met Wesley, but who were influenced by his work in various parts of the country. Groups of laymen, prominent members of the Established Church, and others met together in societies not unlike the Society meetings of Methodism. It is significant that the first centre of this movement was Cambridge University where, under the leadership of Isaac Milner and Charles Simeon, groups of men met periodically for meditation and conversation on religious matters. Through them, young clergymen were influenced who later scattered to parishes throughout the country and spread the Evangelical spirit.

Another centre of revivalism was Clapham, just outside London, where such a group was nicknamed by Sidney Smith 'The Clapham Sect'.[30] Laymen, well known in political, commercial, and social circles, used to meet at the house of Henry Thornton, a banker and Member of Parliament, or at the house of William Wilberforce, who lived at Clapham from 1795 to 1808. Spiritually guided by John Venn, the Vicar of the parish, a revived interest in religion was fostered amongst this group and spread thence into the sphere of politics and social life. The group consisted of Anglicans, Nonconformists, and Quakers, but all were bound together by a common bond: the application of Christian principles to personal, social, and political affairs. Barriers of party, class, creed, nationality, and even colour were broken down. These men were no idle dreamers and talkers. They were practical—and successful—men of affairs. Besides Thorn-

[30] For full details of the Clapham Sect, see Sir James Stephen's Paper in *Essays in Ecclesiastical Biography* (4th ed., pp. 521–82); John Telford, *A Sect that moved the World* (1907); Canon A. R. Pennington, *Recollections of Persons and Events* (1895); G. R. Balleine, *A History of the Evangelical Party in the Church of England* (1908).

ton and Wilberforce (to whom, incidentally, was addressed the last letter written by John Wesley) were Lord Teignmouth, former Governor-General of India, James Stephen, Zachary Macaulay, Thomas Thompson, and Joseph Butterworth, some Methodists, some Members of Parliament, all men of the middle and upper classes. Sometimes the group would meet at Butterworth's town house in Fleet Street, and it was in fact at this house that the first meeting of the British and Foreign Bible Society was held. In England, these men, and groups like them in other parts of the country, fostered the new interest in social matters; popularized the educational theories of Rousseau and Pestalozzi (neither of whom were beloved of Wesley), and encouraged the poor in 'self-help'. Abroad, they stood for peace and goodwill among the nations. Again is seen the Methodist principle of brotherly love.

As far as education was concerned, the primary effect of the revival of religion was humanitarian, and specific examples will be discussed in later pages. Wesley himself was compelled to include education in his sphere of activities because he saw that something must be done for the children of people who could not read and had not the knowledge necessary to understand the Bible story. The wealthy members of the Clapham Sect supported the work being started for primary education. But, though the work started on a foundation of humanitarianism, it quickly awakened interest in social reforms of various sorts for their own sake. It inspired many of the philanthropic movements of the nineteenth century, but it led the leaders of these movements to take a new interest in learning, especially as it applied to the 'humanities' in the widest sense. A new outlook on politics and social problems developed, leading to the passing of the Reform Bill, the abolition of the Slave Trade, the foundation of Missionary Societies, and the reform of education. However narrow-minded some of the earlier Methodists and Evangelicals may have been in certain directions, the work to which they applied themselves was broad in scope, and could not be undertaken by men who were themselves uncultured. Their lives found a new discipline; a demand for education arose among themselves, the first centres for such education being found in the meetings of small groups for discussion on a multitude of topics all centred in the one common theme of humanity. To the house of the Thorntons on Clapham Common 'resorted the good great men of his [Henry Thornton's] day, to seek

30

counsel from his practical wisdom; to devise liberal things for the State, the Church, and for all the world; to relax from the cares of public life in untrammelled conversation, not too grave if not too hilarious; to share the sumptuous family hospitalities and join in the family devotions.' [31] From such intercourse and amongst such men must have arisen an interest in the type of culture which has always been the peculiarity of higher education. Herein lies one of the indirect contributions of Methodism to education, and it is interesting to note that in all the pictures which writers have drawn of the Clapham Sect and the Evangelical centres of revival one gets the impression of a family. Directly arising out of their 'burning love of souls' came a fellowship which gradually broke down class barriers and prepared the way for a time when secondary education should become once more open to all comers, as was the case in the Middle Ages when the peasant child might rise to become Archbishop. The importance of the family principles of Methodism cannot be too strongly stressed. It brought hope to the down-trodden masses as represented in the early Methodist Societies, and it brought a new conception of humanity to the thinking upper classes as represented by the Clapham Sect. Its instrumentality in saving England from a social revolution such as occurred in France forms an interesting topic for conjecture.[32]

As far as Methodist education was concerned, there was evident a spirit which overcame the confines of the Methodist Connexion. Mention will be made later of the admission to Methodist residential schools of children whose parents were not Methodists, but more important than this was a spirit which tried honestly to see the other person's point of view. It was this spirit which caused Matthew Arnold to say, in his Report on the Wesleyan Training College at Westminster in 1856:

'Those at the head of the Wesleyan School system appear to me, I am bound to say, to conduct its operations in a spirit singularly free, so far as their dealings with the Committee of Council are concerned, from all jealousy and mistrust; in a spirit which proves, I hope, the consciousness in them that they have been fairly dealt with by the Committee of Council, and

[31] Abel Stevens, *History of Methodism* (1878 ed.), Vol. II, p. 78.
[32] See Elie Halévy, *History of the English People in 1815*, Book III; J. W. Bready, *England: before and after Wesley*; J. E. Rattenbury, *Wesley's Legacy to the World*, Part 5.

which certainly renders it a matter of pleasure, rather than of difficulty, to deal with them. I find also this spirit eminently present in the great body of Wesleyan teachers with whom I have to deal; I believe that it is a spirit fostered in them by their training, nay, by the principles and tendencies of Wesleyanism itself.' [33]

[33] Matthew Arnold, *Reports on Elementary Schools, 1852–82*, p. 237.

N.B.—This chapter in particular owes much to A. H. Body's research on *John Wesley and Education*, and that work (especially Chapter 3) should be studied by those who would understand more fully that part of this chapter which deals with John Wesley himself.

CHAPTER TWO

John Wesley's Own Contribution

'*TAKE away Mr. Wesley's school and its influence from the Methodist history of the past century, and there would be an immense blank.*' [1]

Enough has been said in the first chapter to show that Wesley, if not primarily an educationist, was yet interested in education. and was not blind to its deficiencies in this country. While Wesley was in Germany in 1738 he saw the University of Jena and the Moravian establishment at Herrnhut, with its carefully organized sections for little children, middle children, big children, young men, and the married, each of the sections being further subdivided. What an impression such organization must have made upon him as he considered the state of education in his own country! The numbers both in the public schools and in the universities of England fluctuated considerably during the eighteenth century. The life in them was hard and rough, with no supervision of pupils out of school hours. In that century, and in the early nineteenth, rebellions occurred at Eton, Harrow, Winchester, and Rugby, largely because of this lack of supervision and the insufficiency of staff. At Winchester the boys held brandy parties and smoked; bullying was rife at all. Cowper, in his *Tirocinium*, though he was probably thinking more of the private boarding-school to which he was sent at the age of six than of Westminster School whither he went later, recalling his schooldays from a distance of forty years when time might be expected to have mellowed his memory, was bitter in his condemnation of boarding-schools. Henry Fielding, a broadminded man who can truly be said to have seen many aspects of life from his vantage-point as a London magistrate, considered the public schools to be nurseries of all vice and immorality. Southey, recalling his education at Westminster and Balliol, told of the 'little or nothing' he obtained there.

Wesley himself remained loyal to his old school, Charterhouse, with which he maintained some connexion long after his schooldays had ended, since a pensioner there, a Mr. Agutter, placed a room at his disposal, whither he sometimes went for quiet talk

[1] *Wesley: the Man, his Teaching, and his Work*, p. 255.

and study in the early years of what we may describe as his active ministry from 1738 onward.[2] The nearest approach made by Wesley to criticism of life at his old school was recorded many years later, when in the *Journal* he remembers that while he was at Charterhouse he had little but bread to eat and not much of that. He believed that that was good for his health![3] Pupils at the public schools worked when they had to work and found plenty of mischief with which to occupy themselves at other times. It is true that the standard of classical learning at that time was high, but that was largely due to the fact that the classics occupied almost the entire curriculum. Other subjects, such as history, mathematics, geography, English literature, and French, had to be taken in out-of-school hours. They were not recognized as 'school business'. In many cases head masters of such schools were Church of England clergymen strongly opposed to dissent in any form.

In addition to the public schools there were a number of private schools, some conforming to the Established Church, some nonconforming, but all varying greatly in efficiency, and tending, since they were unfettered by founders' statutes and tradition, to give a more up-to-date education.

Wesley himself had been educated at Charterhouse and Oxford, while his brother, Charles, had been educated at Westminster School, where an elder brother, Samuel, was an usher. It was therefore with public-school education that John Wesley was most familiar. While he himself found much that was evil in it he admired the hardness of the life, and his subsequent organization of life at Kingswood School shows that he felt such hardness to be an essential part of character training. In an entry in his *Journal* for 1736 [4] occurs a significant phrase in this connexion. He recounts how beneficial he had found sleeping in the open-air in all weathers, as would anyone 'if his constitution was not impaired by the softness of a genteel education'. It seems probable that Wesley was here thinking not so much of public-school education as of a practice which had become common during the century—the employment of private tutors by wealthy parents. These tutors took charge of boys in the family homes until they grew to early manhood, when they undertook the 'Grand Tour' through Europe, or studied in one

[2] *Journal*, Vol. II, p. 137 n.
[3] ibid., Vol. V, p. 373. See also L. Tyerman, *The Life and Times of John Wesley*, Vol. I, p. 19.
[4] Vol. I, p. 258.

of the Inns of Court instead of going up to one of the universities. This type of education had grown increasingly popular
since the publication in 1693 of John Locke's *Thoughts Concerning Education,* in which he had stressed the value of private
education by tutors in place of public education in the schools
of the day. Such education naturally tended to be less strict
and harsh than that given in any institution, though it is only
fair to remember that Locke himself, beside eulogizing such
training, stressed the importance of physical hardening by means
of games as a part of character building. Wesley did not believe
in the games, but he did believe whole-heartedly in the place of
physical hardening in education.

Wesley's conception of the ideal school was one which did
not prepare merely for life in this world, but one which remembered that there was a life to come—one which would last for
ever. He exhorted parents to take this into account in selecting
a school for their sons, for 'otherwise, to send them to school
. . . is little better than sending them to the devil. At all events,
then, send your boys, if you have any concern for their souls,
not to any of the large public schools (for they are nurseries of
all manner of wickedness), but a private school, kept by some
pious man, who endeavours to instruct a small number of children in religion and learning together.' [5] That phrase 'religion
and learning together' has been the keynote of Methodist education from that day to this. Wesley came to believe that the two
words were largely synonymous.

'In the name of God, then, and by the authority of His word,
let all that have children, from the time they begin to speak or
run alone, begin to train them up in the way wherein they
should go; to counterwork the corruption of their nature with all
possible assiduity; to do everything in their power to cure their
self-will, pride, and every other wrong temper. Then let them
be delivered to instructors (if such can be found) that will tread
in the same steps; that will watch over them as immortal spirits,
who are shortly to appear before God, and who have nothing to
do in this world but to prepare to meet Him in the clouds, seeing
they will be eternally happy, if they are ready; if not, eternally
miserable.' [6]

As we have seen, Wesley had been interested in education
while he was at Oxford. He had indeed at one time considered

[5] *Works,* Vol. VII, p. 83.
[6] ibid., Vol. XIII, p. 437.

becoming a schoolmaster. In 1727 he wrote a letter to his mother from Lincoln College in which he said:

'A school in Yorkshire, forty miles from Doncaster, was proposed to me lately, on which I shall think more when it appears whether I may have it or no. A good salary is annexed to it; so that in a year's time 'tis probable all my debts would be paid, and I should have money beforehand. But what has made me wish for it most is the frightful description, as they call it, some gentlemen who know the place gave me of it yesterday. The town (Skipton-in-Craven) lies in a little vale, so pent up between two hills that it is scarce accessible on any side; so that you can expect little company from without, and within there is none at all.'[7]

This extract shows the spirit in which Wesley approached his problems even in his early days. The more difficulties that presented themselves the more eager was he to be at them. The school referred to was Ermysted's Grammar School, one of the oldest northern foundations. Founded in 1492 by Peter Toller, it was refounded in 1548 by William Ermysted, Canon Residentiary of St. Paul's and Chaplain to Queen Mary. Although this project came to nothing and Wesley's thoughts turned more and more to the Church, he never lost his interest in education. In fact, he took active steps to increase his knowledge of it. He began to reconsider his own schooldays and the methods employed at Charterhouse, and those, no doubt, at Westminster, where his brother was an usher. After being ordained he visited various schools in Holland and Germany. He did not visit them to criticize. He had other problems—weightier by far—on his mind at that time, but in all the schools, and particularly in those of this country, he found much that did not meet with his approval. It is with these matters that he deals in his *Plain Account of Kingswood School,* a pamphlet which he published in 1781 in order to correct certain wrong impressions which had appeared concerning the school.[8] Following is a summary of his main points concerning secondary schools in general:

1. Schools were too often situated in the middle of towns where there were distractions to upset the pupils and disturb their work. The numbers of pupils were frequently too large, so

---

[7] *Letters,* Vol. I, pp. 42–3.
[8] For full text of this pamphlet, see *Works,* Vol. XIII, pp. 255–67.

that children were forced to become associated with others not so desirable.

2. Entrance examinations were not sufficiently searching. Wesley felt that would-be pupils of any schools should be more carefully considered by the authorities to discover as far as possible what would be their influence on others in the school. He was always afraid of 'corrupting influences'.

3. Religion was neglected, the master being no less at fault in this matter than the pupils.

4. The curriculum was badly organized, and teaching-methods were defective, textbooks being carelessly selected both as regards content and teaching-method.

5. The teaching tended, not only to give no religious training, but also to destroy its elements by the obscurity of the books prescribed for class use.

Although these views of Wesley's were not published till 1781, they were becoming clarified in his mind over forty years before, and particularly after 1739. In the spring of that year, Whitefield, urged no doubt by the taunts that he ought to go to the colliers of Kingswood if he wished to convert heathen, spent some time in preaching in that mining district near Bristol. He realized that his work could not be a lasting one unless he undertook the training of the miners' children, and in June 1739 he laid the foundation-stone of a school.[9] Immediately afterwards he left for America and asked Wesley to carry on the work he had begun. This was no light task, for Whitefield had not had time to plan the organization of the school. He had merely expressed his belief in practical form that schools were needed. As he had said: 'Were I to continue here, I would endeavour to settle schools all over the Wood, and also in other places, as Mr. Griffith Jones has done in Wales.'[10] He himself had been educated at the Crypt School, Gloucester, and his views on education agreed with those of Wesley, for he felt that the methods employed in training youth had a natural tendency to debauch the mind, to raise undesirable passions, and to stuff the memory with things as contrary to the Gospel of Jesus Christ as light to darkness, as heaven to hell. 'However,' he wrote, 'the first thing I had to repent of was my education in general.'[11]

[9] See *Journal*, Vol. II, p. 323, for Wesley's own account of the school's foundation.
[10] L. Tyerman, *Life of George Whitefield*, Vol. I, p. 192.
[11] ibid., p. 6.

The greatest practical difficulty that Wesley had to contend with in connexion with this school of Whitefield's was that of finance. He overcame it by begging subscriptions in all parts of the country, and in the spring of 1740 the school was completed. It was a day-school for boys and girls, though accommodation was provided 'if it should please God' for the boarding of a few poor children. But the school and its design were not Wesley's, and this fact was not lost upon certain critics, among them John Cennick, a master at the school, who strongly disagreed with Wesley on a fundamental doctrinal principle— that of predestination. This gentleman wrote to Whitefield in America urging him to return, as he did not think that matters were being managed as they should be. He even accused Wesley of perverting Whitefield's design for the building of the school. Wesley's reply to the charge was contained in a letter to White-field, and it illustrated the difficulties of the task undertaken.

'Two years since, your design was to build them [the colliers] a school, that their children also might be taught to fear the Lord. To this end you collected some money more than once; how much I cannot say, till I have my papers. But this I know, it was not near one-half of what has been expended on the work. The design you then recommended to me, and I pursued it with all my might, through such a train of difficulties as (I will be bold to say) you have not yet met with in your life. For many months I collected money wherever I was. . . . In June 1739, being able to procure none any other way, I bought a little piece of ground and began building thereon, though I had not then a quarter of the money requisite to finish.' [12]

From what has already been said it will be evident that Wesley's ideal school would be one in which secular education and religious instruction were one and inseparable. At this colliers' school they were separate, the secular instruction occupying the day-time and consisting of reading, writing, and casting accounts, the religious instruction being given mainly in the early morning or in the evening to older people before or after the day's work. There were 'scholars of all ages'. When the school opened, two unpaid masters were employed, the staff being increased during the first few months as the school grew. From 1741 onward, however, the staff consisted of a master for the boys and a mistress for the girls. The work prospered, and in March 1744 Wesley was able to report to the stewards that

[12] *Letters*, Vol. I, p. 356. See also pp. 338–40.

he found 'great cause to bless God' on behalf of the master, mistress, and children.[13]

During this time, however, Wesley was carrying on another man's work, while at the same time clarifying his own educational views. He may have read the educational theories of Plato, Comenius, Quintillian, and John Locke.[14] He had certainly read, or was at that very time reading, Milton's *Tractate on Education*—a work which he later described as 'admirable'; [15] he had taken to heart the information which his own mother had given him concerning education; only two years before he had visited schools in Holland and Germany, and the impression which his visit to Herrnhut in particular had made upon him can be judged by his carefully tabulated notes set down in his *Journal*, not the least part of which are concerned with the educational side of the work there. He had studied the organization and the curriculum and had found the latter not unlike that of the more enlightened grammar schools of his own country, including as it did reading, writing, arithmetic, Latin, Greek, Hebrew, French, English, history, and geography.[16] He had also visited Halle, where he had seen the Orphan House and marvelled at the great educational work being done there.[17]

He had only been back in England for a few months when the opportunity occurred for him to combine theory and practice as we have seen. But, though the practice was good as experience, Wesley could only regard it as a means to an end. It was not a school which provided higher education. Despite the financial aspect of the affair, the school was not Wesley's, and he was beginning to wish for a school which was his own—the embodiment of educational ideals gradually evolved from theory and his limited practice.

At the first Conference of the Wesleyan Methodist Connexion, held in London in June 1744, the matter of education was brought to the forefront of Wesley's mind when the question was asked: 'Can we have a seminary for labourers?' Unfortunately, the matter was temporarily shelved by the reply: 'If God spare us until another Conference.' [18] At the Conference in the following year the question was again asked, and it was

[13] *Journal*, Vol. III, p. 125.
[14] See A. H. Body, *John Wesley and Education*, pp. 55 ff., where the question of Wesley's reading of educational theory is discussed.
[15] *Works*, Vol. XIII, p. 262.
[16] *Journal*, Vol. II, pp. 50–1.
[17] ibid., p. 17.
[18] *Wesley Historical Society Publications*, No. 1, p. 17.

decided that the matter could not be dealt with 'until God gives us a proper tutor'.[19] Wesley must at that time, and with that reply, have realized that upon him would fall the task of being the proper tutor. He was undoubtedly the man best fitted by his education and ability for such a task. Hitherto, he had been content with his preachers, unpolished as some of them were, but he realized that as the adherents of Methodism increased in knowledge, so must the preachers keep pace with them, or there would arise the danger of their becoming despised by the folk who, previously ignorant, were, since their conversion, becoming more cultured by self-teaching, and especially by that culture which could be, and was being, gained from reading the Bible.

On 9th September 1745 Wesley left London for Newcastle, and no doubt he pondered over his problems as he rode. He could not fail to realize that the work of his helpers would be very much more efficient if some form of training could be provided. The following day, Wesley reached Northampton, where he called on his friend, Dr. Philip Doddridge, Principal of the Dissenting Academy in that town, and the most distinguished dissenter of his day. Since 1739, when the two had first met, they had become very friendly, and evidence of the respect each had for the other is seen in the fact that on this occasion the dissenter, who was about to give his customary lecture on Scripture to the students of the academy, asked the priest of the Established Church to take his place. It would seem probable that one of the topics of conversation between the two friends at their meeting that September was education, for it was only a short time since the question of a seminary for Wesley's helpers had been raised in Conference for a second time.

A few months later, in March 1746, Wesley evidently wrote to Dr. Doddridge from Newcastle, asking his advice concerning books suitable for prescribing for the reading of his preachers, and he received the following reply:

'I am grieved and ashamed, that any hurry, public or private, should have prevented my answering your obliging letter from Newcastle; especially as it has a face of disrespect, where I ought to express the very reverse, if I would do justice either to you, or my own heart. But you have been used to forgive greater injuries. I have unwillingly a guardianship affair on hand, on account of which, I must beg your patience for a little

---

[19] *Wesley Historical Society Publications,* No. 1, p. 27.

longer, as to the list of books you desire me to send you. I presume the list you desire is chiefly theological. Perhaps my desire of making it too particular has hindered me from setting about it. But, if God permit, you shall be sure to have it in a few weeks. . . .' [20]

Three months later came a letter enclosing the promised list: 'I set myself down, as well as I can, to discharge my promise, and fulfil your request, in giving my thoughts on that little collection of books, which you seem desirous to make for some of your young preachers.' [21]

As a 'little collection' the following list appears remarkably comprehensive, and is itself evidence that Wesley's preachers were not so devoid of learning as has popularly been believed.

Logic: Carmichael and Dr. Watts. *Metaphysics:* Dr. Urie, Dr. Watts, and Le Clerc. *Ethics:* Puffendorf and Hutcheson. *Jewish Antiquities:* Lewis, Reland, Calmet, and Prideaux. *Civil History:* Puffendorf, Turselme, and Lampe. *Natural Philosophy:* Rowning, Ray, Cotton Mather, and Derham. *Astronomy:* Watts, Jennings, and Wells. *Natural and Revealed Religion:* Carmichael, Synge, Clark, Gibson, Doddridge, Jefferies, Bullock, Conybeare, Leland, and Chandler.

Dr. Doddridge suggested, too, that there should be some reading of critical literature, and suggested: Beza, Erasmus, Castellio, Heinsius, Patrick, Lowthe, Locke, Pierce, Benson, Ainsworth, Hammond, Grotius, Brenius, Wells, Calvin, Poole, Le Clerc, and Cradock.

Inspired by these suggestions, Wesley formed the idea of making a collection from the most approved writers of the English language in matters of divinity, and of printing them under the title of *A Christian Library.* This was to be for the use of such as feared God. By that time Wesley's original plan of preparing reading-lists for his preachers had been extended. He was beginning to see the necessity for educating all Methodists, and, characteristically, once he had seen the need, he set a high standard. From the list of books suggested by Doddridge and largely adapted by Wesley, it is evident that Wesley planned to give Methodists a higher education and not be content with a mere knowledge of reading and writing, and a smattering of knowledge in general. As Dr. Simon writes: [22]

[20] L. Tyerman, *The Life and Times of John Wesley,* Vol. I, pp. 516–17.
[21] ibid., p. 517. See also *Arminian Magazine* (1778), Vol. I, p. 419.
[22] J. S. Simon, *John Wesley and the Methodist Societies,* p. 218.

'It has sometimes been alleged that the "first race" of Methodist preachers consisted of uneducated men, and that John Wesley employed them because he could obtain none other to do the rough work of the itinerancy. We find it difficult to reconcile that statement with the answer of the Conference to the question, "What books may an assistant read?" The Greek Testament, and more than a dozen books of Latin and Greek authors, appear in the list. The names include Virgil, Horace, Epictetus, Plato, and Homer. Wesley's idealism may have carried him too far, but he never lowered it. He expected that his lay preachers should study the best books; if they would not, he plainly told them that he had no further need of their services.'

The influence of Dr. Doddridge on the educational work of Wesley cannot be overestimated, though Methodist historians have touched but lightly on the subject. Wesley himself calls him 'that amiable man' and nearly twenty years after the Doctor's death he speaks of another acquaintance as being 'as friendly and courteous as Dr. Doddridge himself'.[23] From the present point of view it is important to notice that the period of friendship between the two men (from 1739 to the date of Dr. Doddridge's death in 1751) extended over the greater part of the period in which Wesley was formulating his educational scheme to be put into practice at Kingswood School. During that period, in addition to his evangelistic work, he was keeping a watchful eye on what we may call 'Whitefield's School', he was busy drawing up a list of books suitable for the reading of Methodists, and he was in touch with Doddridge so that he was able to learn something of a dissenting academy. It is impossible to believe that Wesley could have visited that academy and conversed with its principal without being influenced and further inspired to do for his followers what was being done for the dissenters, especially as, even by that time, it was being borne in upon him that his Societies were in fact 'dissenting'.

Wesley, looking back on that time, wrote later: 'After long inquiring, but inquiring in vain, for a school free from these palpable blemishes, at last a thought came into my mind, of setting up a school myself. The first point was, to find a proper situation.'[24] The proper situation was found at the scene of his labours on another man's work, and on 7th April 1746 Wesley

[23] See *Journal*, Vol. III, pp. 244–5; Vol. V, p. 42.
[24] *Works*, Vol. XIII, p. 258.

recorded in his *Journal*: [25] 'I preached at Kingswood, on
Isaiah lx, the seventeenth and following verses, and laid the first
stone of the New House there.' The building was opened on
24th June 1748 by the founder when he preached from the text:
'Train up a child in the way that he should go; and when he is
old, he will not depart from it.' He warned his hearers against
certain dangers which children and those responsible for their
education had to face—atheism, pride, love of the world, anger,
deviation from truth, speaking or acting unjustly—and he asked:
'If these are the general diseases of human nature, is it not the
grand end of education to cure them?' [26] It was in this school,
known as the New House to distinguish it from the older school
established in 1739 (and which continued as a school until 1803)
that Wesley was able to practise his educational theory. When
an educationist founds a school one expects him to spend a great
part of his time there. Wesley did not. He could not, whatever
may have been his desire. As he twice quoted in his *Journal*: [27]
'Man was not born in shades to lie!' Wesley's interests were so
wide that no man who did not possess an unusual amount of
energy and organizing ability could possibly have undertaken
them, but he was a leader of men and knew how to delegate
responsibility. He was interested in humanity in all its varied
aspects, and he spent his life trying to bring back humanity to
its intimate relationship with God. However much he may have
desired it, he simply had not the time to concentrate his whole
attention on any one part of the evangelistic work. He had
helpers, lay and clerical, but even by 1746 Wesley was beginning to realize that if the work was to go on there must be some
institution or organization for training his followers and
preachers. That it was largely due to this realization that he took
the step of founding the school at New House, Kingswood, is
evident, for in the Conference of 1748, just before the school
was opened, the question was asked: 'What is the design of
the foundation at Kingswood?' to which he gave the reply:
'We design to train up children there, if God permit, in every
branch of useful learning, from the very alphabet till they are
fit as to all acquired qualifications for the work of the
ministry.' [28]

Thus there were two Methodist schools at Kingswood, the

[25] Vol. III, p. 238.
[26] *Works*, Vol. VII, p. 90.
[27] Vol. VI, p. 72; Vol. VIII, p. 10.
[28] *Wesley Historical Society Publications*, No. 1, p. 54.

one whose foundation-stone was laid by Whitefield giving elementary instruction to poor children during the day and to working folk, especially the local colliers, before or after their day's work; the other (New House) founded, designed, and opened by Wesley, being a school for boarders and giving instruction of a higher nature, a school which should supply what Wesley considered an ideal education.

During the first eight years of the school's history Wesley was burdened, not only with domestic difficulties in the school itself, but also by its finances. The income received from pupils was quite inadequate to meet expenses, and the income had therefore to be supplemented partly from Wesley's own pocket and partly from the gifts of friends. As Wesley realized only too well, neither of these sources was lasting or even reliable. The matter was brought before the thirteenth Conference in 1756, the Rules of the School were read and discussed, and passed as agreeable to Scripture and reason. Then was taken the step which ranks only second in importance to the founding of the school: It was agreed that a short account of the design and present state of the school be read by every assistant in every Society and that a subscription for it be begun in every place and (if need be) a collection made every year.[29]

This step was vitally important. Firstly, it removed the burden of the school's upkeep from the shoulders of one man and ensured that as long as there was a Methodist Connexion so long would the interests of Methodist education be maintained. Secondly, since the Rules of the School had been discussed at length and approved, the educational ideals of the founder had also been approved and would continue to be practised in spirit at least. Had there been any objections to any of the Rules they would have been brought forward and threshed out. But there was none. The school thus became a Connexional institution, and sufficient has already been said to show that the spirit of higher education and not that of merely elementary education was inherent in its organization. This educational scheme of Wesley's had been officially adopted as the educational scheme of the Connexion.

It has commonly been believed that Kingswood School from its foundation in 1746 was intended for the sons of ministers. That is not correct. Nor is it true to say, as could be said of Whitefield's school in the same place, that it was a school for

[29] *Journal*, Vol. IV, p. 186.

the children of miners in the district. It was a school which should make good the deficiencies which Wesley criticized in contemporary schools, open to all who desired education there, whether they were sons of preachers or not. Would-be pupils had to be between the ages of six and twelve years at entrance and they had to board at the school, for Wesley had no sympathy with 'tender parents' who, by visiting their children during their school life or by boarding them at home, might upset all the good which the school claimed to do. The minds of pupils were to be trained to 'wisdom and holiness, by instilling the principles of true religion, speculative and practical, and training them up in the ancient way, that they might be rational, scriptural Christians.'[30] All pupils, whether the sons of preachers or of laymen, paid the same fees, i.e. £14 per annum, this sum to include board, teaching, books, pens, ink, and paper. But it was plain to all that preachers who wished to send their sons there would rarely be able to afford such a sum, and Wesley realized that better than anyone. Some indication of his interest in the free education of needy children may be seen in the following fact: among the textbooks in use at the school in its early years was Benjamin Franklin's *New Experiments and Observations made at Philadelphia in America* (1754). Wesley's own copy, inscribed with his name, is now in the Library at Kingswood School, but its chief interest lies in the fact that it is bound with certain tracts relating to charitable organizations for children. Since Wesley had thought it worth while to have these tracts bound together with another book in constant use at the school and had autographed the copy with his own name, it seems evident that he had not only read the whole volume himself but desired others to do likewise.

As the number of itinerant preachers increased, so their numbers were swelled by men who had no means of supporting themselves, and once such men had been accepted as preachers it was obvious that something must be done for their financial support. In 1752, therefore, Societies were each ordered to find £12 per annum for this purpose. This sum was later augmented, largely at first by goods in kind, but there was nothing available for the education of ministers' children who became a problem all the more pressing since the father of the family spent so long away from home that parental discipline (on which Wesley set great store) was often completely lacking. It seems that early in

---

[30] *Works,* Vol. XIII, p. 259.

the history of Kingswood School, although it had been founded as a secondary school open to all comers on payment of the requisite fees, a number of ministers' sons were accepted free. The fact that Wesley believed that God would provide for the needs of His servants did not prevent him from being practical and showing considerable generosity himself, and it seems probable that in the very early years of the school he arranged for one or two preachers' sons to be educated free. In his Will he bequeathed the profits made on the sale of his books to his executors, and part of this money he directed to be used for the keeping of such children of travelling preachers at Kingswood School as should be chosen at the annual Conference.[31]

At the discussion concerning the school at the Conference of 1756 it transpired that there were a few ministers' sons receiving a free education, but the first definite record of this practice is found in an old account book of the school relating to the period 1764 to 1770, in which are mentioned nine sons of ministers who were receiving a free education there. In the account of the school which was to be read annually in every Society appeared the following:

'Yet one considerable difficulty lies on those that have boys, when they grow too big to be under their mothers' direction. Having no father to govern and instruct them, they are exposed to a thousand temptations. To remedy this, we have a school on purpose for them, wherein they have all the instruction they are capable of, together with all things necessary for the body, clothes only excepted. And it may be, if God prosper this labour of love, they will have these too, shortly.

'In whatever view we look upon this, it is one of the noblest charities that can be conceived. How reasonable is the Institution! Is it fit that the children of those who leave wife, and all that is dear, to save souls from death, should want what is needful either for soul or body? Ought not we to supply what the parent cannot, because of his labours in the gospel? How excellent are the effects of this Institution! The Preacher, eased of this weight, can the more cheerfully go on in his labour. And perhaps many of these children may hereafter fill up the place of those that shall "rest from their labours".'[32]

Though the majority of the pupils at the school were sons of

[31] See *History of Kingswood School*, p. 44, and L. Tyerman, *Life and Times of John Wesley*, Vol. III, pp. 15–16.
[32] *Works*, Vol. VIII, pp. 333–4.

laymen and came from all parts of Europe, there must have been a gradual increase in the number of preachers' sons and a corresponding decrease in the number of laymen's sons, for at the Conference of 1788 it was resolved that accommodation should be provided at the school for forty ministers' sons and that the number of other pupils should be reduced to ten as soon as possible, the school to become an institution for 'the education of the sons of itinerant Methodist preachers'.[33] From that date onward there must have been an increasing tendency to accept only ministers' sons, for those who wished to become pupils at the school and were unable to do so were given an allowance of £12 per annum to meet the expenses of education elsewhere. When this happened the minister concerned did not receive the usual children's allowance of £4 normally paid to him yearly from the 'Kingswood Collection'. The payment of an educational allowance was obviously open to many difficulties, and it was far more convenient that all ministers' sons should be educated in one institution, though what is the more convenient policy is not always the best.

By 1796 the school was beginning to be recognized as existing primarily for the education of such children, for it was ordained that 'if a preacher cannot give a satisfactory reason why his son should not go to the school, he shall not be allowed the £12 a year out of the collection'. Myles, in his *Chronological History of the Wesleyan Methodists,* fixed the change as having taken place in 1794, but it could not have been until some time later that the school became devoted exclusively to their education, for one who was a pupil there between 1807 and 1813 recalled that at that period of the school's history there were not more than twenty-five boys in residence and that not more than twelve of that number were preachers' sons. If the memory of that writer was not at fault, it appears that pupils other than preachers' sons were still being admitted to the school as late as 1807 to 1813, and no evidence is available as to when the school became devoted exclusively to the education of ministers' sons.

Wesley never forgot that the school was a family. He could not forget it, for that was part of the fundamental educational philosophy which he followed, based on experience in his own home at Epworth under his mother and on his experiences at Hernnhut and Jena. 'My design in building the house at Kings-

---

[33] J. T. Slugg, *Woodhouse Grove School,* p. 11.

wood was, to have therein a Christian family; every member whereof, children excepted, should be alive to God, and a pattern of all holiness.' [34] On many occasions Wesley refers in his writings to the society at Kingswood School—staff and pupils —as 'the family'. He records how, on 25th July 1749, he rode over to Kingswood from Bristol to inspect the school. 'I was concerned to find that several of the Rules had been habitually neglected. I judged it necessary, therefore, to lessen the family —suffering none to remain therein who were not clearly satisfied with them, and determined to observe them all.' [35]

Twenty-five years later, on 12th March 1774, he again 'went over to Kingswood, and put an end to some little misunderstandings which had crept into the family'.[36]

On many occasions Wesley found much that did not agree with his views on the family nature of life at his school, and this apparent failure was emphasized by the excellent spirit shown in another school to which he paid visits—that at Leytonstone. It was a girls' school administered by Mary Bosanquet, who later married John Fletcher, youngest son of a Savoy nobleman, tutor to an English family and subsequently Vicar of Madeley in Shropshire, who was attracted to Methodism and established Methodist Societies throughout his parish. The feature of the Leytonstone Orphan School which particularly attracted Wesley was the fact that it was 'one truly Christian family'. That was, as Wesley comments, what the school at Kingswood should and would be 'if it had such governors'.[37] Later, he became interested in a similar school at Publow, 'which is now what Leytonstone was once. Here is a family indeed. Such mistresses, and such a company of children, as, I believe, all England cannot parallel.' [38]

The family life which Wesley idealized in connexion with his school was not always apparent, even to him, as the above quotations show. But Wesley was proud of his venture and he was convinced that it was based on right principles. In 1754 he wrote to a young clergyman, the Rev. Samuel Turley, who was resident at Queens' College, Cambridge, and who had written to ask for advice as to how he might save himself from the 'perverse generation' at Cambridge. Wesley advised him concerning his studies:

[34] *Works*, Vol. XIII, p. 268.   [35] *Journal*, Vol. III, p. 422.
[36] ibid., Vol. VI, p. 11.   [37] ibid., Vol. V, p. 152.
[38] ibid., p. 484.

'I know no better method you could pursue, than to take the printed Rules of Kingswood School, and to read all the authors therein mentioned in the same order as they occur there. The authors set down for those in the school, you would probably read over (with application) in about a twelve-month, and those afterward named, in a year or two more; and it will not be lost labour. I suppose you to rise not later than five, to allow an hour in the morning and another in the evening for private exercises, an hour before dinner, and one in the afternoon (suppose from four to five) for walking; and to go to bed between nine and ten. . . .'[39]

A scheme such as Wesley had evolved might have some hope of being successful if it was administered by the person responsible for its planning, but it could never be entirely successful if it was entrusted to others who could not thoroughly understand and appreciate it. It must not be forgotten that in the early years of the school the majority of the staff were men selected, not primarily for academic learning nor because they expressed a desire to teach, but for their religious beliefs. A great number of them were, or became, preachers.

What exactly constitutes a spirit of education is hard to say. Either it exists or it does not. There are no half measures. It was found, we would suggest, in the Jesuit schools [40] and in some of the dissenting academies about which more will be said in the next chapter. It is an indefinable spirit depending not upon depth of learning, but upon the relationship between teacher and pupils, and upon the attitude of the teacher toward his vocation: an intimacy which Wesley aimed at cultivating at Kingswood. But unless the person at the head of the school understands truly what such a spirit means and what it entails, no such spirit will exist. In schools where it was alive the head master of the school and the founder were one and the same person; he lived at the school and for the school, spending every ounce of energy in its service. Wesley, as has been pointed out, could not do that. He made a point of visiting the school once or twice every year, but that was the best he could do. The actual control of the school he had to delegate to others—to the masters and matron. The housekeeper was able to write shortly after the opening of the school: 'The spirit of this family is a resemblance

[39] *Letters,* Vol. III, p. 118.
[40] See R. Schwickerath, *Jesuit Education* (1905). Margaret O'Leary, *Education with a Tradition* (1936); *The Catholic Church and Education* (1943).

of the household above.' [41] But Wesley must have had his doubts
about that. The difficulties of starting and maintaining such a
school were immense, especially when education everywhere was
at a low ebb. Wesley overestimated the abilities of many of the
men whom he appointed as masters. Had he been able to live
at the school himself in its early years, no doubt matters might
have been more satisfactory. As it was, crises arose, and most of
the blame for these must be attached to the women connected
with the school. Wesley may have been a good judge of the
character of men, but throughout his life he was continually at
fault where his judgement of women was concerned.

The first of these crises occurred during the first year of the
school's existence, and, as far as the facts can be understood
today, it originated in the domestic quarter, the maids dividing
into two camps, and the housekeeper—that very one who had
spoken so enthusiastically of the household—remaining aloof
from either, being 'chiefly taken up with thoughts of another
kind'. The pupils were not properly cared for, and it was not
long before the academic staff were also upset by quarrels. In
July 1749 Wesley himself paid a visit in order to look into
matters for himself.[42] In March 1750, the staff complained that
a boy had 'studiously laboured to corrupt the rest' and he was
sent home 'that very hour'. Others followed during the course
of that year until by its close there were left only sixteen pupils.
Wesley was determined that the school should be a family, and
if the group could not take on such a semblance then the numbers had to be reduced. Whether Wesley decided that the
housekeeper had much to do with the upsets we do not know,
but by the end of 1750 she too had left the school, together with
four of the masters. Still matters were not right, and in June
1751 there remained only eleven pupils, when Wesley was able
to write: 'I believe all in the house are at length of one mind,
and trust God will bless us in the latter end more than in the
beginning.' [43] But his satisfaction was short-lived, for in 1753
the founder again had to intervene and to exercise all the patience
that he had.[44]

In 1757, the year after the Connexion had adopted the school,
a female unsettling element again appeared, and there can be
no doubt that this was due to Wesley's inability to understand

[41] *Arminian Magazine* (1779), Vol. II, p. 41.
[42] *Journal,* Vol. III, p. 422. (See p. 48, *supra.*)
[43] ibid., p. 531.   [44] ibid., Vol. IV, p. 80.

the female character. It must not be forgotten, however, that Wesley had other things to think about. His life was spent in trying to lead people, often of a depraved character, back to Christ. Miss Bosanquet, the head mistress of the Leytonstone School, had befriended a woman who had three husbands living. Wesley was interested in the case and wanted to help. He appointed the woman as housekeeper at Kingswood! There is no reason for believing that she was not by that time a reformed character, but even so she was not the right person to look after the domestic affairs of a school, especially of a school passing through the difficulties which this one was experiencing. It was difficult enough to find masters under the best circumstances at that time without the added difficulty of finding men willing and able to work with a woman such as had been chosen as house-keeper, however reformed she might be.

This difficulty, combined with the ever-present one of finance, gave rise to a serious discussion at the Conference of 1758. 'Should we drop the school at Kingswood?' Eventually it was decided that the school should be continued if a suitable head master could be procured.

Wesley made no reference to the school again for five years, and this omission, coupled with the evidence that his preachers were taking no little interest in the school, suggests that a suit-able master was found and that, even if the school did not flourish exceedingly, it did at least hold its own and give Wesley no further cause for serious worry.

In 1763 we have the first record—and the only one during Wesley's lifetime—of an evil which is always threatening any institution depending upon voluntary support, especially in those days of bad sanitation and medical deficiencies. (The chief reason for the school's removal to Lansdown, Bath, in 1856, was the lack of an adequate water supply at Bristol.) Riding back from Bath to Bristol, via Kingswood, Wesley met a funeral procession. Until that time he had not heard of anything amiss at the school, but it transpired that one of the pupils had died of smallpox. An epidemic of that sort in a boarding-school often seals the doom of the school, but, as might be expected in view of his outlook on life in this world, Wesley does not appear to have been unduly perturbed. He was gratified that by such means 'God thereby touched many of their hearts in a manner they never knew before'.[45] From those words one gathers that

[45] *Journal*, Vol. V, p. 31.

there occurred something in the nature of a religious revival. Perhaps it was the experience of such a revival and the inevitable reaction later which caused Wesley when he visited the school two years later to write of the pupils: 'They are all in health; they behave well; they learn well; but alas! (two or three excepted) there is no life in them!' [46]

The founder on that occasion left the school dissatisfied, and the following March he returned more than dissatisfied and told masters, domestic staff, and pupils in no uncertain terms what he thought. 'I will kill or cure: I will have one or the other—a Christian school, or none at all.' [47]

In 1766, the question of the school again came up before Conference, and another important step was taken. Until that time, Wesley had attempted to administer the school according to his own ideas and ideals—routine life, financial arrangements, curriculum, and books. He tried to control every side of the school life. And he failed. No man who lived as Wesley lived and who performed the work he did could have succeeded. He visited the school once or twice only each year, and yet he expected to find it developing along the lines he envisaged. It was a hopeless project from the first. A school which is to be the successful child of a man's mind must at least be weaned by that man. Yet Wesley, having, in consultation with his brother, drawn up the Rules of the School and having preached the opening sermon, could not have spent more than the Saturday and Sunday in the neighbourhood, for on the Monday he rode on to Stroud. It seems probable, too, that although the school was officially opened on the Friday, the boys did not begin work there until the following Tuesday.[48] Wesley attempted to form a Christian family there, and yet he, the father under God, was there only once or twice in each year! It is not surprising that Wesley frequently found much to dissatisfy him. By 1766, however, he was growing old, and after a discussion concerning the school it was decided, amongst other things, to appoint three or four trustees and to require each Bristol preacher to spend an hour a week at least with the pupils.[49]

At the same time Wesley appointed Joseph Benson to the head mastership. In view of Wesley's own routine we can imagine that Benson was an ideal person to fill that post, for, on

[46] *Journal*, Vol. V, p. 149. [47] ibid., p. 159.
[48] *History of Kingswood School*, p. 17 n.
[49] *Minutes of Conference* (1766).

entering upon his duties, he resolved to rise at four o'clock in the morning, and to go to bed at nine at night; never to trifle away time in vain conversation, useless visits, or studying anything which would not be to his advantage; to be careful to maintain private prayer, and not to be content without communion with God in it; to spend from four to five o'clock every morning, and from five to six every evening, in devoted meditation and prayer; at nine in the morning, and at three in the afternoon, to devote a few minutes to prayer; to instruct the boys diligently in useful learning and see that they made as much progress as possible; at the same time to endeavour to impress a sense of the things of God upon the minds of his pupils by instructing them in the principles of religion.[50]

Wesley himself was essentially a practical man, and it seems that he realized the dangers of too much bookishness and scholasticism, for in 1768 he wrote to Benson, warning him, 'Beware you be not swallowed up in books: an ounce of love is worth a pound of knowledge' [51]—a statement which might well be remembered by those who accuse Wesley of overburdening the curriculum of the school.

Mention of these readjustments at the school (only some amongst many) has been made here in order to make clear that Wesley himself had to contend with those same difficulties which were to occur in the later days of Methodist education; to show how he worked to overcome those difficulties; how, having decided that his aim was true, he fought for the realization of an ideal. We are dealing with Wesley as an educator and, in particular, with his conception of higher education as he expressed it in practical fashion at his own school. To the reader of Wesley's *Journal* it may seem that Wesley had merely passing enthusiasm for his project, and that, having founded the school, he merely visited it occasionally to see how matters were going and to adjust difficulties. On the surface that is true. But there is no doubt that he had in his own mind a scheme of education which was an essential part of his scheme for evangelizing the whole country. As Dr. J. S. Simon wrote, John Wesley 'patiently thought out a scheme for the higher education of Methodist boys'.[52] He was, too, an autocrat. If those to whom he entrusted the government of his school did not carry out their

[50] *History of Kingswood School*, p. 56.
[51] *Letters*, Vol. V, p. 110.
[52] *John Wesley and the Methodist Societies*, p. 314.

duties in accordance with his own preconceived plan, there was trouble. He shows this in his correspondence with Joseph Benson, to whom he wrote:

'When I recommend to anyone a method or scheme of study, I do not barely consider this or that book separately but in conjunction with the rest. And what I recommend I know; I know both the style and sentiments of each author, and how he will confirm or illustrate what goes before and prepare for what comes after. Now, supposing Mr. Stonehouse, Rouquet, or any other to have ever so great learning and judgement, yet he does not enter into my plan. He does not comprehend my views nor keep his eyes fixed on the same point. Therefore I must insist upon it, the interposing other books between these till you have read them through is not good husbandry. It is not making your time and pains go so far as they might go. If you want more books, let me recommend more, who best understand my own scheme. And do not ramble, however learned the persons may be that advise you so to do. This does indulge curiosity, but does not minister to real improvement, as a stricter method would do. No; you would gain more clearness and strength of judgement by reading those Latin and Greek books (compared with which most of the English are whipped syllabub) than by fourscore modern books. I have seen the proof, as none of your Bristol friends have done or can do. Therefore I advise you again, keep to your plan (though this implies continual self-denial) if you would improve your understanding to the highest degree of which it is capable.' [53]

The autocratic attitude adopted by Wesley with regard to his reading scheme applied no less to his conduct of the school. In another letter to the same gentleman, Wesley wrote: 'Your grand point is, Bring the boys into *exact order,* and that without delay. Do this at all hazards. . . .' [54] Although Wesley desired a Christian family, he never made the mistake of believing that correction and all that is connected with formal discipline were unnecessary. If instant obedience was not forthcoming from the pupils, then steps had to be taken to produce it. He himself, by his striking personality, inspired instant attention and obedience. One has only to consider the many occasions when he quelled an angry mob to realize that. And, like many another man with such a gift, he was blind to the failings of others in this respect. He regarded the whole of life upon earth as a constant and

[53] *Letters,* Vol. V, pp. 118–19.   [54] ibid., p. 123.

disciplined campaign against evil. Again and again we find that spirit of militant discipline breathed out in the hymns written by his brother Charles. It was because of this outlook that John Wesley laid down such strict rules for the pupils of Kingswood School. He was no shirker of hard work himself, and he could not find an excuse for it in others. But—and this is often over-looked by critics of Wesley—he was not blind to the fact that the rules were strict. He meant them to be, and he acknowledged that they were. Before the opening of the school he wrote to a Mrs. Jones of Fonmon Castle, who was thinking of sending her son there: 'If your son comes there, you will probably hear com-plaints; for the discipline will be exact: it being our view not so much to teach Greek and Latin as to train up soldiers for Jesus Christ.'[55] It was well that he had warned her! The son was one of the first pupils to be expelled. Whether the expulsion was permanent we do not know, but on 27th August 1784 he wrote a most friendly letter to the boy, then a grown man, and it is obvious that, whatever cause for dissatis-faction there may once have been, none remained thirty-five years later.

In 1781 was published the *Plain Account of Kingswood School*.[56] Wesley's decision to publish the pamphlet seems to have been taken after a careful inquiry had been made into affairs at the school, when Wesley wrote indignantly: 'I found some of the Rules had not been observed at all, particularly that of rising in the morning. Surely Satan has a peculiar spite at this school! What trouble has it cost me for above these thirty years! I can *plan*, but who will *execute?* I know not; God help me!'[57]

Up to this time the right choice of masters to carry out his educational scheme had been an almost insuperable difficulty, and one of which Wesley was all too conscious. The words quoted above were spoken from the heart. His troubles in connexion with the school were not over, but they were at least on the mend. We have referred to one change in staffing arrangements. There were many others. In that, though Wesley did not, per-haps, fully realize it, lay the clue to the future successful organi-zation of the school.

Two years later, Wesley again had his attention called to the school when rules were once more being neglected and

[55] *Letters*, Vol. II, p. 128. [56] *Works*, Vol. XIII, pp. 255–67.
[57] *Journal*, Vol. VI, p. 334.

favouritism was being shown toward fee-paying pupils at the expense of sons of preachers. The school was, in fact, 'perfectly disorganized', and the person responsible was the head master's wife, Mrs. Simpson, who ruled husband and school with a rod of iron—of her own pattern. Wesley's wrath and indignation were voiced in the Conference of that year, and there was left no doubt that either the school must be closed or steps taken to ensure the proper observance of the Rules passed in 1756. The head master, against whom Wesley appears to have had no personal grudge, was dismissed, mainly, one gathers, that the evil influence of his wife should no longer corrupt the place. Thomas McGeary was appointed head master and matters improved.[58] A strong personal interest and influence was needed, and that the new head master supplied whole-heartedly. He was only twenty-two, but he regarded teaching as his vocation. He was assisted by another professional schoolmaster, Thomas Welch, son of the principal of a dissenting academy in London. He came to the school with some experience of teaching, having been on the staff of a school at Coventry. In spite of all that had happened, Wesley's attitude had not changed one jot from that which he had shown when the school was first opened. He wrote to Welch:

'Dear Thomas,—You seem to be the man I want. As to salary, you will have £30 a year; board, etc., will be thirty more. But do not come *for money*. (1) Do not come at all unless purely to raise a Christian school. (2) Anybody behaving ill I will turn away immediately. (3) I expect you to be in the school eight hours a day. (4) In all things I expect you should be circumspect. But you will judge better by considering the printed Rules. The sooner you come the better.'[59]

The appointment of these two masters marked the end of the more flagrant evils at the school. Wesley was now an old man, though as active as ever, and he was content to look on as these two men set about their task of reforming the life of the school. A year later that family spirit which was the desire of the founder was once more evident, and after a visit in 1786 Wesley wrote in his *Journal*[60]:

'I walked over to Kingswood School, now one of the pleasantest spots in England. I found all things just according to my desire,

[58] *History of Kingswood School*, pp. 79–80.
[59] *Letters*, Vol. VII, p. 188.
[60] Vol. VII, p. 190.

the Rules being well observed, and the whole behaviour of the children showing that they were now managed with the wisdom that cometh from above.'

Again, in the following year, he spent an evening there and was much pleased with the management of it.[61] Two years before he died, Wesley made the last reference to the School in his *Journal* [62] and was able to record peace after the strain and stress of the previous forty years. 'I went over to Kingswood. Sweet recess! where everything is now just as I wish. But "man was not born in shade to lie!" Let us work now; we shall rest by-and-by.' Wesley then, it seemed, did not regret the toil and care which the school had caused him. He regarded this life as a campaign in which there was no time for rest. Ever since he had first turned his thoughts toward education he had remained true to the principles which thought and experience had created within him. Proof of the careful way in which he had evolved his educational scheme is seen in the fact that he never found reason for toning down the strict and almost monastic nature of that scheme. His insistence upon a broad curriculum, upon small classes, and upon the need for personal interest in each pupil is not unlike that found in the best schools today. There is, too, a strong resemblance to the practice of the schools of Port-Royal with their aim of solid intellectual power subservient only to character training.[63] Wesley would have agreed whole-heartedly with this aim. It was from his own attitude toward the content of education that his idea of a Christian family came. Wesley was an evangelist, and an evangelist must look to the interests, not only of the individual, but of the individual's in-fluence on, and place in, society. If the principle was understood adequately in Methodist education, we should expect to see the strict discipline which Wesley advocated combined with a close association between master and pupils. That was one of the reasons for Wesley's wanting small classes. He realized that the mere enforcement of strict discipline upon a child would not necessarily train that child's character. That could only come from mutual regard between teacher and taught. The teacher must first be a man who has been converted—to use Methodist phraseology. Unfortunately, Wesley relied too much upon that one requirement, and forgot that a teacher has need of other

---

[61] *Journal*, Vol. VII, p. 329.
[62] Vol. VIII, p. 10.
[63] H. C. Barnard, *Little Schools of Port-Royal.*

qualifications. The troubles at Kingswood during its first forty years arose largely from his failure to realize that. The converted master must have also a genuine interest in boys so developed that he will make a conscious effort to understand them, while still imposing the strict rules imposed on the school by the founder.

CHAPTER THREE

The Tradition of the Dissenting Academies

*I*N *the attention paid to the religion of students lies the prime excellence of the dissenting academies.'* [1]

Study of the curriculum laid down for Kingswood and later for Woodhouse Grove School reveals a closer affinity to dissenting academies than to the public and grammar schools of this country.[2] Wesley himself was influenced by both. Educated himself at Charterhouse, one of his brothers an usher at Westminster and later head master of Blundell's School, Tiverton, with a strong affection for the classics, he believed in the value of the classical education given in the public and grammar schools. In his youth he had no doubt been influenced and biased against the dissenting academies, for his father, although he had been educated at Veal's Academy, Stepney, and later (on failing to enter Oxford) at the Newington Green Academy where Daniel Defoe was once a pupil, vehemently attacked all dissenting academies in a *Letter from a country divine . . . on the education of the Dissenters in their private academies in several parts of the nation.* It was an outspoken diatribe, and in it Samuel Wesley charged all scholars of such academies with defect of learning, loyalty, sanctity, and respect for the Church, and their tutors with lack of integrity.[3] This letter started a controversy which, if it did nothing more, gained for the writer a reputation as an upholder of the Established Church and an opponent of Dissent. It was answered by a London dissenting minister, Mr. Samuel Palmer, and his reply called forth a second lengthy attack. Although, at the end of his life, Samuel Wesley had considerably modified his hostility, parental views must have had some influence on his children.

Whatever influence there was, however, John Wesley was not so biased in later years as to be hostile to dissenting academies, and though he was deeply disturbed by the growing realization of the separation of the Methodist Connexion from the Church

---

[1] Bogue and Bennett, *History of Dissenters*, Vol. IV, p. 304.
[2] See *A Short Account of the School in Kingswood, near Bristol* (1768), reproduced as Appendix A, p. 324, *infra*.
[3] Bogue and Bennett, op. cit., Vol. II, pp. 90–1.

and of its thus becoming ranked as a dissenting sect,[4] in the educational work which he began in Methodism can be clearly seen the influence of dissenting education. An outline of this form of education is necessary to understand what Methodism owed to it.

During the seventeenth century a group of men worked and spread abroad their views in this country and abroad—men such as Samuel Hartlib (labelled, as was Wesley later, an 'enthusiast'), John Milton, John Dury, John Amos Comenius, and William Petty. These men had a common interest in social and educational reform, though their work in education tended to centre on higher education. Milton's *Tractate on Education* (1664), for example, deals only with secondary education, and it is Milton alone whose views on education are expressly mentioned by Wesley.[5] They were all interested in religion, they believed in the value of the Roman and Greek literatures as educational media and for their own sake, but at the same time they were essentially realistic in their outlook. It was necessary, they implied, to move with the times no less in education than in other matters. Comenius, for example, who came to London in 1641 by invitation, wanted to open in London a college which would give an encyclopedic education, a utilitarian education which would appeal to the professional, the commercial, and the middle classes.

Unfortunately, the Civil War put a stop to such schemes, and the Restoration authorities did not approve of anything suggestive of revolution, however non-physical. They feared that views were becoming too advanced, and steps were taken to crush all tendencies toward independence of thought and action in education and religion. From 1662 date the various Acts of Conformity whose suppressive measures drove social reform underground. It was in this period and endued with this reforming spirit that dissenting academies began, and they continued to flourish until after 1800. While the grammar schools sunk lower and lower into their rut of dull classical tradition, their teachers able to obtain their salaries from endowments without having to bother about pupils,[6] the dissenting academies grew into the

[4] See J. S. Simon, *John Wesley and the Methodist Societies*, pp. 17–18, 211–13; *John Wesley and the Advance of Methodism*, pp. 36–8, 291, 295–300, 329.

[5] *Works*, Vol. XIII, p. 262.

[6] For an interesting account of one such case, see A. W. Gibbon, *The Ancient Free Grammar School of Skipton in Craven*, pp. 58 ff.

greatest schools of the day. Two points must be remembered about them, however. Firstly, they were not merely schools. They were institutions of university status, giving a four-year course to youths from the age of fifteen to seventeen years at entrance, and these youths were expected to have a knowledge of the classics before appearing in the academies. They were 'seminaries, which, but for a malignant policy, would never have existed . . . opened in various parts of the kingdom to meet the wishes of such as would otherwise have sent their sons to the universities'.[7] Secondly, since they were dissenting institutions providing training for those who refused to take the oaths of allegiance to the Established Church and therefore the chief training-grounds for dissenting ministers, the theological course was the most important in their studies, including in its scope divinity, Greek, Hebrew, ethics, natural philosophy, metaphysics, practice in sermon-writing, and instruction in pastoral care. But they also trained many who had no intention of entering the Ministry.[8] Most of the pupils in the seventeenth and early eighteenth centuries appear to have been intended for a professional career—academic, legal, or medical. There were, in fact, occasions when members of the aristocracy were pupils—men like Robert Harley, Earl of Oxford, and Henry St. John, Viscount Bolingbroke—and in the eighteenth century the doors of the academies (no doubt owing to the intentional laxity with which the various laws of conformity were used) were widely opened to students who were not entering any profession, but were interested in commerce and industry. There was a distinct return in curriculum to the original realist movement of the seventeenth century. Modern subjects took a more prominent place, and English displaced Latin as the ordinary mode of speech in lectures. The growth of the idea of a higher education for lay dissenters gathered acceptance, largely owing to the teaching and practice of Dr. Joseph Priestley (1733–1804). His views, widely accepted, were expressed in his *Essay on a Course of Liberal Education for Civil and Active Life* (1765), in which he insisted on the necessity for altering the curriculum to suit the needs of the day and the view that education was not a monopoly of the clergy. He specifically advocated the teaching of history (with which he included geography), enough Latin to permit the

---

[7] Toulmin, *Historical View of the State of the Protestant Dissenters in England*, Vol. II, p. 217.
[8] Bogue and Bennett, op. cit., Vol. II, p. 75.

reading of easy classics, French, and practical mathematics. In these academies 'both tutors and students breathed in a pure air, and having no cause for an idolatrous veneration of antiquity, they sought every improvement within their reach, in order to enrich their course of study. The newest books in the several departments of science displaced the older and more imperfect manuals of the preceding age—and some of the tutors drew up abstracts as textbooks for their own use.' [9] Wesley followed the same plan at Kingswood School and in his publication of the *Christian Library*.[10]

One of the best-known academies in the middle of the eighteenth century was that of Dr. Philip Doddridge at Northampton, and there this same plan concerning textbooks was followed. We have already seen how interested John Wesley was in this academy immediately prior to his establishing Kingswood School and his most friendly relations with its principal. It was no chance that took him to Northampton that day in September 1745. However suspicious Wesley may have been of dissenters, he realized the truth of what Bogue and Bennett said later in their *History of Dissenters:* [11] 'In the attention paid to the religion of students lies the prime excellence of the dissenting academies.' That fact alone would cause him to consider them with interest, while the fact that they were illegal institutions subject to persecution through no fault of their own, yet flourishing in spite of, or because of, that persecution, would draw the sympathy of a man who himself knew what it was to fight against odds. That, however, is mere sentimentality. John Wesley, the loyal Churchman, was attracted toward the dissenters, and especially toward their educational practice, because he was essentially a practical man, and it is in the practical sphere that we can most usefully observe the influence of the dissenting tradition on the work of Wesley.

From what has already been said, it is evident that Methodism owed much to the principles of dissenting education. In four main ways this can be seen:

First, there was, especially in the early stages, a close relationship between the theological training and more general education. The life of every Methodist school has always been closely linked with religion. In the case of the boarding-schools, chapels

[9] Bogue and Bennett, op. cit., Vol. III, p. 301.
[10] See *History of Kingswood School*, pp. 33, 39.
[11] Vol. IV, p. 304.

have been built, or rooms set aside as chapels, corporate prayers are held at least twice each day, and an important part of the education provided is the creation of a balanced life with religion as the co-ordinating factor. Wesley regarded this life as a preparation for life after death, and was not satisfied with a purely classical curriculum. He required a broader view of life, one that dealt with things as well as with people, but above all one that regarded the development of character as more important than intellectual attainment.

Second, the importance of the individual was realized. 'There is no doubt that with the rise of Puritanism the sixteenth century saw a strengthening and a crystallizing into definite shape of the Reformation idea of the recognition of the individual,' writes Irene Parker in her *Dissenting Academies in England*.[12] This has resulted, as did the Methodist revival in the eighteenth century, in a more general interest in religion, in politics, and in education. Just as the formalism of the Church was condemned, so was the worthless formalism of grammar teaching in the schools.

Third, 'Things, not words' had been the battle cry of the seventeenth-century educational reformers. There had been a genuinely healthy interest in educational advance, and at that time it was advance rather than reform that was needed. Comenius had maintained this principle of realistic education in his *Great Didactic*, and whether Wesley had read that work or not, he did owe much to Moravian educational practice. His visit to the Moravian community at Herrnhut had certainly impressed him, as we have seen, and it is noticeable that ever afterward he advocated two of these realistic principles, and, it might be added, was in advance of contemporary educational theory in doing so. He advocated that the teacher should proceed from the known to the unknown [13] and that children should be interested in things rather than in words. However ridiculous some of Wesley's views on education may appear today, there is no denying his place as an educationist when it is remembered that he put forward and practised these principles in the eighteenth century.

Fourth, education must be adaptable (and adapted) to the needs of the day, and teachers must be practical men, in touch with the subjects they taught and with the pupils being taught. McLachlan, in his *English Education under the Test Acts*,[14]

[12] pp. 23-4.   [13] *Works*, Vol. XIII, pp. 261-2.   [14] p. 22.

states that tutors of academies met the need for satisfactory books by writing their own. Wesley did precisely the same, and when he founded Kingswood School, the majority of the text-books in use were written, edited, or abridged by him to suit the ages of the boys for whom the books were intended, and each book contained instructions to the teachers as to their use.[15] Care was taken that no book contained anything profane or obscure which might corrupt youthful minds. Wesley was always suspicious lest any matter or being should 'corrupt'. To this question of books Wesley devoted a large part of his *Plain Account of Kingswood School,* and he took special care to select a certain order for the reading of those books, beginning with the easiest and working upward by gradual stages.

'Another point which has been carefully considered is, the order in which the books are read. The harder are never learned before the easier; we begin with the plainest of all; next read such as are a little more difficult; and gradually rise to those that are hardest of all, that is, of all those which are read in the classes that belong to the school. The most difficult are reserved for those who have gone through the school, and are employed in academical exercises.'[16]

Wesley's greatest achievement in this direction, however, was his publication of the *Christian Library,* which consisted of fifty volumes of extracts or abridgements of the best books published in the English language with a direct or indirect bearing on religion. He asked Dr. Doddridge to help him, as we have seen, in the drawing-up of a list of books suitable for the widening of Methodist preachers' knowledge, and the painstaking reply that he received did much to help him. Publication of this Library cost him over £200 loss from his own pocket in the first eight years, but he did not begrudge that expenditure, regarding it as a solid contribution to education. 'Perhaps the next generation may know the value of it,' he wrote in his *Journal.*[17]

Perhaps the greatest similarity between Kingswood School and a dissenting academy, however, is to be found in that part of the school's organization which Wesley called 'the Academic Course'. In the *Plain Account* he made it clear that Kingswood was more than a school. It was intended to be not unlike one

[15] For a list of these books, see Appendix A and also 'List of Works' in *Works,* Vol. XIV, pp. 215–331.
[16] *Works,* Vol. XIII, p. 262.
[17] Vol. IV, p. 48.

of the academies proposed by Milton and Comenius. He had been loath to adopt any scheme which might appear to compete with the universities, for he himself was a lover of Oxford. But the attitude of the university authorities toward dissenters had compelled him to make plans of his own for the education of Methodists. Those plans he discussed in the following extract from the *Plain Account:*

'It is true, I have for many years suspended the execution of this part of my design. I was indeed thoroughly convinced, ever since I read Milton's admirable 'Treatise on Education', that it was highly expedient for every youth to begin and finish his education at the same place. I was convinced nothing could be more irrational and absurd than to break this off in the middle, and to begin it again at a different place, and in a quite different method. The many and great inconveniences of this, I knew by sad experience. Yet I had so strong a prejudice in favour of our own universities, that of Oxford in particular, that I could hardly think of any one's finishing his education without spending some years there. I therefore encouraged all I had any influence over, to enter at Oxford or Cambridge; both of which I preferred, in many respects, to any university I had seen abroad. Add to this, that several of the young persons at Kingswood had themselves a desire of going to the university. I cannot say I am yet quite clear of that prejudice. I love the very sight of Oxford: I love the manner of life; I love and esteem many of its institutions. But my prejudice in its favour is considerably abated: I do not admire it as I once did. And whether I did or not, I am now constrained to make a virtue of necessity. The late remarkable occurrence of the six young students expelled from the university, and the still more remarkable one of Mr. Seagar refused the liberty of entering into it (by what rule of prudence, I cannot tell, any more than of law or equity), have forced me to see, that neither I, nor any of my friends, must expect either favour or justice there. I am much obliged to Dr. Nowell, and the other Gentlemen who exerted themselves on either of those transactions, for not holding me longer in suspense, but dealing so frankly and openly. And, blessed be God, I can do all the business which I have in hand without them. Honour or preferment I do not want, any more than a feather in my cap; and I trust most of those who are educated at our school are, and will be, of the same mind. And as to the knowledge of the tongues, and of arts and sciences, with whatever is termed academical learning; if those who have a tolerable capacity for them do not advance more here in three years, than the generality of students at Oxford or Cambridge do in seven, I will bear the blame for ever.'[18]

The statements that Wesley then proceeded to make throw an interesting light on certain aspects of university life in the eighteenth century. To those who stressed the advantages which a university had over such an institution as Kingswood, Wesley replied by wondering whether the university professors and tutors were so influential after all. It frequently happened that they lectured to one or two persons only, and when there were audiences very few members of them understood what was being said. Some tutors were worthy of all honour, some were not. Of those who were genuinely learned there were many who could not impart their learning, while there were others who had none to impart. To those who pointed to the social advantages of the universities, Wesley showed the evil influences that were often found in the society there. He admitted that those who sought preferment in Church or State ought to go to Oxford or Cambridge, but, he wrote:

'There are still a few, even young men, in the world, who do not aim at any of these. They do not desire, they do not seek, either honour, or money, or preferment. They leave collegians to dispute, and bite, and scratch, and scramble for these things. They believe there is another world; nay, and they imagine it will last for ever. Supposing this, they point all their designs and all their endeavours toward it. Accordingly, they pursue learning itself, only with reference to this. They regard it merely with a view to eternity; purely with a view to know and teach, more perfectly, the truth which God has revealed to man, "the truth which is after godliness", and which they conceive men cannot be ignorant of without hazarding their eternal salvation. This is the only advantage which they seek; and this they can enjoy in as high a degree, in the school or academy at Kingswood, as at any college in the universe.'[19]

These quotations show clearly the place which Kingswood was intended to hold in English education. How necessary it was to Methodism will be realized when it is remembered that it was not until late in the nineteenth century that Gladstone himself introduced the Universities Tests Act by which religious tests were abolished at Oxford, Cambridge, and Durham, though even

[18] *Works*, Vol. XIII, pp. 262–3.   [19] ibid., p. 266.

then the Act did not apply to degrees in Divinity.[20] It says much for Wesley that when he found the universities closed against his young followers he proposed an alternative scheme and took steps to implement it.

At the same time, as can be seen, Wesley was not afraid to indict the universities for their shortcomings, showing how they lacked true learning, morals, and religion. In the school at Kingswood Wesley showed in practical fashion his conviction of the close connexion between religion and education. He knew that would-be students would find a place and means of learning. He was not convinced that they would take the trouble to find a place and the means which would give a truly broad Christian education.

There are no figures available to show how many pupils stayed on at the school to take the academic course, nor how many students entered after their normal school career. There was, however, one young man who entered for that purpose— Adam Clarke, who was later to become President of the Conference on three occasions. In his youth, Clarke caught the attention of Wesley, who advised him to enter Kingswood and to take the academic course. Most of the information available concerning the school prior to 1782 comes from Wesley himself, and that information had, at best, to be scrappy and biased. (It is only fair to remember, however, that it was not one of Wesley's faults to whitewash even cherished schemes such as Kingswood. When he found cause for criticism, he made it.) In the *Life of Adam Clarke*,[21] however, there is no longer any need to read between the lines to understand what life there was like. Methodism may, as it has been stated, have been cradled in the university, but Methodist education owed most to the domestic education of the home and family, hard as that often was, and to the educational traditions of Dissent.

'The dissenters have, however, something yet to acquire in order to perfect their system of education for the ministry. One of the most important of these desiderata they have already begun to supply—grammar schools for the early initiation of their youths into classical knowledge. For when these institutions become more common, it may be expected that a greater proportion of those who enter the ministry will have had an introduction to the learned languages, which will render their

[20] See Sir Charles E. Mallet, *History of the University of Oxford,* Vol. III.
[21] Published by John Stephens (1834).

future studies more easy, and their attainments more considerable.' [22]

It must be stressed that the dissenting academies were of
university status, just as the upper course of studies at Kingswood was of university status. Their students had to attain a
considerable standard of learning before they entered, and to
meet the demand for this earlier education there must have been
a large number of dissenting schools. Unfortunately, although
a fair amount is known of the academies by reason of the
eminence frequently attained by former students, little is known
of the schools which must have existed, most of them small, all
of them dependent upon private individuals, to supply a stream
of promising scholars to the academies. Research is made more
difficult owing to the fact that many of them, though the
standard of their studies was incomparable to that of the
academies, yet gave themselves the title of 'Academy'.

Such schools became more common after 1779 when an Act
of Parliament allowed Protestant dissenters to follow the teaching profession except at the public schools and universities.
They were founded mainly in the industrial areas, where there
were many manufacturers and business men who demanded a
more practical education for their sons than was provided in the
grammar schools, and a more advanced course than was possible
in the local dame-schools. These were of all denominations, and
included at least some Methodist schools among them.[23] They
were founded to meet a need, and were not bound by tradition
as were the older public and grammar schools. Their curriculum included English, French, mathematics, history, geography,
and science, and such subjects as might be provided to meet the
local needs of their particular district.[24]

Such a school was founded by a Mr. May, a Methodist local
preacher, at Northmolton, Devon, in the middle of the eighteenth
century. The school co-operated with the local farming community by accepting at least some of its pupils for only parts of
each year so that boys should be free to learn their trade of
farming by working on the land for the remainder of the year.
John Gould, a farmer's son, for example, attended this school
for thirteen weeks in each year from November to February
between the ages of twelve and seventeen, and during those

[22] Bogue and Bennett, *History of Dissenters*, Vol. IV, p. 307.
[23] See *Wesley: the Man, his Teaching, and his Work*, p. 253.
[24] See *Report of the Spens Commission on Secondary Education*, pp. 12–13.

years, in addition to the normal subjects mentioned above and taught in such schools, he learnt land-surveying and navigation.[25]

Further evidence of the manner in which these schools were founded can be gathered from the story of another farmer's son in the same district. Arthur Packer, after leaving Tiverton Grammar School at the age of sixteen, started a school of his own at Winkleigh, which he moved in 1810 to Barnstaple. He was no firm adherent to any particular denomination, but when he opened his school at Barnstaple he came under the influence of the Rev. Cradock Glascott whose father had been a friend of Wesley's and one of those reputed to have been present at the Methodist Conference in Bristol in 1746. The son, after being ordained in the Church of England, became one of Lady Huntingdon's chaplains, and was employed as an itinerant preacher until in 1782 he was presented with the living of Hatherleigh. This clergyman appears to have had considerable influence on at least two schoolmasters. Packer, partly owing to his influence and partly owing to the influence of Methodist friends in Barnstaple, became a Methodist, and in spite of the forebodings of many his school prospered and quickly had a hundred pupils on its roll, his brother opening a classical branch of the same school.[26] The other schoolmaster was a Mr. Roberts, who gathered a large school, numbering as many as sixty youths, principally boarders, the children of farmers of near and distant parishes. These were brought under the pastoral direction and instruction of Mr. Glascott.[27]

Another example of the setting up of a dissenting school of a similar nature is found in the biography of the Rev. William Barber, a Methodist missionary. The son of a Wesleyan father and a Baptist mother, he was, as might be expected, 'carefully educated in the nurture and admonition of the Lord'.[28] The results, however, do not appear to have been all that might have been hoped, and when he was seven or eight years old, owing to 'the wildness of his habits and those of the associates with whom he was invincibly connected',[29] he was removed from a day-school in Bristol and sent to his uncle's classical academy at Wellington, Somerset. His age at entry proves this to have been no academy in the accepted meaning of the word. It was indeed

---

[25] *Methodism in North Devon*, pp. 33–4.
[26] ibid., pp. 125–6.
[27] ibid., pp. 165–6.
[28] cf. Fol. 542 *Memoirs of the late Rev. William Barber*, p. 1.
[29] ibid., p. 2.

one of the dissenting schools which prepared boys for admittance to the dissenting academies proper, and was under the head mastership of the Rev. John Cherry, a Baptist minister. After spending three or four years here he was 'deeply convinced of his awful alienation from God and exposure to eternal wrath', became a Methodist local preacher, and hoped eventually to enter the ministry. Knowing this, the Baptist Academy accepted him as a student without fees.

On completing the course at this academy he accepted the offer of a post as tutor in the 'classical and commercial academy' of Mr. William Clarke at Chew Magna, near Bristol, of which in 1819 he became acting head master. Illness forced him to retire from this work, however, and for seven months he was unable to undertake any duties. When he had recovered, there being no vacancy at that time for entrance to the Methodist ministry, he decided to open a 'classical, commercial, and mathematical academy' of his own at Longford, near Gloucester.

A gentleman of the neighbourhood, on being asked whether he intended sending his son there, is said to have replied: 'No. From what I have heard, the young man (Barber) is polite enough, and able enough, but I understand he is a Methodist, and I would as soon send my children to —— (presumably the Devil) as to a Methodist!' [30] Nevertheless, despite prejudiced opposition of this sort, the school flourished, and Barber found it necessary to employ an assistant, while his elder sister acted as matron-housekeeper. The age of the pupils is not mentioned, but it is clear that they were children rather than young men of university age. Another fact of interest is that the life of the school centred round the Methodist Class-meeting which Barber established from the first.

Within a year of opening the school, Mr. Barber married, and an account of the reception which the school prepared for the bridal couple makes amusing reading and throws some light on the type of discipline which prevailed in the school. The bridegroom wrote in a letter to his parents:

'We took tea at Ross and reached Longford about eight in the evening. The weather was remarkably fine, and nothing unpleasant was permitted to disturb the hilarity of the evening. The boys were in a high tone of preparation, they had provided themselves with a Christian song and a poetic address of welcome to the bride, and they feasted like princes on the cake and

[30] *Memoirs of the late Rev. William Barber,* p. 120.

wine prepared for them by Mrs. W. (the bride's mother). Nothing but entire satisfaction was visible, nothing but cordial congratulation was to be heard: it was indeed a solemn—happy—Christian day, for we had no boisterous nor irrational mirth.' [31]

The school continued to grow in numbers to such an extent that the house at Longford soon proved too small to accommodate all who wished to enter, and plans were made for moving to larger premises near Gloucester. Those plans never materialized, for within six months Mrs. Barber died of an infectious illness.

Infectious illnesses, even today, are a serious problem in any boarding-school. Apart from the disturbing influence on the school curriculum and its consequent bad effect on efficiency, they affect the reputation of the school. Contrary to one trend of thought, parents do not, and did not in the nineteenth century, often send their children to boarding-schools in order to be rid of a nuisance. They send them because they sincerely believe that in such schools their children will achieve the best results. Considerable thought is naturally given to the choice of a school and not the least consideration is that of health. Many great schools have come near to disaster, especially in the nineteenth century, owing to the outbreak of a serious epidemic. There are no records to show how many actually met complete disaster. We do know that in this particular case a school ceased to exist.

There must have been many private dissenting schools in the early nineteenth century, but because they were purely private schools not one of them has survived today. In some cases they continued for several generations, successive head masters or mistresses being members of the family who owned them. Some, like the day-school at New Buckenham, Norfolk, whose head master was a Methodist local preacher, were little more than dame-schools and gave even the rudiments of education inefficiently. Others, such as the Mackworth Academy in Derbyshire, tried to carry on the best traditions of higher education and character-building. In 1837, the head master of this school was Thomas Russell, who had been educated at Kingswood School (1817-22), and such a school succeeded because of the efficiency and the sense of vocation shown by its staff and particularly by its head master, who in this instance 'exerted an influence none the less lasting and extensive because so quiet and gentle, not only on the mental habits of his pupils, but also on their

[31] *Memoirs of the late Rev. William Barber,* p. 125.

manners, and on their character and spiritual life'.[32] To such schools the more prosperous Methodists sent their sons [33] and at this particular one were educated a number of men who became leading Methodist ministers.

Nevertheless, the education of future dissenting ministers was not their chief aim, as it was no longer the chief aim of the dissenting academies proper. Already these schools and academies were concentrating on the subjects which later were to form the staple subjects of public and grammar schools' curricula. It was, we read, a matter of regret 'that the elegant classic, the profound metaphysician, often lost the spirit of the man of God in the taste of the man of letters, and studied to recommend himself to the great by his literature, rather than to the good by his usefulness. . . . Many liberal friends of our religion were induced, therefore, to project the formation of seminaries in which the time of education should be shorter, and the objects of attention should be only those which were essential to the plain useful pastor.' [34] Here is seen the first mention of dissenting colleges for the study of theology only, but Methodism did not institute such colleges until well into the nineteenth century.[35] At first, as will be shown in the case of the schools at Taunton, Shebbear, and York, the tradition of dissent was followed in that specialized training for the ministry was provided in schools, as was envisaged in 1744 when the question (repeated annually for many years) was first asked in Methodism: 'Can we have a seminary for labourers?' [36]

That was the transition stage when general education was mixed with a more specialized theological training. By the close of the eighteenth century the need for theological colleges separate from dissenting schools and academies was becoming a real need, and by 1808 the number being educated for the ministry among the different denominations of dissenters was far greater than at any former period.[37]

John Wesley was not the only clergyman who was influenced by these ideas. In 1782, John Newton formulated a scheme for

[32] Benjamin Gregory, *Autobiographical Recollections*, p. 204.
[33] Similar schools for girls are mentioned later, in Chapter 16 (pp. 267 ff., *infra*).
[34] Bogue and Bennett, op. cit., Vol. IV, p. 300.
[35] 1834, when a small theological institution was opened at Hoxton. This was followed during the century by Didsbury, Manchester (1842); Richmond (1843); Headingly (1888); Victoria Park (1872); Handsworth (1881); Hartley (1881); and Wesley College, Cambridge (1921).
[36] *Wesley Historical Society Publications*, No. 1, p. 17; cf. p. 39, *supra*.
[37] Bogue and Bennett, op. cit., Vol. IV, p. 303.

the establishment of a school in the tradition of the dissenting academies for the education of students who would, at the close of their studies, be prepared to serve as clergymen either in the Church of England or in the Churches of Dissent. His scheme was published in a pamphlet entitled *A Plan of Academic Preparation for the Ministry*. William Cowper was interested, and it was he who sent a copy of the pamphlet to the Rev. William Bull, urging him to establish such a school. By the efforts of a number of friends subscriptions were raised, and in January 1783 Mr. Bull opened a school at Newport Pagnell organized on the lines suggested. A school of a simliar nature was later opened by another clergyman, the Rev. Cornelius Winter, at Painswick, Gloucestershire.

Although it had never been laid down that Kingswood School was intended to produce future Methodist ministers, the idea—and the result—has always been present, and the hope that a school of this sort would in fact produce future ministers was felt when, as will be shown in the next chapter, a second Methodist school was founded.

CHAPTER FOUR

A Second Methodist School

AT THE CLOSE of the eighteenth century Kingswood was the only Methodist Connexional school giving higher education to its pupils, and from the early nineteenth century that school was confined to the sons of Wesleyan Methodist preachers. At that time the Connexion was passing through a critical stage. It had passed its infancy and was proving its ability to stand on its own legs. Its founder and source of life, as it seemed to many, died in 1791. Any system of philosophy—religious or otherwise—may flourish during its founder's lifetime, but if it is a true system its essentials will last for all time. Was Methodism to show some fundamental contribution to the spread and practice of Christianity, or was it to sink back into evangelical conformity? The years following the death of John Wesley were to prove decisive. It was fortunate for Methodism that in 1799 the Connexion received as one of its preachers a man who was essentially a statesman. Like Wesley himself, he was an autocrat, and his dominating personality made him many enemies, but his life was one of selflessness, and the organization which he helped to give to Methodism was brilliant. That man was Jabez Bunting (1779–1858), a man remembered in Methodism as second only to John Wesley. In the eyes of the world, until the early years of the nineteenth century, Methodism was merely another sect of dissenters. It was due to the far-sighted understanding of Jabez Bunting that Methodism came to take its place as a widely recognized religious sect which played a part in national life, and from which were to arise many of the leaders of the trade-union movement. It was Bunting who realized how great a part organization has to play in the firm establishment of religion in national life. He followed Wesley in his insistence upon the realization of personal redemption and the need of vocation on the part of men who became whole-time preachers. He followed his own genius in his insistence on the formation of those preachers into a strong organization, working toward one common end: the introduction of God to those who did not know Him. He played a leading part in sowing the seeds of understanding of the slogan:

74

'Union is strength'. To achieve such results he organized the Conference into the weighty legal machine which it now is, and in so doing he built up a force of clergy in no way inferior to that of the Established Church. This is no place to deal with the details of Bunting's work in achieving such a result, but it is significant that, like Wesley, he early realized the importance of education in that work.

We speak glibly of 'apostolic succession' in many contexts, but we see it working clearly in the history of Methodism. It was Joseph Benson, one-time governor of Kingswood School, who started Jabez Bunting on his work. It was he whom Bunting called his 'spiritual father'. Bunting was fifteen years old when he became a member of the Methodist Society and met Benson, and from that time onward the young man studied the organization, or the lack of organization, of Methodism with watchful eyes.

When Wesley died a storm of controversy broke out in the Connexion. There had been low rumblings during the founder's lifetime, but his presence had tended to still them. When the master hand had gone, however, quarrels broke out and Bunting (though only twelve when Wesley died) watched it all with interest.

'Of an eager disposition, and naturally apt at the solution of questions of practical difficulty, he noted every phase and change of the controversies of that period, as they rose; he acquired a thorough insight into their nature and meaning; he became familiar with their essential principles; and he laid up a store of facts, precedents, and opinions which were of great and lasting service to him, during the whole of his subsequent course.'[1]

It was controversy which for half a century and more distracted the majority of the Methodist leaders from the needs of education as part of religious training, but it acted on Bunting in a different way: it awoke in him a realization of the need for education if such controversies were to come to an end and if Methodism was to become a force for national good. In a letter written in 1805 he wrote deploring the lack of distinguished writers and theologians in Methodism, for that seemed to him its chief defect.[2] While still only seventeen years of age he became the founder of a 'Society for the Acquirement of Religious Knowledge' whose object was the improvement of religious

[1] Thomas P. Bunting, *Life of Jabez Bunting, D.D.*, p. 71.
[2] ibid., p. 234.

knowledge, experience, and practice in individuals to make them more desirous of being, and more able to be, useful members of the Church of Christ in this world. It was in this Society that Bunting laid the foundations of his work as a preacher and as one of the great religious statesmen of his time.

After Wesley's death the clergy who used to help him fell back into full support of the Established Church, in many cases becoming the leaders of the Evangelical party in that Church. They were men of culture. The Methodist preachers, considered in general, were not men of culture. Their sermons were evidence of that, being evangelical rather than reasoned arguments. At that time there was an increasing number of people who formed their opinions on reason and not on slavish imitation or mob influence through emotionalism. The power of literature began to make itself felt, and there is always danger lest literature may become anti-religious, the spiritual being swallowed up in purely intellectual considerations. Sir Walter Scott's biographer claimed that Scott's services, direct and indirect, toward repressing the revolutionary propensies of his age were vast. If fiction could wield such power—and there is no evidence for doubting it—then the printed word of a religious body could also do much, and should do much. Bunting showed himself a true follower of John Wesley in realizing the power of literature and of the Press, which at that time, with the increasing facilities of communication, printing, and transport, was beginning to show itself. 'That mode of influencing public opinion, and of saving souls from death, we grossly neglect; a neglect, however, which is one out of many evils resulting from an uneducated ministry.' [3] Those last two words reveal the incentive of Bunting's first work for education. He saw that, unless its ministers were educated, Methodism could not advance beyond a certain point. He was not alone in that view. There was a growing feeling in the Connexion that there should be more systematic training of approved candidates for the ministry. Bunting himself had a deep sense of the responsibility of men who took upon themselves the pastoral charge, and he wanted to see them intellectually developed for the responsibility. He felt that many first-class scholars were being wasted through lack of opportunity and training. True, many ministers spent long hours in learning Greek and Hebrew that they might read the Scriptures in their original form and understand the various

[3] Thomas P. Bunting, *Life of Jabez Bunting, D.D.*, p. 234.

commentaries upon them, but such self-education, commendable as it was, could rarely reach the highest results, since it lacked the inspiration of a teacher who had himself experienced the difficulties of a beginner and who could give the necessary stimulus to minds often dulled by the daily routine of their pastoral duties.[4] It was mainly owing to his efforts that the Theological Institution was founded in 1834, with Bunting as its first Principal, for 'through him, more than through any other man, the value of education for the ministry was realized in the Methodist Church'.[5]

That, however, did not take place till nearly thirty years after the period with which we are now dealing. It was the result of a great deal of work by, at first, a small group of men. All the proposals concerning higher education during the first hundred years of Methodism were connected with either a raising of the educational standards of preachers, or with the charitable care and training of preachers' children. There was confusion of aims. Methodism did, in fact, follow the same method as that of the eighteenth-century dissenting academies, in which theological training was often mixed with more general training. The education given at Kingswood, Woodhouse Grove, Shebbear, Queen's College, and Elmfield aimed in part at least at the production of future ministers, and in each of these schools, except Woodhouse Grove, there was in the first years of their existence a specialized theological course for ministerial candidates.

The training of ministers was a work which Bunting believed to be essential if Methodism was to spread; that was his chief interest in education in the very early stages of his ministry, and once he had realized its importance he worked unceasingly toward its attainment. Whatever education was given must be distinctly and doctrinally religious. Throughout his life he stated that emphatically, and Methodism has taken his words as one of its educational principles. It was what Wesley himself had said of education. That was why his Rules for the pupils at Kingswood were so strict and apparently harsh. That was why there was so much hostility on the part of official Methodism to State provision of schools during part of the nineteenth century.

'I think that education, so called, without religion, is not education. I think that an education which looks only at the

---

[4] An excellent illustration of the breadth and depth of preachers' reading can be gathered from Benjamin Gregory's *Autobiographical Recollections*, pp. 165 ff.
[5] Maldwyn Edwards, *After Wesley*, p. 156.

secular interests of an individual, which looks only at his condition as a member of civil society, and does not look at him as a man having an immortal soul, as a being bound to prepare for eternity, is not education.'⁶

Those words were spoken by Bunting at the age of seventy-six. They might well have been spoken by Wesley nearly a hundred years before. The thought is precisely the same.

It was Adam Clarke (who had, incidentally, laid the foundations of his scholarship under the patronage of Wesley himself) who first proposed a definite scheme for the extension of educational facilities in Methodism, and in 1806 a paper on the subject was read in Conference. It was referred back to District Synods for further consideration, and there, officially, the matter rested for five years. But interest in education was steadily growing, and the fact that there was opposition to any advance in this direction only helped to make it grow the more healthily. There was a strong feeling that more should be done to raise the cultural standard of preachers; there were some who felt that the educational facilities already provided were insufficient; there were others, mainly unmarried, who strongly objected to the foundation of another school, describing such a project as 'a grand trick of the devil'.⁷

There were others—the largest party—who wanted more education, but who were alarmed at the financial aspect of such extension, and adopted a laissez-faire attitude. Alexander Suter, in a private note on the Paper read at the 1806 Conference, said: 'About a grammar school, or academy, Butterworth sent a letter on the subject, in which are very indifferent reflections.'⁸ The lack of enthusiasm which these words suggest was typical of many.

For five years the question was discussed without any official step being taken, though the District Synods in the north made some practical inquiries, as will be shown later. Meanwhile, Bunting, the growing power behind the Methodist ministry, watching and listening, waited until there was a more general concurrence of opinion in favour of another school.

In 1811 it became clear that there was a majority opinion in favour of a second school, and Jabez Bunting's patient exertions to increase the interest of Methodism in higher education was rewarded. On 29th July the sixty-eighth Conference opened in

⁶ T. P. Bunting, op. cit., p. 735.   ⁷ ibid., p. 281.
⁸ ibid.

78

Sheffield under the Presidency of the Rev. Charles Atmore, and at this Conference three separate proposals were made for the establishment of a second school for ministers' sons. Preliminary inquiries had already been made concerning suitable property in the north of England, for it was felt that since Kingswood was situated in the south, a second school would be most usefully situated in the north. As a result of these preliminary investigations, it was proposed that a school should be established in one of the following places: 1. Mansfield, where a suitable house was for sale, plans of which were produced. 2. Bramley, four miles west of Leeds, where suitable land had already been purchased and on which a new building could be erected. (Nothing more is known of this purchase, but it is a strange example of a *fait accompli* when the poor financial state of the Connexion is considered.) 3. Apperley Bridge, near Bradford, where a suitable house and estate, the former residence of a Quaker gentleman named Elam, were on sale cheaply.

The proposals were carefully considered, for the respective District Synods had been most careful in their investigations. The Halifax District put forward a very strong claim in favour of Apperley Bridge, where the estate was known as Woodhouse Grove. The debate was long, the final vote being taken by ballot. A large majority voted in favour of Woodhouse Grove. It was possibly not the geographical position merely that was attractive, for Yorkshire Methodists were recognised as 'sensible and liberal'. The decision of Conference is best recorded in its original Minute form:

'1. That it is highly expedient to provide an additional school, without delay, for the education of those sons of preachers who cannot be admitted at Kingswood, or whose fathers may prefer another situation to that of Kingswood.

'2. That the house and estate of Woodhouse-Grove, near Leeds, in Yorkshire, are the most eligible that have been offered for this purpose: and that they be immediately purchased on behalf of the conference, by the president.

'3. That the premises thus to be purchased shall be designated, in honour of our venerable father in the gospel, *The Wesleyan Academy* at Woodhouse-Grove.

'4. That the estate, when purchased, shall be legally conveyed to twenty-three trustees, on behalf of the conference; and that the following brethren shall be the trustees, viz. James Wood,

Dr. Coke, Joseph Benson, Henry Moore, Joseph Taylor, Adam Clarke, John Barber, Charles Atmore, James Bogie, Walter Griffith, Jonathan Crowther, John Gaulter, George Highfield, William Bramwell, Richard Reece, Joseph Entwisle, Thomas Wood, John Stamp, Samuel Taylor, John Stephens, George Marsden, Jabez Bunting, Robert Newton.

'5. That a committee shall be appointed to superintend the fitting-up and furnishing of the academy, and to prepare it for the purposes of education;—that the said committee shall consist of the following preachers and others. . . . [Here followed the names of the committee members.]

'6. That a subscription be immediately opened by the preachers now present; and that the chairman of the committee shall be directed to send a circular letter to every absent preacher, requesting him, in the name of the conference, to contribute a sum not less than one guinea (and more if his circumstances will permit) toward the intended purchase.

'7. That the superintendents shall be directed, in the said circular letter, to make immediate application for the same purpose, to our principal friends in their respective circuits, and to forward the monies which may be raised to Mr. Wood, at Leeds.

'8. That lists of the subscribers shall be published from time to time, on the cover of the Methodist magazines.' [9]

If Wesley's views about the geographical position of a school were remembered, a more suitable spot could not then have been chosen. Wesley, in choosing a site for his own school, had written: 'The first point was to find a proper situation; not too far from a great town; which I saw would be highly inconvenient for a large family: nor yet too near, and much less in it; which would have been attended with greater evils.' [10]

The site chosen for this second school was thus described in the *British Register* for November 1811: 'Woodhouse Grove, near Leeds, the estate recently purchased by the Methodists for a large seminary of education, is, without exception, one of the most delightful situations in this country. It is situated in a rich and highly cultivated valley on the banks of the river Aire, abounding in wood and water. To the north is the beautiful scenery of Esholt; the south aspect presents the bold and in-

[9] Jonathan Crowther, *History of the Wesleyan Methodists*, pp. 147–8.
[10] *Works*, Vol. XIII, p. 258.

teresting landscapes of Rawdon and Horsforth, and the west the towering woods of Calverley. The estate, which, besides the mansion, consists of about fifteen acres of land, cost the Methodists only £4,575, a sum scarcely equal to the value of the buildings.' [11]

A modern traveller passing the school might smile when he beheld the 'beautiful scenery of Esholt', but it requires little imagination to realize what must have been the real beauty and advantages of such a locality in those early years of the nineteenth century.

Toward the cost of purchase £428 15s. was at once raised amongst the ministers attending the Conference. A total of £1,377 12s. was subscribed by Conference before its close, and the ministerial aspect of the school was emphasized by the fact that before any appeal for funds was made to laymen, each minister had undertaken to contribute at least one guinea. It is significant, too, that this was the largest financial undertaking in which Conference had engaged up to that date. There is often cause for grumbling even today that a penny spent on education is a penny wasted. There is also, even today, an impression that Methodism, especially in its early stages, has not done all it might for education. But the facts of the purchase of the Woodhouse Grove estate speak for themselves, especially when it is remembered that in 1811 the Methodist Connexion had no really wealthy members, and that it had to consider the most effective way of spending every penny. One would imagine that an economic survey of the first hundred years of Methodism would show many instances of the faith required by Christ: 'Take no thought for the morrow, what ye shall eat. . . .' The evangelical side of Methodism was dominant at that time, and sometimes there was a tendency to overlook the importance of the educational factor. But again, it is only fair to remember that the majority of the preachers were men who had taught themselves all the book-learning they had, and most of them had some. Education lacked organization—as it did everywhere in England —and its scope in relation to winning souls for God had not been generally realized, but enlightenment was increasing, and now and again an individual or a small group of men kindled a spark, and as Methodist organization grew so did educational facilities. In 1811 the fact stands out: the largest financial outlay yet made by Conference was given to education, and

[11] Quoted by J. T. Slugg, *Woodhouse Grove School*, p. 5.

the 'Wesleyan Academy of Woodhouse Grove' came into being.

Immediate preparations were made to receive boys from the north of England who could not be accommodated at Kingswood. No attempt was made to build a new school, and little was done in the way of adapting existing buildings. The committee, which included six Yorkshire laymen, consisted of practical men who may not have had particularly enlightened views on education, but who knew how to tackle a job, and they set about their task of turning a private residence into a school. The barn was fitted up as a schoolroom; a room adjoining was furnished as a form-room for senior boys; the stable was turned into a chapel. Thirty beds were purchased.

Dr. Thomas Arnold has been claimed as the first head master to centralize school activities around the school chapel, but he did not become head master of Rugby until 1828, and in 1811 the committee of Woodhouse Grove School was converting a stable into a chapel. Financial considerations compelled the keeping to bare essentials, but a chapel was considered to be one of those essentials. It would be wrong, however, to suggest that this school was a pioneer in centralizing the chapel as the focal point of school routine. Roman Catholics in their educational work on the Continent and in this country had for long made it their central feature. Most of the dissenting academies did likewise, and Wesley himself had insisted on the central position of the school chapel at Kingswood. The Grove committee was merely following his example, and his expressed wish. The time-table of daily routine shows the importance attached to religious observance.[12]

The school was opened in the early part of 1812 with twenty-seven boys. There is no need to go into details concerning the school staff nor the organization during the following seventy years.[13] There is one point, however, about which there has been some confusion—the connexion of the Brontë family with this school. This is admittedly a digression from the theme of this work, but it is an interesting one and has at least a slight bearing on the matter in hand.

It is not known how the first head master came to be selected, but he was a layman who afterwards became a clergyman in the

---

[12] See Appendix C, p. 330, *infra*.
[13] The story is told by J. T. Slugg in his *Woodhouse Grove School*, and by H. W. Starkey in his *Short History of Woodhouse Grove School*.

Church of England. His name was John Fennell, and his wife was appointed to look after the domestic arrangements of the new school, the two together receiving a salary of £100 per annum. The Rev. Patrick Brontë, then curate of Hartshead, a small village east of Huddersfield, became the first examiner of the pupils, for in those days it was the custom to appoint an external examiner to conduct examinations annually or at more frequent intervals. No doubt he was glad to undertake this work, for he had himself opened a school in Ireland at the age of sixteen and continued it for four or five years until he became tutor to the Rev. Tighe, Rector of Drumgooland. He was therefore interested in education, and during the course of his duties as tutor he had probably become interested in Methodism, for Mary Tighe (wife of Henry Tighe, M.P., a member of the family) was a Methodist. There was soon a third reason—the strongest of all—for wishing to visit the school, for in the summer of 1812 Maria Branwell, daughter of a Penzance merchant and niece of John Fennell, came to visit her uncle. Mrs. Gaskell in her *Life of Charlotte Brontë* [14] states that Mr. Fennell was then a Church of England clergyman who had previously been a Methodist minister, but in fact he was a layman and did not become a clergyman until later. It would have been easy to make the mistake of believing him to be a Methodist minister since he was head master of a Methodist school for ministers' sons. Thomas Fletcher, brother-in-law of Jabez Bunting, wrote to his son: 'Early in 1812 the school at Woodhouse Grove was opened. At the following Conference it was stated that the young man who had been appointed class teacher was not competent and the Conference requested that I should take his place.' [15] Mr. Fennell cannot have been as young as Mr. Fletcher implied, for he had a daughter of marriageable age. Possibly his youthfulness was suggested by rumours reaching Mr. Fletcher of certain things which were happening in the head master's household, for while Maria Branwell was staying there she met Patrick Brontë and the friendship thus started quickly ripened into an engagement. Mrs. Gaskell speaks of picnics at such places as Kirkstall Abbey, in which, no doubt, the Fennell family, Maria, Patrick Brontë, and his clergyman friend, Mr. Morgan, took part. Maria's parents made no objection to the engagement, and the marriage was arranged to take place in that same year.

[14] Routledge New Universal Library Edition, p. 36.
[15] H. W. Starkey, op. cit., p. 21.

H. W. Starkey [16] continues the story: 'Mr. Fennell's daughter Jane was at the time engaged to a clergyman of the name of Morgan, and it was decided that the two marriages should be celebrated on the same day, and at Guiseley Church. The Rev. Patrick Brontë performed the ceremony for the Rev. Morgan and Miss Fennell, while Mr. Morgan in his turn married Mr. Brontë and Miss Branwell, the Governor in each case giving the bride away.' It was in memory of the connexion between the Brontë family and the school that the preparatory school for Woodhouse Grove, opened in 1934, was called Brontë House, especially as it was at Upperwood, on the site of which Brontë House now stands, that Charlotte Brontë was at one time a governess.

It appears probable that such distractions as would be occasioned by this double courtship would hardly make for the watchful care and organization which the successful opening of a new school would demand, and it is not surprising perhaps that Conference took steps to get rid of the head master who was their first choice.

As far as the school and Methodism were concerned, it was not an auspicious beginning, nor did matters improve for some time. When one considers the difficulties of the administration it is a matter for surprise that the school continued to exist at all, and that, as a school, it quickly earned for itself a sound reputation. It started with no settled scheme of instruction, no governor who might have watched developments on behalf of Conference, a head master who proved far from capable, and a miscellaneous collection of pupils of all ages whose previous education had been sketchy in the extreme. It was administration and staffing that proved the greatest problem. During the first four years of the school's existence there were five head masters and five governors. Domestic difficulties were continually arising, and were only set right finally by the wife of a governor who 'came and discharged all the servants at once!' [17] Men were appointed to the governorship who were too old for their work and who had no knowledge of children. One of the head masters of the early period, in a fit of despondency as to the management of the school, threw up his appointment and emigrated to America! On the other hand, even among the misfits, there were men who, though they might not have been schoolmasters, had character and personality which made them

[16] H. W. Starkey, op. cit., p. 20.   [17] ibid., p. 25.

remembered by former pupils long after the more practised schoolmasters were forgotten. Such a man was the Rev. Miles Martindale, who went to the Grove at the close of those four anxious years and who set the school on a surer course. The period of his governorship (1816–24) was a vital one in which were shaped the traditions and destinies of the school. The governor was 'everything a governor needed to be, and far more than that officer was expected to be. In the field he was a farmer, in the household a head, in the playground an observer, in every department a ruler, in the pulpit and at prayers a Christian sage, and in all places and at all times a father and a friend.' [18]

As has already been pointed out, Methodist secondary education was instituted and organized by individuals. The individuals were inspired by the evangelical spirit of Methodism. Individuals undertook the education of the young, and it was not till late in the nineteenth century that the Methodist Connexion as a whole took an active hand in helping to provide secondary education on a wider scale than that provided at Kingswood and Woodhouse Grove. The work was left to individuals of genius and foresight. Miles Martindale has a strong claim to be ranked among this group of Methodist educationists. He was not, in the theoretical sense of the word, an educationist. He was not even interested primarily in education, but he was a Methodist of the best type and a hard worker who accomplished to the utmost of his ability any job that was entrusted to him. He was a self-made man—if that epithet can be applied to a man of religion—a type common enough in the nineteenth century, but less common in the eighteenth century when Martindale was busy 'making' himself. He was a thinker, and when a young man he had passed through the various stages of scepticism—atheism and materialism. But he had that type of inquiring mind which went to the best authorities for his philosophy. He read Voltaire and Rousseau and was perforce compelled to learn French. He found the classics necessary for a satisfactory solution of his religious and spiritual difficulties, and was compelled to learn Greek and Latin. Not until he had undergone such a rigid course of learning and reading did he come to believe that Methodism's approach to religion was the sound one. The fact which arouses admiration about Martindale, however, is that during the whole of this vast amount of work, self-inflicted, he

[18] H. W. Starkey, op. cit., p. 25.

was carrying on the work which supported his wife and family. Once persuaded that Methodism was the creed of his choice, he gave himself up to evangelistic work, and in 1789 entered the Methodist ministry. After travelling for twenty-seven years and becoming twice chairman of the District, he was appointed governor of Woodhouse Grove School in 1816—the fifth governor to be appointed since the opening of the school. Previously, Martindale had never had much to do with children apart from those of his own family, but at once he set himself energetically to learn the new task to which he had been called, and a diverse one he found it.

'With fully eighty pupils clothed, boarded, and lodged at the institution, some ten or twelve domestics, a large house, and a considerable farm under his care—the whole establishment open every hour to the visits of such of the boys' parents as might be stationed near, or whom chance might bring into the neighbourhood, and no less so to the lay friends and patrons of the school —it may easily be seen that his duties and responsibilities were not light, though his excellent wife was no less active than himself, and his three daughters took part in the domestic management. The responsibility rested upon him. . . . He was the first to rise in the morning, and generally the last to retire at night, and, after the boys had retired to bed, he would go round the various rooms to see that each boy was in his own bed, and that all was right.' [19]

This sketch of one aspect of life at the school will help one to appreciate the difficulties with which a man like Martindale had to deal. But what entitles him to a place among Methodist educationists is the fact that once he had mastered the theory of secondary education as practised at Woodhouse Grove he began to expand the theory into a more common-sense practice. He quickly saw that the standard of reading in the school was low and that the pupils' ability to speak aloud and express original thought in speech or writing was limited. He promptly took steps to improve matters, and herein showed himself a reformer. The standard of speech and composition in the native tongue was a subject for criticism in various educational inquiries made at the close of the nineteenth century and in the twentieth century in all types of school, including the public schools. [20] It is not

[19] H. W. Starkey, op. cit., pp. 46–7.
[20] Report of the Committee of the Secondary School Examinations Council appointed by the President of the Board of Education in 1941 (Norwood Commission), p. 92.

right to claim that one of the characteristics of Methodist secondary education in the nineteenth century was an ability to use the native tongue correctly and elegantly in speech and writing, but we do know that English reading and, to a lesser extent, speaking were encouraged in these schools.[21] It was Miles Martindale who led the way in this matter. Instead of filling his pupils to saturation point with Greek and Latin classics, and especially with their syntax, he encouraged the reading of English poetry and prose, particularly in the higher Forms. No talking was allowed at meals either at Kingswood or at Woodhouse Grove, and until at least 1930 it was the custom—though the no-talking rule had long since lapsed—for boys to read at meal-times. But Martindale did not consider it sufficient that books should be read in silence: they had to be read aloud, and with the proper pause, intonation, and emphasis. At all times, in and out of school, he strove to influence boys in this matter of literature. Public speaking too was encouraged, and here the governor discovered a method of doing two things at once. Both he and his wife were missionary enthusiasts, so they started missionary meetings (which have remained a feature of life at Woodhouse Grove to this day). These meetings had to be properly conducted. Boys then, as now, frequently lost the use of their tongues through nervousness. One young speaker at one of these early missionary meetings rose to deliver his carefully prepared speech—and found that he could not start. In the midst of the awkward silence which ensued and just as the boy was going to resume his seat, Mrs. Martindale called out: 'Take your speech out of your pocket, my lad; it's worth it!' It would be well if modern English masters took as much care over spoken English as this untrained governor and his wife did.

Such an incident as that just related gives some indication of the atmosphere which prevailed in the early years of last century. The life was hard and sometimes over-severe; corporal punishment was the normal method of maintaining discipline; but there was an intimacy and a homeliness about it all which one looks for in vain in most boarding-schools of the time. Wesley's family spirit was alive.

One other innovation of Martindale's should be mentioned. He not only encouraged the spoken word: he also encouraged

[21] Wesley himself had several things to say on the subject of the written and spoken word, and he always practised what he preached. See *Works*, Vol. VIII, p. 317, Vol. XIV, pp. 312–13; and Sir Leslie Stephen: *English Thought in the Eighteenth Century*, Vol. II, p. 410 *et passim*.

written composition by offering prizes—from his own not-too-well-filled pocket—for the best essays on given subjects. Such encouragement was not often found in other schools at that time.

Appendix C to this work [22] shows the routine and curriculum in use at the school only a few months after its opening. The non-appearance of Greek on the time-table is explained by the fact that the boy who wrote the letter on which this table is based was a junior who had not started to learn Greek. That subject was not taught until the middle school, the time of starting being dependent upon progress in Latin. The chief books studied were Xenophon, Homer, and the Greek Testament.

Latin was the backbone of the instruction—as it was in the public and grammar schools of the day. The new boy of eight years old was confronted with the *Eton Latin Grammar* on arrival, and that book remained with him throughout his school career, as the chief interpreter of the many Latin texts studied. 'The range of classical reading would startle the present-day schoolboy of fourteen to fifteen—and most schoolmasters,' wrote an Old Boy of the school, Dr. Benjamin Gregory.[23]

The scope of the curriculum at this school varied considerably during the course of the nineteenth century, depending upon the head master, but instruction in the classics did not vary. It was felt to be only fitting that the education at Kingswood and Woodhouse Grove should be predominantly classical. 'The ministerial vocation of the parents, the advantages of reading the Greek Testament, the tradition of the schools, the possible future calling of a few of the boys to the office of the ministry, the chances of a university success—all these considerations led irresistibly to the conclusion that Kingswood and Woodhouse Grove Schools should never cease to be the home of a thorough teaching of Latin and Greek.' [24]

The authorities determined from the first, therefore, that the classical instruction should not be inferior to that of the public schools, and with that end in view they tended, perhaps too slavishly, to copy the curriculum of such schools.

But the scientific side of education was not forgotten. When the original buildings were adapted as a school, one room was set aside as a science lecture-room and a number of scientific instruments were installed. That was in 1812, and science teaching did not find a place in the public school curriculum till

[22] pp. 330–1, *infra*.   [23] *Autobiographical Recollections*, p. 91.
[24] J. T. Slugg, op. cit., p. 156.

after the publication of the *Report of the Clarendon Commission* in 1864.[25] Again can be seen the influence of the dissenting academies. However, enthusiasm for scientific training outran understanding of it, for the school committee at first prescribed as a textbook the one in use at Kingswood, John Wesley's *Natural Philosophy*, a book long out of date even then. When this was realized, Blair's *Grammar of Natural and Experimental Philosophy* was substituted, but not until Samuel Parker became head master in 1816 did the teaching of science serve any practical purpose. With the frequent changes of head master in the first four years of the school's history the science lecture-room was often disused for months on end in spite of the committee's openly expressed disapproval.

Samuel Parker, like Dr. Joseph Priestley (1733–1804), principal of Warrington Academy, believed in a broad cultural background for all intellectual matters. He taught classics in such a fashion that even young boys were able to appreciate them. But he was primarily a mathematician, publishing a textbook himself —*Arithmetical Grammar*—which was used in the school. He must be ranked as one of the pioneers of science teaching in the schools of this country. When he first came to the school he instituted weekly science lectures which were followed by a test on the following morning. This organized science teaching in 1816 is remarkable when one considers the backwardness of such teaching in other secondary schools, particularly the public schools. As late as 1850 Rugby alone made any real effort to teach science. At Eton, Winchester, and Charterhouse, occasional lectures were given in out-of-school hours, but that was all. They were not considered 'school business'. On the other hand, the dissenting academies had for some time shown a practical interest in science, and it was following their example that this science teaching became a part of the Woodhouse Grove curriculum. It was, as J. W. Adamson has pointed out,[26] 'owing to the private schools of the country that an interest in science was disseminated in the public and grammar schools'.

One of the boys who was taught science by Parker was John William Draper, who entered the school in 1822. On leaving, he continued the study of chemistry and mathematics at the newly founded London University before emigrating to America where,

[25] See J. W. Adamson, *English Education, 1789–1902*, pp. 236 ff., and the *Report of the (Spens) Consultative Committee on Secondary Education*, pp. 21–3.
[26] In his *Short History of Education*, p. 270.

three years later, he graduated at the University of Pennsylvania. From then onward he had a distinguished career as a scientist, eventually becoming President of the Science and Medical Department of the University of New York, and author of a number of scientific works. It is impossible to believe that Professor Draper did not owe much to the scientific head master of Woodhouse Grove, who in that age of misunderstanding of boy nature had the love of teaching and patience which 'made him delight in explaining difficulties in a clear and lucid style'.[27] Organized science-teaching seems to have lapsed after Parker left, though in 1858 the head master's report refers to instruction in photography, to lectures in chemistry and biology, and to lessons in 'common things' for junior boys.

The school curriculum, like that of dissenting academies, also included instruction in book-keeping. Nor were games and athletics overlooked. Gymnastics were introduced as a subject in 1842, and in the following year a report stated that the boys were diligent in that subject. Yorkshire appears to have led in this inclusion of physical training in the school time-table, for Mr. J. G. Fitch, one of the assistant commissioners reporting on secondary education for the Schools Inquiry Commission (1868), visited the school and was impressed by the facilities provided, not only at this school but at other denominational schools in Yorkshire. He wrote: 'In regard to secondary advantages, such as cricket fields, swimming-baths, gymnasia, workshops, reading-rooms, libraries, etc., several of them, especially Ackworth, Wesley College, Woodhouse Grove, and Bootham, possess a completeness of equipment which almost amounts to luxury.'[28]

This statement scarcely seems to reflect the tradition of Wesley, but at least it proves that Methodism was awake to the changing needs of education. There was a change, too, in another direction. When Wesley founded Kingswood School he refused to allow pupils to return home at any time during their school career. He knew the unsettling influence of fond mothers and anxious fathers and refused to allow his plan of education to be upset by such factors. No child was received unless the parents agreed to observe all the rules of the school and not to try to take the child home for short temporary periods. The rules were later relaxed, however, and in 1803 Conference resolved that Kingswood boys should be given a holiday of two

[27] J. T. Slugg, p. 131.
[28] *Report of the Schools Inquiry Commission*, Vol. IX, p. 244.

months every two years. This was repealed when it was reported as 'highly detrimental to morals and learning'.[29] From 1811, however—and from the foundation of Woodhouse Grove—an annual holiday was granted, though the time at which it was taken varied during the first half of the nineteenth century, the duration being approximately one month. For one brief period parents could select their own time! During school term the only days on which there was no instruction were Christmas Day and Good Friday, with half-holidays each Saturday, on the fifth of November, the governor's birthday, once a quarter on 'Committee Day', and once a year on the boys' Missionary-meeting day. Holidays were therefore short, but educationally there were advantages in this, and in his *Report* for the Schools Inquiry Commission,[30] J. G. Fitch stated:

'Relatively to the age of the boys, the standard of scholarship attained in languages, mathematics, and general knowledge is exceptionally high. This is probably due to the fact that by the regulations of the institution all the boys are admitted at the age of nine, and are expected to remain for a fixed term of six years. Scholarships, which are open to competition, may enable a promising scholar to remain without further payment, until the age of seventeen, but otherwise the term of residence is the same for all. Hence the plans of the teachers are more uniform, and are less susceptible of interruptions from the caprice of parents than any other School in the district.'

The public served by this school, and by Kingswood, was a small one, since both schools during the greater part of the nineteenth century took as pupils only the sons of Wesleyan Methodist ministers. They were, in fact, as the Schools Inquiry Commission pointed out, almost private institutions, under the special care of the Wesleyan Conference. Their chief importance lies in the type of boy who went out from them. The list following shows in some measure the type of life for which the schools were fitting their pupils, but the statistics (taken from the *History of Kingswood School*) are approximate only. As will be shown in a later chapter, Kingswood and Woodhouse Grove later in the century formed a unique combination, so that it is at least possible to consider them during the nineteenth century as one unit. Of 2,613 pupils of whom any records remain, their careers on leaving school were as follows:

Business, 689; Wesleyan Ministry, 470; education, 271; medical

[29] *History of Kingswood School*, p. 90.   [30] Vol. IX, p. 240.

(including dental), 243; pharmacy, 203; Holy Orders, 113; banking, 96; law, 94; engineering, 91; Government services, 90; farming, 40; accountancy, 38; architecture and surveying, 34; journalism, 34; sea, 27; art, literature, music, 27; ministers of other denominations, 24; and miscellaneous, 29.

All came from poor homes, many knew full well that their parents had made great sacrifices to give them their education, they knew that when they left school they would find no wealthy or influential patron to gain them entrance to some worthwhile or well-paid job; they had to make their own careers. These facts must be realized before the influence which these schools exercised can be understood. In their school-days the boys not only gained information: they had before them the example of self-sacrifice and unselfishness shown by their parents and mas- ters, and during a period of six years or so they came to under- stand these qualities and to imitate them. Perhaps the results of that understanding were best expressed by those many Old Boys who became missionaries. One of the most striking features of nonconformity in general in the nineteenth century was its missionary activity, and this branch of Methodist work was especially well supported by former pupils of the two Con- nexional schools.

CHAPTER FIVE

Religious Revivals in Schools

THE LETTERS AND DIARIES of eighteenth- and nineteenth-century Methodists are full of rapturous accounts of conversions and revivals. Conversion was a feature of Methodism, for the first objective in saving souls for God was the breaking-down of the individual's natural reserve to make him publicly acknowledge his sins and dedicate himself to the service of God. The outward effect of the 'breaking-down' process varied. Sometimes it took the form of inward assurance, as with John Wesley when he felt his heart warmed within him; sometimes it was a dramatic outburst. Such manifestations usually make the modern reader feel faintly uneasy, but whatever the modern view, the remarkable results of these conversions in the eighteenth and nineteenth centuries cannot be denied. Normally, they were obtained by direct appeal, often in crowded assemblies where the emotionalism of the group could be worked upon and in turn affect the individual, but such direct appeals were not normally made to children. Although there was widespread misunderstanding of the child mind, most people realized that their minds and hearts were immature, and interest in religion was encouraged by quiet, and often sentimental, instruction and catechism, but not by direct appeal.

There were, however, others who did not realize any difference between an adult and a child. As E. E. Kellett in his *Religion and Life in the Early Victorian Age* has stated, in early Methodism Christ's well-known dictum became 'Except ye be converted and become as grown people, ye shall in no wise enter the Kingdom of Heaven'. Unfortunately, it was often those good but mistaken people who made children deceitful or miserable, for an adult was sometimes so filled with evangelistic zeal himself that he tried to pass on his feelings to a child, asking him if he were saved and other questions which no child could understand. But the child did understand what he was expected to reply and he had a choice of two courses: either he could lie to please the grown-up; or he could be silent, knowing that he ran the risk of being punished as a sullen and awkward child. That is, baldly stated, the type of thing that happened in individual cases, and examples of children being 'brought to God' can be found in most memoirs and biographies dealing with early Methodism. They would, no doubt, provide excellent material for psychologists, but we are not here concerned with that aspect. There are recorded some amazing examples of mass conversions and religious revivals amongst the pupils of Kingswood and Woodhouse Grove Schools in the first seventy years or so of their history, and it is necessary to mention these here since they show the way in which certain individuals tried to introduce an evangelical spirit into education with complete disregard of the immaturity of the child mind, and since they did have an influence on Methodist education and therefore on the contribution which that education made to national life. For that reason this chapter has been included here.

In 1765, James Hindmarsh was appointed English and Writing Master at Kingswood School, under the head mastership of Joseph Benson, who was also newly appointed in that year. Whatever may have been Hindmarsh's academic qualifications, he was a dangerous person to undertake the care of children. Honest and sincere himself, his whole life was centred in God and his whole ambition was to save people from their sins. Like his fellow Methodists, he was far more interested in the life to come than in the life of the present. He had no knowledge of children. He regarded them as men and women in miniature, swayed by the same influences and having the same outlook as grown men and women. He was in fact a religious fanatic. On 5th May 1768 Wesley wrote in his *Journal:* 'About this time a remarkable work of God broke out among the children at Kingswood School.' This note was occasioned by the receipt of a letter from Hindmarsh, who had written:

'On Wednesday the 20th God broke in upon our boys in a surprising manner. A serious concern has been observable in some of them for some time past; but that night, while they were in their private apartments, the power of God came upon them, even like a mighty, rushing wind, which made them cry aloud for mercy. Last night, I hope, will never be forgotten, when about twenty were in the utmost distress. But God quickly spoke peace to two of them. . . . A greater display of His love I never saw; they indeed rejoice with joy unspeakable. For my own part, I have not often felt the like power. We have no need to exhort them to pray, for that spirit runs through the whole school; so that this house may well be called "an house of prayer".

While I am writing, the cries of the boys, from their several apartments, are sounding in my ears. There are many still lying at the pool, who wait every moment to be put in. They are come to this, "Lord, I will not, I cannot, rest without Thy love". Since I began to write, eight more are set at liberty, and now rejoice in God their Saviour. . . . Their age is from eight to fourteen. There are but few who withstand the work; nor is it likely they should do it long; for the prayers of those that believe in Christ seem to carry all before them. Among the colliers likewise the work of God increases greatly; two of the colliers' boys were justified this week. . . . I had sealed my letter, but have opened it to inform you that two more of our children have found peace. Several others are under deep conviction. Some of our friends from Bristol are here, who are thunderstruck. This is the day we have wished for so long; the day you have had in view, which has made you go through so much opposition for the good of these poor children.'[1]

Not a single person seemed to realize the dangers of such religious hysteria, and Wesley himself, though more level-headed than some of his followers, had no misgivings about the events reported to him. A few days later another person wrote from Kingswood School:

'I cannot help congratulating you on the happy situation of your family here. The power of God continues to work with almost irresistible force; and there is good reason to hope it will not be withdrawn, till every soul is converted to God. I have had frequent opportunities of conversing alone with the boys, and find the work has taken deep root in many hearts. The house rings with praise and prayer, and the whole behaviour of the children strongly speaks for God. The number of the new-born is increased since you received your last information. I have been a witness of part; but the whole exceeds all that language can paint.'[2]

A revival had started at the school of the type which was well known to Methodists in all parts of the country, though never before had they experienced such religious fervour in children. The age of the boys concerned is significant—eight to fourteen, the impressionable age on which the sincere but dangerous evangelistic outpourings of a man like Hindmarsh would have full effect, especially when set against the background of hardness and cold routine which was a feature of the school. During the

---

[1] *Journal*, Vol. V, pp. 259–60.   [2] ibid., p. 260.

following two years it seems that the influence of that first revival never entirely died away. It is doubtful whether a man like Hindmarsh would allow it to do so. In 1770 came another climax. On 18th September of that year some of the boys were taken to view the body of a man who had been known to them. It is not difficult to understand the morbid results of such a pilgrimage on boys whose school routine, separated from the emotional outlets which home life would give, enforced much silent meditation. Hindmarsh followed up the inspection of the corpse with an exhortation 'suited to the occasion' and by the singing of the hymn: 'And am I born to die, to lay this body down?' It is not surprising to read that on this occasion the religious hysteria spread to the girls of the domestic staff! [3]

It is noticeable that although Wesley records in his *Journal* the letters received and the events as they occurred, he does not comment upon them save to label them as a remarkable work of God. But then Wesley made a habit of thus labelling anything untoward which occurred in his experience. Frequently in his *Journal* he comments ecstatically upon outward signs of conversion in adults, but upon these events at the school he is comparatively silent. When he worked out his scheme for education there he never envisaged religious results of this nature amongst the pupils. Had he done so, he would undoubtedly have commented upon the successful results as they occurred. All he desired at Kingswood School was a Christian family, developing and living in accordance with a carefully planned routine. The plan was good, but the execution, as has been shown, had to be left to men who were not John Wesleys—good, honest men, chosen by Wesley himself, but men whose religious fervour outweighed any understanding of education and children that they may once have had. The constant changes in staff did not help matters, for school traditions can be built up only on continuity, and when masters were constantly changing there could be no continuity in work or method. Matters improved in this respect after 1770, when Joseph Benson left to become principal of Trevecca College, and Wesley asked the advice of Conference concerning the appointment of masters. It was suggested that each applicant for a post at the school should be asked whether he intended to be a teacher, or whether his ultimate aim was to be ordained and become a preacher. This simple scheme was

[3] See also *History of Kingswood School*, pp. 58–64, and A. H. Body, *John Wesley and Education*, pp. 122–3.

96

adopted, and for the rest of Wesley's life only one other head master left to become a minister. This helped to ensure continuity in the school, and, equally as important, it helped to ensure that the masters were men who genuinely wished to teach. Men like Hindmarsh would not apply for such posts. The men who would, and did, apply were those with academic qualifications whose desire was to impart something of their knowledge to others and to show them how to work and live. In short, the school was no longer an educational establishment always on the verge of becoming a revivalist meeting, but a school.

Only one further scene similar to those described above is recorded, and that was in 1773, occasioned by a visit from a preacher named Ralph Mather.[4] It is curious, however, that many years later, in the early days of Woodhouse Grove School, similar events did occur there. The first happened within a year of the opening of the school and is thus recorded by the first head master, writing to a member of the school committee:

'The wonder-working Lord is still going on with His blessed work. I have had the pleasure of witnessing two or three revivals of religion among young and old. I have seen half, and sometimes two-thirds, of a congregation affected. I have heard *children pray*, and speak of the work of God upon their hearts: *but any thing* to equal this, where there is scarcely any exception, I have not seen. The work on many of their souls is *really deep*. Your son, W., you know, is generally solid and steady; but J. exhibits the most striking proofs of a change, and a *real deep rational work* is wrought in both their souls; as well as in 20 others. Yesterday was a glorious day among them. They spent the time, from school-hours till supper, in prayer to God in a part of the school-room. One of the servants put her ear to the key-hole of the door, and *God smote her heart!* Another of them stole unperceived into the school, and had not hearkened long before she began to cry for mercy. The third must needs see and hear for herself, and she also was deeply affected, and has set out, I hope, in good earnest. Thus, by the instrumentality of these *dear boys*, are three thoughtless girls brought to an acquaintance with themselves in the space of one short hour; and they are determined for heaven. After supper, they gathered round me like bees, telling me how the Lord had been amongst them, and earnestly intreating that they might be permitted to spend a few hours more before bed-time, in prayer. Love for their souls, and

[4] *Journal*, Vol. V, pp. 524–5.

a desire to indulge them in any thing that might do their souls good, *on the one hand*; and feeling the indispensable necessity of keeping all things in order, and mixing *prudence with piety on the other*, caused such a struggle in my mind, that I was at my wits' end while surrounded with the loud clamour of *"Do, Sir, do Sir, let us, if it be but one hour."* "Well", said I, "but I have a little good news to tell you, before you go, if you will sit and hear it." All was still, and soon the little group was seated around me to hear, with great attention, this good news. "But", said I, "perhaps I might say, 'tis you that have some good news to tell me." Immediately a burst of praise made the room ring, and the artless tales of the manifestations of God amongst them broke my heart. Surely the kind friends who have contributed to this Institution will rejoice to hear that they have been purchasing and furnishing a house for God: *and that no sooner had they finished their part, than the Lord came down, took possession of it, and began His part; and a blessed work it is! Lord, carry it on—and while we are preparing these children for this world, do Thou prepare them for another.'* [5]

If one can say so without irreverence, one is not surprised to find that this head master stayed no more than a year in the school! However, he was not the only man connected with scenes of this sort at that school. During the head mastership of Samuel Parker there were similar incidents. As a teacher he was great, but he was, especially toward the end of his head mastership, approaching dangerously near to religious fanaticism and was fond of telling the boys of 'his experience'. Daily between five and six o'clock after a hard day's work he would conduct a prayer-meeting in the chapel which was attended by an average of twenty to thirty out of the hundred pupils then at the school.

Toward the end of his head mastership, in 1829, he preached a sermon one Sunday in which he described in graphic detail 'how an unhappy spirit entered the eternal world'. The speaker claimed to have had divine revelation on the matter, but whatever the sources there was no doubt of the result. One boy fainted, and ninety-three out of the hundred boys were converted. 'During the ensuing week school-work was almost impossible, and indeed next to nothing was attempted, and play was discouraged and discontinued for a considerable time.' [6]

The modern reader instinctively condemns as unhealthy such

[5] *Methodist Magazine* (1812), Vol. XXXV, pp. 395–6.
[6] Benjamin Gregory, *Autobiographical Recollections*, p. 97.

manifestations of religious hysteria, but it is wrong to condemn them too harshly, especially if the conditions prevailing in Kingswood and Woodhouse Grove Schools are compared with those in other boarding-schools of the period. From a purely disciplinary point of view, indeed, the pictures painted of such incidents as the above are preferable to the pictures painted of public schools. For example, the following diatribe on Eton was published in 1834:

'Before an Eton boy is ready for the university he may have acquired at a place of education, where there is much less effective restraint than at a university, a confirmed taste for gluttony and drunkenness, an aptitude for brutal sports and a passion for female society of the most degrading kind, with as great ease as if he were an uncontrolled inhabitant of the metropolis and were responsible neither to governors, teachers, spiritual pastors, nor masters.' [7]

Just previous to 1834, the general tone of Woodhouse Grove School had badly deteriorated, and although there is no suggestion that vice was as rampant there as it appears to have been at some of the public schools, yet there was little enough of the family spirit that Wesley had looked for, and still less of religion, while discipline, owing to the laxity of masters, had fallen to a low standard. In the winter of 1833–4 the Rev. Robert Aitken asked for permission to hold services at the school, and the result of his efforts was that 'for some months Woodhouse Grove presented a spectacle which would have made the heart of Wesley dance for joy. The whole establishment: boys, masters, servants, were intent on living thoroughly Christian lives', and the 'genuineness of the revival was proved . . . by a most perceptible and long-lasting elevation of the moral tone of the whole school'.[8] The occasional outbursts of revivalism may startle and even disgust, but at least they had the effect of raising the general average of religious feeling in the schools, and in this connexion it is interesting to read the words of one of the most distinguished Old Boys of Woodhouse Grove School—one who was a pupil at the time of at least one of these revivals—Sir William Atherton (Attorney-General 1861–3), who, speaking at the Jubilee celebration in 1862, said: 'Religion did not change, nor sound principles of morality, nor the principles of a sound education. The cardinal point of the education given in the

[7] *Quarterly Journal of Education* (1834), Vol. VIII, p. 286.
[8] Benjamin Gregory, op. cit., pp. 112–13.

school was, and always had been, the connexion of religion with literature.' [9]

It seems, then, that however unhealthy religious revivals may appear today, they did maintain a standard of tone in the schools. That was their direct influence. But indirectly, they affected Methodist education still more decisively, for in the memoirs of Old Boys of both schools can be read the acknowledgement of how religious awakening came to them in their teens and provided them with a standard of conduct throughout their lives, affecting not only themselves but those with whom they came in contact and the affairs with which they dealt.

[9] *Jubilee of Woodhouse Grove School,* p. 16.

CHAPTER SIX

The Bible Christian Contribution

ONE OF THE most challenging stories of the Methodist contribution to nineteenth-century education is supplied by the Bible Christian Connexion. It seems that where there is a religious revival an increased interest in education is not far behind. No sooner was James Thorne converted than he started to teach in the Church of England Sunday-school. The reason is not far to seek. Conversion must mean introspection, and this is perforce honest and sincere, so that one begins to appreciate one's cultural shortcomings. Men who have been converted are not for long satisfied with the emotional experiences of short duration: they turn to books, partly no doubt to justify to themselves the new experience and the new outlook they have gained, partly to satisfy the mental and spiritual craving which a mind suddenly opened up to spiritual influence feels.

But before one can appreciate the extent of the Bible Christian contribution it is necessary to know something about this branch of Methodism, and to appreciate the pioneer nature of the school which was later to be established at Shebbear it is necessary to have some idea of the type of people in the parish and of the lives they lived. The district was purely agricultural. There were a number of squires and clergymen who spent the greater part of their time in riding and hunting, drinking and gambling, and who all-too-often took no notice whatever of their social inferiors, as they considered the peasantry and yeomen farmers. The labourers were little better than serfs, whose average wage when wheat was at famine prices was one shilling per day. Their staple food was barley bread, supplemented by turnips and blackberries. Utterly ignorant and living in abject poverty, there was only one circumstance which made their state better than that of the lower classes of the towns, and that was the purer air of the country, the lower concentration of population with its resultant lessening of ill health. There were few schools, and many of the farmers could neither read nor write. As far as their religious life was concerned, therefore, even if there had been no scarcity of Bibles, they would not have been able to read them. They were dependent on a hard-drinking, hard-swearing clergy for their knowledge of Scriptural truth. The closest connexion between the clergy and their parishioners was found in the collection of tithes about which there were never-ending disputes. Cock-fighting and bull-baiting, the chief pastimes, also on occasion brought the upper and lower classes together.

Amid such surroundings and in such society grew up the Bible Christian Church. To the village of Shebbear in North Devon there came in 1813 a curate named Daniel Evans who had already shown himself a man true to his calling. He taught the need of a new spiritual birth and the village began to think more seriously about religion. Among these inhabitants were John Thorne and his wife Mary of Lake Farm. John Thorne had always been a 'good man'. He was a typical Devon farmer, upright and honest, punctual and exact in all his dealings, so that he had been nicknamed—much to his wife's disapproval—a 'Methody', though Methodism up to that time had scarcely touched that area of Devon. He surprised his neighbours by holding family prayers each day. In this he was actively supported by his wife, though she distrusted the Methodists, being herself a devout Church woman. She certainly had no intention of being labelled a Nonconformist, for she regarded all dissenters as 'false prophets' and 'deceitful workers', but one day, under the influence of Daniel Evans, she found herself compelled to stand up in church and make public testimony of her assurance of sins forgiven. The tide of such self-revelation spread, and in that parish of Shebbear there grew up a tiny centre of Christianity which was essentially Methodist in character but which owed its inception to the work and character of a Church of England clergyman who, together with a fellow Anglican clergyman—the Rev. Cradock Glascott, mentioned earlier in this work—was the first to bring spiritual reality and the hated 'enthusiasm' to Devon.

Meanwhile, a man named William O'Bryan was preaching in neighbouring districts. He was a farmer and wanted to give himself wholly to the work of preaching, but no opportunity offered itself until at last he was asked to supply the place of a Methodist preacher called away to another part of the country. O'Bryan did much to bring about that revival of religion which took place in Cornwall after Wesley's death, but his irregular methods did not please the Wesleyan Methodists. Looking for 'method' perhaps they lost some of the fire and enthusiasm which their primitive simplicity had kindled. Be that as it may, they did not approve of William O'Bryan. Nevertheless, the close affinities between the Wesleyan Methodists and the Bible Christians must not be overlooked. Although, until 1932, the two Connexions were separate in name, there was no essential difference between them, nor was there the slightest hint of rivalry at any time. The Bible Christians were never loath to acknowledge the spiritual help given them by the much larger and older established Wesleyan Methodist Church.

Hearing that there were fourteen parishes on the borders of Cornwall and Devon where there was no evangelical preaching, O'Bryan resolved to go there, and in 1815 he was invited by John and Mary Thorne to go to Shebbear.

So were brought together the 'primitive simplicity' of religious zeal and the evangelicalism of the Church of England, and from these two influences was born the Bible Christian Church on 9th October 1815 at Lake Farm, Shebbear.[1]

It grew and took its strength from a number of influential farmers whose properties were scattered around that district. The religious society which O'Bryan formed became their school and centre of interest, while the Bible was their text-book. Those who could not read taught themselves to read—because they had to read the Bible—and that self-tuition had to take place after the day's work was done. It needs a farmer, working without the aid of modern machinery, to appreciate what that meant. It is scarcely surprising that such men and women came to look for a school in which their sons might be taught in their youth the things which they had had to learn by lamplight. Amongst the best-known and most influential of these farming folk were the Reeds of Holwell, the Thornes of Lake Farm, the Courtices of Winslade, the Cottles of West Youlstone, and the Rattenburys of Milton Mill. These people, after their day's work on the farm was done, settled down to reading and writing, or else 'took their way from the farmhouses in various directions to assist in the evangelistic services that were being successfully conducted within a radius of some miles. Returning at different hours of the night, each party retired at once to rest, for all must be ready at five next morning to resume the daily task'.[2] Could John Wesley have seen those Devon farmers and their families,

[1] For an account of the actual formation of the Society, see S. L. Thorne, *William O'Bryan*, pp. 101-2.
[2] *James Thorne of Shebbear*, pp. 37-8.

he must have been well satisfied by those who carried on his work in spirit if not in name.[3]

The problem of education appeared early in the history of the Bible Christian Connexion, for it was realized that their cause would be greatly strengthened if there was a school in which could be educated future leaders. A developing interest in education can be seen in the lives of two of the sons of John and Mary Thorne, who were present at that first historic gathering at Lake Farm in 1815. It is with those two sons that this work is particularly concerned, for they were the founders of what is today known as Shebbear College. Their names were James and Samuel and, as in the case of many pioneers, they owed much to their parents.

In an age when many people, especially those who were engaged in agriculture, could find any number of house and farm tasks for even the smallest child and when compulsory education was not even being considered, John Thorne and his wife sent their children to a village school at Langtree. It would have been easier to keep them at home, for the family was large enough for the mother to have been considerably helped by the elder children. This school was typical of the village school of the eighteenth and early nineteenth centuries, presided over by a master who believed in the rod as the cure for all evils and the source of all knowledge.[4] It is not what they learnt at the school, but the fact that they were sent there that is to be noted here, for there is little doubt that any cultural development that there was came from the mother and father rather than from the school. The home library was meagre, but again it is to be remarked that one existed at all. *Jack the Giant-Killer, Jack and the Beanstalk, The Whole Duty of Man,* and *The new week's preparation for the Sacrament*—a quaint collection, but the parents supplemented what their children learnt at school and at the Church Sunday-school by instruction at home, by careful restraint, and a guard on the too-easy gossip of the day, and by family devotions.

Growing up in such an environment, the children did not realize how they differed from others. Less than two years after

[3] Although the official title is 'Bible Christian', the Societies were for long called 'Bryanite'—a name still heard amongst older folk today. It is interesting to note that John Wesley, writing to Joseph Benson in 1779, said: 'If you tread in the steps which my brother and I did, you may be the means, under God, of raising another set of real Bible Christians.'

[4] For a picture of such a school, see Thomas Jackson's *Recollections of my own life and times* (1874), pp. 18–21.

the coming of William O'Bryan to Lake Farm, James Thorne (who, with his brother Samuel, had joined O'Bryan as a travelling preacher) was distributing tracts in London when, 'to his surprise', as he noted in his diary, he found that the folk to whom he was talking could not read. It was then that James Thorne realized the need for education, and from that time onward he took a keen interest in it. Though it was his brother Samuel who actually founded the school later, it was James who supplied the practical, as well as the moral, support when there seemed a danger of its failure. James's diary was not a reflection of the times as was John Wesley's *Journal*, for it dealt almost entirely with matters of purely personal interest and had not the evidence of culture that Wesley's had, but it is noteworthy that he recorded an intimate interest in education. He mentioned with enthusiasm the opening of Sunday-schools in various places, watching how the numbers of pupils increased. He was interested too in the theory of education. 'It was a good discourse on education,' he wrote after hearing a sermon.[5] Unblessed with a Charterhouse education, still less with the cultural background which a university offered, he determined to improve his own powers that he might improve those of others, and at a time when he was fully engaged in his ministerial work he yet found time to study the Greek and Latin classics. This was the man who came to have more influence on the Bible Christian Connexion than any other man, save possibly the founder, William O'Bryan.

It was his brother, Samuel, however, who actually founded Shebbear College. His educational work also began after the historic meeting at Lake Farm in 1815. As he realized the broader vision which his conversion brought to him, he felt a new intellectual longing within him, and at once set about satisfying it. No learning was outside his scope. He sought to improve what he had already attained by sheer hard work and self-restraint. When he was appointed to the Michaelstow Circuit in 1821 there was some consternation among the local inhabitants when he arrived with a large box of books, for there was a general feeling in those days that a Nonconformist preacher ought not to be too learned or the congregation would not be able to understand him. But Samuel Thorne's learning never obscured his common sense, and during the period in which he was in circuit work there was no more popular or more understandable preacher than he. Languages, history, mathematics,

[5] *Memoir of James Thorne*, p. 203.

theology, general literature, law, politics: he read them all widely and well.

It is necessary here to attempt to show how it was that this man who had received his own education at a village school was inspired to found a secondary school amongst an agricultural community who viewed education—like machinery—as a new-fangled and time-wasting pursuit.

At the Conference of 1819, Samuel Thorne's name appeared in the *Minutes* as one of those 'received on trial', and he was sent to the Ringsash Circuit. From that time onward for six years he worked as a Bible Christian minister, though his interests were wide and were not narrowly centred on pulpit preaching. It was during those years of ministry that his thoughts on education became crystallized as he saw the dangers of an uneducated public. It was during those same years of political struggles which led to the Reform of 1832 that thinkers began to realize the dangers of an uneducated public from a political point of view. Samuel Thorne realized the dangers from the Christian standpoint, as he was brought more and more into touch with the uneducated masses of Devon.

In November, 1820, he wrote to a Mr. Chapple of Burrington the following letter:

'This is to acquaint thee a little about the things which thou desirest me, viz., 1st. We much want a *good* school in Shebbear. 2nd. But there seems to be a few difficulties in the way. One with respect to a schoolroom. The chapel is large enough, but then it is cold, is it not? Another is, thou art not sure of having a larger number of children than thou hast now, though I rather think thou wouldest. I should like to have a school in this parish kept by a man who feared God, and would keep the children under subjection, and if thou art willing to try I will gladly do all I can to promote it. . . .'[6]

It is probable, though not certain, that the school here referred to was to be a Sunday-school, but from remarks made by Samuel Thorne later it is clear that his thoughts were not only of Sunday-schools. It was education for the children of the district that he wanted, and he knew well that a worth-while education must be given on seven days of the week and not merely on one.

Mr. Chapple and he must have had many interesting talks on the subject, for both were self-educated men; both knew the hardship and difficulty of self-education all the greater for the

[6] S. L. Thorne, *Samuel Thorne, Printer*, pp. 76–7.

fact that they lived in a district far from great cities. The power of the Press was growing, but it had not then reached the agricultural district of Devon; books were hard to obtain; the ability to read and understand them harder still to obtain. Not the least of the difficulties of the self-educator who happened to be a member of a Nonconformist church was the suspicion with which book-learning was often viewed by the Nonconformist congregations. Even Chapple wondered whether it was fitting for him to attend classes at a newly opened Mechanics Institute, for Samuel Thorne recorded in his Diary: 'Jonathan Chapple came to have my advice whether he should commence being a member of the Mechanics' Institute. I gave him leave.' [7]

What Samuel Thorne realized in theory his wife realized in practice, and to her he owed much of the inspiration which led to his later actions. It must not be forgotten that it was not until the man had had the opportunity of exchanging views with the lady who was to become his wife that we find educational schemes taking practical shape in Samuel's mind. In 1825, Samuel was married to Mary O'Bryan, daughter of the founder of the Bible Christian Connexion, and herself a preacher who had 'travelled' from the age of seventeen—in London; Jersey, where she found her ability as a linguist invaluable; in the Isle of Wight; and in Portsmouth; so widely had the Connexion spread its influence in eight years. As has been seen in the case of other Methodist educationists, much importance must be attached, we believe, to the environment and the upbringing of youth. This was no less the case with Mary O'Bryan.

Twenty-two years before, on 9th July 1803, William O'Bryan, her father, had married Catherine Cowlin of Perranzabuloe, a village of north Cornwall. The lady was of good family, her father a strict churchman and her mother one-time governess to a clergyman's daughter at Roche. For some considerable time Catherine had attended a good girls' school at Truro, and the education she received there was not wasted in later years. When her children were in bed, and while she waited up for her husband to return from his preaching, she would write religious poetry, some of which found its way into the Bible Christian collection of hymns in later years. Gifted and educated as she was, it was largely due to her that the prejudice against women preachers was broken down, for she herself was not averse to going out with her husband, or alone, to preach Christianity,

[7] S. L. Thorne, *Samuel Thorne, Printer*, p. 117.

yet she did not forget her duties as a wife and mother. Though no data is available, we can imagine that it was largely from her that her daughter Mary gained the best of her education and was inspired to impart it to others less fortunate.

Mary was born in 1804 and was converted to take part in active Christian work at the age of fifteen. She was largely responsible for the opening of a mission in London in 1822, and it is remarkable that a girl—for she was no more than that—should have recorded in her diary at that time words which might well have been taken from the journal of one of Wesley's earliest preachers: 'Missionaries are just as much wanted as in the interior of Africa. Yes, in the very metropolis, so great and famous, whence missionaries are sent out to almost all parts of the discovered globe.'[8] The style and matter even of so short an extract are some indication of the gifts and breadth of view of this young lady. She was, too, a fluent speaker of French, and one whose 'accomplishments' compared favourably with those of ladies who had been educated at great expense in private schools and by private tutors in their own homes.

During these years Samuel and Mary met occasionally and corresponded frequently, but both were troubled about what was their duty: whether it would be right for them to marry, or whether they ought each to continue the work being done. At that time there began in Samuel's diary a sequence of curious jottings, half English, half French, concerned with his feelings for Mary O'Bryan. It was Mary who had taught him all he knew of the French language—during those infrequent meetings in Devon. One can imagine the girl and the zealous preacher walking or riding along the Devon lanes, on their way to an appointment which one or other of them was to keep with a congregation, forgetful for a time of those around them, and immersed in the conversation of all lovers, she at times lapsing mischievously into the foreign language, he picking up odd phrases which later found their way into his diary. Such a picture brings a more human touch to the puritan background of chapels and conversions in which their lives were spent. But the conversation of lovers is not always as slight and fatuous as novelists would have us believe. Both Mary and Samuel were wise beyond their years, they were both inspired by the great ideal of Christianizing in practical fashion the drab and often hopeless lives of their fellows. Their future life proved them to be

[8] S. L. Thorne, *William O'Bryan*, pp. 121-2.

utterly unselfish, and as they walked those lanes they discussed many of the problems which Christian leaders and thinkers have discussed through the ages. After all, though young, both were already builders of the Bible Christian Connexion, and they were not blind to their responsibilities. Mary told him, and even more showed him, the value of a good home and careful upbringing. Samuel had for some years been teaching himself that he might be better fitted for the work he had undertaken. Education was one of the problems they discussed as they tramped along those lanes, and in this girl Samuel found inspiration to persevere with his ideas for the education of children—ideas which as yet were still shapeless. As he quaintly recorded: *'Elle instructions sont toujour bon au moi.'* [9]

In 1825 Samuel Thorne read John Locke's *Essay on the Understanding*. What his reactions were to the section dealing with education are not known, but entries in his diary at that time showed that he was becoming more and more interested in the subject and that a practical scheme had begun to take shape in his mind. William O'Bryan had been informed of the scheme and made no objections, but Samuel was conscious of his own shortcomings as a teacher and proposed inviting a professional schoolmaster, a Mr. Hamilton, to assist in the scheme. O'Bryan 'thought it right' for him to do that, and arrangements were made for a fellow preacher to take over the school to be vacated by Mr. Hamilton. Then arose the difficulties which have dogged most educational undertakings—those of finance. The salary which was to be paid to Hamilton was not considered large enough by that gentleman, and he wrote to Samuel telling him that unless it was increased he would accept another post which had been offered in Jersey. The salary could not be raised, and the whole scheme fell through for a time. Samuel recorded: 'On friend O'Bryan's advice, I gave up the thoughts of having any preparation made for a school when I was home at Lady-Day, or rather in April, as he thought, he said, we could not now determine how things would be till Conference.' [10]

Although the scheme had come to nought, Samuel had no intention of giving it up altogether. In this connexion appears a rather puzzling entry in his diary. Two weeks after the refusal to raise Mr. Hamilton's salary, he wrote: 'This evening friend O'Bryan again expressed his thoughts on Mr. H——'s coming

[9] S. L. Thorne, *Samuel Thorne, Printer*, p. 95.
[10] ibid., p. 120.

to conduct the printing business. Does he think that I expect after all to stay? and so he wishes me to give up all such thoughts. Well, I am preparing to keep a school at Lake, and do feel quite willing to go from hence.' [11]

At that time Samuel was considering retiring from the active ministry and he had discussed the matter with O'Bryan. What is not clear is whether one of his chief reasons for desiring to retire was in order that he should be free to devote his whole time to keeping a school. That is a problem which will probably never be cleared up. What is certain is that at the Conference of that year Samuel Thorne resigned from his work as a travelling preacher because he was satisfied that he was in his proper place in a local sphere. He took that step in spite of the protests of his friends and of their strong persuasion. After seven years of active ministry his name was removed from the *Minutes,* though he was reappointed manager of the Connexional printing affairs, a member of the Book Committee, the General Committee, and Treasurer of the Missionary Society. Later that same year (1825) he recorded in his diary:

'Monday, November 28th. This day Mary O'Bryan and I joined hands in the Lord, to live together according to God's holy ordinance of matrimony. I have taken this step in His fear, with a sincere desire to glorify my Maker.' [12]

During the next ten years little or nothing was heard of the school project. This was not due to any cooling of interest in the scheme, but to a variety of Connexional circumstances in which Samuel and his brother James took a leading part. As we have seen, Samuel at the 1825 Conference had been reappointed manager of the Connexional printing affairs. This side of the Bible Christian work had been started because there had been difficulties in obtaining copies of the Methodist Hymn-book. In 1823, the Connexion had decided to publish a hymn-book of its own, and from the first Samuel Thorne took a prominent part in this extension of evangelical activities, which soon afterwards included the publication of a magazine. Like Wesley earlier, he and other leaders saw the usefulness, and the need, of reading matter for those converted to Christianity, and it is typical of the spirit of these men that they did not hesitate to undertake work of which they knew nothing, but which they were only too willing to learn. Passing through London in 1822, James Thorne

[11] S. L. Thorne, *Samuel Thorne, Printer*, p. 127.
[12] ibid., p. 134.

bought a printing-press which was installed in an office at Mill Pleasant, Stoke Damarel, Devonport, and Samuel was appointed by Conference to superintend its working. Perhaps it is hardly surprising that the finances of this publishing concern were a problem from the first. But Samuel and James Thorne were confident that they were undertaking a useful work in thus helping to tempt people to read and so to think. William O'Bryan, who, as head of the Connexion, was responsible for its finances, was in debt from the start of the publishing business, while Samuel Thorne found his time and energies more and more occupied. This is no place to deal in detail with the history and difficulties of the Connexional Press in the 1820's, but enough has been said to show that Samuel Thorne, as long as he retained his interest in it, had little time to devote to the problem of founding a school.

In 1829 came even greater difficulties, and Samuel had still less time to give to idealistic educational schemes of his own. William O'Bryan since 1815 had called himself 'General Superintendent', and he claimed to govern the Connexion. For some years many of his followers felt that they had some right to a share in the Connexional organization. There was autocracy on the one side, dissatisfaction on the other, and at the Conference of 1829 came the disruption, and William O'Bryan left the Bible Christian Connexion.[13] Such an upheaval in a small and immature organization might easily have caused its complete collapse. It was largely due to the Thornes and their farmer neighbours in North Devon that this did not happen. Steadied by James Thorne's example, by his resourcefulness, ability, tact in administration, and untiring devotion and selflessness, the Connexion struggled on.[14]

Although Samuel Thorne had had little time to put into effect his plan for a school, he had been able to prepare the building for it, and in 1829 Prospect House was completed. The site had been selected by William O'Bryan and Samuel's father, on the edge of the latter's estate—a site on which a notable 'camp meeting' had been held in the early years. But, though the walls of a school existed, the school did not begin then. We have already noted the two great difficulties which Samuel was

[13] Six years later a reunion took place between those who had remained loyal to O'Bryan and those who had remained loyal to the Connexion, though O'Bryan himself had gone to America in 1831, where he died in 1868.
[14] F. W. Bourne, *The Centenary Life of James Thorne of Shebbear*, pp. 215–16.

helping to face—disruption in the Connexion and bankruptcy in the publishing business—nor should those other offices that he held be forgotten. These, too, took up much of his time and energies. Three years before, the printing-press had been removed from Devonport to Lake Farm, Shebbear. When Prospect House was ready, the press was removed thither, and at the same time Samuel helped the Connexion considerably by buying up all the interests in the publishing affairs, thus relieving the Church of much financial strain. But he did not do that of his own free will. He was urged to it by his brother James and by others of his friends who promised their assistance, for they knew that the project most dear to his heart was that of keeping a school.[15] They knew too that the Bible Christian Connexion could not bear the financial liabilities of the publishing business for much longer.

Settled in his own house, understanding from practical experience the management of the printing-press, and helped by friends around, Samuel might even then have started the school had his wife been able to give him her help, and we can imagine that Samuel regarded that help as essential. But she was busy rearing a family. Between 1826 and 1835 four children were born, and the time was hardly ripe for increasing such a family by housing a school at Prospect House. It has been suggested that the school did indeed start at this time, but the omission of any mention of it in Samuel's diary disproves the idea. We know that the school project was dear to him, and it is impossible to believe that one was started without any mention being made in the diary. In it are recorded intimate thoughts and hopes, accounts of journeyings made by himself and with his wife, the births of his children, certain vague thoughts of emigrating to America—no doubt inspired by his father-in-law —but there is no mention of a school, apart from the Sunday-school work in which he was naturally keenly interested.

The school probably did start, however, in 1834 or 1835,[16] by which time the Connexional upheavals had died down, and its organization was working smoothly. By that time, too, the printing-press, if it was not paying any dividend, was no longer a liability, so that conditions were more favourable for the undertaking of a new work. In 1835, Samuel wrote a long letter to his

[15] S. L. Thorne, *Samuel Thorne, Printer*, p. 139.
[16] The date 1834 is supplied by the Rev. Ford Reed, a descendant of the Reed family of Holwell, to whom I am indebted for much valuable information.

112

sister-in-law in New York, and this was evidently written at the beginning of a school holiday, for he says: 'Although we are now ten less to the family than we were a few hours ago, the boarders and apprentices being gone to see their friends, still we are thirteen of us. As to work, we are always busy, but the profits lie too long in our ware-rooms.' [17]

The school at its foundation was a purely private venture, administered by Samuel Thorne and his wife, and receiving boys and girls, day and boarding pupils, some of whom probably stayed on at the school serving their apprenticeship to the printing trade—which, we remember, was carried on in the same house—and to agriculture, the neighbouring farmers assisting in this part of the work. Publication of the *Bible Christian Magazine* and of various books continued, and included a spelling- and reading-book compiled by Samuel for use in his school. In addition he edited *The Youth's and Child's Magazine* and published *The Western Herald*. A schoolmaster in 1835 who was also an editor, printer, and publisher must surely have been unique, and during the six or seven years he spent in such work, encouraged and helped by his wife and brother, he showed others that there was a need for education which should have a close connexion with the Bible Christian Connexion itself. He laid the foundations of practice for the time when the Connexion would make education one of its vital interests. If Samuel Thorne had not set that example, and if James Thorne had not been convinced of the need for it, Shebbear College as we know it today would not have come into being.

'The Thornes were a family of strong and clear intelligence. They saw beyond the horizon that bounded the peasant community amidst which they lived and, recognizing the need of schools and education, started the school. It was with them an enlightened enthusiasm.' [18]

For three or four years, the school maintained its way. It was not an overwhelming success, and one would be surprised to find that it had been. Its chief importance during that period lay in the service it rendered in inspiring others with the enthusiasm which the Thorne brothers already possessed. In 1838 the first signs of that increasing interest in education were seen when some of the leaders of the Connexion began to discuss the possibility of a Connexional school which would serve the double

[17] S. L. Thorne, op. cit., pp. 158–9.
[18] MS. letter of the Rev. J. Ford Reed.

purpose of giving a general education to the young and of training future leaders of the young Church. In this spreading of interest it was James Thorne who took the leading part, for he had realized for some years that private enterprise was not sufficient alone and that unless the Connexion itself took steps to educate its youth it would suffer, for there was a growing demand for education amongst its members, and what could not be found inside the Connexion must be looked for elsewhere. In November 1839 a circular letter was issued to ministers; the matter was discussed in Conference, but at that time this body did not feel that it could undertake the responsibility, involving as it did considerable financial outlay. A number of influential men, however, were persuaded that a school was needed. The drawing up of a definite scheme took a considerable time, but in 1841 four ministers—Paul Robins, James Way, Richard Kinsman, and James Thorne—together with Messrs. W. and H. H. Newcombe, R. D. Gay, James Horswill, and a few other laymen, formed themselves into a Company to organize and put into practice a scheme of education closely connected with the Bible Christian Connexion. Some of these men had received a very slender education, and it is a tribute to their vision and character that they were willing to invest capital in a scheme which held little promise of financial return. No fixed sums had to be invested, nor was there any stipulated maximum as there was later in other Methodist Company schools. No doubt the members of the Company were all too conscious of their own financial limits to make such a maximum necessary. It is a fact which should not be forgotten: that no man of wealth assisted in the founding of this school. Wesley College, Sheffield—the only other Methodist Company school founded by 1841—could not claim great wealth amongst its promoters either, but compared with the wealth attached to Shebbear it was immensely rich. Realization of the financial limitations imposed on those who had the courage to go forward with this scheme only increases our respect for the members of the Company. On 20th January 1841 a meeting of the shareholders was held and the Rules and Regulations of the 'Bible Christian Proprietary Grammar School' were formulated and approved. The total sum subscribed was £150! It was agreed that shares should be repaid 'when the clear proceeds of the Institution will admit of it, with lawful interest paid annually'.[19] But, as the Rev. F. W. Bourne (who

[19] Richard Pyke, *The Golden Chain*, p. 122.

may be called the official historian of the Bible Christian Connexion) has pointed out, the shareholders 'got no dividend beyond the satisfaction of doing good',[20] and the capital was never redistributed. The Company bought the school which had been founded by Samuel Thorne, and it was reopened under its new management on Lady Day, 1841. From the first it was intended to be a place 'where the sons of the more affluent members of the body might receive their education, without going outside the Connexion for it'.[21]

Samuel Thorne had begun to farm Lake when his elder brother John moved thence to Broadwoodwidger in 1838, and when the school was taken over by the Company he moved with his wife and family to that farm. (A man of many parts was Samuel: preacher, self-educator, printer, editor, publisher, schoolmaster, and farmer!) The Company appointed as head master of the school an Irish clergyman, the Rev. H. C. O'Donnoghue, M.A., formerly of St. John's College, Cambridge. He had been one of William the Fourth's chaplains, but had seceded from the Established Church for conscientious reasons. A scholar and a good organizer, he proved during the short time he carried on his duties in the school an excellent choice. From the first, he included in the curriculum the Latin and Greek classics in addition to the usual subjects of instruction. He even found time, while at Shebbear, to complete his lengthy *History of the Church and Court of Rome,* a work which Samuel Thorne published. Unfortunately, however, he died suddenly of apoplexy at the close of school prayers on 22nd March 1842, only a year after taking up office. A Mr. Sanderson, an Independent minister from Cheshunt College, was appointed in his place, but this choice was not a success. It would have needed a man of outstanding ability, determination, and tact to have been successful, for the sudden death of the head master at the very start of the school's history was a blow from which it could not soon recover. School routine had scarcely had time to settle down, and in addition there was already considerable debt. Many doubted whether it was possible to carry on, but James Thorne never lost hope of ultimate success, and it was due entirely to his encouragement that the school was not given up. Mr. Sanderson did give up, and it was realized that only one step was possible if the school was to continue at all: it would have to be placed under the

[20] F. W. Bourne, *The Bible Christians: Their Origin and Story,* p. 263.
[21] F. W. Bourne, *The Centenary Life of James Thorne of Shebbear,* p. 241.

general supervision of a man who had the interests both of education and of the Connexion at heart. There must be complete understanding and sympathy with all that the school stood for and with the movement which had led to its foundation. There was only one man of such weight and influence as could save the school, and in 1844 the Conference released James Thorne from circuit work at Bideford to take over the responsibility of the government of the school, his wife, formerly Catherine Reed, undertaking the duties of matron, for the root of many of the school's difficulties lay in bad domestic management.

Not the least of the difficulties with which James Thorne had to contend were apathy, timidity, and prejudice. As we have already seen, there were many people in those days who felt that evangelicalism had no place or time for education. Some even went so far as to feel that education was contrary to the laws of piety and Christianity, but a movement which led to the stamping out of such views, as far as the Bible Christians were concerned, started in 1842, when, at the Conference held at Truro, one of the largest increases ever recorded in Connexional membership was announced, and for the first time serious consideration was given to its causes and to its possible conservation. On the negative side it was pointed out that neglect of mental improvement among the converted and the unconverted led to much of the un-Christian spirit against which Methodism was contending. Such a realization must have done much to convince waverers of the need for carrying on the school at Shebbear. But it did not completely convince them, and the Conference only 'reluctantly consented to relieve the shareholders of their responsibilities'.[22] The reluctance shown then came later to be regretted, but the taking-over of the school has never been regretted.

James Thorne was designated 'Secretary', a title he retained until the Conference of 1866 changed it to 'Governor'. We have already recorded something of his early upbringing, and we cannot do better than quote from his biography a summary of his character which, apart from his burning zeal for education and Christianity, accounts for the success of the school:

'Although Mr. Thorne had not received a liberal education in his boyhood, he had made some efforts to supply the deficiency, and records attempts at the study of the classics during his first

[22] F. W. Bourne, *The Centenary Life of James Thorne of Shebbear*, p. 102.

appointment to Kent, which it can well be imagined could hardly have fair play for their development. But his great natural powers had been supplemented by diligent reading in general literature of the practical school, and he was prepared to sustain a respectable place among well-informed men. His manners, free from a particle of affectation, wore a simple dignity of their own, and constitutionally averse to harshness or rigour, he contrived to maintain an admirable discipline, under circumstances of such difficulty as only practical acquaintance with them can teach. He sustained a fatherly relationship to the boys, interested himself in their welfare, mingled in their sports, in those spare moments of relaxation which his manifold engagements permitted, and ever kept their spiritual improvement before him as the chief end of their connexion.' [23]

For over twenty years James Thorne and his wife struggled against enormous difficulties. There was lack of the capital necessary to equip the school, and although some few people had by then come to believe in the venture and supported it by sending their sons, the majority still felt that higher education was not necessary and was even a hindrance to work, especially to agriculture. There were, too, constant changes in the teaching staff, many of those appointed being inexperienced or incompetent, for the Connexion could not afford to pay high salaries.

Amongst those educated at the school at that time was the son of one of the original shareholders, James Way. In 1850, the father sailed as a missionary to Australia, leaving the boy behind to finish his education at Shebbear. That boy, Samuel Way, was to become the most distinguished Old Boy of the school: The Right Honourable Sir Samuel Way, Baronet, Chief Justice of South Australia, Chancellor of the University of Adelaide, a D.C.L. of the University of Oxford, an LL.D. of the University of Cambridge, and a member of the Privy Council.

That education does not destroy evangelism in a personality is shown in the case of another pupil of that period—Samuel Keene, who became a well-known English evangelist. It appears probable that this man was one of the first to receive a certain amount of theological training at the school after he had passed through it as an ordinary pupil, for, as in the case of Queen's College, Taunton, the school at Shebbear for a number of years served both as a school and as a theological college. Another pupil of that time who received similar training was William

---

[23] F. W. Bourne, *The Centenary Life of James Thorne of Shebbear*, p. 243.

O'Bryan Reed, who later became the Governor of Edgehill—
the Bible Christian Girls' School which will be mentioned in a
later chapter.

During the period 1842 to 1864, there were four head masters
—the Mr. Sanderson mentioned above, a Mr. Kelly who had
been an Independent minister, and Messrs. Cloke and Loase,
both of whom were Old Boys of the school. Their difficulties were great, but they were surmounted, and it was during
those years of testing that the best traditions of the school were
laid, the fact that the school was situated in the village where
the Bible Christian Connexion had had its origin assisting the
indefinable growth of tradition. From that little village, the
Bible Christian influence had spread out to all parts of the
world, especially to Canada and Australia, and it was to that
village of North Devon that thoughts turned continually. There
is little wherewith to colour the picture of the school during
those testing years, but one figure stands out—that of James
Thorne. At the celebration of the school's Jubilee in 1891, Sir
James Way, who was on a visit from Australia at the time, was
the chief speaker, and looking back at those twenty years of the
school's comparative obscurity he recalled that the 'dominant
influence in the school at that time was undoubtedly the gracious
and benignant personality of James Thorne. No one who had
the privilege of knowing him can forget his devotion, his piety
and his zeal.' [24]

James Thorne did give his whole energy to the work of the
school, believing that it was intimately linked with evangelistic
work, and it is not surprising to find that, in the latter half of
the century, when the question of State help for education was
raised which divided educationists and those concerned with
religion into two loudly speaking parties, he opposed all State
interference, believing that the voluntary principle was right and
most effective. Unlike some men who opposed State aid for
education, he had twenty years and more of practical experience
on which to base his views. It was James Thorne who laid the
foundations and built up the traditions of the school at Shebbear
as a Connexional institution, but it was a professional schoolmaster who built up its reputation as a school.

Thomas Ruddle was appointed to the head mastership in
1864, owing to a fortuitous sequence of events which proved
the salvation of the school. In that year the head master of the

[24] F. W. Bourne, *The Bible Christians: Their Origin and Story*, p. 265.

British School at Portland preached on Sundays for a Bible Christian minister who was ill. This came to the knowledge of the school committee of management, who did not approve and ordered the master to cease preaching or to resign his school appointment. He resigned. The minister whose pulpit he had been occupying—a former President of the Bible Christian Conference—knew that there was a head master wanted at the Shebbear School and advised his friend to apply. The school, however, required an unmarried man. The Portland schoolmaster was married, and there were other reasons too why he did not wish to apply. He therefore took no action himself, but he did pass on the advertisement in the *Bible Christian Magazine* to a friend of his, another schoolmaster who lived at Weymouth. This man was Thomas Ruddle. He applied for the post and was appointed. It is interesting to notice that he had been trained at the Borough Road Training College during the period when Joshua Fitch (later Sir Joshua, a Government inspector and an assistant commissioner in the Schools Inquiry Commission and a lifelong friend of denominational schools) was principal there.

Thomas Ruddle is another of the group of professional schoolmasters of whom Methodism is rightly proud. He took up his duties as head master of Shebbear at the age of twenty-three and carried on that work for forty-five years until ill-health caused his resignation in 1909. He died only three months later. During the period he was in office, the school became one of the best-known secondary schools in the west of England.

His former college principal used to say that freshness and vigour, variety and versatility were of the essence of successful teaching. Ruddle had those qualities. He possessed a vivid personality, as a study of his life and letters shows, was eager in his pursuit of new interests, yet without being in any way a dilettante, never content to stand still in the present—a danger which besets most schoolmasters—he was always looking to the future, never content merely to expound and teach others; he was throughout his life a pupil himself. He had that gift which in a schoolmaster is invaluable—the ability to use common sense, not only as a young man but throughout his busy life. When he was appointed to Shebbear he was not a Bible Christian. He was, in fact, inclined to despise what he had previously considered their narrow-mindedness and sectarianism, and on most religious and social questions he differed from all that the Bible

Christians held most dear. Always outspoken, of deeply rooted principles, until the closing years of his life he caused uneasiness amongst certain individuals who had been brought up in the traditions of the Bible Christian Connexion. But in spite, or perhaps because, of his unswerving principles, he gradually gained the whole-hearted confidence of the Conference and of most of the Connexion, who, though they might differ from him in detail, yet sent their sons to the school of which he was head master. It was not long before Ruddle's prejudice against the Bible Christians gave way to admiration, and before many years had passed he was a willing and a welcome occupier of the village pulpits in the neighbourhood of the school. This changed attitude owed much to the quiet influence and the understanding sympathy of James Thorne, who was governor during the first six years of Ruddle's head mastership, and who had been largely responsible for his appointment. Ruddle objected to pretence in any form. Under no circumstances would he allow the use of translations (or 'cribs') in classics, for example. The clever boy found him an interested and an interesting teacher; the dull boy found him sympathetic; the lazy boy found that laziness did not pay.

The school premises had been altered and improved considerably in 1862, but when Ruddle arrived he found the structure and equipment inadequate. The school life appeared at a low ebb. There were twenty-two boarders only, some of them candidates for the Ministry, so that the mode of education was of necessity tutorial, the usual division of the school into Forms being practically impossible. The routine was rigid and exacting, resembling somewhat the early routine of Kingswood School. The only redeeming feature, in Ruddle's eyes, was the sincere friendship and understanding between the governor and pupils. Like all those who have a genuine love of work, difficulties only called forth greater efforts. The curriculum already included English, history, geography, arithmetic, classics, and French. To these subjects he added, at any rate for certain pupils, land-surveying, music (when one boy wished to learn to play the violin, Ruddle himself learnt in order to teach him!), Spanish, and Italian. Nothing came amiss to him, and yet, in spite of the wide scope of his interests and occupations, he was thorough in them all, and it was not long before his fame as a teacher and his reputation as a man began to come to the ears of the Connexion as a whole.

In 1868, the Conference *Minutes* recorded: 'We believe that the time is now come when we may with a united effort make the institution a great success.'

The Connexion had become conscious of its own school as never before; it now had working in it a head master who had the ability and the will to guide its destinies, and the Conference expressed its willing support—unanimously for the first time. Hitherto its support had been forced from it by the enthusiasm of such men as James Thorne.

In 1870, James Thorne resigned from his position as Governor. Just as his brother had taken over the Connexional printing-press when it was an impoverished and losing concern, and had laid down his duties when it was a paying concern, so James Thorne had taken over the superintendence of the school when its future was, to say the least, doubtful, when it looked as though it might have to close down altogether, and he resigned when it was achieving a reputation which spread far beyond Devon. There is no need here, however, to deal in detail with the various changes. Suffice it that it did develop as an educational power, spreading its influence beyond the shores of this country to other parts of the world. During the 1870's there was rapid progress in all directions, though the number of pupils did not exceed fifty until 1875. By then the head master had won his way to the respect and confidence of the Connexion. Respect he always had; confidence he gained more slowly. But once it was gained, the Connexion had no cause for regret, and allowed him a free hand on the educational side. Ruddle did more than his duty. His curriculum was too wide for the Staff which the school could employ, but, rightly or wrongly, Ruddle refused to narrow it to suit the staff. Instead, he gave extra tuition himself in out-of-school hours, and his work was made the more difficult in that he was coaching young men, candidates for the Ministry, who were sent to the school year by year at the direction of the Conference, in addition to the ordinary school pupils. He was able to impart to all some of his love of learning, his hatred of affectation and pretence, and in doing that he gave his pupils more than they could learn from books. The aim of the school at this time can best be expressed in Ruddle's own words:

'We put on no airs. We have no more ambition to imitate the aims and methods of our great public schools than we have ability to rival their numbers, wealth, and prestige. Few of our pupils will proceed to the universities; should any do so, we trust they will do us no discredit there; but this is not our general aim. We wish to prepare our pupils thoroughly for the duties of professional life, for situations in the Civil Service, or for mercantile and agricultural pursuits. And for this purpose we hold it to be of great importance to be intelligent and true, as to be familiar with grammars and lexicons; to be of even more consequence to know how to deny one's self for another's sake, than how to enter a drawing-room or pick up a pocket handkerchief.' [25]

The number of pupils increased steadily, and Ruddle was not averse to encouraging a competitive spirit amongst them. There were yearly and half-yearly examinations organized within the school, and as soon as there were pupils who were capable of the work and who would profit by it Ruddle entered them for the Oxford University Local Examinations, whose inception owed much to the local Member of Parliament, Sir Thomas Dyke Acland,[26] a true friend of the school at Shebbear. One night, after addressing a meeting at a village in his constituency, Sir Thomas found himself benighted—no uncommon happening in that part of England even at the end of the nineteenth century—and received hospitality at Prospect House. James Thorne was at home that night, and though no detailed record exists of the talk between these two men, it certainly centred on education. Sir Thomas was greatly impressed by the sincerity of his host and by the work he was doing at the school, and told James Thorne that he might count on him for any help that he could give. That was no idle thanks given in return for a night's shelter. Again and again, the school found him a true friend, and Sir Thomas himself was especially pleased when, some years later, a boy from Shebbear, H. W. Horwill, won the Dyke Acland Scholarship straight from the school, having taken first place in the Senior Oxford Local Examination. This scholarship was open to candidates from Somerset, Devon, and Cornwall, so that the winning of it by a boy from Shebbear did much to bring prestige to the school. Nor was that an isolated case. As we have already seen, Ruddle did not aim at producing genius nor

[25] G. P. Dymond, *Thomas Ruddle of Shebbear*, pp. 64–5.
[26] Sir Thomas was keenly interested in education, and his interest was not confined to mere theory. He was one of the Commissioners appointed in 1864 to inquire into education not already examined by the Newcastle Education Commission. He was largely responsible for Chapter 3 of the Schools Inquiry Commission Report—the chapter dealing with the local distribution of endowments. Previously he had drawn up for the Commissioners five elaborate memoranda mainly on the statistics of middle-class education and on local and central administration. See E. G. Sandford, *Memoirs of Frederick Temple*.

a succession of university honours. He aimed at a knowledge of how to work rather than the material success of the work itself. However, success is bound to attend any organization with such an aim at some time or other, and on another occasion a Shebbear boy gained first place in all England in the Oxford Junior Local Examinations in classics, and others followed with similar successes in English and mathematics.

During this period (1864–80 approximately), the school was as well known in parts of Australia as it was in Devon. Largely owing to Sir Samuel Way's influence, contingents of boys came year by year from that country, and when the Rev. John Thorne, youngest son of James Thorne and fellow-pupil of Way, went out as a missionary to Australia in 1872, the fame of the school spread even more widely, and an influx of pupils thence continued steadily until 1892, when he was largely responsible for establishing a school, similar to that at Shebbear, in Australia. He and the Rev. Thomas Piper toured the land, arousing interest —and collecting subscriptions—in the project of founding a school in Australia for those boys who had been making the long journey home to England for their education. Way College, so called in memory of the Rev. James Way, one of the first Bible Christian ministers in Australia and father of Sir Samuel, was opened in 1892. In 1903, it was taken over by the Government to be incorporated in the scheme of high schools which was being organized throughout southern Australia, under the leadership of the Premier, himself a Methodist. During the short existence of Way College as an independent school, 1,109 boys were educated there, and it became the centre of the Bush Mission, from which missionaries and ministers went out to all parts of Australia, just as they went out to all parts of England and the world from the centre of Shebbear.

In 1876, at the suggestion of the Rev. John Thorne, who was on a visit to this country, the name 'Bible Christian Proprietary Grammar School' was changed to 'Shebbear College', the name by which the school is known today. For three years previously the school had been growing rapidly and the number of pupils had outgrown the premises. Extensions were essential. On 5th April 1877 the foundation-stone of the new buildings was laid by the Earl of Portsmouth, and a year later the buildings were formally opened by him and Lady Portsmouth. One name should be mentioned in connexion with this. Although Conference had sanctioned the extensions there was still some unwillingness in certain quarters to spend money on education, and it was largely due to the efforts of the Rev. William Higman that the extensions were made possible. He travelled the country arousing interest in, and sympathy for, the ideals which the Bible Christian leaders centred in their school. Over £3,000 was subscribed in this way, despite active opposition on the one hand and indifference on the other. Further extensions took place in 1879 and 1883.

'The buildings grew as did the school. There were no men of wealth to direct the development or to enrich it with endowments. As a consequence, the additions made from time to time were of a modest character, as a close scrutiny of the fabric at once makes apparent. But if the structure is plain, it has through the years commended itself to expert visitors whose comment has been that they were "an eminently serviceable set of premises".' [27]

In 1891, the school commemorated its Jubilee, the special speaker on that occasion being the Right Honourable Sir Samuel Way. After distributing the prizes to the boys, he presented a prize to the school itself—Lake Farm, the birthplace of the Bible Christian Connexion—saying:

'When I acquired Lake Farm, it was because of the interest I took in it as the cradle of the Bible Christian Connexion. I purchased it, not for the purpose of making money, but in order that the land which had so many sacred associations to us Bible Christians all over the world might be secured for the benefit of the Denomination in perpetuity. And after considering the matter, I dare say you will think for too many years, I have come to the conclusion that the best way in which the interests of the Bible Christian Denomination and the cause of learning and religion can be furthered by this estate is that I shall present it to the Bible Christian College. I have executed a deed of gift of the estate to certain trustees named in it. The deed has been enrolled in Chancery, and I have now the pleasure of presenting it to the President of the Conference on behalf of the Bible Christian people.' [28]

By this action Sir Samuel signified his own belief in the close relationship between religion and education.

Thomas Ruddle in a short address at the Ecumenical Conference at City Road in 1900 said: 'I always think that a good

---

[27] *The Story of the United Methodist Church*, p. 153.
[28] F. W. Bourne, op. cit., p. 535.

test of organic life is its power to reproduce itself. I believe all scientists say that the real proof of life is—whether life can reproduce itself. The highest form of life that a man knows anything about is the Christian life, and it seems to me that the time is coming when we have to be tried, and all Christian forms will have to be tried, by their power to reproduce Christian gentlemen, and the Church which cannot do that cannot live or will not live permanently.' [29]

The Bible Christian Connexion was a small one. Today it is part of The Methodist Church, from which in spirit it has never differed. It can be proud of its leaders and particularly of Samuel and James Thorne, who from the first realized that it is largely through the youth of a Church that the spirit of that Church is reproduced, and who, in spite of opposition and disinterestedness, struggled on and maintained a school such as Shebbear College which has sent and is sending former pupils into all parts of the world to spread Christianity.

[29] G. P. Dymond, *Thomas Ruddle of Shebbear*, pp. 83–4.

CHAPTER SEVEN

Lay Influence on Methodist Education

'I T HAS BEEN SAID that the British Empire was founded in a fit of absence of mind. The rebuilding of our educational system in the nineteenth century was equally unpremeditated. Institutions were established or ideals realized as the occasion required, and the originator was now some great head master or head mistress, now a religious community, now a city guild, now an examining body, now a public authority, whether central or local, but most often a small group of public-spirited men and women—like the founders of the great University of London— who saw a crying need, hoisted a banner, set up an association, collected the funds, and if they succeeded, as they generally did, bequeathed to the nation one more wing of our haphazard scholastic structure.'[1]

Thus wrote Professor Dover Wilson concerning the schools of England regarded from a national point of view and looking back over the nineteenth century. In the same spirit had written Matthew Arnold in 1867, looking forward from the haphazard education of his present to an organized system of the future. This country lacked the nationalized outlook on education which was growing rapidly in Germany and France, but it is not right for this reason to belittle the education that did exist in this country. There were tragic shortcomings, but there were men, and institutions who by their unhampered efforts did much to make this country what it later became, and Methodism took its share in the work.

During the period from approximately 1780 to 1835 Methodism had more indirect influence on the general education of the country than it had direct influence on its own education. It was during this period that criticism of the public schools reached its climax, and it is suggested that the appeal to the heart spread abroad by the Evangelicals in the Established Church, by the new outlook on the arts labelled 'Romanticism', and by the reactionary influence of the increasing use of machinery with all its attendant heart-searchings and awakenings was at least assisted by Methodism. As an educational historian has said:

[1] Dover Wilson, *The Schools of England,* pp. 11–12.

'In the eighteenth century there was a renaissance of emotional interest in morality and intellect. . . . Its spearhead was Wesley and its first manifestation was Methodism. It thus began as a lower-middle-class movement, and was radical in that it appealed to the heart rather than to dogma. At first it gained adherents chiefly among those outside the Church, but later it spread, under the name of Evangelicalism, to the ruling classes, and in this way affected the public schools. Most of the reactionaries were Evangelicals.' [2] If Methodism did indeed have such far-reaching influence, that influence could not be entirely due to the mere handful of travelling preachers. The work of the laymen of Methodism, no less in the early stages than in the present day, cannot be overestimated. As has already been shown, Wesley had no desire to dissociate himself from the Established Church and to form yet another dissenting sect, but when such a step was forced upon him, the usual congregational system of dissent was discarded and the connexional system took its place. The Wesleyan minister did not depend upon the vote of the people: he took his authority from God, and any control imposed upon him could therefore only come from other ministers of God. Herein lay the extreme importance and authority of Conference which is still exercised today. A number of Methodist Societies formed a circuit under the control of a superintendent minister; the circuits formed Districts under the general surveillance of another minister, and those Districts formed the Connexion under the authority of Conference. But, though the minister controlled, he did so largely through laymen. There were class leaders, stewards, local preachers, and other lay officials, and these all acted together so that we see the curious paradox of the Methodist Connexion with its appeal to the individual and its individualistic philosophy finding its chief strength and glory in the reality of its fellowship.

This excellent state of affairs did not happen suddenly. It could not be imposed, nor could it take root without considerable disturbance and 'growing pains'. It was the gradual evolution of the fellowship and organization of the Connexion which largely occupied the energies of Methodists in this particular period.

At first the Methodist Connexion was controlled by its ordained ministers. It was this autocratic ministerial control which caused Alexander Kilham to rebel and to found the

[2] Edward C. Mack, *Public Schools and British Opinion, 1780–1860*, pp. 120–1.

Methodist New Connexion in 1797—a Connexion in which laymen had a greater share of control and in which there was from the first a more democratic form of government. It is significant that in the years following Kilham's expulsion the laymen of Wesleyan Methodism were given a greater share in government, and leaders of local Societies were given the right of veto on the admission or expulsion of members and officers of the Society. Today there is a Representative Session at District Synods, and Conference is composed of ministers and laymen, while Connexional Committees contain a large proportion of laymen.

That is the position today, but it has taken two hundred years to reach it. The foundations were laid in the period immediately following the death of John Wesley. It was a period of unrest—unhealthy, irresponsible unrest, it must have appeared to many leaders of Methodism in those early days. Only in the light of historical perspective can it be truly judged. There is no doubt that the difficulties and heart-searchings in the early years of the nineteenth century made for the strength of the Methodist organization which at length appeared.

Nonconformists have frequently been accused of narrow-mindedness, often with reason, but Methodism has never been so narrow that it has not been influenced by external affairs nor exercised equally strong influence on those affairs.

The foundation of the Bible Society in 1804 had an incalculable influence on education throughout the world, an influence all the greater for the undenominational nature of the Society. All thinking men at that time were constantly being stirred as social abuses were made public. The movement which led to the abolition of slavery in that same year turned men's eyes beyond the limits of their own country. It is worthy of note that it was in 1817 that the Methodist Missionary Society was founded. The gradual correction of social abuses in England itself held attention on internal affairs, but not to the exclusion of affairs overseas. It was an age of humanitarianism in its widest sense. Although this cannot be claimed as an achievement of Methodism alone, yet, on the other hand, it is equally incorrect to take away from Methodism all the credit. John Wesley emphasized the importance of the individual and this resulted gradually in the recognition of the rights of the common man. A parallel spirit is seen in the literature of the time. Individualism became sometimes dangerously rampant. Wesley, however, guarded against the dangers by insistence on the greatness and the Fatherhood of God and the necessity of social religious life, i.e. fellowship. It is but a short step from this to an interest in politics. Bentham could not but find supporters there with his sometimes apparent paradox: 'Every man the best judge of his own interests' and 'the greatest happiness of the greatest number.' The political change which he advocated was, too, a peaceful change, and fear—fear of violence—was no small factor to be considered at the turn of the century. Again, Bentham did not like 'highbrows'. The Established Church said: 'I know because I am told I ought to know.' Methodism said: 'I know because my heart burns and tells me so.' Reason was opposed to emotion, and the Methodist people were on the whole ranged on the side of emotion. Its leaders, especially those who held views precisely similar to those of the Wesleys, were, however, heartily opposed to the violence to which unrestrained emotions were susceptible. The Conference, for example, strongly opposed Chartism and on several occasions passed resolutions against it.[3] Official Methodism disliked the Chartist demand for secular education as much as it disliked its anticlericalism. It was this which caused them to oppose the proposed Education Bill of 1839. It is an interesting fact that, although the Methodist appeal to emotion had woken people up, it was the conservatism of the Methodist leaders which steadied them in years of social unrest. Lord Egerton, in a speech in the House of Commons in 1839, referring to the presentation of petitions by the Methodists, said: "I must say I am inclined to attribute more weight and authority . . . to the expression of opinion of this great body than to the leaders of the Establishment. I think the former opinion [i.e. of Methodists] would carry more weight throughout the country." [4] There was indeed a spiritual vitality in Methodism which led to progress in many directions, but led to it through paths of peace because it was based on loyalty to established order. The value of tradition was recognized.

This sketch of the political and philosophic background of the period has been drawn in order to emphasize two important facts: firstly, that Methodism was beginning to play a not unimportant part in national affairs, and secondly, that within Methodism itself, as in the country generally, there were con-

[3] Maldwyn Edwards, *This Methodism*, pp. 11ff., and *Methodism and England*, pp. 44–8.
[4] *The Watchman*, 14th June 1839, pp. 206–7.

flicting opinions which caused many spirited exchanges in the annual meetings of Conference.

Methodism made its first appeal to the depressed working classes, and in its early years not the least of its practical difficulties was that of finance. Nevertheless, the influence of Methodism worked upward socially, and by the beginning of the nineteenth century there was increasing wealth amongst the laity.

John Wesley resembled Calvin in his distrust of the natural man. His hatred of sloth, luxury, and indulgence is evidenced in many of his writings and sermons. The Christian's duty was the carrying out of his business in life in a conscientious manner and in a way which would not injure his neighbour nor his own mental, physical, and spiritual health. The Society Class and the Chapel were the social as well as the religious centres of Methodism, and Wesley always insisted on the use of every moment to the fullest possible advantage. As far as money was concerned, he exhorted his fellows to gain all they could.[5] This advice, put alongside of his other statements concerning the shunning of luxury and indulgence, set some of his followers on a dangerous path. Methodists, spending their energies on their businesses and in the company of those of similar outlook and practice, led to the creation of worldly fortune, and many of them overlooked Wesley's other warnings about the dangers of amassing wealth and his reminders about the need of giving it away to the poor. Wesley realized during his lifetime the dangers of his dictum 'Gain all you can', and again and again he warned his followers against too much prosperity.[6] Nevertheless, the lay element in Methodism was growing increasingly prosperous as far as wealth was concerned, and in the nineteenth century wealth was all-important. By the time Wesley died Methodism was becoming middle-class in social status. Its membership was growing. It included artisans and workmen, but the Connexion was beginning to be controlled not by manual workers but by the middle-class folk of Tory outlook. As this happened, Methodist laymen began to feel the need of Methodist schools wherein their children might be brought up in the moral and social atmosphere of the schools which catered for higher education. At the same time, they demanded a

[5] *Works,* Vol. VI, p. 126.
[6] See his sermons on 'The Danger of Riches', 'Riches', 'Worldly Folly', 'The Danger of Increasing Riches'.

religious environment such as they had known—the religious atmosphere of friendliness and love of family peculiar to Methodism.

A system never begins at once. Wesley, for example, did not organize his preachers for some years. His own personality gave the spark of life to minds which had grown dull and lethargic; it inspired other personalities, and Methodism grew, but it did not become 'Methodism' as the world knows it until there was organization, and it was part of Wesley's genius that he was not only able to give an initial drive, he was also able, when he realized the need, to organize, though the name which is outstanding as far as organization is concerned is that of Jabez Bunting. Only because of organization has Methodism been able to become the world-wide power it is today. First the individual and his ideals, then the society practising those ideals. And this needs organization.

Education, as we have seen, occupied a foremost position in Wesley's mind. 'Before the actual genesis of Methodism, Wesley had recognized education as part of his great mission work, and it was much the best part, too, of his work at Savannah. But after his conversion education, as well as evangelization, was placed at the very root and basis of his great work.'[7]

As far as higher education was concerned, however, Kingswood School was Wesley's only contribution. Originally, this school was to have educated any boys whose parents wished to send them there, but Wesley was 'reluctantly compelled to abandon his original intention, at least for a time, and to fill up the school with the sons of his preachers, making public collections to defray its expenses'.[8] This step was necessitated by lack of public understanding of the scheme; by the impossibility of obtaining masters with the requisite literary and religious qualifications, combined with willingness to carry out the rigorous rules of Wesley; and by the resolution of the two Universities not to admit as students any who had been educated at Kingswood School.[9]

Wesley knew the intimate connexion there must be between evangelization and education, but evangelization came first. As it was, he did the work of several men during his lifetime, but all his efforts centred in evangelization. He had to leave some

[7] *Wesley: the Man, his Teaching, and his Work*, p. 251.
[8] *The Wesleyan Proprietary Grammar School, Sheffield*, p. 13.
[9] See also *Wesley: the Man, his Teaching, and his Work*, p. 255.

matters for others to deal with, and he is not to be blamed if others did not appreciate the importance of education as he did. They followed him and copied him, as is evidenced by the foundation of Woodhouse Grove School, but their efforts were severely limited. It is not right, however, to accuse official Methodism of neglect in the matter of young people. As will be shown later, much was being done for the primary education of young Methodists, and Methodism did not lag behind the various advances in education and social reformation which were beginning to occupy the country before the passing of the Reform Bill in 1832. In the *Minutes of Conference* for 1838 [10] appeared this 'direction':

'The attention of our Preachers is earnestly directed to the necessity and importance of making some effectual arrangements in every town where a preacher resides for obtaining pastoral access, at stated times, to the young persons of Methodist families, between the ages of fourteen and twenty, with a view to promoting their spiritual welfare by instruction, exhortation, and prayer.'

That, in Wesley's view, would have meant education. Again, if official Methodism, as represented by Conference, had no direct connexion with secondary education apart from Kingswood and Woodhouse Grove, there were a number of Methodist private schools, many of whose head masters were Local Preachers— schools such as that at North Walsham under a Mr. Crickmore, Edenfield House, near Doncaster, whose head master was an Old Boy of Woodhouse Grove, or Thistleboon House, Swansea. These were secondary schools catering for boarders as well as day boys. In 1844, the President of the Conference, who, during the course of his duties, travelled extensively throughout the British Isles, speaking on higher education, maintained that there did exist many Methodist schools, though they were private schools.[11]

Because official Methodism did not quickly realize the need for an educational system in direct connexion with itself, it is not right to say that those who came immediately after Wesley had no use for education and did nothing to extend that branch of evangelistic work. Wesley himself was educated at a public school and Oxford; many of his followers had no education at all, though one must not forget what a reading of some of *The*

[10] p. 114.
[11] Benjamin Gregory, *Sidelights on the Conflicts of Methodism*, pp. 371–2.

Lives of the Early Methodist Preachers shows clearly: that many of Wesley's preachers at least were educated men.[12]

'Methodism, it is true, was born and cradled in a university, but she soon left her native place, and it took a very long time to get her back again.'[13]

After all, England herself was no more enterprising in her development of education. There was for long a *laissez-faire* attitude far too pronounced. In the Middle Ages the Church organized education, and appears to have done so most effectively.[14] The Roman Catholics, as soon as the Penal Laws against them slipped into abeyance in the eighteenth century, started to build up an organized system of education in this country, modelling it on the highly efficient organization of the Continental Jesuit schools.[15] But by the eighteenth century schools other than Roman Catholic ones and a few dissenting academies were in a poor state, and of an organized system there was not the faintest sign. It was the superficiality and scantiness of what existing schools did offer and the almost complete neglect of religious instruction that caused Wesley to found his own school at Kingswood.

Methodism was an evangelical movement. It was new. Its appeal, initially, was to the lower classes—to miners, labourers, and to those who did not know whence their next meal would come; even to criminals. It is scarcely surprising that no general attempt was made to organize a system of higher education during its early years. The struggle through which the infant Church was passing in order to survive taxed all its resources and all the leadership of its greatest figures. Yet it is interesting to read in 1839 that 'it has always been understood that good schools for the literary, scientific, and religious instruction of the youth of the societies was a part of the original plan of Methodism; a part which has been unavoidably postponed by the necessity of circumstances, but never finally given up. Indeed, for the last thirty years, its immediate adoption has been a subject of frequent conversation in different parts of the Connexion; and while the unnecessary introduction of any invidious remarks into this sketch should be carefully avoided, it must be said that

[12] See T. B. Shepherd, *Methodism and the Literature of the Eighteenth Century*, pp. 143ff.
[13] *Wesley: the Man, his Teaching, and his Work*, p. 251.
[14] See A. F. Leach, *The Schools of Medieval England*.
[15] See A. S. Barnes, *The Catholic Schools of England*. P. Guilday, *English Catholic Refugees*.

133

the necessity for such institutions has not been superseded by any improvement in education during the last century.'[16]

One of the men who, no doubt, took part in such conversations was the Rev. S. D. Waddy. He was the son of a Methodist minister, grandson of the master of a Charity School at Nunmonkton, Yorkshire, but little is known of his education apart from what he himself wrote later in his diary. In this he recalled how, at the age of eight, he was sent to school:

'May 22nd 1813. I was removed to the Wesleyan Academy, Woodhouse Grove, Yorkshire, where I remained six years, keeping pace with the regular classical routine, and somewhat excelling those of my own age in mathematical studies. The only distinction I ever obtained was in my last year, when the best prize was awarded for an heroic poem on the nativity of Christ. My principal competitor on that occasion was John Hare.'[17]

The work of Waddy is an example of the way in which Methodist secondary education developed from within itself. A very large percentage of the men who guided and organized the educational schemes of Methodism were themselves educated in Methodist schools, especially at Kingswood and Woodhouse Grove. What advance there has been in education has been due to impulses from within rather than from without.

After leaving school, Waddy was apprenticed to a linen weaver, and the period spent in that occupation he counted the most unhappy of his life. But the experience he gained at that time no doubt helped to broaden his outlook, and one cannot help feeling that all he saw and felt then was later an added inspiration when he took up the cause of education. One has only to glance at the pictures of Hogarth or to read the stories of Dickens to obtain an idea of the type of life an apprentice might have to lead in a great city like London under an employer lacking any trace of humanitarian feeling. Waddy was a sensitive, though strong-willed, youth, and the sights he saw, the experiences through which he passed—not made any easier by the cruel and grasping character of his employer—turned his thoughts more intensively to his own home. After thinking for long of the nature of that home, and of the meaning of Methodism as it had been shown him there and at school, he came to a turning-point in his life. He records in his diary:

'It was on Saturday morning, November 26th, 1822, while

---

[16] *The Wesleyan Proprietary Grammar School, Sheffield*, p. 14.
[17] A. Waddy, *The Life of the Rev. Samuel D. Waddy, D.D.*, p. 7.

wrestling with God in earnest prayer, that my sorrow was turned into joy, my despair vanished, and I was enabled to believe on the Lord Jesus Christ with the heart unto righteousness, and the Spirit of God bore witness with my spirit that I was a child of God.' [18]

The writer might have been consciously copying the words of John Wesley on a similar occasion. Perhaps he was. But there is no doubt about the reality of his experience. His whole future life is a testimony to that experience. He became a Local Preacher and subsequently entered the Wesleyan ministry.

In his diary for 1831 appears a significant entry:

'Removed to Northampton with my father. There I endeavoured to establish a proprietary school on the plan of those already established in connexion with other religious communities. I went to look at land in a suitable situation, and published prospectuses to obtain subscribers and shareholders; but the school met with no adequate encouragement and was for the present dropped.' [19]

Whence had Waddy gained this interest in secondary education? He was a man of wide interests and there was none of the narrow-mindedness sometimes associated with Nonconformist ministers of the time. It seems possible that Waddy had met the brothers Hill of Birmingham. At the Conference of 1827 he was appointed to the Birmingham Circuit. At that time the town was not the great city of today, and one circuit sufficed for the work of Methodism in the area. There Waddy spent two years. In 1817 the Hill family, of which Rowland Hill of 'penny post' fame was a member, established a school at 'Hilltop', Birmingham, and so successful was it that two years later larger premises were acquired at Hazelwood.[20] The peculiarity of this school, and of another established by the family at Bruce Grove, Tottenham, in 1826, was the belief that boys should be trained to educate themselves. It was, in fact, the first example of self-government in schools, about which much was heard in the period between the last two wars. A boys' committee, elected by the boys and containing one or two masters, proposed, discussed, and administered such rules as were found to be necessary. Another feature of the school was the 'charitable fund'—

---

[18] A. Waddy, op. cit., p. 19.
[19] ibid., p. 68. The schools of other religious communities to which he refers were schools such as Mill Hill (1807), Fulneck (1753), and Ackworth (1779).
[20] J. W. Adamson, *English Education, 1789–1902*, p. 51.

the practical outcome of a keen interest shown by the founders in social welfare. There is no need to tell of the life of the schools, but it is worth noting that later when Waddy became governor of Wesley College, Sheffield, he believed in interfering as little as possible in the routine of the school, allowing the boys to administer things for themselves, though no committee of boys was set up for that purpose. When asked by a pupil to supervise a certain activity in the school, Waddy replied: 'If I come, I shall alter the whole thing. You will feel more constrained. You shall do the work yourselves; but be humble.' [21]

There does appear to be some reason for believing that Waddy may have had some association with the school at Hazelwood. If he never saw its routine in practice, it is probable that he heard of it during those two years in Birmingham, and possibly the seed of his interest in secondary education was sown at that time, for he must have viewed with dissatisfaction the two existing schools of Methodism—dissatisfaction because there were only two of them and both were for the sons of ministers. Methodism by that time counted its adherents in thousands, and included a number of families who desired an education for their sons more advanced than that given in such primary schools as existed. But, as T. G. Osborn said in an address at City Road Chapel commemorating the centenary of Wesley's death, Dr. Waddy 'was a man before his time in this great question of higher education in our Connexion. He was before his age, as Mr. Wesley was, on this subject. He maintained the true tradition in times when there were few to support or to sympathize with him. . . .' [22]

The project of a school at Northampton came to nothing. Waddy, in spite of personal canvassing and the prospectuses he had printed and circulated, received no encouragement, and the scheme was dropped for a time. It is possible that one reason for this lack of interest was the great excitement throughout the country caused by the projected Reform Bill, which had repercussions in the Methodist Connexion by reason of the high feelings aroused and the extreme views expressed even among ministers.

The Conference of 1834 appointed Waddy to Sheffield, and there again a scheme for the establishment of a proprietary school was promulgated. Sheffield was a town in which resided

[21] A. Waddy, op. cit., p. 196.
[22] *Wesley: the Man, his Teaching, and his Work,* p. 256.

a number of Methodists of means. After canvassing in the neighbourhood, Waddy realized that it would be possible to found the type of school which he had in mind. No doubt his desire to establish such an institution was strengthened at that time by the strength of the Roman Catholics in the town. Like many other Methodist ministers, Waddy feared and distrusted anything which savoured of Popery, and in Sheffield he found grounds for fear. There was a considerable Irish element in the town; the building of a Roman Catholic cathedral was being considered, and it seemed that Roman Catholicism was on the increase. It would be natural therefore for him to press on with his scheme for ensuring a Methodist education for the Methodist children of the district.

In 1836 a meeting of various gentlemen of Sheffield was called, and it was unanimously decided that the time was ripe for building a Methodist school for higher education, and that in Sheffield were to be found the means for its provision. A Committee was appointed, a prospectus drawn up, and the co-operation of the whole Connexion invited. It was then that difficulties started. The Connexion was not at all decided that it wanted such a school. The point, however, which brought the matter into the open was a request by the School Committee to Conference to appoint a minister as governor and chaplain of the proposed school. When this question was raised in the Conference of 1836 a lively debate occurred and extracts extant giving verbatim accounts reveal the struggle that was going on within Methodism. It was a struggle largely between a handful of the ministers supporting a majority of the laity and the conservative ministerial leaders of the Connexion. The reasons given for opposing the appointment of a minister to the proposed school was the fear lest ministers should be distracted from their primary duty as pastors and should tend to concentrate all their energies on education.[23]

The real reason for opposition appears to have been a sounder one: realization that if the Connexion was to interest itself in education at all, it must interest itself in it fully, and during the course of the 1836 debate on the matter it was revealed for the first time that the establishment of other schools was also being considered—in fact, the nucleus of a Methodist system of higher education under the surveillance of Conference, in support of which a speaker showed how the American Metho-

<hr />

[23] See Benjamin Gregory, op. cit., p. 226.

dist system of higher education had developed upward from elementary schools.[24]

But, as Conference was only too well aware, it lacked both funds and men to undertake such work adequately. Though matters were improving in both directions, Methodism was still in the growing stage and had still to concentrate all its energies on the main lines of 'saving souls for Christ', and education was no longer generally accepted (as it had been in Wesley's day) as one of those.

The following resolution was therefore passed by Conference:

'The Conference has heard with great pleasure that some highly respected gentlemen in Sheffield have determined to establish, in that vicinity, a proprietary school, uniting the advantages of a sound classical and literary education with a religious and Wesleyan training. The Conference deeply feels the great value and importance of the object in view, and admires the spirit and zeal with which the gentlemen have pursued it; and, as they have been the first to propose a plan which, it is hoped, will be extensively beneficial to that important neighbourhood, and may possibly be followed in other parts of the Connexion, the Conference consents that they shall be at liberty to make an arrangement with any preacher who now is, or may hereafter, by consent of the Conference, become a supernumerary, if one sustaining that relation to our body can be found, who is suitable for the office of house governor and chaplain to this proposed seminary, and willing to undertake it.' [25]

It was unfortunate, as events were to prove, that Conference did not make a bold experiment and appoint a minister in his prime instead of one who had already spent much of his active ministry and was due to become a supernumerary on grounds of age. The obvious choice was the Rev. S. D. Waddy, who had already done so much toward arranging for the foundation of the school and who had the implicit trust of the laymen who were supporting the scheme. However, the mistake was made, and at least the blessing of official Methodism had been obtained. The work of establishing the school proceeded.

On 29th March 1837 the foundation-stone was laid, beneath which was deposited a parchment inscribed:

'The foundation-stone of this, the first Wesleyan Methodist Proprietory Grammar School, was laid by the Rev. George

[24] See Benjamin Gregory, op. cit., p. 227.
[25] A. Waddy, op. cit., pp. 101–2.

Marsden, on Wednesday, March 29th, 1837—Treasurer, J. Jones, Esq.—Secretaries, Rev. Samuel D. Waddy, and Mr. Thomas Branson, Solicitor; Rev. G. Marsden, Superintendent of the Sheffield East Circuit—Rev. Edmund Grindod, Superintendent of the Sheffield West Circuit. Trustees . . .'

And here followed a list of fifteen Methodist laymen. Many proprietary schools founded at about that time had as their trustees men of different religious views, selected because of their humanitarian views or because they were wealthy and influential. This school was to be essentially Wesleyan Methodist as far as administration went, though it was to be open to members of any denomination who wished to send their sons there. The Methodist character of the school was to be its most prominent feature, and a Chapel was to be the centre of its life, as was the case at Kingswood and Woodhouse Grove Schools. Educationally, the importance of this focal point was being realized, popularized as it was being by Thomas Arnold at Rugby.

The money required for building and equipping the school was collected by the formation of a limited liability company. Shares were in £50 units, but in order to extend interest in the school and at the same time to obviate pecuniary speculation, no person was allowed to hold more than three units. A Deed of Settlement was drawn up, the main items of which were:

1. To settle the freehold of the property in the shareholders.

2. So to restrict their power in its disposal that it might never be completely separated from its original purpose or from the Wesleyan Methodist Connexion.

3. To secure such a fair and public mode of appointing masters that the places might be always most effectively filled, and learning and ability never sacrificed to mere patronage.

4. To secure not only the religious but the decidedly Wesleyan character of the school.

On 8th August 1838 the school opened with 161 pupils on its roll. After a lunch attended by 'about two hundred persons, consisting of the committee and proprietors, many of their ladies, the governor and masters, with the young gentlemen',[26] there was a religious service in which the Rev. James Dixon alluded to the difficulties which the founders had had to face. It would have been comparatively easy for a number of the Sheffield business men to found a school in their town which

---

[26] *The Watchman*, Vol. IV, p. 263. This article contains a full account of the opening of the School.

would instruct Methodist youth in the fundamental principles of Methodism. The constitution, mode of education, and government of the school had to be framed in harmony with the outlook of the whole Methodist body.

'The erection of this school may be considered as indicative of the growing intelligence of the Wesleyan body. We have been considered an illiterate, ignorant, and barbarous people,' said Mr. Dixon. Methodists were despised; they were regarded as ignorant, and that was due not only to the deep-founded traditions of a conservative Church of England; it was due to a fact. The initial appeal of Methodism had been made to the illiterate poor. It was only by the middle of the nineteenth century that that appeal was becoming widely extended to include the middle classes of England, and that could perhaps have been done more effectively had there been more scholastic establishments similar to the one at Sheffield, for higher educationists were in the van of those who despised Methodists. As Mr. W. D. Bersey, the newly appointed second master, said: 'I have in schools experienced, on account of my connexion with Methodism, ridicule and obloquy.'

At the very opening of this school was expressed the feeling which lies at the core of Methodist life. The Rev. John Maclean, governor and chaplain appointed by Conference, said that he miscalculated if they would not be able to form a family of love while they continued together. He alluded to this same matter again three years later when, in his first *Report* on the school, he stated:

'From the beginning, we have thought that the most effectual way to benefit our young friends would be to keep them constantly under the influences, instructions, and restraints of a well-regulated and happy Christian family; which, in connexion with the ministry of the word, and other opportunities, when desired, for fostering experimental godliness, seemed the most likely means of promoting a healthy, youthful piety. The results thus far have not disappointed me. . . . Our influence is not confined to the shores of Great Britain: we have pupils from Egypt, Malta, and Rome; from the East and West Indies, South America, and Australia; through whom we may hope, by the blessing of the Great Head of the Church, to contribute, in some humble degree, to the conversion of distant nations.' [27]

[27] *First Report of the Sheffield Wesleyan Proprietary Grammar School*, 1841. (Privately printed.)

Those words were written when the school had, as is evident, become known in Methodism throughout the world. This publicity was due in no small measure to the business acumen of the laymen of Sheffield, who in 1839 caused to be published a booklet, *The Establishment, Principles, Discipline, and Educational Course of the Wesleyan Proprietary Grammar School, Sheffield,* in which is described the site of the buildings, something of the life of the school, and its objects. It is, in fact, a detailed prospectus. From it we learn that there were 'besides all the rooms, kitchens, apparatus, etc., necessary for the domestic department of such an institution, one large and six smaller schoolrooms, nine dormitories, in which each pupil has a bed to himself, a spacious dining-room, amphitheatre for lectures, laboratory, museum and library, reading and music room, warm and shower baths, and lastly a beautiful and commodious chapel. There is also a spacious swimming-bath on the premises, detached from the main building.' [28]

This description is interesting. Reference has already been made to Waddy's possible connexion with the Hills's school at Birmingham. Mention of a swimming-bath further strengthens the possibility, for swimming was taught at Hazelwood, and there were very few other schools in the country where that was the case. Certainly none of the public schools possessed swimming-baths at that time. It seems that this school may be classed as a pioneer in secondary education, though the curious ideas which persisted in educational matters in those days are typified in a further description of the premises: There were cloisters 'where the studious youth may walk at any time, when he wishes not to be disturbed by boisterous mirth'.[29] A touch of the Middle Ages seems to linger round that description!

Although the school was frankly denominational, there was no objection to the sons of parents of non-Methodists entering it. Soon after the foundation of the school, indeed, there were included in the list of pupils the sons of a Unitarian and of a Roman Catholic. But for all pupils attendance at school chapel and observance of a certain course of religious instruction were ordained, as follows:

SUNDAY.   Morning: Attendance of the whole school at one of the Wesleyan chapels in Sheffield.

[28] *First Report of the Sheffield Wesleyan Proprietary Grammar School,* 1841, p. 16.
[29] ibid., p. 17.

> Afternoon: Learning of the Wesleyan Methodist Conference Catechisms.
>
> Evening: Attendance at service in the school chapel.
>
> WEEKDAY. 7 a.m.: Attendance at a Bible class conducted by the chaplain 'with practical and experimental expositions'.

Each morning and evening: Family devotions, consisting of singing, reading, and prayer.

Once a week there was a Scripture lecture, the governor giving a critical exposition. Presumably this was given to the whole school gathered together, for in addition there was, once a week, religious instruction in the various Forms in their own rooms. For those pupils who were members of the Wesleyan Methodist Society there was a Class-meeting each week conducted by the chaplain. The school was one of those which came under review by the Schools Inquiry Commission of 1868, and in the *Report* is mentioned the 'Family Prayers' which were held each morning and evening.[30]

Although from the first there were many day pupils, the school was primarily for boarders, each of whom had to have a minimum of two suits of clothes, six shirts, three nightcaps, six pairs of stockings, three pairs of shoes, six pocket handkerchiefs, and two black silk cravats! Mention of the nightcaps is omitted from the next prospectus issued (dated 1854)! There was a master sleeping in a room adjoining each dormitory whose duty it was to call up his pupils at 6 a.m., see that they all knelt down for private prayer, and that all were washed and in the schoolroom by 6.30 a.m. The curriculum was as follows: mathematics, German (optional), Italian (optional), classics, Hebrew, music and drawing, commercial subjects (including penmanship, ciphering, book-keeping, land-surveying, mental arithmetic), and occasional lectures in a variety of subjects.

The school's daily routine was as follows: 6.45 a.m., grammar and exercises; 7.45 a.m., prayer and breakfast; 8.15–9 a.m., free; 9–12 (12.30 for seniors), school (with change of classes at 10.55 a.m.); 12 (12.30) p.m. free; 1 p.m. dinner; 2–5 p.m., school; 6 p.m., tea; 6.30 p.m., preparation; 8 p.m., supper, followed by bed for the juniors, or an hour's reading for the seniors.

Although S. D. Waddy had done so much to bring about the opening of Wesley College—to give the school the name by

---

[30] *Report of the Schools Inquiry Commission*, Vol. XVIII, p. 662.

which it is best known—it was not he, but the Rev. John Maclean who in 1837 was appointed first governor and chaplain of the school. This gentleman did not live on the school premises, nor was he at first actively engaged in its affairs, so that it was fortunate that Waddy continued for another three years as a minister in the Sheffield West Circuit and was thus able to continue to guide its course in association with the directors and head master.

At the Conference of 1840, however, he was appointed to the Hull Circuit. Mr. Maclean moved to live in the school, but so convinced were the directors, only too rightly as events were to prove, of the need of Mr. Waddy's direct interest in the school that they persuaded him to retain the secretaryship and to travel from Hull once a month to attend the Board meetings. From Hull, Mr. Waddy was appointed to Bath (1841–3), whence it was impossible for him to travel once a month to Sheffield. He therefore resigned his secretaryship. At once, matters at Wesley College began to go wrong. Mr. Maclean was an excellent minister, but he had little understanding of either business or school affairs. An agitation was started to gain the appointment of Mr. Waddy to the governorship when Mr. Maclean announced his intention of resuming regular circuit duties. A speaker at the Conference of 1842 put the matter succinctly when he told his fellow representatives: 'It is a short question. Is the school worth saving? If it is, you must send Mr. Waddy. If it is not, don't.'[31] By that time the school had been mortgaged for £10,000. There was a heavy overdraft at the bank; the buildings needed renovating, but there was no money for the purpose; the number of pupils had fallen from just under 200 to 100. To try to economize in every direction, the Directors had reduced the masters' salaries—a step which would hardly make for efficiency—and had reduced the pupils' fees to attract more boys. The result was a slight influx of poorer boys and a falling-off in the number of boys from better-class homes, for the latter objected to sending their sons to a second-rate school, as they began to regard Wesley College. In those days, parents, especially those of the middle class, were class-conscious, and nowhere was this fact more clearly seen than in the boarding-schools of the country.

Discussion in Conference during the first years of the school's existence was not made less bitter by the knowledge of these

[31] A. Waddy, op. cit., p. 153.

matters. The school was not proving the success that had been envisaged. Conference, however, was unwilling to admit the mistake it had made in not appointing Mr. Waddy as governor from the first. The supernumeraries who were appointed impressed neither directors nor school committee, while they found their own position increasingly intolerable. In presenting his resignation from the governorship, one of them alleged that in the eye of the directors 'the governor is little more than an authorized spy upon the youths, the masters, and the domestics residing in the establishment. According to their regulations, the governor may dismiss an underservant; he may send a boy on errands, he must carry on the correspondence with the parents of the youth, and it is his privilege to do the whipping of the institution, but the internal government of the house is incessantly interfered with from without.'[32] He did not, in fact, effectively represent, nor was he allowed to utilize, the full authority of Conference.

In 1844, as in the first deliberations on the subject eight years before, the root problem was the extent to which official Methodism was to be responsible for higher education.[33] It had become increasingly obvious that half-measures were useless. At that Conference, therefore, though not without considerable opposition, the Rev. (by then Dr.) Waddy was at last appointed governor, and with his appointment matters improved.

He inspired the bank with confidence and persuaded it to increase the overdraft, he had the buildings renovated, raised the fees—and the masters' salaries—and gradually cleared the debts and reduced the mortgage.

The early history of Wesley College has been dealt with in some detail in order to show wherein lay the foundations of Methodist secondary education. It lay in the enthusiasms and in the business acumen of individuals who did not allow their dreams to carry them away from reality. Here, as in other examples mentioned in this work, can be found the truth of R. L. Archer's remark: 'The living force of education has always sprung from movements of the human mind and aspirations of the human heart; legislation and administration are mere tools which these movements and aspirations use.'[34] The

[32] Benjamin Gregory, op. cit., p. 370.
[33] The pressure that was being brought to bear upon official Methodism as regards higher education is illustrated in a lengthy letter which appeared in *The Watchman* of 24th May 1843.
[34] R. L. Archer, *Secondary Education in the Nineteenth Century*, p. 147.

same truth can be seen in all the Methodist secondary schools.

Conference approved when individuals had brought about a satisfactory state of affairs; it disapproved when the reverse was the case. If any excuse for such an attitude is needed, it is found in the fact that Conference had its own adult problems which occupied every moment of the time available when representatives from the circuits of Methodism met together annually. It is easy to be critical today, but the twentieth-century Methodist should remember, perhaps with a twinge of conscience, that Methodists of the mid-nineteenth century felt and thought about religious matters more deeply than they do today. They had to. Methodism in those days was attacked, or, worse still, silently despised by a section of the nation. By many in the Established Church it was regarded as a bastard growth. Men who became, or were, Methodists had to be very sure of themselves. Their Connexional organization was not what it is today. It was being built gradually as new demands were made. The deeper the feelings, the greater the animosity which might be engendered in people's minds. This is no place to deal with the quarrels and the discussions which arose in Methodism in those days. They existed; they were fierce, and they were bitter. It is not altogether surprising that the Conference drew up no schemes for higher education. It was not that it was not interested; it was due to its enforced obsession with other interests. At least it did not interfere with individual members of the Connexion whose interest lay in education. Such a man was S. D. Waddy.

He first put forward the project for a Methodist secondary school for the sons of laymen, he was responsible for the fulfilment of that scheme, and he, when things became difficult and had been allowed to drift, brought back the school to the position of one of the two best schools for boys in Sheffield. He was a man who can, not unfavourably, be compared with the head masters who led public schools back to a position of respect. When he was appointed governor of Wesley College, he assembled the whole school and said : 'I am determined to be obeyed, and to be obeyed without question.' [35] That might be taken as his motto, not only in the school, but in family life too. He was a 'Victorian father', as we like to think of a certain type of man today. When, eighteen years later, he resigned from the governorship, he again assembled the school and spoke of its

[35] A. Waddy, op. cit., p. 177.

history. 'I could often have been exceedingly popular by omitting to notice irregularities, by relaxing the laws and regulations which seemed so stringent, and by endlessly multiplying your holidays. I could have sought my own ease and (for a time) my own reputation among you by these means. I have never done it. I have not asked myself "What will these boys like?" but "What will they think of my mode of government when they are men?" ' [36] That remark alone, sincerely expressed as it was, shows the type of man he was and the influence he must have had on at least three generations of boys at the school. In many respects he resembled Thomas Arnold. He was in fact a great admirer of that gentleman, and at Sheffield he tried, as he stated in a *Report* on the school, 'to combine what the late Dr. Arnold appeared to consider so desirable—a full recognition of the paramount claims of religion, without diminishing the real importance of learning and science; and such a recognition of religion as shall unite the largest charity to our fellow Christians, and the most respectful consideration of their peculiar views, with a decided and intelligent preference of the community to which we conscientiously belong.' [37]

'Be Christian gentlemen' was a favourite maxim of Waddy's. Deceit and distrust were hateful to him and, like Arnold, he relied implicitly on a boy's word.

Methodism as a Connexion had still (in 1839) not awakened to all its educational duties, but individuals were beginning to appreciate the need for more effort than had been made in that direction. The Sunday-schools were flourishing and, as will be shown in the next chapter, more systematic steps were being taken at that very time to deal with primary education. As far as higher education was concerned, the matter which chiefly worried Methodist was the lack of religious instruction in the existing (non-Methodist) schools to which the new Methodist middle classes were beginning to send their children. Religion itself was indeed all-too-often treated with careless indifference —a state of affairs which was utterly at variance with the deepest principles of Methodism.

[36] A. Waddy, op. cit., pp. 281–2.
[37] *Report on the Sheffield Wesleyan Proprietary Grammar School* (1854).

146

CHAPTER EIGHT

Connexional Interest in Primary Education[1]

IT IS NECESSARY to retrace our steps to consider briefly the development of Methodist interest in primary education, since higher education must be based on a solid foundation of primary education if it is to be of lasting value. In Wesley's own day there was no system of primary education in England. There were various charitable trusts and orphanages; most villages had their dame-schools; but it was a haphazard supply of education at its best, and it was not until the Sunday-schools started as an organized assault on irreligion and illiteracy in 1780 that anything resembling a system was seen.[2] Once the idea had been popularized by Robert Raikes it spread rapidly, and on 18th July 1784 Wesley recorded in his *Journal*:[3] 'I preached, morning and afternoon, in Bingley Church; but it would not near contain the congregation. Before service I stepped into the Sunday-school, which contains two hundred and forty children taught every Sunday by several masters, and superintended by the curate. So many children in one parish are restrained from open sin, and taught a little good manners, at least, as well as to read the Bible. I find these schools springing up wherever I go. Perhaps God may have a deeper end therein than men are aware of. Who knows but some of these schools may become nurseries for Christians?' Wesley published Raikes's appeal for Sunday-schools in the *Arminian Magazine* in 1785 and for the rest of his life did whatever lay in his power to support them and to spread a knowledge of the valuable work they were doing. Many years before, he had himself taught in Sunday-schools in Georgia.

Wesley took a practical interest, too, in weekday primary

---

[1] While this book was being written, another work on Methodist education was also being prepared, the two authors being unaware until later of each other's work. This chapter is necessary to the continuity of any study of Methodist secondary education, but for a fuller treatment of the Methodist contribution to primary education the reader is referred to the Rev. H. F. Mathews' work, *Methodism and the Education of the People, 1791–1851* (Epworth Press).

[2] Sunday-schools were not a new idea in 1780. There were traces of them in the days of Luther and Knox. Hannah Ball started her well-known school in 1769 at High Wycombe, but all efforts before 1780 were merely sporadic efforts by individuals.

[3] Vol. VII, p. 3.

education. At the end of 1739 he set up the headquarters of London Methodism at the Foundery near Finsbury Square, and it was not long before he found himself concerned by the 'abundance of children' who were nothing better than a wild rabble. As he wrote in his *Plain Account of the People called Methodists:* 'At length I determined to have them taught in my own house, that they might have an opportunity of learning to read, write, and cast accounts (if no more), without being under almost a necessity of learning heathenism at the same time: And after several unsuccessful trials, I found two such school-masters as I wanted; men of honesty and of sufficient knowledge, who had talents for, and their hearts in, the work.' [4] So started the Foundery School. An outline of the manner in which Wesley undertook the foundation and administration of Whitefield's school for colliers' children at Kingswood has already been given. There, from the first, Wesley had realized that education would not be confined to children, but that there would be 'scholars of all ages, some of them grey-headed',[5] for whom instruction would have to be arranged in the early morning or late evening, so that there need be no interference with their normal work.

In 1742 Wesley bought ground at Newcastle-on-Tyne on which to erect a headquarters for his work in the north. In his original plans he intended to found an orphanage there, modelling it on that which he had visited at Halle. His project was never fully realized, though the buildings at Newcastle came to be known as 'The Orphan House', which was at once 'A place of worship, a school for orphans, a refuge for the injured and oppressed, the northern home of Wesley, and the theological institution of his preachers'.[6]

In each of the schools at the Foundery and the Orphan House there were approximately sixty pupils, who were instructed in reading, writing, arithmetic, and religion. The rules followed the lines of those later enforced at the new Kingswood School, viz.:

1. No child is admitted under six years of age.

2. All the children are to be present at the morning sermon (which took place at 5 a.m.).

3. They are at school from six to twelve, and from one to five.

4. They have no play days.

5. No child is to speak in school, but to the masters.

[4] *Works*, Vol. VIII, p. 266.
[5] *Letters*, Vol. I, pp. 339–40.
[6] L. Tyerman, *The Life and Times of the Rev. John Wesley, M.A.*, Vol. I, p. 543.

6. A child who misses two days in one week, without leave, is excluded the school.[7]

Strict rules, but they need to be considered against the background of the times, when there was a crying need for a stricter discipline in living, and for the foundation of rigid principles. One innovation made at the Foundery School requires specific mention, for it further reveals the practical common sense of Wesley: He started a weekly meeting of masters and parents, revealing his understanding of practical education—that there must be co-operation between school and home—an educational principle evidenced today in Parents' Associations.

Apart from these individual efforts by Wesley himself, little was done for primary education during the eighteenth century, though many of the small private schools were administered by Methodists. There are few specific records of such schools. All the information concerning them has to be gleaned from passing references in diaries, biographies, and local histories, and even when they are mentioned it is often impossible to tell whether the school was purely a primary school or whether it provided higher education as well. In this connexion it is interesting to read what A. E. Dobbs wrote in his *Education and Social Movements, 1700–1850*:[8] 'The practice of recruiting the clergy from yeoman families made it necessary that the village school should combine, in some measure, the function of an academy with that of a place of elementary instruction for the poor; among whom, in turn, some "love of Greek and Latin" was found to diffuse itself after the disorderly fashion of that time and place.'

Though official Methodism showed little initiative in the provision of primary education in the eighteenth century, it was always ready to help, and the germs of later endeavour can be seen. Nearly every minister conducted a Saturday-afternoon class for children. The object was religious instruction, but in attaining that object pupils acquired a fair standard of reading and writing. Sunday-schools were encouraged everywhere, but their very popularity and their undenominational character seems to have caused a *laissez-faire* attitude, so that it was not till 1827 that any attempt was made to make them part of the Connexional system. In that year were published rules for the management of Wesleyan Methodist Sunday-schools.

[7] *Works*, Vol. VIII, p. 266.
[8] p. 68. See also *Report of the Schools Inquiry Commission* (1868), Vol. IX, pp. 903ff.

Apart from what had been done in relation to Kingswood and Woodhouse Grove schools, that was the first official step toward making education a part of the Methodist organization, but interest was awakening, and at the Conference of 1833 the question was asked: 'What is the sentiment of the Conference with regard to the formation of weekday schools in connexion with our Societies?' To which the reply was given: 'The Conference has heard with satisfaction of the formation of weekday schools in immediate connexion with some of our Societies, and recommends their establishment wherever the means of supporting them can be obtained; as such institutions, when constructed on strictly Methodist principles, and placed under an efficient spiritual control, cannot fail to promote those high and holy ends for which we exist as a religious community.'[9] Little was done, however, until 1836, when Richard Treffry, William Atherton, and Samuel Jackson were authorized to make inquiries of every superintendent minister and to prepare reports concerning 'the actual state of education in immediate connexion with Methodism throughout Great Britain'.

Methodism was following the lead of the Government which, urged on by an increasing number of social reformers and by the fear of an uneducated electorate to whom the franchise had been extended in 1832, was beginning to realize the necessity for State interest in education. In 1833 J. A. Roebuck, Member of Parliament for Bath, moved in the House of Commons 'That this House, deeply impressed with the necessity of providing for a due education of the people at large, and believing that to this end the aid and care of the State are absolutely needed, will early during the next session of Parliament proceed to devise a means for the universal and national education of the whole people'. The resolution was defeated, but it was the first move toward State interest in education—the expression of a need increasingly realized, and in the following year £20,000 was voted for the erection of schools for the poorer classes.

The official movements toward a system of national education which started in 1833 awoke many apparently dormant educational ideals. All denominations realized afresh that they needed schools in which to train their young. There were at that time, as far as religious education was concerned, two main principles: the first, that religious and secular education could not be separated, that the two had to work together and be allowed to mingle freely to produce a well-balanced and cultural education; the second, that education could be secular, with religion tacked on as a curriculum 'subject', as a sop to the Churches. Each of these views was sufficiently dangerous to awake the Churches out of their lethargy. If the first was adopted in practice, the question arose: What denomination was to be responsible for the various schools? If the second, then all the denominations united in condemning it. The National Society and the British and Foreign Schools Society had been doing most useful work in setting-up schools in all parts of the country for more than twenty years, but they had not been able to supply the needs of the whole country. These Societies and all those organizations which had founded 'voluntary' schools took the view that religion and secular education could not be separated, since religion could never be made a mere 'subject'. While those voluntary schools were supplying all they could of the demand for popular education there grew up with the changing circumstances of life —the increasing enfranchisement of the people, the growing power of the Press, the better facilities for travel and transport, and the shifting of population as the industrial areas were developed—the fear of an uneducated populace who, though uneducated, had a share in the government through their parliamentary vote. It is easy to make too much of this fear and to explain it all by memories of what had happened in France. Nevertheless, there was a certain amount of fear present, and the Government began to realize its responsibility in the matter. When that happened, the Established Church awoke to the fact that she had been responsible for education in this country since earliest times and that it was a responsibility that she did not wish to see taken from her. She felt that she was still the rightful director of popular education. At the same time the Nonconformists prepared jealously to guard their own interests and hard-won rights against such a directorship.

In 1837 the three Methodist ministers appointed by Conference to inquire into educational matters made their report—that there were 3,339 Sunday-schools with 59,277 teachers and 341,442 pupils, that twenty-five per cent. of the chapels had no Sunday-school, that there were only nine weekday schools for infants and twenty-two for older children. The Report included this statement:

'That on account of various circumstances which have occurred since this Committee was appointed, and in consideration, especially of the manner in which the subject of General Education has been lately brought under public attention, both in and out of Parliament, and of the movements which have been made in the Houses of Lords and Commons, the business confided by the Conference to this Committee has, in their judgement, assumed much additional importance, and must now be viewed more distinctly in connexion with the discussions which have already taken place, and with the possible results of the inquiries going on before the Committee of the House of Commons, and of the measures actually introduced into the House of Lords.

'That the Committee therefore deem it necessary that further time and deliberation should be afforded to the subject, before any definite and organized plan of operation be recommended to the adoption of the Wesleyan Connexion; and that their present duties must, therefore, be regarded rather as provisional and preliminary, than as directed to the immediate formation and execution of any permanent plan.

'That the Committee are, however, very deeply impressed by a sense of the magnitude and urgency of the subject, as affecting the obligations and privileges of the Wesleyan body; and will forthwith apply themselves with earnestness and assiduity to the task of collecting information; of exciting in our Connexion an increased attention to the utility and necessity of Wesleyan Infant and Day-schools, conducted on those principles which, as Wesleyan Methodists, our people are bound to prefer, wherever practicable, to the utmost extent of their power; of watching over the rights and interests of our Societies, as they may be involved in any legislation or other proceedings on the question of National Education; and of preparing, as soon as they shall find themselves able to do so, with confidence and advantage, some specific plan for the promotion of Religious Education in connexion with the Wesleyan body, which may be submitted to the consideration and sanction of our friends and of the Conference.' [10]

Interest in education was being awakened by the actions of the Government, and Methodism was beginning to realize both the possibilities and the dangers. The 1837 Conference approved the *Report* submitted and ordered it to be printed and circulated, while a provisional Education Committee was set up to administer both Sunday- and Day-schools.

[10] Extract from the *Report of the Methodist Education Committee* presented to the Conference of 1837.

Meanwhile, the Government was continuing to act. After the granting of the £20,000 for educational purposes in 1834, a Committee was set up to administer such moneys as might be voted for education from time to time, and this remained the ruling force in national primary education until the passing of the Board of Education Act in 1899. This Committee immediately formulated a scheme for the setting-up of a training college for teachers, to which were to be attached two practising schools in which religion was to be an integral part of the curriculum, not as a mere subject, but as the basic principle of the instruction and discipline. The special periods set apart for 'doctrinal instruction' in religious matters were to be taken by a Chaplain who would instruct Church of England children, and by a licensed minister who would instruct Nonconformist children. At once there was a storm of protest. The Church of England protested because it saw its authority being undermined; the Nonconformists protested because they saw their hardly-won rights being lost through the youth of their Churches being led astray by 'false doctrine'. Amongst those who protested most strongly were the Wesleyan Methodists, who said that the proposed scheme was corrupt and anti-scriptural. The scheme was hurriedly dropped. It had nearly proved the undoing of the Committee of Council on Education. But the upheaval achieved one useful result. It awoke finally the religious communities to the importance of education as a part of their organization.

In 1841, Conference approved the 'General Plan of Wesleyan Education'. This had been drafted by the provisional Education Committee as a basis for all future operations in education. It set up a General Committee of Education, consisting of at least fifteen ministers and fifteen laymen who would be appointed annually—

'1. To exercise a general supervision of the affairs of Wesleyan Education; to connect and combine the whole of our School operations, *in their aggregate character* for the purposes of public utility; to be a medium of communication for the Connexion, on Educational subjects, whether with the Government of the country, or with other public bodies; and to promote and facilitate the adoption, in Wesleyan Schools, of such regulations as shall tend at once to secure the greatest practical efficiency, and to preserve connexional harmony;

'2. To direct the application of any Funds which may be entrusted to their care from any sources whatsoever;

'3. To superintend the selection and training of *Teachers*; and to recommend such Teachers to Schools, on application from the Local Committees;

'4. To collect information on matters relating to the general interests of Education; to correspond with the Local Committees and Friends of Education, on various questions connected with Teachers, Inspection, etc.; to promote the formation of New Schools, wherever practicable, as well as to encourage those already formed, especially by advice and friendly co-operation;

'5. To prepare, from their official documents, and to present to the Conference, an Annual Report of their proceedings, and of the general progress of Wesleyan Education.'

Then followed details concerning the principles to be adopted in the various schools, under the following headings: Religious instruction, government, financial support, teachers, accommodation, and routine reports on the state of the schools and their development.[11]

In 1843, this new Committee put forward a plan for the building of seven hundred new day-schools throughout the country. The plan was approved by Conference and the work started, a portion of the Centenary Fund being allocated to it. From the first a major difficulty had been realized: that of staffing. The monitorial methods used by Bell and Lancaster for training teachers while at the same time instructing children could be, and was, adopted, but it was soon realized that there must be at least a nucleus of more highly trained teachers. Here Methodism was confronted by a double deficiency: there were only two secondary schools, excluding Kingswood and Woodhouse Grove (which were for ministers' sons only), from which potential teachers might be recruited; there were no teacher-training facilities.

This difficulty was one which had confronted the Government when it had started taking a practical interest in education, for the monitorial system of Bell and Lancaster was no substitute for the specialized training of teachers, though it might lay the foundations. In the type of man or woman who offered as a potential teacher there was, nearly always, a complete lack of any cultural background. Those who had received a secondary education rarely wanted to become teachers, and those who offered to become teachers had rarely been to a secondary school.

[11] See *Report of the Wesleyan Committee of Education* (1841), pp. 11–16, and *Minutes of Conference*, Vol. IX, p. 243.

Primary education was therefore bound up with secondary education through the demand for teachers. In the early days the best that could be done was the establishment of institutions which combined the functions of primary school (for practice), secondary school (for instruction in actual knowledge), and training college (for specialized training).

One of the most successful of the teacher-training institutions was founded by David Stow at Glasgow in 1836—the result of twenty-nine years of experiment in Sunday- and Infant-schools. Stow worked on the principle that education must aim at the development of religious and moral character. Such an openly expressed principle was bound to attract Methodism when it turned its attention to the problem of teacher-training. The success of Stow's methods influenced the Committee of Council, too, when it began to consider the same problem.[12]

In 1839, the Methodist Education Committee advertised for four young men who would be willing to train as teachers, two at Stow's 'Normal Seminary' and two at the British and Foreign School Society's institution at Borough Road. It was intended that these four should afterwards train other teachers. There were thirteen applicants, but none was considered suitable. Eventually, however, acceptable candidates were found, and in 1840 there were six young men in training at Glasgow, and shortly afterwards there was a lady being trained there too. For the following eleven years a small but steady stream of young Methodists, men and women, attended there, all expenses being paid by the Methodist Education Committee.

But the difficulties arising from lack of secondary schools were becoming more and more acute. Stow refused to educate his students. His task, he maintained, was the training of teachers. He objected to the attempts made in other training institutions to combine the three functions of primary school, secondary school, and training-college. The potential teachers selected by the Methodist Education Committee had therefore to have reached a certain standard of education; and Methodism had not the means of supplying that standard.

The authorities did what they could to supply it by means of the primary schools which were steadily being built all over the country, and in this they were helped by parents. The universities, public schools, and many of the grammar schools were, until the second half of the nineteenth century, closed to Metho-

---

[12] See J. W. Adamson, *English Education, 1789-1902*, p. 135.

dists, though there were, before then, many Methodist tradesmen, farmers, and others of the lower middle classes who had begun to realize that they could afford to give their children a better education than that normally given in the primary schools of the day. They began therefore to demand a better education, and they obtained it.

'The Wesleyan schools have established, generally speaking, a rate of payment on the part of their scholars higher than that which is made in the other elementary schools that I have seen. This rate of payment varies from 2d. to 8d. per week for each scholar; in some schools a majority of the scholars pay 3d.; in others 4d.; but in none less than 2d. It is obvious that these rates of payment must generally exclude the children of the very poor; and although these are not altogether excluded (for arrangements are sometimes made in Wesleyan schools by which poor children are admitted at a reduced rate of payment, either by subscribers' tickets, or on the recommendation of members of the school committee), yet on the whole, the Wesleyan schools which I have seen must be considered as existing for the sake of the children of tradesmen, of farmers, and of mechanics of the higher class, rather than for the sake of the children of the poor. In fact, these schools are sometimes nothing else than private schools, in which the salaries of the teachers, the school furniture, and the books are provided out of the school pence, the managers supplying little more than the building in which the school is held. It is evident that schools of this kind have not the first claim to assistance from public funds, which are designed to promote the education of the poor. And I think it may well be a question for the managers of the Wesleyan schools to consider whether it is not desirable for them to extend the basis of their educational operations and to confer on a wide circle the benefits of their excellent schools. A lower rate of payments would, in my opinion, greatly extend their sphere of usefulness, while their present high character for respectability need in no degree be impaired.' [13]

That is an extract from Matthew Arnold's general report for the year 1852. As Arnold points out, Wesleyan Methodist primary schools were by that time catering for a class above the very poor; they tended in certain districts to be a type apart: they represented the filling up gradually of the gap between the top and bottom sections of education—between the university

[13] Matthew Arnold, *Reports on Elementary Education, 1852-82*, pp. 3-4.

and the primary school. They catered for children whose parents desired a higher standard of training, and who were willing to pay more for it.[14] There was a danger therefore of a snobbish feeling growing up in Methodism—a sense of satisfaction that their children were being better educated than those of their neighbours. Many Methodists could afford to keep their children longer at school, too, and there was in many cases, long before compulsory education was considered, a genuine desire on the part of these parents to do their best for their children. With that desire came a need for some system of secondary education in Methodism. Arnold felt the danger of snobbishness, and hoped that steps would be taken to alter circumstances which caused the danger. He wanted secondary education, but he was never blind to the needs of the very poor, and he wanted education for all. He foresaw a time when there would be no provision made by Methodism for those who most needed its help. As soon as his fears on this subject were made known, he received assurance from the authorities, and it can truly be said that Methodism has done as much as any other denomination for the education of the very poor, even though in some districts Methodist schools did develop into early examples of higher-grade schools.[15]

If one is tempted to criticize Methodism for not taking bolder measures and trying to build up a system of education to meet the demand, there is a very good answer: that of finance. Methodism had begun to wake to the needs of education; it was growing increasingly wealthy, but it was not yet wealthy enough to meet the demands which any system of education would necessitate, especially when it is remembered that Methodism was not primarily a social service organization, but a Church. A vast amount of money was required during those years for the building of chapels and Sunday-schools. It is to the Connexion's credit that it did so much for primary education, and if some of those attempts did not go far enough it was at least ready to experiment. In those days there was no 'payment by results', and individual schools were left largely to their own devices, so that the education given in some schools tended to be more advanced than in others. There was no average standard; there were a great number of educational aims—or none at all. No wonder

---

[14] Matthew Arnold, op. cit., p. 19.
[15] See A. W. Harrison, *The Methodist Church; Its Origins, Divisions, and Reunion*, pp. 210–11.

that Matthew Arnold, as one of H.M. Inspectors of Elementary Schools, with his wide knowledge of Continental education, was dissatisfied. He wrote:

'The fact is that at the present moment all is so undetermined in England with respect to public education—one system, one body of persons is so little in possession of the entire field—that everything depends, in each locality, on special circumstances, which are continually changing, and on individual agencies, which cannot be calculated beforehand. Public education is perhaps too vast a matter to be advantageously left to these individual agencies, but, where it *is* left to them, it is absolutely necessary to take into account their inherently fortuitous and independent character. It is necessary to leave each of them to produce freely its natural fruits, without attempting to prejudge its character and chance of success.' [16]

This gradual building-up of education from the bottom on the part of the Methodist authorities continued steadily from 1837 onward, but it was not till the 1870's, as will be shown later, that a general move was made to fill in the gap at the top of the educational ladder. The Education Committee kept its finger on the pulse of the new educational life by appointing an Inspector of its own in 1845—Mr. H. Armstrong—who toured the existing schools, advising on questions of curriculum, staffing, finance, and the planning of new schools. It was no doubt the work of Armstrong which convinced the committee that something more definite would have to be done about obtaining a larger stream of trained teachers, and in 1844 the first reference was made to a possible Methodist Training College. In 1847 the committee reported that a suitable site for such an institution had been found. As we have seen, Matthew Arnold's objection to the Methodist primary schools of that day lay in the fact that on the whole they did not cater for the very poor. Paradoxically, these were the very folk that Methodism most wished to help, and in looking for a suitable site for a training college they looked for it, and found it, 'in the very heart of that part of Westminster which is most densely and extensively occupied',[17] for the committee did not wish their students to be spoiled in training and, by a lengthy stay away from the dwellings of the poor, amongst the attractions of 'superior life', to grow disinclined or be ren-

[16] Matthew Arnold, op. cit., pp. 50–1.
[17] *The Westminster Club Bulletin* (Privately printed), 59th season, 1945–6, p. 4.

dered unfit to undertake the arduous and self-denying duties of school teachers. It hoped that, surrounded, as the students would be at Westminster, by the families of the very poor and unprivileged, their best instincts of service would be awakened by their realization of the poverty of fellow men with all its attendant degradation and misery.[18]

On 6th October 1851 Westminster College was quietly and unspectacularly opened, with the Rev. John Scott, who had been chairman of the Methodist Education Committee since its start, as principal. There was accommodation for one hundred students, men and women,[19] and practising schools with 1,333 pupils. The site had cost £9,391 and the buildings £38,259, toward which the Committee of Council had contributed £7,000, so that the new educational project was no small one for the Methodist Connexion.

Methodism never set bounds to the scope of primary education. Even in the poorest districts it never stated dogmatically that a child's education should begin and end at any definite age. There was indeed a tendency to give an education whose scope was wider than that normally given in primary schools, but it was never purely utilitarian. Its outlook on all forms of education has never wavered, and it has been based on John Wesley's own views: that religion and education are so closely connected that they are the same thing. It has been a close observance of this principle which has caused a struggle, still not entirely ended, concerning religious instruction and denominationalism in schools. Guided always by this principle, Methodism has never been content merely to follow, or to take up arms against education provided by the State merely because other Nonconformist sects have objected to such education. Increasingly as the nineteenth century passed, Wesleyan Methodism in particular has had little use for intolerance and the petty jealousies between nonconforming sects. That was evidenced as early as 1840 when the storms began to rage round the provision of education. So long as the State did nothing contrary to the spirit and principles of Methodism, Methodism loyally supported the State, as John Wesley had always done.

'We were never whole-hearted believers in denominational education. In country districts especially, the intolerance of Anglican clergy often made defensive measures necessary,' wrote

[18] Matthew Arnold, op. cit., pp. 232–3.
[19] Until 1872, when a separate College was opened for women at Battersea.

Dr. A. W. Harrison,[20] speaking of the struggles in which Methodism has been forced to take part. In 1847 it was Wesleyan Methodism, alone of all the nonconforming sects, which supported the Minutes of Council by which Lord John Russell laid the foundations of a primary-school system in England.[21] When, later, School Boards were introduced, there was a strong minority in Wesleyan Methodism which, led by the Rev. William Arthur, strove to have sectarian education abolished altogether. Methodism wanted education at its best, just as it wanted religion at its most sincere, and it was prepared to support any measures which seemed to have that object in view.

It is not within the scope of this work to deal with primary education, but it is necessary to refer to these matters to show, firstly, that Methodists, once they became interested in education, were not interested merely in one section of it; and secondly, that at the very start of the Connexional interest in education there was a tendency to give instruction in primary schools which is today more associated with secondary schools.[22]

[20] op. cit., p. 211.
[21] J. L. and Barbara Hammond, *Lord Shaftesbury* (Pelican Edition), p. 235.
[22] See *Report of the Consultative Committee (Hadow) on the Education of the Adolescent* (1926), p. 7.

CHAPTER NINE

A Proprietary School in the South

JUST AS WESLEY COLLEGE had been founded to meet the demand for higher education among the wealthy Methodist families of the north, so a similar school came to be founded at Taunton a few years later, though the immediate cause of its foundation lay in the exclusiveness of the Church of England in and around that town. It was further encouraged by new opportunities presented to Nonconformists by the foundation of the University of London, a foundation which also was caused by that same exclusiveness.

Early in the century many thinkers began to express disapproval of the aloofness of Oxford and Cambridge, so that at the same time that an interest in education was being awakened at the bottom, or primary end, a move was beginning to break down the exclusiveness of the top. Oxford and Cambridge at that time catered only for those who conformed to the Articles of the Church of England. There was a narrowing element, too, in the severely classical nature of the curriculum. A group of reformers turned their attention to this among other social problems. Jeremy Bentham, Zachary Macaulay, Lord John Russell (who used to attend Great Queen Street Methodist Chapel on occasions), James Mill, Henry Brougham, George Birkbeck, and others took up the cause of education on behalf of the Nonconformists, aiming amongst other things at a more utilitarian form of education. They decided to found another university— in London. The project, which had originated with the poet Thomas Campbell, was carried through and 'London University' was opened in October 1828, with a curriculum which included languages, mathematics, physics, mental and moral sciences, law, history, political economy, and medicine.

To avoid difficulties over religious instruction, religion was omitted from the curriculum altogether. Churchmen objected strongly to this and founded another College in London. This was opened in 1831 as King's College, and it was expressly stated that, while the various branches of literature and science were made subjects of instruction, an essential part of the curriculum was the teaching of the doctrine and duties of Christianity as practised in the United Churches of England and Ireland.

The importance of these foundations lay in their influence on education in general and on Nonconformity in particular. The broad scope of their curriculum influenced the proprietary and private schools founded during the century so that their curricula also tended to be broader. An interesting feature was that both 'London University' and King's College had attached to them schools to act as training-grounds for future students, just as at the end of the century, public schools began to organize preparatory schools to act as nurseries for themselves. The idea of university and school in close connexion was not, of course, new. William of Wykeham had founded complementary institutions: New College, Oxford, in 1379, and Winchester College in 1382. Eton had its particular College (King's) at Cambridge. Comenius and the other educational reformers had advocated a close connexion between school and university in the seventeenth century. John Wesley had attempted the same plan at Kingswood when he drew up his 'Academy Course'.

Although King's College was founded mainly by Churchmen, there was no religious test to prevent Nonconformists entering, and in this appears the first evidence of the breaking-down of the Church of England reserve. The Principal of King's College in 1872, Dr. Alfred Barry, was in fact one of the educationists consulted by Methodism in making an inquiry into higher education.

The direct influence, however, which the founding of 'London University' exercised on Methodism came through its examinations. In 1836, 'London University' was incorporated by Royal Charter as University College, London, and an entirely new body, 'The University of London', was created and incorporated to grant certain degrees. The students of University and King's Colleges were to be examined for degrees by this body. The important point was that other institutions, incorporated or not, might be added to these two Colleges with the same relations to the examining body. Thus Wesley College, Sheffield, was affiliated to it in 1844, when Samuel Waddy became governor of the school. No one realized more clearly than he the disadvantages of pupils in Methodist secondary schools, who, on leaving school, had either to renounce the denomination in which they had been brought up, or to forgo a university degree. The

matter was further complicated at Wesley College by the fact
that the original school Deeds had ordained that the head
master must be a graduate of Oxford or Cambridge. This of
necessity debarred a Methodist from holding the appointment,
since no man could graduate at either of those universities unless
he signed a declaration that he conformed to the Articles of the
Church of England. Waddy, therefore, as soon as he was
appointed governor, took steps to have the Deeds altered, and
H. M. Shera, M.A., who for the previous five years had been
head master of Kingswood School, was appointed head master.
Shera, in collaboration with Waddy, at once took steps to increase the academic efficiency of the school, making full use of
the opportunities offered by the University of London. He
introduced the 'Gallery' system of instruction and internal
organization, rearranged the time-table so that the most important
subjects were taught during the mornings while the afternoons
were freed for 'accomplishments', and divided the school into
three divisions, the first of which was known as the University
Division. Boys who had already qualified or were working to
qualify as undergraduates of the University of London were in
this division. This was made possible by the fact that Waddy
and Shera, having affiliated the school to the University as a
college, were empowered to instruct boys as candidates for all
the university examinations. All the prizes and honours of the
university were henceforth open to pupils of Wesley College,
including degrees, boys being required to visit the university
only when the time came for them to sit for the actual
examination.

The Senate of the new university consisted according to its
Charter of 'Persons eminent in literature and science to act as a
Board of Governors and to perform the functions of the
examiners in the Senate House of Cambridge'. Thus this new
University of London was purely a body of examiners who henceforth provided a common standard of examination at various
levels for all students who wished to make use of them. The
Matriculation examination, originally an entrance examination
for colleges affiliated to the university, from 1850 onward came
to be used as a leaving examination for pupils of secondary
schools who were not proceeding to any university. It formed
an excellent standard at which to aim, and was therefore one
of the strongest dictators of the curriculum in schools. Since
that time, examinations have perhaps tended to become too

dictatorial,[1] but the fault does not lie with the originators of the system in 1850. The lead of the University of London was followed by the College of Preceptors in 1853, the Indian and Home Civil Service Commissioners in 1855, and by Oxford and Cambridge Universities with their Local Examinations in 1858. A standard for secondary schools was thus provided and its importance was stressed in the *Report of the Schools Inquiry Commission*[2] in which it was recommended that the system should be further developed by the setting up of a 'Council of Examinations', consisting of twelve members, six to be nominated by the Crown, two each by the universities of Oxford, Cambridge, and London.

The Methodists had set some sort of standard for their secondary schools from the first. There is no specific mention of examinations at Kingswood School during the eighteenth century, but on several occasions Wesley recorded in his *Journal* how he visited the school and found, or did not find, matters to his liking. His chief standard of education was a religious one, but it is impossible to believe that a scholar like Wesley did not at times, during those hours he spent with the pupils in his school, inquire into their learning as well as into their religious convictions. Phrases such as 'I inquired into the state of Kingswood School', 'Spent an hour with the children at Kingswood', and his *Journal* entry that the scholars there 'learn well' suggest it. He himself set the standard during his lifetime, and that an academic standard was aimed at is borne out by the fact that when Woodhouse Grove School was founded in 1812, from the very beginning, an 'external' examiner was appointed to conduct an annual examination, the first being the Rev. Patrick Brontë. In 1815, the Committee of Management of Woodhouse Grove arranged that examinations should be held twice a year, and in 1816 a sub-committee was appointed 'to witness the examination'.[3] Later references make it clear that a great deal of attention was paid by the committee to this question of examinations. At one time the writing was found to be unsatisfactory; at another, too much time was being given to classics and too little time to science, while from time to time there were complaints about spelling and composition. Academic standards was certainly not being neglected by Methodism, and it must have been

[1] See *Report of the Committee of the Secondary School Examinations Council*, 1941.
[2] Vol. I, pp. 649ff.
[3] J. T. Slugg: *Woodhouse Grove School*, p. 132.

a relief to those responsible for testing the standard when 'external' examinations, such as the London Matriculation and the Oxford and Cambridge Local Examinations, were instituted. The early age at which pupils left Kingswood and Woodhouse Grove in those days made it practically impossible for them to avail themselves of the London Matriculation. The first pupil at either school to sit for that examination—and to pass it while still at school—was C. A. Clulow in 1864. The head master of Kingswood in 1858 availed himself of the Cambridge Local Examinations as soon as they were instituted, and in that year five pupils passed. The action of the head master in entering candidates evoked criticism—a criticism which, unfortunately, showed the worst type of snobbishness, for the objection was raised on the grounds that entry of pupils of the two Connexional schools to these examinations meant that they would have to mix with young tradesmen and clerks. The Grove Committee refused to allow boys to enter at first because it was understood that the object of the examination was to extend the influence of the Church of England among the middle classes [4]—unfortunate evidence of that Nonconformist narrow-mindedness so much deplored by Matthew Arnold. It was not until 1860 that Woodhouse Grove School entered candidates.

Nevertheless, as early as 1840, the value of external examinations, especially those instituted by the University of London, was recognized in some sections of Methodism, and was largely responsible for the foundation of another Methodist secondary school.

Wesley College, Sheffield, had been founded by the efforts of a Wesleyan Methodist minister, inspired by a genuine realization of the need for higher education among the Methodist laity. The founders of the 'West of England Wesleyan Proprietary Grammar School', Taunton,[5] were inspired by similarly sound ideals, though they were considerably influenced by the deep cleavage between the Church of England and Nonconformity in and around Taunton.

In 1522, Richard Fox, Bishop of Winchester, had founded a Grammar School at Taunton. Like many other ancient endowed grammar schools, it had fallen into decay by the middle of the nineteenth century, though it was still attended by the children

[4] *History of Kingswood School*, p. 228.
[5] To commemorate the Jubilee of Queen Victoria's accession, the school was renamed in 1887 'Queen's College'—the name by which it is called in the following pages.

of middle-class tradesmen and farmers of the district. There was much animosity between the sons of known Nonconformists and Church of England pupils, and the former were often refused admittance as pupils. Such a refusal confronted William French when he wished to send one of his sons to the school, and he and another Methodist layman, James Barnicott, determined to found a Methodist secondary school. They had before them the example of Wesley College, Sheffield, and they appreciated the opportunities offered by the University of London examinations. They found others who shared their views and a company was formed to procure the capital necessary for the building of a school. In 1843 the school was started in a portion of the Norman Castle, and thirty-three pupils were enrolled in the room where Judge Jeffreys is said to have held his 'bloody assize'.

Following the example of Wesley College, Sheffield, the Company issued one hundred and fifty £25 shares, and no subscriber was allowed to hold more than five shares. Should anyone acquire, by will or otherwise, more than that number, he was compelled to sell the excess or to forfeit them to the Company. This arrangement was similar to that laid down at Sheffield and was introduced in order to ensure that no one person should acquire a controlling interest in the school. With the concurrence of three-fourths of the holders of shares, directors might claim an annual dividend not exceeding £5 per cent. on paid-up capital. Any surplus moneys above these dividends were to be applied to the liquidation of debts, the establishment of scholarships, purchase of equipment for the school, or as a donation to any Methodist Connexional fund.

The object of the school, as laid down in the Deed of Settlement, was the provision of an efficient course of religious, literary, and physical education. No pupil was to be admitted until he had completed his eighth year.

Over the appointment of a governor for this school difficulties arose similar to those which had occurred at Wesley College. In 1844, the Company applied to Conference for the appointment of the Rev. R. Ray (superintendent minister of the Taunton Circuit) as governor, and this, as in the case of Wesley College, evoked discussion concerning the extent of responsibility which official Methodism was prepared to undertake in regard to such schools. Dr. Jabez Bunting was President, and he objected strongly to the way in which Mr. Ray appeared already to have committed himself to the school's affairs. A stormy scene followed and the President ruled, somewhat autocratically, that no governor should be appointed—a ruling which disturbed Conference considerably. Dr. Bunting, as we have seen, was a true friend to education, but he was not prepared to commit the administration of Methodism to any responsibility whose nature had not been fully examined. In his view, any school, over which official Methodism had any jurisdiction, should be wholly a Connexional school as were Kingswood and Woodhouse Grove. However, when, at the following Conference, the matter was again introduced, though he made no secret of his doubts about the advisability of Conference involving itself in educational matters without obtaining complete control of them, he admitted that if Mr. Ray had particular gifts for the work, then he was the proper man for the post. Mr. Ray was appointed governor.[6]

This school showed the tradition of the dissenting academies —and of Wesley's 'academic course' at Kingswood—in that it was intended to be more than a mere school. It was to provide a course of instruction whose upper section should be parallel to that of Oxford and Cambridge. It was, in fact, a 'Collegiate Institution' of the University of London, and it availed itself of the opportunity of combining school and university work. For a time, too, its scope was further extended by the presence of a number of theological students training for the ministry, so that 'no clear differentiation was made between the training candidates for the ministry and the school itself'.[7] But by that time both Richmond and Didsbury Theological Colleges had been opened, and this branch of the school's activities was not long continued.

Funds were not large and it was impossible to erect elaborate buildings, additions having to be made as they became essential. From the first this caused difficulty, and it must have made the establishment of any sort of school tradition an almost insuperable task. The school started in a portion of Taunton Castle, with boarders sleeping in two houses near the centre of the town, but by 1845 there were over one hundred pupils and it was imperative that new accommodation should be found. A committee made inquiries, and in the following year the foundation-stone of the present buildings was laid, the architect being Mr. Wilson of Bath, who shortly afterwards designed the new Kingswood School at Lansdown, Bath, and Westminster Col-

[6] Benjamin Gregory, *Sidelights on the Conflicts of Methodism*, p. 387.
[7] *Wesleyan Education Report* (1937–8), p. 15.

lege. The Taunton buildings were not completed until 1852, but the school moved into the completed parts in 1847. In that same year another Nonconformist school was founded in Taunton by the Independents on the model of Mill Hill (founded 1807). This school, now called Taunton School, was also started owing to the animosity between Church and Nonconformity in that district, though some incentive appears to have been given by the success of Queen's College.

For, despite the ambitious scope of its aims, the school was successful, and for this much of the credit is due to its first head master, Thomas Sibly.[8] Like Wesley and Waddy, he was a great personality. 'Your head master is the best I have found in England,' wrote an inspector who had nothing to gain by flattery; yet at one time it scarcely seemed that this man would succeed as a schoolmaster. He was studying medicine at Bristol when the governor of Kingswood School came to ask if any senior would supply the place of a master who was ill. Somewhat unwillingly, Sibly found himself volunteering, and his study of medicine was pushed aside, though the love of science was never lost, and in later years at Taunton he broke away from the old rigid classical curriculum of the public and grammar schools and made Queen's College a pioneer in recognizing the needs of contemporary life and a more scientific outlook. His unwillingness to take the post at Kingswood was not helped by his first experiences there. He found the life of a schoolmaster distasteful, and wrote to his sister: 'I only wish I were quit of this honourable profession. Let me be an astronomer, let me be a doctor, let me be a quack! Let me be a scrivener, let me be a rat-catcher!!! but don't let me be a schoolmaster.'

Unpromising material apparently for outstanding success in the teaching profession, but Sibly quickly changed his attitude, and one wonders what it was in the life of Kingswood School that caused the change. It seems certain that at least a contributory factor was his real understanding of boy nature. He was a good disciplinarian, but he had not been at Kingswood long before he dispensed altogether with corporal punishment as far as he himself was concerned, believing that education could best be served by the power of personal example and character. That was the man who was chosen after ten years at Kingswood to be the first head master at Taunton.

[8] Most of the information concerning Thomas Sibly is supplied by his daughter, Miss Blanche Sibly.

The rapid increase in the number of pupils (one hundred in the first two years) tells its own tale. From the first, Sibly introduced his own scientific interests into the school, and he had that gift—so necessary in a schoolmaster—of being able to impart to others not only his learning but also his enthusiasm. He was particularly fond of geology and was able to find scope for that interest in the neighbouring Quantock Hills, whither he took numbers of his pupils from time to time. He started school gardens and made the boys enthusiastic about them. Incidentally, this cultivation of school gardens, which was considered an innovation in preparatory schools and other institutions for small boys in the second half of the nineteenth century, was practised at Kingswood School in the second half of the eighteenth century. One of H.M. Inspectors who visited Queen's College in its early days told Sibly that it was the first school in which he had found science taught as a regular subject. That was the period when T. H. Huxley, Spencer, and others were agitating for more time being given to science in school curricula, and it was largely the example set by proprietary schools of this type which caused a reform in the old public and grammar schools. Sibly broke away from the rigidly classical curriculum and made his school a pioneer in the teaching of science and mathematics.

But it was not Sibly's up-to-date outlook on education alone which made him such a great head master and his school a success. 'Mens sana in corpore sano' was one of his guiding principles. Anything attempted had to be done thoroughly; he tried always to act as a Christian gentleman; his power of making others enthusiastic was not confined to matters of mere learning. It embraced everything—religion, humanity—everything that was worth while. The Rules of the school, in framing which he naturally took a leading part, stated: 'Cultivate uniform promptitude particularly in obeying the signals and orders of the institution.' As an Old Boy of the school said: 'He ruled with the authority of a king and the wisdom of a sage.' [9]

Learning was important, enthusiasm and the wish to learn were important, but they were not everything. 'I have always regarded the formation of character as the main object of education,' he said in 1881. The governor of the school was responsible for the moral welfare and religious instruction of the boys. He gave a weekly lecture on theology to the whole school, took

[9] *Queen's College Old Boys' Directory* (1932), pp. 12–13.

the seniors for the study of the Greek Testament, and conducted family prayers morning and evening. But, in Sibly's time. it was the head master who, by his example and character, moulded the life of the school and made it one which would have won Wesley's approval. At Wesley College, Sheffield, the reverse was the case. There it was the governor who was the real power.

From its earliest days, Queen's College attempted to keep in touch with the two Methodist Connexional schools. As we have seen, Sibly himself came from Kingswood to become its first head master. The Rev. Samuel Simmons (Kingswood 1818–24), the Rev. William P. Slater (Kingswood 1831–3), and the Rev. C. E. James (Woodhouse Grove 1868–73) became governors of Queen's College; J. J. Findlay, M.A., Ph.D. (Woodhouse Grove 1871–5, and Kingswood 1875–7), became the head master of Queen's College at the start of a distinguished career as an educationist, while a number of former pupils of Kingswood and Woodhouse Grove Schools became at some time assistant masters at Queen's College.

Another way in which this connexion was maintained occurred through the 'Taunton Scholarship'. Pupils left Kingswood and Woodhouse Grove at such an early age that the only external examination they were able to take while still at school (in the mid-century) was the Oxford and Cambridge Local Examination. They were not able to sit for the London examinations, and this was a serious handicap, since these offered openings to the professions which were otherwise closed to boys whose parents had but moderate means and who could not afford the fees required at Oxford and Cambridge. Queen's College, however, did prepare for the University of London examinations and had had considerable success. In order to do what she could to help the sons of ministers, a scholarship was offered first to Kingswood and later to Woodhouse Grove as well, which took the form of a year at Queen's College at half the usual fees. Wesley College, Sheffield, quickly followed the example, for it was obvious that this scholarship did not benefit only a few scholars. Those who received it were, normally, the best scholars at Kingswood or Woodhouse Grove who could, and did, increase the reputation of their school by their academic honours. Thus the best scholars left the two Connexional schools and became pupils of Wesley or Queen's College—and, later, of certain private schools which, realizing the reaction upon their own standing, offered similar scholarships—and increased their own reputation thereby. In 1869 J. A. Vanes, after seven years as a pupil at Kingswood, won this scholarship, passed his Matriculation examination at Queen's College, and was then invited to become head master's assistant—a post which he accepted for two years. This brought him into close touch with Thomas Sibly, about whom Vanes wrote: 'It seemed very clear to me that his mind had been the formative influence which had stamped on the college its characteristic features.' It is interesting to note what were these characteristic features in the eyes of a former Kingswood boy.

'The system of prefects, classified as seniors and sub-seniors, popular science lectures throughout the school, the rule which he made at Kingswood that he would never enforce discipline by corporal punishment, the recognition of organized sport with its annual exhibition, such things were the offspring of his fertile brain.' [10]

The clearest view of the course of instruction at the school during the first twenty-five years of its history can be obtained from the *Report of the Schools Inquiry Commission*.[11] There were, by 1868, 172 boarders and a few day boys, and these were organized into three departments:

1. The Junior Department, in which instruction was given in elementary Latin, French, natural science, and the usual English subjects.

2. The Middle School, in which instruction was continued in these subjects, and Greek and book-keeping were begun.

3. The Collegiate Department, whose curriculum was based on the syllabus of the Matriculation and higher examinations of the University of London.

Five years after the publication of that *Report* the head master stated in his *Annual Report*: 'Four of our students have passed the first B.A. examination since the last annual meeting, and one has taken his B.A. degree. Three have matriculated in the first division. Several have successfully taken the preliminary legal and medical examinations, and at least ten of our students have acquitted themselves well at Oxford and Cambridge, one having gained a high position in the list of wranglers.'[12] The number of successes at Oxford and Cambridge have continued from that date onward, but the 'Collegiate Department' gradually

[10] *History of Kingswood School*, p. 233.
[11] Vol. XIV, p. 492.
[12] These words were, of course, spoken after the older universities had been thrown open to Nonconformists.

disappeared, as more universities came into being and religious tests disappeared. Today, it would appear that the existence of this department must have implied a great waste of labour, for at no time were there a large number of scholars in it, but in those years before 1870 it did provide, in conjunction with the University of London, a means by which clever boys from Nonconformist families could equip themselves with the knowledge and the academic distinctions which were denied them at Oxford and Cambridge. On the other hand, the fact that Queen's College was primarily a school was never forgotten, and its success is proved by the steady increase in numbers. New houses were acquired in 1862, 1874, and 1878. They were placed in charge of housemasters, but the public-school system of Houses (with personal financial profit to the housemasters) was never adopted by this or any other Methodist school. Full use was made of the opportunity for masters to come into closer relationship with pupils, especially during a rather difficult period when J. J. Findlay became head master and pulled the School out of a temporary period of ill fortune. There was healthy rivalry between Houses, but they never became the self-contained units which were seen in many of the public schools of the time. The opportunities that were made possible for a closer relationship between teacher and taught did much to solidify the tradition of family relationship which was characteristic of all the Methodist secondary schools.

Unfortunately, the close of Thomas Sibly's head-mastership was marred by personal disappointment. In 1882, he resigned after holding the office for forty years. For the last few years of that period he had relied increasingly upon his son, G. W. Sibly, who was one of the assistant masters. Latterly the son had become senior resident master, since his father had always lived away from the school, at first at Hope House and then at Flook House, which was two miles from the school. It was natural, therefore, that both father and son should expect that the son would, more or less automatically, be offered the post of head master on the resignation of the father. The directors thought otherwise. The school was theirs; Thomas Sibly had, by his outstanding work, made it virtually his, and perhaps the directors felt this to be unwise. There is no need here to consider the pros and cons of the affair. The directors appointed Mr. H. Jefferson to the vacant post, and G. W. Sibly, disappointed, took his brother and two other masters with about fifty boys to Stonehouse, Gloucestershire, where he founded Wycliffe College, whose head master until recently was W. A. Sibly, grandson of the first head master of Queen's College. When Thomas Sibly heard the decision of the directors, he wrote in his diary:

'I recognize the hand of Divine Providence in this as in other cases and, as the action of the college directors sent him elsewhere, I fully believe that in his new sphere he will be more happy and prosperous and useful than he could have been at Taunton. I feel assured that with him, as with myself, the great aim will be to promote sound, religious education, to train boys after a generous, manly, earnest, intelligent type, fitting them for usefulness in the world as well as in the Church. By the Church we understand no bigoted sectarianism but the Church universal, that which Christ established and of which, in His simplicity and purity and nobility and true spirituality and self-sacrifice, He is at once the supreme Head and an unerring model for all His followers in all ages.'

CHAPTER TEN

Awakening of the Middle Classes—1845-70

ALTHOUGH DURING THIS twenty-five-year period the actual achievements in Methodist higher education appear to be disappointing, only three schools being founded in the period, and none of them by English Wesleyan Methodism, a number of influences were at work which made this the most important formative period in Methodist secondary education. They may be summarized as follows: The work of establishing a system of Methodist primary schools was going forward steadily in all parts of the country and, as more schools were built, so more people found an interest in education as a whole; a new conception of the content of secondary education was being preached and practised, and the middle classes especially were realizing their opportunities—and their responsibilities; educational experiments and achievements at home and on the Continent were arousing interest and emulation, the knowledge of these matters being spread abroad by individuals and by groups formed for the purpose.

As was shown in a previous chapter, the beginning of a Methodist primary-school system was made in 1837, and by 1870 there were 743 schools. That in itself was an achievement of which to be proud, especially as some of these ranked among the best in the country.[1] The very fact of such large-scale action increased interest not only in primary but also in higher education, and coupled with that was the upward trend of curriculum standards, already noted, which was due mainly to the fact that the poorer classes were anxious to 'better' themselves, the Methodists being on the whole hard-working, conscientious, and desirous of an education which went beyond the three R's; and that the middle classes who could afford to pay more for their children's education supported such schools. For example, the reputation of one of the Methodist schools in Hull had become so high that there was almost an embarrassment of applications from parents of higher rank than those who normally sent their children to primary schools.[2]

[1] See A. W. Harrison, *The Methodist Church: Its Origins, Divisions, and Reunion*, p. 211.
[2] *Report of the Schools Inquiry Commission*, Vol. IX, p. 246.

Matthew Arnold knew only too well the increasing power and potentiality of those who saw educational facilities being extended for the poorer classes, but for whose own children there appeared to be no increasing opportunities for higher education. It was that realization that led him to formulate his famous call for action: 'Organize your secondary schools!' It was that realization that led the group of men who had been responsible for the foundation of the University of London to study the Continental theories of education and to attempt to copy the practical examples set by men like Père Girard, Wehrli, and Fellenberg in the setting-up of high-grade primary schools organized on the monitorial system.

Once again, at the risk of redundancy, must be stressed the fact that Methodism, which had started as a religion of the lower classes, did not confine itself to them. Even in Wesley's day some of these same classes had lifted themselves above their fellows. Methodism in Wesley's day meant sobriety and thrift, but by the nineteenth century sobriety and thrift had produced wealth, and wealth, as Wesley had well known, did not mean a continuation, still less an increase, of piety. During his lifetime he had ruthlessly expelled from the Methodist Society any who became rich and ceased to live as he believed followers of Christ ought to live. After his death, this expulsion did not continue to be practised as strictly, and by the middle of the nineteenth century there were many wealthy members. In Leeds, for example, between 1830 and 1860, the 'Best People' were Methodists.[3] There is no need to inquire too closely into the meaning of the term 'Best People'. Suffice it that wealthy Methodists were not necessarily impious. In the majority of cases religious fervour and sincerity continued with the amassing of wealth, and the poverty which had been known was not forgotten. It was only natural, therefore, that parents who, by sheer hard work and self-restraint, had gained some knowledge and standing should wish to give their children a better education than they had had. Hence the increasing demand for higher education, a demand not limited to Methodists. Thomas Arnold and a number of public-school head masters, together with the educational reformers nicknamed 'the education-mad party',[4] had put a new conception on higher education, and the emphasis now lay more

[3] E. E. Kellett, *Religion and Life in the Early Victorian Age*, p. 28.
[4] Known also as 'Philosophical Radicals', the men responsible for founding the 'London University', men who based their political beliefs on the philosophy of Jeremy Bentham.

on character-building and the development of a balanced personality than on the mere attainment of knowledge. Many members of the Church of England and the majority of the Nonconformist denominations believed that such an education could be provided only in schools under the direct control of the Church or of a particular denomination.

Another factor which contributed to the demand for secondary education was the need for teachers in the primary schools, which were rapidly increasing in numbers. As far as Methodism was concerned, potential teachers had to have something more than a certain standard of learning: they had to be trained in Methodist principles and doctrine. Gradually was being formed the vision of an educational ladder, but to realize that vision in practice, secondary schools were needed. New ones were required and old ones needed re-formation.

One man at least understood the difficulties, and though he made many scathing comments on the Philistinism of Nonconformity he expressed on many occasions his appreciation of the sincere attempts being made by Methodism to further education. Matthew Arnold, the son of Dr. Thomas Arnold, a man of culture, a school inspector, and one whose duties allowed him to travel and to study the Continental systems of education, was in a unique position to comment and to help, for he had many contacts with Methodism.

He recognized the existence of too-well-defined social classes in England, the cleavages between them all the more disturbing because of the denominational differences which caused friction instead of providing a cement to bind different social strata together. He saw in education a means of softening the sharp edges. It was the middle classes that gave him most concern. Already the Committee of Council and a number of voluntary bodies [5] had started providing schools for the poor, and the middle classes were saying: 'What about us?' Unless something was done to provide education for them, there would soon be active opposition to further broadenings of the educational facilities for the lower classes.

On the other hand, the upper classes were beginning to be well-provided for. Changes were occurring in the public schools which gave pupils in these schools something that was unique—

[5] National Society (1811), British and Foreign Schools Society (1814), Home and Colonial School Society (1836), Wesleyan Education Committee (1837), London Ragged School Union (1844), Catholic Poor School Committee (1847), Church Education Society (1853).

a confidence, spirit, a style. Such schools had been swept away in France, and new institutions had been put in their place. This had not happened in England, and Arnold hoped it never would, and that a process of gradual change would continue to function quietly and naturally from within. All the signs showed that this was in fact happening.

The middle classes had for their higher education the grammar schools, which needed reform as urgently as the public schools had done, but in which reforms were occurring too slowly, and a large number of private schools, some doing useful work, but belonging to no system, subject to all the evils of competition and business which had to succeed financially or cease to exist. Because they were private schools, they were immune from a common standard of inspection and criticism which might have improved them, and which alone would help to guarantee a healthy life. Arnold worked for a system of secondary schools organized under State auspices. He believed that such a system would not only meet the growing demand, but by competing with existing schools would improve the whole organization of English higher education by healthy stimulation. State interest would not mean a rigidly despotic control, especially if the State's actions were directed, as they would be, by that middle class which was already renowned for its strength, energy, zeal, and industry. Schools whose fees were graded and so accessible to all would be one means by which the middle classes could reach their ideals. They would provide a tradition and a cultural pride which was then obtainable only by attendance at a public school. 'It would', said Arnold, 'really augment their self-respect and moral force; it would truly fuse them with the class above and tend to bring about for them the equality which they deserve.' [6]

Bishop Butler in 1745 had preached a sermon on behalf of the charity schools of London and Westminster in which he said, 'Of education, information itself is really the least part,' but it took a hundred years for that idea to become generally recognized, though it was always a guiding principle in the Methodist secondary schools, where Lacordaire's desire was portrayed in practice: 'Let us form Christians in our schools, but first of all let us form Christians in our hearts. The one great thing is to have a life of one's own.' [7] Thomas Arnold had called

[6] *The Popular Education of France*, p. 40.
[7] Quoted by Matthew Arnold in *A French Eton*, p. 26.

for a Christian and a gentleman as the product of education. The Methodists had striven for the same object since John Wesley had made education a part of his evangelical work.

Matthew Arnold was appointed H.M. Inspector of Elementary Schools in 1851, and he continued to hold that post till 1886. His work took him to all parts of the country and brought him into contact with all types and classes of people, but especially with the Nonconformist middle classes, for since the National Society had made an arrangement whereby their schools were only to be inspected by Church of England clergy, the lay inspectors' work was in schools other than those provided by the Church of England. This brought Arnold into contact with Methodism. He met the teachers of the new primary schools and the staff and students of Westminster Training College, but there was another more intimate link, for over a period of eighteen years Thomas Healing, a Methodist Local Preacher and Sunday-school worker, was assistant to Arnold in his work as an inspector.

Thomas Healing (1838–1902) represents a type of Methodist who did much to help Methodist education behind the scenes at a time when it was important that the State and its representatives should know clearly what was being done by the denominations for education. Though Healing's work as a day-school master did not last long, he remained essentially a teacher during the whole of his life. He never forgot the teacher's viewpoint—and made sure that Matthew Arnold did not forget it either.

At the age of fourteen, when about to leave his primary school in Cheltenham, he attracted the notice of Matthew Arnold, then recently appointed an inspector, and was apprenticed as a pupil-teacher. In 1858, after gaining first place in the Queen's Scholarship examination, he entered Westminster College as a student. There he spent the usual two years and on leaving was appointed head master of the new Wesleyan school at Highbury. During his four years there 'his capacity as a teacher and his practical insight into educational principles so impressed Arnold that he asked the Education Department to appoint him Inspector's Assistant'.[8] That was in 1864, and the relation between these two men 'during eighteen years' association developed from that of disciple and master in educational matters to that of colleagueship and friendship. The influence of Arnold is seen in his assistant's continued encouragement of all that tended to a

[8] C. Arnold Healing, *Thomas Healing*, p. 29.

broader culture in the teachers, in his insistence on the tincture of letters in the school curriculum, as shown in the improvement of the school reading-books, in the heightened standard of the poetry memorized, and in the humanizing of the arid methods employed in the teaching of geography. On the other hand, the assistant supplied the lack of his chief in the practical applications of educational principles, a department which Arnold viewed, as he himself was the first to confess, from the standpoint of the cultivated amateur. In estimating methods of instruction, school fittings, and architecture, and the standard of testing efficiency, he relied greatly on the opinion of his assistant, whose technical training and practical teaching genius made his judgement on such points swift and reliable.' [9]

Thomas Healing, largely through his work as a Sunday-school superintendent, in which capacity he was well known throughout Methodism, was able to influence his fellow Methodists with a fuller understanding of what teaching meant, and at the same time he was able to imbue them with something of the ideals which he had learnt from Matthew Arnold for a broader and deeper culture among the Nonconformists.

Matthew Arnold has often been criticized for unfairness to Nonconformists ('Philistines' as he labelled them in his *Culture and Anarchy*). It is true that in his zeal for a spreading of culture he overlooked the difficulties with which Nonconformists had had to contend for three hundred years. He disregarded the work of the dissenting academies and the enlightenment which Methodism in particular had brought to the country. The words of another leading educationist of that time are apposite here: 'In like manner the eighteenth century saw in the Church of England decorum, learning, and many other estimable qualities, but also coldness and a notable absence of religious fervour or of strong conviction. And it was to Wesley and Whitefield, and not to ecclesiastics in high places, that we owe the evangelical revival of that century. We have, as a nation, been in fact saved from moral corruption in the seventeenth century, and from religious apathy and indifference in the eighteenth, not by the influence of the educated and privileged classes, but by the great and steadfast qualities of that very class of British Philistines against whom Matthew Arnold directed all his earnest condemnation and all the lighter artillery of his sarcasm and his wit.' [10]

[9] C. Arnold Healing, *Thomas Healing*, pp. 31–2.
[10] J. G. Fitch, *Thomas and Matthew Arnold*, pp. 227–8.

Yet Arnold's very cruelty was in a sense kind, for it awoke action, and whatever may have been his neglect of the achievements of Nonconformity he was sincere in his struggle for the enlightenment of the future. The respect which Healing had for his chief is evidenced by the fact that he named his son after him.[11]

On Arnold's side, he saw much in Wesleyan Methodism to admire,[12] especially in the early efforts of the Connexion to provide primary schools and the teachers required in them. In a Report on Westminster and speaking of the students there he wrote in 1856: 'Their training is studiously addressed to "form in them habits of right feeling and of good conduct, as well as of correct thinking"; to develop in them a spirit of peaceableness and affectionateness; "the spirit of teaching for the good of others as well as for their own livelihood". They are exhorted to labour, "not only that they may have their schools in a creditable state at the visit of the Inspector, but that their scholars, when they come to be men and women, may remember their school-days with pleasure, may think of their teacher with affection and mention him with honour, when Blue-books are shelved and forgotten". This is the spirit which, I truly believe, those who conduct the Wesleyan training institution do their best to develop and to promote.'[13] These words suggest flattery, but Arnold had no occasion to use flattery, least of all in an official report. Nor did he ever dream of flattery where 'Philistines' were concerned —satire, ridicule, but never flattery. He was perfectly sincere and honest: he did admire the manner in which Wesleyan Methodism was setting about its educational task. What he did not admire was the small breadth of vision shown by many Nonconformists who lived 'a life of jealousy of the establishment, disputes, tea meetings, openings of chapels, sermons.'[14] He objected, too, to the narrow conception, as he deemed it, of Methodist religious instruction which neglected the historical and comparative aspects of religion.[15] Arnold, the practical reformer and school inspector, was not afraid to criticize and to show his disapproval; but Arnold, the poet and dreamer, who saw far

[11] The Rev. C. Arnold Healing.
[12] In a letter to Dr. Rigg, Arnold wrote: 'I have a real attachment to the body of Wesleyan Methodists.' See John Telford, *Life of James Harrison Rigg*, p. 271.
[13] Matthew Arnold, *Reports on Elementary Schools, 1852–82*, pp. 237–8.
[14] *idem, Culture and Anarchy* (Cambridge 1932), p. 58.
[15] *idem, Reports on Elementary Schools, 1852–82*, pp. 139–40; 259–61; 262–5.

beyond the confines of his duties which demanded of him comment on the workings of an inadequate system, was appreciative and friendly. He came to respect those responsible for Methodist education, but that very respect only made him regret the shortcomings the more. It was to bring a greater breadth of vision, more 'sweetness and light', to Nonconformity in general that he wrote his *Culture and Anarchy*.[16] And against the scathing sarcasm and apparent injustice of that book must be set such remarks as 'I found the children human'[17]—a favourite expression of his, but one which he used only of schools which deserved it, and the fact that many of them did, even in the difficult days of 'payment by results', is a tribute to Nonconformist education, as he himself realized.

The fact that Arnold was an inspector of Nonconformist schools might have meant nothing, but Arnold was not only a man whose job took him into Nonconformist preserves: he was also a man who wanted to meet people, to learn of them their ideas and ideals, and such a man could not help giving in exchange some of his own brilliance and vision. He was a romantic, albeit a practical one. He knew the potentialities of Nonconformity, which, by the Reform Bill of 1867, formed a majority of the English electorate, and he feared lest narrow-mindedness and short-sightedness of policy should come to dominate national life.

For this reason he rallied his fellows in the organization of secondary education, for he felt that only through the medium of higher education could the outlook of the growing middle classes be broadened. As an Assistant Commissioner under the Schools Inquiry Commission he was sent to report on higher education on the Continent. Previously, in 1859, he had visited France, Holland, and Switzerland on behalf of the Newcastle Commission, and the unofficial report on those journeyings is contained in three books: *Popular Education on the Continent* (1861), *A French Eton, or Middle-class Education and the State* (1864), and *Schools and Universities on the Continent* (1868). 'Organize your secondary education' was the theme of all these books, and Methodist leaders (and in particular James Rigg, William Arthur, and John Scott) read them critically. One fact especially interested—and alarmed—them: the fact that the State, and the State alone, was envisaged as the provider and

---

[16] Published in 1869, with a completely revised edition in 1875.
[17] *Wesleyan Education Report* (1902–3), p. 110.

organizer of secondary education. Indeed, their immediate reaction might be said to prove the truth of the criticism of narrow-mindedness. William Arthur and James Rigg alone at that time seemed to see beyond the denomination. Methodists were not alone in their fear and the consequent donning of denominational armour. The country did indeed suggest

> *a darkling plain*
> *Swept with confused alarms of struggle and flight,*
> *Where ignorant armies clash by night.*[18]

It is unfair to Nonconformity, however, to suggest that it alone provided the 'confused alarms'. The Roman Catholics have always followed a strictly denominational path in education, and have done so with dignity, courage (for they have been much persecuted), and extreme cleverness; the Church of England found it necessary to join issue in the denominational battle of education, and made a notable contribution to higher education through the Woodard Schools.

Amongst the Nonconformist denominations, however, the educational struggle was particularly fierce and often bitter, but it achieved one valuable result: it produced widespread interest not only in primary education in connexion with which the battle at first raged, but also in education as a whole. In Methodism there were, during this period, two parties. There was a majority who said, 'We must provide our own schools', and there was a minority who said, 'Let us give up what schools we have that other denominations may do likewise, and let us help by so doing to provide a State system of education'.

The Rev. John Scott may be taken as the Methodist leader of the majority party during this period. It was during his first term as President of the Conference (1843) that he showed his advocacy of Methodist education and tried to show Methodism its duty toward national education. In that year he laid before Conference his scheme for the building of seven hundred primary schools. He became Chairman of the Education Committee, and on the opening of Westminster Training College was appointed first Principal, holding that office during the difficult early days of popular education.

The Rev. William Arthur may be taken as the leader of the minority party. Always a keen educationist, brought up in Ireland where he had before him examples of what Roman

[18] Last lines of Matthew Arnold's *Dover Beach*.

Catholicism was doing for education—and for itself—he had lived for many years in France and knew and admired the system of State education there. As he grew older he became more and more convinced that education of all types must ultimately be provided by the State. He never underestimated the difficulties of providing Christian education in such schools, and he sympathized with those who clung to the narrower denominational view of education, but he felt that if only all denominations would agree to disagree on non-essentials, the essential achievements of education would become established fact with no loss to any individual denomination. It was his knowledge of the wealth and power of the Roman Catholics in Ireland and France which mainly brought him to that view, for he felt that as long as the denominational 'voluntary' principle persisted, so long would the most wealthy denominations have the advantage.

During this period, however, there appeared a Methodist minister who came to act as a link between the two schools of thought—using the best of both views to achieve results—and who had more influence than any other minister on the establishment of secondary schools on a larger scale. That man was James H. Rigg, D.D. Of the five years spent at Kingswood School as a pupil and four years as a master he wrote: 'The advantages which I received at Kingswood School—advantages which are not excelled in any school in the kingdom—prepared me for certain studies, theological and otherwise.' [19] When he left Kingswood he intended to continue teaching as a career and became an assistant master at a school near Leeds whose head master was a Rev. Firth. Already Rigg had proved himself to be a young man with drive, but in his enthusiasm he rather over-reached himself, for he opened a school of his own in Ruston Street, Islington, which was a complete failure. No doubt the experience stood him in good stead later, bitter as it must have been for the young man of twenty-one. He again became an assistant master, this time at Dr. John Conquest's Academy at Biggleswade, where he taught classics and mathematics for £40 a year. This was one of the many Methodist private schools scattered throughout the country at that time, a school of which its head master used to say: 'I am exceedingly anxious that my establishment should not merely assume the name of a religious one, but be so in fact.' [20]

[19] John Telford, *The Life of James Harrison Rigg, D.D.*, p. 152.
[20] ibid., p. 23.

Rigg seems to have come to realize the difficulties of achieving such an aim, though he himself was filled with a desire to follow the precepts of Wesley. It was while he was on the staff of this school that he became a Local Preacher and began seriously to consider entering the Ministry, though that was in no way due to unhappiness in his work of teaching. He became a minister and was sent to the Woodhouse Grove Circuit for a time. There he went out of his way to meet the boys from the school and to see something of their life. While still a probationer in 1847 he and his friend William Arthur were allowed to attend one of the Methodist Education Committee's meetings when the question of national education was being discussed. It was a time when State interest was causing Samuel Jackson and W. M. Bunting and other Methodist leaders to stress the importance of the Churches in all educational work.[21] During that same period of probation, when Rigg was closely connected with the Spitalfields Chapel, his educational interests were further stimulated by informal talks which took place in the homes of the number of Methodist professional and business men who attended the Chapel. One such talk in particular took place at the home of a well-to-do gentleman who had invited some of his friends— among them Mr. and Mrs. Lycett (afterwards Lord and Lady Lycett) and Mr. Edward Corderoy—to discuss the project of a Methodist Connexional school for the sons of laymen—a project which was revived at intervals but did not find fulfilment until the establishment of The Leys thirty years later. Rigg's brother, Frank, kept a private school, Strathmore House, at Southport. Thus, from his earliest years he had every opportunity of studying education, and there is no doubt that the problem of its supply to people who were crying out for it was one which occupied him much.

After Dr. Rigg's death in 1909, M. E. Sadler wrote of him: 'I have long thought of him as one of those far-seeing men who stood out at a critical time against the false ideal of secular education. He knew, and he made others realize, that spiritual beliefs are necessary presuppositions to all educational work which fortifies character. He knew, and he made others understand, that the inner life of the great religious societies is a necessary factor in religious education and that the task of the State is, not to compete with the religious bodies, but to welcome their

---

[21] For full account of this important committee meeting, see James H. Rigg, *Reminiscences*, pp. 103–14.

aid and extend their opportunities of service. He stood out manfully, at a time of momentous change, against a false conception of the place and work of schools in national culture. He was a link between two schools of thought. He mediated between them and made each realize the strong position of the other. He was a peacemaker, because he refused a false truce, and our debt to him is very great. Much that he did, most of what he did, has passed into the very structure of the national life. It does not bear his name, but it is the outcome of his thought and reasoning and insight. And I trust that, in his declining years he knew that what he had done was increasingly appreciated by those who are students of the problem to which he gave, through a long life, the passion of a balanced mind.' [22]

Thus spoke one who did more than most men in the early years of this century to shape English education. The tribute was not a mere empty eulogy, nor was it based only on the fact of close personal friendship. It was occasioned by a review of the achievements and by a knowledge and understanding of the man's mind. The closing phrase is most apt: 'The passion of a balanced mind.' Therein lay the secret of Dr. Rigg's success. Passion there always is and must be in evangelical religion. Too often, however, there is passion without balance, spirit without body, and when that occurs there can be no lasting achievement. A flame is lit, flickers, flares up, and at the end of life is extinguished, leaving not even smoke behind. Rigg's work, like that of others mentioned in these pages, was lasting, and it was so because it was inspired by passion and guided by balance born of experience. Rigg may have lacked the human touch: he is criticized by one of the students who was at Westminster College when Rigg was Principal as 'unapproachable', but he was an able educational statesman.

It was because of that that Rigg was able to do so much to further the cause of Methodism in State education, and of education in Methodism. His position was not one of mere compromise. He was a stern and resolute fighter when need be, and would connive at no easy way out of difficulties. His own view was that the adequate provision of schools of all types was something that Methodism could not hope to achieve alone, even for its own adherents. He advocated, therefore, a combination of the 'voluntary' principle and State aid.[23] Today, such a view

---

[22] Quoted in John Telford, op. cit., pp. 195-6.
[23] See James H. Rigg, *Essays for the Times*.

seems to be the only common-sense way of regarding the matter, but before we condemn our forefathers who thought differently it is well to remember the reason for their different view. The Act of Uniformity of 1662 and those Acts (The Corporation, Test, Conventicle, and Five Mile Acts) which were known collectively as the Clarendon Code were intended to stamp out Nonconformity in the seventeenth and eighteenth centuries by making it illegal for a Nonconformist to preach in a chapel or to teach in a school. Later, in 1713, the Schism Act ordained that 'No person in Great Britain should keep any public or private school, or act as tutor, that has not first subscribed the declaration to conform to the Church of England and obtained a licence from the diocesan, and that upon failure of so doing the party may be committed to prison without bail; and that no such licence shall be granted before the party produces a certificate of having received the Sacrament according to the communion of the Church of England within the last year, and also subscribed the oaths of allegiance and supremacy.'

Till 1779 it continued to be illegal for a Nonconformist to act as a schoolmaster, while the Test and Corporation Acts survived till 1829. Tests on admission to degrees in the universities were not finally abolished by Parliament till 1871. Thus for three hundred years Nonconformists were excluded from universities and schools, and therefore from the higher professions and public services. It is hardly surprising, therefore, that the nonconforming Methodists showed a wary and habitual dread of State interference in any matter which affected them. They had suffered from such interference in past days, and were not going to be caught again if they could help it.

On the death of the Rev. John Scott, Conference appointed Dr. Rigg Principal of Westminster Training College. It was an obvious choice, for by that time he was recognized as an educationist outside the Connexion and was friendly with many of the leaders of the reforming party in English education. W. E. Gladstone called him one of the ablest men he had met on committee; and said that when he had spoken on the subject of education there was no need for any other person to speak on the same side. He presented the question in such a clear, convincing, and reasonable manner that he carried conviction to any mind.[24] Soon after Dr. Rigg went to Westminster he was elected a member of the London School Board, the first Methodist minister to

[24] John Telford, op. cit., p. 181.

achieve such a distinction. He was a personal friend of Sir James Kay Shuttleworth, first Secretary of the Committee of Council on Education, and of Michael E. Sadler who, when they first met, was Professor of the History and Administration of Education Department at Victoria University, Manchester.

But Dr. Rigg was not content with a near view of education. He made it his business to study education in other countries, and read Matthew Arnold's reports on Continental systems with particular care. In fact, he reviewed at least one of them for the *London Quarterly Review*. He became almost as well known, largely through his writings, in America [25] as in this country, and became especially friendly with Abel Stevens, the Methodist historian. When he visited America he regarded himself as an unofficial educational commissioner and made a special study, in so far as the comparatively short periods of his stay would permit, of the educational problems of that country. In Canada he became an intimate friend of Dr. Egerton Ryerson, who did more than any other man to found and organize the school system of Ontario. In 1886 Rigg was appointed a member of the Cross Commission on education and championed the 'voluntary' principle in the primary-school system. Long before that, however, he had become well known to many prominent educationists, though this work gave him added opportunity to meet and exchange views with Dr. Temple, then Bishop of London, Cardinal Manning, and Canon Gregory. His views on religion and education were further broadened and strengthened by talks at Westminster with Dean Stanley and Lady Augusta. Nor was the broadening influence all on one side, for frequently the Dean borrowed books, particularly on Wesley, from the study at Westminster College.

Dr. Rigg, especially during those years he spent at Westminster, had more influence in the educational sphere than any Methodist had had previously. And this was not due to the offices thrust upon him and which forced him to become a student of education; in himself he seems to epitomize the principle of religion and education being one indivisible whole. To him Methodism was everything, and bound up with that loyalty was a genuine interest in education. This outline of some of his offices and interests has been written to show that fact. He realized the difficulties of denominationalism. He understood,

[25] In 1851 he was appointed English correspondent of the New Orleans *Christian Advocate*.

more clearly than most of his fellow-Methodists, the vastness of the work of establishing a system of education in this country. He came to realize that no one denomination could hope to cope with it, and he had seen enough in committee to know that the various denominations would not unite whole-heartedly in undertaking the task. At the same time he was passionately convinced of the need for freedom of religious conviction in all schools. Dr. Rigg marked the intermediate stage between the voluntary system and complete control by the State.[26] He had realized before the passing of the 1870 Act that the Churches could not unaided provide education for all and at all stages, but throughout his life he remained a staunch supporter of the voluntary schools. He did not believe in leaving everything to others; he believed that every little counted and that the Methodists, if they were to be true to themselves, their founder, and their God, must take education as part of their evangelistic work, must provide what schools they could—the more the better—but at all times must be prepared to co-operate with others, and especially with the State, in any sincere effort to forward the scope and the structure of education.

Certain individuals have been considered in some detail because they typify the varying development of opinion on education during this period, and because they had in their various spheres considerable personal influence: Matthew Arnold, poet and educationist whose reputation became national; Thomas Healing, Methodist layman and educationist who acted, as it were, as the chief connecting link between Matthew Arnold and Methodism; William Arthur and John Scott, ministerial leaders of the Methodist Connexion with conflicting views concerning the supply and administration of education but wholeheartedly desirous of a wider provision of education; James Rigg, Methodist minister who became better known as an educationist than as a minister, in America if not in this country.

There is another individual who must be considered, for he exercised considerable influence on education, especially on denominational education. Nathaniel Woodard was a Church of England clergyman who, like Matthew Arnold, saw the needs of the middle classes, but who, unlike him, believed that the education necessary could and should be provided by the

---

[26] Dr. Rigg's plan for combining 'voluntary' and municipal schools under Governmental control was similar to that later laid before Parliament by W. E. Forster.

authority which had first provided it in England—the Church. He formulated a great scheme for secondary education and he put the scheme into practice. He had no money and, when he began, no influence, but 'whilst others wrote and talked about the evils of ignorance and irreligion, here was a man ready to devote his whole life to providing the only remedy; that is, the organized means of training the neglected youth of the middle classes at a cost which they could bear'.[27]

In 1847, Nathaniel Woodard, curate-in-charge of New Shoreham, Sussex, founded a school for the special purpose of supplying secondary education to the sons of the middle-class parents who wanted a better education than that provided in the primary schools, who were dissatisfied with the slackness and inefficiency of the average grammar schools of the time, and who could not afford the fees of the public schools.[28] Woodard had a clearer insight into contemporary social conditions than most men had. He was also a keen Churchman. He saw the spread of irreligion throughout the country and the comparative failure of the Church to stop it; he saw the numerical strength of the Methodists growing while that of his own Church stood still; he saw and appreciated the measures being taken to educate the poor, but, he wrote: 'The poor cannot be successfully educated, or really benefited unless you educate their employers'.[29] These employers were mainly to be found amongst the middle classes, and it was there that the growing strength of the Methodists was being recruited. Woodard felt that a system of avowedly Church schools, catering specially for the needs of the different social strata of these classes, would help to check their estrangement from the Church of England. Such an idea did not take sudden shape. Woodard was a practical man, and he regarded his school at Shoreham—a day-school held in the dining-room of his own house with one man to help him—purely as an experiment. Makeshift as it was, it succeeded, and he found others keen to help and to provide the necessary capital. In the following year his plan for a system of Church schools to be established throughout the country was publicly mooted.[30] By that time his idea had been clarified, and its essentials may be summarized:

The schools must be boarding-schools. More was required of

[27] Sir John Otter, *Nathaniel Woodard*, p. 2.
[28] For full accounts, see Sir John Otter, op. cit., and E. E. Kirke, *The Story of the Woodard Schools*.
[29] Sir John Otter, op. cit., p. 38.
[30] Nathaniel Woodard, *A Plea for the Middle Classes*.

education than could be provided in the classroom. Woodard entirely agreed with what Lord Lyttelton wrote to him in 1866: 'I do not consider that a day-school is in any full or half-full sense a place of education at all. It is a place where certain parts of instruction and knowledge are imparted. Greatly do parents delude themselves if they suppose that by sending their children for perhaps one-sixth or one-seventh of their time to a day-school they are educating them.' [31]

Fees must be moderate and graded to meet the means of the various strata of the middle classes.

The aim of the schools must be the maintenance of loyalty to the Church of England.

The moral and intellectual aspects of school life must be kept separated, directed by two separate persons.[32]

The scheme produced an encouraging response. The day-school was given up and a boarding-school, accommodated in a number of private houses, took its place. A society was formed —the Society of St. Nicholas College—which had as one of its aims the provision of education for the sons of the middle classes on terms suited to their means. In 1849 a second boarding-school was opened at Shoreham with fees only half those charged at the first school, and in 1850 the school was moved to its present home at Hurstpierpoint.

Development took place rapidly, and in 1851 Woodard, in a letter to the clergy of the Chichester diocese, proposed the foundation of schools of three grades—similar to the grades adopted eighteen years later by the Schools Inquiry Commission. To give practical effect to the proposal, the first school at Shoreham was moved to Lancing, and in its place was founded a third school known at St. Saviour's,[33] for the education of the sons of lower-middle-class parents, with fees fixed at £13 per annum to meet their means.

The scheme was a magnificent one, though Woodard was fortunate in finding a number of wealthy men sufficiently enlightened in educational and religious views to support the venture.[34] One feature of the schools in their early days which made for economy was the smallness of masters' salaries. As in

[31] Quoted by Sir John Otter, op. cit., p. 185.
[32] As was largely the case in existing Methodist Schools. This peculiarity is dealt with in the next chapter.
[33] Now Ardingly.
[34] £250,000 was spent in twenty years, and Woodard estimated that £2,500,000 would be necessary for the carrying out of the whole scheme.

the early days of Kingswood School and in certain Roman Catholic schools today, this meant that a master who accepted a post in one of the schools did so through a sense of religious vocation and duty to his Church. As the Schools Inquiry Commission later reported: 'The success of the schools must in some measure be ascribed to religious zeal.' [35] For the same reason, the staffs came to be drawn largely from old boys of the schools —as in the case of the Methodist secondary schools.

The success of these schools, and still more the formulation of the scheme of which they were a part, did much to influence those members of the Methodist Connexion whose thoughts were turning more and more toward higher education. It was possible for pupils in a lower-grade school to be moved to a higher-grade school and so to the university. There was therefore an educational ladder leading to high honours for the sons of the lower-middle classes. Perhaps it is not without significance that it was after the successful start of the Woodard scheme that the Scholarship plan was formulated whereby promising pupils at Kingswood and Woodhouse Grove Schools were moved to Queen's College at Taunton in order to undertake higher studies.

But, more than anything else perhaps, it was the denominational character of the Woodard schools which influenced Methodism. The Woodard scheme was widely publicized. In particular, great meetings were held in London and Oxford in 1861, in Cambridge in 1864, in Shrewsbury, Chester, Wolverhampton, Leicester, Nottingham, and Derby in 1869-70, and these were fully reported in the daily Press. The very fact that there was some opposition to the scheme in the Church of England itself ensured greater publicity being given to it. W. E. Gladstone moved the first Resolution at the Oxford meeting in 1861: 'That considering the growth of intelligence among the lower classes, owing to the impulse given of late years to education, the establishment of public boarding-schools for the education of the lower-middle classes which may be cheap and self-supporting is of great national importance.' His speech was fully reported in *The Times* of 23rd November in that year and was certainly read by most Methodist leaders, especially as Woodard made no secret of his hope that dissenters would be won back to the Church through the work of his schools. That this hope was realized is shown by what he wrote in a letter to the Marquis of Salisbury in 1868: 'Our schools will, I know by experience,

---

[35] *Report of the Schools Inquiry Commission*, Vol. I, p. 49.

be as much used by good Dissenters as by Churchmen, which confirms my hopes that a large proportion of the Dissent of the country is far from hostile to the national religion.' [36]

It was becoming clear that if Methodism did not soon provide education for the middle classes on a wide scale parents would send their children to schools of other denominations.

Before closing this review of influences which affected Methodist education during the period 1845 to 1870, mention must be made of the three Methodist secondary schools founded during the period, two of which owed their foundation partly to the need which had led Wesley to found Kingswood School— the theological training of potential ministers. The schools are Elmfield, York; Wesley College, Dublin; and the Methodist College, Belfast.

Elmfield was the first attempt on the part of Primitive Methodism to give secondary education to its children, and is interesting in that it is the first practical achievement in higher education undertaken by the Liberal element in Methodism as a whole. Since its secession from the Wesleyan parent body, Primitive Methodism had been essentially Liberal in its social outlook, but it was only in the middle of the nineteenth century that signs appeared in Wesleyan Methodism of a similar tendency. It is ironical that one of the ways in which John Wesley had offended the Church of England was his open-air preaching, and that the chief bone of contention between Wesleyan and Primitive Methodism was Hugh Bourne's practice of holding open-air 'camp meetings'. In 1807 the Wesleyan Conference condemned such meetings as 'highly improper and likely to be of considerable mischief'. Feelings ran high and led in 1811 to the establishment of 'Primitive Methodism'. That, however, is by the way. Suffice it that from the first Primitive Methodism represented a Liberal element in Methodism. Until 1859 it did nothing to promote higher education, though as early as 1843, under the influence no doubt of what was being done in Wesleyan Methodism, education was being discussed.[37] In that year the establishment of a ministerial training college was suggested by the Rev. Gordon Black, but the suggestion was overwhelmingly defeated in the Primitive Methodist Conference. There was considerable disagreement about education in this

[36] Quoted by Sir John Otter, op. cit., p. 211.
[37] Hugh Bourne himself, who in 1802 was teaching in a day-school at Harrisahead, was frequently exhorting his followers to 'take care of the children'. See A. W. Harrison, op. cit., pp. 218–19.

branch of Methodism, the north being, on the whole, in favour of providing schools, the south being unanimous in opposing all such projects. John Flesher said in 1849, however, 'We have three kinds of Connexional schools, and one kind in prospect: namely, Sabbath, Day, and Night schools; the one in prospect is designed for the education of preachers' children.' [38] It remained 'in prospect' until 1859, when the suggestion was put forward that a school should be provided 'for preachers' children and the children of members'. [39]

1860 saw the Jubilee of Primitive Methodism, and a special Jubilee Fund was inaugurated, part of which was to be set aside for the establishment of a middle-class school and the provision of education for ministerial candidates. The project was not over-popular, for it was, as one member said, too vague, and a number of Conference members said bluntly that the money would be better spent on foreign missions.

No further step was taken therefore until 1863, when the Primitive Methodist Conference was held at York. In that district there were a number of comparatively wealthy members who were beginning to express their anxiety lest their sons should be lost to Primitive Methodism through their being compelled to be educated in schools of other religious denominations. [40] At that time laymen had more power in the government of Primitive Methodism than they had in Wesleyan Methodism, and these northern laymen swayed Conference to their way of thinking. The establishment of a Connexional school for boys was at last authorized and it was to be called 'The Primitive Methodist Jubilee School'.

A house in the Malton Road, York, was rented, and in January 1864 the school was opened—with so many pupils that the building could not house them! The Conference therefore, after authorizing the purchase of the property and the setting-up of a committee of management, gave orders for its enlargement. So Primitive Methodism founded its first secondary school whose object was the education of the 'middle classes of society, specially (though not exclusively) for youths belonging to the Primitive Methodist denomination'. [41]

These words were written in 1868, by which time Elmfield (as

[38] H. B. Kendall, *The Origin and History of the Primitive Methodist Church*, Vol. II, p. 520.
[39] ibid., Vol. II, p. 521.
[40] *Report of the Schools Inquiry Commission*, Vol. IX, p. 241.
[41] ibid., Vol. XVIII, p. 676.

it came later to be called) was a school and nothing more. Until that date, however, ministerial candidates had been trained under the same roof—twenty of them to one hundred and twenty boys—for it was only in that year that the Primitive Methodist Conference decided to open a separate ministerial training college at Sunderland.

Meanwhile Irish Wesleyan Methodism had also been making a contribution to secondary education. In 1844 a deputation from Northern Ireland asked permission of the Irish Methodist Conference to proceed with a scheme for opening a secondary school in Belfast. The proposal was warmly welcomed, so warmly that it was further suggested that the school should be situated at Dublin where it could better serve the needs of Irish Methodism. After much discussion this suggestion was adopted and a Company was formed to establish a school on the lines of those recently established at Sheffield and Taunton. On 1st October 1845 the 'Wesleyan Commercial and Classical School' opened with three boarders and nine day-boys, though soon it was filled to its capacity of forty boarders and forty day-boys. This was one of the schools to which George Bernard Shaw was sent as a pupil (in 1867) and where he usually occupied a place near the bottom of the Form, though on one occasion he showed an unexpected knowledge of Scripture and rose temporarily to second place. During most of his time there, however, as he recalls, 'I instinctively saved my brains from destruction by resolute idleness, which, moreover, made school meaningless and tedious to me'.[42] One of the masters there did impress him—the elocution master, Alexander Bell, who was 'by far the most majestic and imposing-looking man that ever lived on this or any other planet'.[43] This was the school which is known today as Wesley College, Dublin, occupying premises to which it moved in 1879.

This school served a useful purpose, but it was not enough for Irish Methodism, and from 1855 onward there was agitation for something more ambitious. In that year a Fund for the increase of Methodist Agency in Ireland was launched, and one of its chief lay supporters was William McArthur, a wool merchant who later became Lord Mayor of London. Son of a Methodist preacher, he knew the difficulties of those who wanted higher education and could not get it, and he wanted to get most of

[42] Archibald Henderson, *Bernard Shaw* (New York 1932), p. 13.
[43] ibid., p. 119.

the Fund devoted to the foundation of a central educational institution, in which sons of ministers and laymen should be trained together, for he saw serious dangers in segregating them, as was done at Kingswood and Woodhouse Grove. The various projects connected with the Fund languished, however, until 1863, when a group of Methodist business men, led by William McArthur, took action.

There had been, especially in Northern Ireland, a quick and considerable commercial expansion, and many of those responsible for this were Methodists—wealthy men, who wanted to give their sons and other children a better education than they themselves had been able to get. They also wanted to see Methodism spreading its influence through the intellect as well as through the heart. A school, or schools, in direct connexion with Methodism was considered essential, and they resolved to found such a school, one which should be modelled on the best of the re-formed English public schools, open to any who wished to send their sons there. From the first the Irish Methodist Conference did all it could to help, and ministers and laymen worked in complete unanimity, a fact which no doubt explains the success of the venture, for it soon became an ambitious one. A Committee was set up with the avowed intention of making a real contribution to Irish education while at the same time assisting Methodism. Early in the discussions the example already set in England was followed, in that part of the school's function was to be the training of potential ministers. This, it was hoped, would also help to produce a religious atmosphere in the school. The scheme was in fact not unlike that adopted by the Roman Catholics in their residential schools.[44]

But the Irish Methodists went farther. Dissatisfied with the strictly secular Queen's College founded by Sir Robert Peel, they resolved to set up a University Department, following the tradition of John Wesley and his 'academic course' at Kingswood. Land was bought in Belfast, and in 1864 the Committee laid its proposals before the Irish Conference, for the setting-up of a secondary school for boys of any denomination, a hostel for students preparing to graduate at the Queen's College or at any other approved College, and a training department for potential Methodist ministers.[45]

[44] See A. S. Barnes, *The Catholic Schools of England*; John Gerard, *Stonyhurst College* (1894); H. N. Birt, *Downside* (1902); C. Almond, *History of Ampleforth Abbey*.
[45] See *The Watchman* for 19th June 1870, p. 22.

No sooner had the foundations been laid than the Committee encountered the difficulties that had beset every Methodist educational undertaking—those of finance. The story of the struggle for funds, a struggle which was carried out of Ireland to England and America, is a long and intricate one which need not concern us here, but amongst those who came to the rescue were English Methodists. In 1866 the whole of the Irish contribution to the Wesleyan Missionary Society Jubilee Fund was allocated to the school, thanks to the interest of the Rev. William Arthur, the Society's General Secretary. From what has already been said of this minister it will be evident how whole-hearted was his support of this project for higher education in Ireland. He was an Irishman himself, but apart from that it was a project after his own heart. When the school was officially opened on 18th August 1868 he was appointed its first Principal.

Three schools is a small contribution to higher education during the course of twenty-five years, but, though the actual achievements were small, the increased interest in education was real and was soon to show itself in solid achievement. Nor was Methodism alone in her apparent failure in higher education. Material advance on the national level was lacking at that time, though the latter part of the period saw the seeds of future advance sown in a number of Royal Commissions. These were appointed, not by a Government anxious to be original, but by one which reflected the demands of the electorate. They were the result of the increased interest in education of which some trends have been traced in this chapter. There were many different standards—of living, of wealth, of culture—but there was a general demand for education. In 1850, a Royal Commission was appointed to inquire into affairs at Oxford and Cambridge. This was largely due to Nonconformist power. For more than twenty years the Nonconformists had been keeping a watchful eye on the universities, representing as they did the prejudices and traditions of the Church of England. No doubt a certain amount of envy mingled with the watchfulness. Wesley's sorrowful realization of the position of Methodists at Oxford has been noticed. Petitions had been sent to Parliament praying that Nonconformists might be admitted to the older universities, and some of the signatories were themselves members of the universities—heads of colleges, professors, and tutors. The spirit of these petitions is typified in the following words taken from one of them and written in Cambridge in 1834: 'Your petitioners conscientiously believe that if the prayer of this petition be granted, the great advantages of good academic education might be extended to many excellent men who are now for conscience' sake debarred from a full participation in them, though true friends to the institutions of the country.' [46]

The growing power of Nonconformity lay in its Liberalism, but Wesleyan Methodism, ever since the time of John Wesley, had been a stronghold of Toryism.[47] The last words of the quotation above suggest that the petitioners were thinking primarily of the Wesleyan Methodist section of Nonconformity, for not all Nonconformists were 'friends to the institutions of the country'. The Wesleyans, especially during the first half of the century, were. They had shown themselves no friends to the Luddites; the Chartist movement had been condemned by them; even after the 'Peterloo Massacre' their sympathies had appeared to be with the Government.[48] while in 1833 a Methodist Journal, *The Christian Advocate,* had been severely censured by the Wesleyan Methodist Conference because its views were considered too Liberal. Official Wesleyan Methodism, following the example of its founder, supported the Government in spite of its sometimes glaring shortcomings, and was suspicious of reformers, especially of political reformers. She did, simply because of her Tory leanings, look forward to a time when the ancient traditions (by then often grown into prejudices) of Oxford and Cambridge might be broken down or amended so that she might re-enter. 'Methodism, it is true, was born and cradled in a university, but she soon left her native place, and it took a very long time to get her back again.' [49]

But she did come back again, and one of Kingswood's claims to greatness has been the number of Fellowships at Oxford and Cambridge obtained in the last seventy years by Old Boys. Only a few years before the words quoted above were spoken at the centenary remembrance of John Wesley's death there were among one single generation of pupils at the school eight future Fellows of Cambridge Colleges.[50] The appointment of the Royal Commission in 1850 was the beginning of Methodism's re-entry into the older universities.

[46] *Quarterly Journal of Education* (1834), Vol. VII, p. 370.
[47] Though from the Conference of 1848 onward the Tory autocracy began to be challenged.
[48] Thomas P. Bunting, *Life of Jabez Bunting,* pp. 526–9.
[49] T. G. Osborn, in *Wesley: The Man, his Teaching, and his Work,* p. 251.
[50] E. E. Kellett, *As I remember,* p. 263.

Between 1858 and 1861, another Royal Commission was inquiring, under the Chairmanship of the Duke of Newcastle, into the state of popular education in this country, and considering the measures needed to extend primary education to all classes of the people. This was followed in 1861 by a Royal Commission under the chairmanship of the Earl of Clarendon to inquire into public school education. Finally, that section of education which had been more neglected than any other, because the class which mainly supported it was comparatively new, was covered by the Schools Inquiry Commission, appointed in 1864 under the chairmanship of Lord Taunton, to consider schools which had not been dealt with by the two earlier Commissions —the secondary grammar schools of the country. Since the *Report* of this Commission affected Methodist secondary education closely, further reference will be made to it later. First, however, it is necessary to consider a peculiarity of Methodist secondary schools—a peculiarity which was also reflected in the Woodard Schools.

CHAPTER ELEVEN

A Peculiarity of Methodist Secondary Schools

A S ONE READS the records of Methodist secondary schools in the nineteenth century one is sometimes confused by the constant use of the words 'Governor' and 'Head Master' applied to the chief officers of each school—applied to two men whose duties appear sometimes to be synonymous, sometimes to overlap in certain particulars, but never to be clear cut. This dual control is a feature of nineteenth-century Methodist secondary education.

Writing his *Report* for the Schools Inquiry Commission and dealing with Wesley College, Elmfield, and Woodhouse Grove, J. G. Fitch, one of the assistant Commissioners, wrote: 'The moral discipline in these schools has exercised considerable influence on their organization. There is in each of them a head master, usually a graduate, who takes the entire responsibility of the school teaching. But above him there is, generally, a governor or superintendent, who takes the oversight of the establishment as a whole. In the Wesleyan and Primitive Methodist schools, this arrangement seems always to prevail, and it exists in a modified degree in the institutions of the Friends and Moravians. The governor is generally a minister of mature years, chosen rather for the weight of his moral influence than for his scholarship. Yet he is supreme over the school as well as over the household, and appeals may be made to him from the plans and decisions of the head master.' [1]

This dual control was not confined to Methodism, as this quotation shows. Nor indeed was it confined to Nonconformity. At the foundation of Cheltenham College in 1841 the Rev. Francis Close was rector of the parish which he had made a centre of evangelicalism, and he was responsible for the separation of the moral and intellectual aspects of education at the school, employing separate masters for each. Nathaniel Woodard, too, kept separate the moral and intellectual aspects in his schools, entrusting their direction to different persons. In all these schools, initially, the founders looked to one end: the saving of souls for God. Their denominational founders feared

[1] *Report of the Schools Inquiry Commission*, Vol. IX, p. 241.

lest the purely academic side of education, conducted in the main by laymen, should overshadow the religious side until education found no place for religion. They failed to realize that in their very actions to prevent it they were tending to draw a line of cleavage between education and religion—the very thing which Wesley had wished to avoid. Mere organization in a school is not enough. Personal influence is needed to take the place of parental influence at home. They realized that and they appointed an elderly man to give that personal and religious influence, but what they did not realize was that a boy cannot serve two masters. On the whole there might tend to be a compromise, but from time to time circumstances inevitably arose when pupils came near to loving one and hating the other. Dual control, however excellent in theory, was not easily workable in practice, yet Methodism, able as it proved itself in organization, maintained the system for the greater part of the nineteenth century. The reason lay in the fact that it helped to preserve Wesley's educational principles.

John Wesley required a high standard of character in his assistants, and in selecting masters for his school at Kingswood he tells us that although he was fortunate in having a wide knowledge of people in all parts of the country he yet had difficulty in finding teachers who reached the required standard. That is not surprising. There was no means of training the teachers who, to meet Wesley's demands, had to have 'learning sufficient for their several departments . . . and a fear of God, producing an unblamable conversation', and who had to be 'men who were truly devoted to God; who sought nothing on earth, neither pleasure, nor ease, nor profit, nor the praise of men'.[2] What he required was, in fact, a separate order of Methodists pledged to the sacrifice of themselves to God and teaching. Mention has already been made of Wesley's conception of a school as a family, and he wanted the head master —the classical master as he was in Wesley's day—to act as the father of that family. But Wesley never found such a master, and in spite of the scarcity and the brevity of his visits to the school it was Wesley himself who came to be regarded as the father of the family there.

In the early days the classical master was a travelling preacher. In other words, he was equivalent to an ordained minister to-day; a preacher first, a teacher second. But toward the end of

[2] *Works*, Vol. XIII, p. 259.

Wesley's lifetime the staff were appointed primarily as teachers and a man who had any intention of entering the ministry was not appointed. This made for the success of the school as a school, but one can understand how anxious Wesley and other preachers were to keep a watchful eye on the religious life of the school, since the object of its foundation was the provision of education in which religion played a dominant part. While Wesley was alive he could keep an eye on affairs, and because he did so and acted himself as 'father of the family' records were kept in his mind rather than on paper, and the organization of the staff was not clearly defined, frequent changes having to be made to meet new circumstances. The classical master was only a head master in theory. Thomas Simpson, who was appointed to that position in 1770, could not even receive a new pupil without Wesley's permission.[3] Thomas McGeary who followed in 1783 was the first to be in fact a head master, and this was due to the combined fact that Wesley was growing too old to keep such autocratic control as he had previously done and that McGeary was a man of exceptional character and ability. This was the man who was in charge at Kingswood School when Wesley died, and for four years there is no evidence of any minister being directly connected with the school.

Mention of the title 'Governor' was first made in 1795 when the Rev. Joseph Bradford went to live at the school. In an obituary notice of the Rev. Robert Wood who was a pupil there from 1796 to 1802 there is a description of the school and of the man who had charge of it:

'The establishment at that time consisted of a minister and his wife, two masters, two maid-servants, one man-servant, and about thirty scholars. It was under the wholesome rule of the Rev. Joseph Bradford. Scorning the idea of making fine gentlemen of his pupils, and knowing that most of them would have to "rough it" in their future career, Mr. Bradford endeavoured to prepare them for the encounter of life. Mr. Wood was accustomed to relate with pleasantness the impressions made on his boyish imagination by the tall, gaunt figure of the "governor" as he stalked into the dormitory. One stroke on the ground with his oaken staff was expected to rouse the youthful sleepers. Then, with his watch in his hand, he counted three minutes, at the end of which their simple toilet was to be completed. Another

[3] J. B. B. Clarke, *An account of the Infancy, Religious and Literary Life of Adam Clarke* (1833), pp. 136–7.

signal was then made for them to kneel down to their morning devotions. After this their ablutions were performed in a long, low gallery, open on one side to the air, which, as they rose at five in summer and six in winter, was chilly enough. Their diet and studies were regulated with the same uncompromising strictness.'[4]

That is the first mention of a governor, and at that time the duties appear to have been synonymous with those of head master.

A few years later a layman was appointed classical master, and though he tried to combine the duties of schoolmaster and pastor to his pupils he does not seem to have been successful. At any rate, his attempt was suspect by the Conference, for in 1808 when the President of the Conference, the Rev. James Wood, was reappointed to the Superintendency of the Kingswood Circuit a note was added to the list of 'stations': 'The Conference consider the appointment of their President a third year for this circuit as highly expedient for the interests of Kingswood School —so expedient as to be considered an exempt case, and sufficient to justify their deviation from their important law in respect of the two years' station.'[5] In the following year, a house adjoining the school was rented as quarters for the Kingswood Circuit minister. Conference had made it clear that it wished to keep direct control of the school, and henceforth, instead of a schoolmaster combining lay and ministerial duties, a minister, in co-operation with the classical master, was to combine the duties of circuit superintendent and school pastor. The duties of the latter appear quickly to have become extended, for in the same year we learn that he was expected to superintend the provisioning of the school and a large vegetable garden was provided for his use!

In 1812 the new Woodhouse Grove School was founded, and after the experiences, often unhappy, of administration at Kingswood School it is surprising to find that the first head master was a layman and that no minister was specially appointed to look after the school. This gentleman did not survive long as head master, as has already been shown, and in 1813 we have the first clear evidence of the appointment of a governor and a separate classical master at each school. 'It is the unanimous opinion of the Committee that a preacher and his wife be

[4] Quoted in *The History of Kingswood School*, pp. 84-5.
[5] ibid., p. 118.

stationed over this school, and to be Governor and Governess of this institution.' [6] Those words applied to Kingswood School, but the same principle was applied to Woodhouse Grove, for in that same year the Rev. James Wood was appointed governor there. This was the start of dual control in Methodist secondary schools, a form of control which was to last for the greater part of the nineteenth century. The governor was always an ordained Methodist minister appointed by Conference and he was responsible for religious instruction and pastoral oversight. He was the supreme executive authority out of school and for all matters not specifically under the head master's direction. The head master could be a layman and was selected by the school committee of management. He was responsible for the choice of books, method of teaching, arrangement of classes, and general educational management of the school. He was, in fact, the executive authority in school hours.

That was the theory. In practice, the duties overlapped, and the co-ordination which was essential was often lacking. A particularly unfortunate example of this was seen at Wesley College, Sheffield, but otherwise the worst examples of friction occurred in the two Connexional schools of Kingswood and Woodhouse Grove.

John Wesley, in practising his theory of education centred in religion, had made many mistakes, but he was an educationist and he was a practical man. His followers were often neither, and far too many of them after Wesley's death neglected education altogether. When schools were founded and when the official notice of Conference, as the representative authority of Methodism, was called to them, the only way in which the place of religion in the education could be ensured by Conference was by appointing a minister to the pastoral oversight of the school —a minister whose duties had no connexion with normal school work. Unfortunately, in doing this, Conference did the very thing which Wesley had wished to avoid: it separated education into two distinct departments. It is true that the experiment of having one man at the head of all the school's administration had been tried and had proved a failure (William Wragge at Kingswood, 1807–9, and Thomas Fennell at Woodhouse Grove, 1812–13), but perseverance and a more careful selection of the men appointed would have achieved a better result.

In these days we remark with surprise the appointment of a

man in his twenties to a headmastership, but during the nineteenth century many of the head masters, especially of Kingswood School, were extremely young. For example, Mr. Horner was nineteen when he was appointed; Mr. Lomas twenty; Mr. Shaw twenty-three; Mr. Griffith twenty-one; Mr. Osborn twenty-three; Mr. Workman twenty-five; Mr. Shera twenty-eight; and Mr. Crowther twenty-one. In most cases it seems that these head masters were chosen young intentionally in order that the greater age of the governor should combat any tendency on the part of the head master to control the governor. Such a view, however, shows a complete misunderstanding of psychology. The responsibilities of the head master were not light, and a young man willing and able to undertake them would find the presence of an older man, one of whose duties was the keeping of a watchful eye on affairs generally, more than irksome. No man can achieve his best under such circumstances, and the worst examples of friction naturally arose when men of real ability and strong personality held the respective posts.

At Kingswood in 1836 the Rev. Robert Smith, who had been governor since 1820, met with an accident and the head master, Samuel Griffith, naturally undertook the duties which would normally have been performed by the governor. This did not meet with approval and led to strained relations between the governor when he returned, the staff, and the school committee. Two years later discord had reached such a pitch that a committee of inquiry was appointed. Samuel Griffith was a man of considerable personality who had, as it were, grown up with the school. Educated there, he became usher in 1832 at the age of fourteen and then successively writing master and second master within the space of five years. He was only twenty-one when he was appointed head master, and during the course of his career in that office he appears gradually to have gained power in the organization and administration of the school while the governor lost it. One wonders whether the fact that he became the governor's son-in-law had anything to do with this! Until this period the governor was responsible to the committee of management for school requisitions, but in April 1838 the head master (who was not a member of the committee though the governor was) managed to insert the thin end of a wedge and obtain permission to buy maps. A little later he was also authorized to buy prizes. Small, petty matters these, but they were evidence of changing views. The head master was becoming more and more responsible for purely academic affairs and school equipment. In 1841 the committee tried to secure better co-ordination between governor and head master by stating that 'the head master is considered to be responsible for the discipline during school hours and should he find any difficulty his appeal shall be made to the governor'. Obviously this would not help matters: it merely told the head master that he was subservient to the governor. Two years later the 'Rules for Internal Management' at Kingswood were drawn up and a note was added to the effect that they were not to be taken as altering any previous instruction concerning the powers and duties of the governor out of school or of the head master in school.

Another dispute arose in 1844 concerning religious instruction. Both the governor and the head master wished it to be given, but trouble started over the amount of time to be set aside for it. The head master felt that it would be sufficient if the Catechism was taught only on Sundays; the governor wished the Catechism and other specified devotional books to be included in the curriculum of ordinary school work. The school committee, as usual, supported the governor and ruled that the head master was to meet the boys on a Sunday if the governor was away and was also to include religious instruction in the ordinary school curriculum. To placate an evidently irate head master, they added, however, that the governor was to consult the head master before granting holidays. 'The governor', they concluded, 'must be upheld in the exercise of his supreme and undoubted authority.'[7] It is scarcely surprising to learn that the head master shortly afterwards resigned—and opened a private school at Westbury-on-Trym, near Bristol.

Lord Taunton, the chairman of the Schools Inquiry Commission, showed special interest in the relationships between governor and head master, and between both and the school. Questioned by Lord Taunton himself, Thomas Sibly, then head master of Queen's College, Taunton, said that the functions of a governor were to provide for the pupils, 'in fact,' he said, 'to act as the father of the family'. He controlled the provision of food and had the general oversight of pupils out of school, particularly looking after their spiritual welfare and religious discipline. The head master was more particularly responsible for the discipline during school hours, though even during

[7] Quoted in *The History of Kingswood School*, p. 131.

those hours the governor was responsible for the school as a whole.[8]

Obviously, a considerable amount of friction might arise between the two. The friction that did occur was not confined to Methodist schools. The first head master of the Woodard foundation, Shoreham Grammar School, resigned after only one term because of the 'undue prominence' of the man responsible for the moral and religious training of the boys. Later, the head master of Lancing resigned for a similar reason. But Woodard, like the Methodist authorities, attached so much importance to the principle of dual control that he retained it as long as he lived.

From time to time, Methodism tried to ease the position, though until late in the century no general proposal was made for the abolition of dual control. As a result of serious differences between governor and head master in the 1850's, a Committee of Inquiry was appointed to review past difficulties and to draw up a statement clarifying the governor's position. When it appeared, however, the statement did nothing to ease the position: 'The selection, appointment, and powers of the governor are regulated by these principles, viz. that, having regard to the weighty and paramount considerations of religion, morals, and humanity, the Conference seeks a minister of such character and qualifications as will admit of his being entrusted with *large general powers*; that a minister so appointed is in a peculiar manner and degree placed *in loco parentis* . . . and he ought to be in a position to promote reasonable wishes and to redress grievances. He is *not* expected personally *to do the teaching*; but he *is* expected to be eyes and ears for the parents and the Conference, and must therefore be understood to have a general right of inspection and oversight in all departments of the institution. . . . It has, so long ago as 1844, been judged needful [to declare that] "the governor must be upheld in the exercise of his supreme and undoubted authority". The sub-committee understands this clause comprehensively as foreclosing any pretension on the part of the head master to equal or co-ordinate authority.'[9]

On the publication of such a statement, in which the governor was stated, *inter alia,* to be a Connexional spy, the head master

[8] A verbatim record of the evidence of Thomas Sibly is given in the *Report of the Schools Inquiry Commission*, Vol. V, pp. 337–45.
[9] Quoted in *The History of Kingswood School*, p. 252.

not unnaturally appealed to Conference. That body upheld the committee. The governor (and not the head master) resigned.

The head master was always in a weak position, for the governor was appointed by Conference while the head master was appointed by the School Committee of which the governor was a member. On the other hand, the governor, though he was a member of the committee, was not answerable to it: he was only answerable to Conference. On paper, therefore, he was the real power of the school. But schools do not work to paper designs. The pupils themselves exercise more power than is often credited to them. A school in which the staff as a whole is genuinely respected is very different from one in which that is not the case, as any chance visitor to the school can appreciate. Boys quickly discover whether there is any member of the staff whom they cannot respect. It should be noted, though, that a person whom they do not respect is not necessarily one whom they do not like. They can dislike a person most intensely and yet respect him. Once the spirit of alliance—or otherwise— between boys and staff is roused, it acts in the form of a circle and other elements are absorbed only slowly. Herein the head master usually had an advantage over the governor. The former saw the boys many times every day, and they came in most cases during the nineteenth century to respect him. There are few greater loyalties than those between pupil and master when there is genuine respect. Thus it sometimes happened in a tussle between head master and governor (of which pupils in a boarding-school would become conscious in a very short time) that the boys wholeheartedly supported the head master, whatever might have been laid down on paper by Conference or the School Committee.

These were the thoughts in the mind of S. D. Waddy, who could rightly claim to be an authority on the matter, when in 1858 Kingswood was about to have a new governor. He gave his views on what was required of a governor in these words: 'Unless the governor have some pretensions to learning, and can stand a very decent comparison with the boys and with the masters, and even with the head master, the idea that he will ever be able to secure and maintain authority is perfectly ridiculous. He can only maintain his position by one of two alternatives, either of which is lamentable—by a sort of old womanish kindness to the boys and masters, which makes his position one of mere toleration; or by an amount of severity, which cannot be justified on any principle whatever. I mean this: the power and ability to interfere with the head master will save the necessity for such interference. The governor should be able to sit during your examinations and detect common inaccuracies either in classics or in any other department of education. He should not sit there as a mere automaton; but it should be seen and felt by the boys that he understands what is going on.' [10]

In 1875 Conference adopted the Scheme for the Management of Kingswood and Woodhouse Grove Schools as one. In the scheme were several references to the governor and head master but none of them showed any advance on the circumstances which had caused difficulty throughout the century. The governor was held responsible for religious instruction and over-sight of the school. It was this last phrase that had caused the difficulties throughout, yet no further attempt was made to define exactly what 'oversight' entailed, apart from the fact that it included superintendence of the domestic affairs of the school. The head master controlled, as before, the choice of books, methods of teaching, arrangement of classes, entrance examinations, and the educational management of the school. Here, obviously, 'educational' was considered in its narrowest sense— the very thing which Wesley had wished to avoid. The head master, subject to the Committee of Management, was the supreme executive authority in respect of school duties and discipline in school hours; the governor in all other respects. Expulsion had to be approved by both governor and head master, as also did the appointment and dismissal of assistant masters. The governor and head master had to submit separate reports annually on the general condition of the school.

In the face of so many difficulties arising directly from dual control it is strange at first sight that all the Methodist secondary schools founded before 1870 adopted this form of control. As we have seen, Wesley College, Sheffield, insisted on the appointment of a governor, one who should be not merely a chaplain but a supreme authority. In fact, when it was decided in 1888 that the post of governor should be discontinued at that school both the governor and the head master resigned. At Queen's College, Taunton, it was required that there should be a minister appointed governor to take charge of domestic, moral, and religious affairs. The same principle was applied at the opening of

[10] Quoted in *The History of Kingswood School*, pp. 252-3.

Belfast Methodist College in 1868 when the Rev. William Arthur was released by the Missionary Society to become its first principal, which was only another name for governor.

It is interesting to note that dual control appeared independently in the schools of the other (non-Wesleyan) Methodist Connexions. In the case of Shebbear College, for example, there is no reason to suppose that there was conscious imitation of the plan adopted in the Wesleyan Methodist schools. Dual control was established there because it seemed the only way of saving the school, and the importance attached to the post can be judged from the fact that when the Bible Christian Conference agreed in 1844 to make themselves responsible for the school it felt it necessary to appoint one of its foremost personalities to the work—the Rev. James Thorne. From that time until Thomas Ruddle was firmly established as head master, James Thorne was the real power at the school, though he had no part in the affairs of the schoolroom. At the school he represented Conference, at Conference he represented the school and acted as adviser in matters concerning it. Such was his personality and grip on affairs that he, under the title of 'secretary' (yet another name for 'governor') was a far more important person than the head master. By the time he retired in 1870 Ruddle was firmly established and thenceforward it was the head master and not the secretary who was the real power. But dual control continued, and it worked more or less smoothly according to the respective personalities of the men in charge of the school. In fact, the system worked more smoothly at this school than at any other, and continued for longer—until the retirement of the Rev. Richard Pyke from the secretaryship in 1922.

The Primitive Methodist Connexion also adopted the system of dual control when Elmfield College was founded in 1864, a resident governor who was a minister being appointed by the Conference to have general supervision of the whole school, subject only to the Committee of Management, of which he was a member, and which was appointed by Conference.

Today the dual system of school government no longer exists in any Methodist school, the religious life being supervised either by a chaplain appointed by Conference (an arrangement first proposed by the Rev. John Scott in 1838) or by the local circuit minister. It is significant that at the foundation of The Leys School no governor was appointed, though the head masters of that school until 1934 were Methodist ministers. In the nineteenth century, however, dual control was the normal practice, and its effect should not be minimized. It typified the close relationship between religion and education, it carried on the tradition of strict Methodist principles which John Wesley had taught, and thus was instrumental in enabling Methodism to make a peculiar contribution to secondary education. For this reason a separate chapter has been devoted to the matter. No attempt has been made to gloss over the difficulties or the imperfections of this form of government. In fact, the difficulties have been stressed, but outweighing them was the fact that through it Methodism maintained close contact with its schools and passed on through them something of its evangelical spirit by which pupils were led to see the central place of religion in life. It is no accident that so many former pupils of the schools in which dual government was practised entered what might be called 'social service' professions. For example, out of approximately 2,600 former pupils of Kingswood and Woodhouse Grove Schools in the nineteenth century, 607 became ministers or clerks in holy orders, 243 entered the medical profession, and 271 became schoolmasters. The governor (early in the century nicknamed 'Daddy') was the outward and visible sign of the father of the school family, and when the right man held the post he was more than a mere figurehead: he represented the union between religion and education. The dual system, with all its shortcomings, did more than any other single feature of the organization of Methodist secondary education to keep the schools in close touch with the Connexion and to perpetuate Wesley's family spirit.

CHAPTER TWELVE

The Schools Inquiry Commission and Methodism

'THERE IS NOT (with the exception of some schools for the
military and naval services) a single school in England above
the class of paupers over which the State actually exercises full
control. A few are under the control of the municipal authorities
of a borough. The rest are under private individuals or private
companies, or special ecclesiastical or eleemosynary corporations,
or bodies of practically irresponsible trustees. There is no public
inspector to investigate the educational condition of a school by
direct examination of the scholars, no public board to give advice
on educational difficulties, no public rewards given directly to
promote educational progress, except those distributed by the
Science and Art Department, hardly a single mastership in the
gift of the Crown, not a single payment from the central Government to the support of a secondary school, not a single certificate
of capacity for teaching given by public authority professedly to
teachers in schools, above the primary schools. In any of these
senses there is no public school and no public education for the
middle and upper classes. If direct pecuniary assistance is not
required, the State offers nothing. It might give test, stimulus,
advice, dignity: it withholds them all, and leaves the endowed
schools to the cramping assistance of judicial decisions, which
may be quite right as regards the interpretation of the founder's
words and quite wrong as regards the wise administration of the
schools they founded.' [1]

That is part of the *Report* of the Commission appointed in
1864 to inquire into the education given in schools not already
investigated by the Clarendon (Public Schools) or Newcastle
(Primary Schools) Commissions, and to make recommendations
for its improvement. It shows clearly the confusion that existed.
Assistant Commissioners were appointed to inquire into the
details of secondary education, not only in this country, but also
in Wales, Scotland, France, Germany, Switzerland, Holland,
Italy, Canada, and the United States of America for purposes of

[1] *Report of the Schools Inquiry Commission*, Vol. I, p. 107. This Commission is variously described as 'The Schools Inquiry Commission', 'The
Endowed Schools Commission', and 'The Taunton Commission'.

comparison. The scope was vast and to simplify the inquiry English secondary schools were divided into three classes— Endowed, Private, and Proprietary. The latter [2] were found to combine to a certain extent the character of Endowed and Private schools.

'They resemble private schools in owing their origin to private enterprise, in their consequent attempt to adapt themselves to the needs of the day, in their tendency to rest on social distinctions. They resemble endowed schools in providing some security that the master shall be fit for his duties, and in the general character of their management. To this may be added that in the end they generally pass into one of the other two classes. Those which do not succeed under proprietary management are generally sold and become private schools; those which are successful enough to become permanent end with being devoted irrevocably by deed to the purposes of education, and are thus transferred to the rank of endowed schools.' [3]

These proprietary schools were of comparatively recent origin, their history normally extending over a period of not more than forty years, and they owed their origin either to lack of schools of a more public character than private enterprise could supply, or to the desire of religious denominations to have a school in which religious instruction could be given in accordance with their views. Among such schools were Stonyhurst and Oscott (Roman Catholic); Wesley College, Sheffield; Queen's College, Taunton; and Woodhouse Grove School (Wesleyan Methodist); Taunton School, Silcoates, and Mill Hill (Congregational); Fulneck (Moravian); Ackworth, Bootham, and Tottenham (Quaker); Elmfield (Primitive Methodist); Finsbury and Palestine Place (Jewish). 'The history of these schools is in a great degree the history of recent struggles for the improvement of secondary schools', stated the *Report*.[4] This was due to the fact that such schools were not profit-making concerns: they were the outcome of religious zeal. They met a certain demand and the standard of their education was high, their curricula differing from that of grammar schools in that considerable attention was paid to English, geography, history, and science, while classics and mathe-

[2] For example, Cheltenham (1841), Marlborough (1843), Rossall (1844), Radley (1847), Wellington (1853), Epsom (1855), Haileybury (1862), Clifton (1862), and Malvern (1863).
[3] *Report of the Schools Inquiry Commission*, Vol. I, p. 310.
[4] Vol. I, p. 314.

matics were merely regarded as a groundwork for mental training instead of the whole content of education.

The inquiry took three years to complete, but by the end of 1867 a survey of secondary education had been made which was wider than any previous one. It was found that the distribution of secondary schools in this country was inadequate, especially in the more populous areas of the north; there was no clear conception of the purpose of secondary education, some educationists believing that their schools should supply a liberal education based on the classics,[5] others that they should provide still wider scope based on the humanitarian principles practised in the Prussian gymnasia since the time of William von Humboldt; there was no adequate attempt to deal with the groups of pupils who left their schools at different ages; few schools used the university examinations which had been available since 1858; still fewer schools sent pupils to the universities; private schools were usually 'lamentably unsatisfactory'; teaching was bad everywhere, and there was an entire absence of standards.

As a starting-point for its recommendations, the Commission divided all secondary schools into three grades:

First Grade: Schools whose pupils left at the age of eighteen or nineteen, to pass to the universities.

Second Grade: Schools whose pupils left at the age of sixteen or seventeen to enter the army, the professions, or the Civil Service.

Third Grade: Schools whose pupils left at fourteen or fifteen after receiving an education fitting them for 'small tenant farmers, small tradesmen, and superior artisans'.

It was with the second-grade schools that the increasingly wealthy and powerful middle classes were chiefly concerned, and by many of this class the third-grade schools were considered inferior. It must have come as a shock to some of the Methodists when they realized that the leaving-age of fourteen at Kingswood and Woodhouse Grove Schools caused these two to be classed as third grade.

The Commissioners had some comment to make on religious instruction which brought satisfaction to Nonconformist readers of their *Report*, though at the same time it showed the need for continued vigilance. Religious instruction was considered essen-

[5] As portrayed by Joseph Priestley in his *Course of Liberal Education for Civil and Active Life* (1765), by Vicessimus Knox in his *Liberal Education* (1789), and by F. W. Farrar in his *Essays on Liberal Education* (1867). See also the *Spens Report on Secondary Education* (1938), Appendix II, pp. 403 ff.

tial in giving 'a higher tone and character to the whole of school life', and in presenting 'education both to parents and to boys in its only true light'.[6] The inevitable question arose: Who was to give this religious instruction? The Commissioners gave a vague answer but it satisfied Methodism for the time: Parents were to be allowed to withdraw their children from periods of religious instruction if they wished.

The Report recommended:

1. The organization of a system of education graded according to the age at which pupils left school.

2. The establishment of a central authority to administer the system, presided over by a Minister of Education. Amongst the duties of this authority would be the consideration of schemes for the reorganization of educational endowments; the appointment of inspectors; the auditing of accounts; and the allocation of doubtful endowments.

3. The division of the country into provinces for the purpose of administration. Towns of over 100,000 inhabitants would have their own secondary-school boards.

4. The establishment of an examining body.

5. The introduction of natural science into all schools.

One can find little to criticize in these recommendations. Sound as they appear today, however, they were too far-reaching for the 1860's and English education had to wait until this twentieth century to see most of them realized in practice. For the reasons given in preceding pages, Methodism was keenly interested. The few secondary schools it possessed had for the first time, and in common with other Nonconformist schools, come under independent review. But more important than review was the future. A 'system' of education such as that recommended would produce all the discussion and high feeling over denominationalism which had been called forth by the steps already taken in primary education. In that dispute the Wesleyan Methodists had been able to point to the schools they had established all over the country to prove their interest. Such material facts carried more weight than merely theoretical arguments. But in the sphere of higher education there would be no such material facts. All that could be shown were four Connexional Schools and five proprietary schools. On the other hand, given the will to do it, it would not be overwhelmingly difficult to do for secondary education what Methodism had done

<hr>

[6] *Report of the Schools Inquiry Commission*, Vol. I, p. 43.

for primary education, and a small group of Methodists began their task of interesting fellow Methodists in such a scheme.

Dr. Rigg was one of the group. It is scarcely surprising that he was keenly interested in the recent *Report,* knowing as he did many of those responsible for drawing it up. He realized that, although Methodism was making a useful contribution to primary education, it was doing very little for higher education, and as principal of the Methodist teachers' training college he had practical reasons for regret. He agreed wholeheartedly with his friend William Arthur on the need for extending the training of Methodist schoolmasters, and he knew that that could not be done without secondary schools. But, unlike Arthur, he believed that Methodism alone could not supply the whole of the need. In his *Essays for the Times on Ecclesiastical and Social Subjects,*[7] published just before the appearance of the *Report of the Schools Inquiry Commission,* he had written:

'For ourselves, we are prepared to demand that the State go yet farther than it has done, and make some provision not only for elevating (as it is doing) the education of the working classes, but for defending the middle classes from that educational imposition which has, ever since there were middle classes, been commonly inflicted upon them. We do not wonder that the Irish are petitioning for middle-class schools, as a completing link to connect their National Schools and their Colleges. For England we should make no such demand. But we are prepared to require that Government should take means to encourage the formation of colleges, under its own inspection, for the training of masters for middle-class schools. Why should quackery in medicine be proscribed, but no means afforded of discriminating between quackery and science, plausible pretension and true art, in education?'

The Watchman, semi-official journal of Methodism, did what it could to help. On the publication of the *Report of the Schools Inquiry Commission* it reprinted extracts from it; it opened its columns liberally to correspondents anxious to rouse Methodism to its educational shortcomings. It was one of those correspondents, signing himself 'X. Y. Z.', who did much to sow the seeds which later grew into a Methodist secondary-school system. The writer was Henry French, mathematics master at Queen's College, Taunton.

One of the men responsible for the foundation of this school

[7] pp. 496-7.

in 1843 had been Henry French's father, whose son, Henry's brother, owing to the family's Nonconformist views, was refused admittance to the grammar school that had been founded in the town by Richard Fox, Bishop of Winchester, in the sixteenth century. Henry French never forgot that. He had himself experienced the difficulties of a Nonconformist undergraduate at Cambridge, for he had been at St. John's College when religious tests were still applied. He had remained loyal to his family's Church but as a result he had not been allowed his Degree, and he knew many young men who had not thus been able to remain loyal. In a series of letters to *The Watchman* he pointed out these facts in an attempt to arouse sufficient interest to enable Methodism to establish more institutions for its sons' higher education. He pointed out that Methodism was totally unprepared for the new order of higher education foreshadowed in the *Report of the Schools Inquiry Commission*. Although Conference had, on numerous occasions, affirmed the right and duty of Christian Churches to train in their own principles the children of their charge, it had scarcely extended its duty beyond Sunday- and primary-schools; it had failed utterly to appreciate its duty in relation to secondary education, and French quoted one of the questions put by Mr. Acland, one of the assistant Commissioners: 'Do you think that your Connexion (the Wesleyans) are not desirous to have facilities of entrance into the grammar schools different from those which they now have, or do you think they are content with the present state of things?' And the answer: 'I think they are content with the present state of things. I have never heard any complaints.' [8] French was not content, and he bitterly regretted that any Methodist witness had stated such a view.

The *Report* foreshadowed recognition of, and help for, schools other than Church of England schools, but, French pointed out, there could be no help for schools which did not exist, nor for schemes not properly drawn up. He then proceeded to lay down the first constructive scheme for a system of Methodist secondary schools, the points of which were as follows:

1. The appointment by the following Conference of a Secondary Education Committee to take charge of the whole matter.

2. The recognition of this Committee as an Education Authority by the Government when the time came for the recom-

mendations of the Schools Inquiry Commission to be put into action. The Commission had recommended that, as part of the necessary machinery for carrying out their suggested scheme for secondary education, as many 'Provincial Authorities' should be set up as there were Registrar-General's divisions in the country, i.e. eleven. Provision would be made, however, for the withdrawal of a County from the jurisdiction of such an Authority, for the formation of a County Board of its own. If this arrangement were made, then the proposed Methodist Secondary Education Committee would be able to make out a strong case for being considered an educational Authority to deal with all Methodist secondary schools, and to stand in the same relation to the Charity Commissioners as the existing Wesleyan Day-schools Committee stood to the Privy Council.

3. The institution of a system of Wesleyan middle-class or secondary schools of the various grades defined in the Schools Inquiry Commission's Report, i.e. Third-grade schools for the lower section of the middle classes (small shop-keepers, skilled artisans, and others). These would be established in all large towns. In addition there would be Second- and First-grade boarding-schools established in suitable places for the training of boys up to the age of sixteen and eighteen respectively.

4. The organization of these schools would possess a 'conscience clause' to make them acceptable to others besides Wesleyan Methodists. The existing Connexional, Proprietary, and Private Methodist schools would be associated with the other schools to be founded under the scheme.

5. The most promising of the boys in the 631 Wesleyan primary schools might be sent by means of Exhibitions to one of the secondary schools, and thence possibly to the university.

6. 'Should some of the Colleges at Oxford and Cambridge be assigned to us, these of course would form a highly important department of the arrangements here contemplated. From the schools they would receive their chief supply of students, and they would contribute in return Masters and Examiners.' [9]

Such a scheme, with its 'ladder' for the poor boy from the primary school to the university, does not deserve to have dropped into the oblivion from which it has been taken in this work. It contained bold proposals, made by a man who wanted to see something of the enterprise which had been shown by

[9] *The Watchman,* Vol. VI, p. 175.

Methodism in regard to primary education directed to higher education.

The Government, however, was as tardy in carrying out the recommendations of the Schools Inquiry Commission as was Methodism in taking to itself the practical working of a plan for higher education, and this tardiness on the part of the State was a contributory factor to the failure of Methodism to take action. As always, one of the considerations which deterred both Government and Methodism was that of finance. Henry French had not overlooked this, however, and in presenting his plan he had gone on to draw up proposals as to the manner in which it could be financed. Payment for the necessary land, premises, and equipment was to come from two main sources: (1) Connexional funds; (2) the State organization for higher education.

The Schools Inquiry Commission had recommended that existing secondary-school property and endowments should be redistributed by the central authority which was envisaged. Once a start had been made, the proposed Methodist Secondary Education Committee could claim its fair share. Since, however, the recommendations of the Commission were not carried out, this important source of income was not forthcoming.

The plea for secondary education evoked no response, therefore, but it did produce evidence of the widespread demand for such education in Methodism. It started a sequence of letters in *The Watchman* and further roused the Connexion to a realization of a serious danger. One minister pointed out that young people were asking: 'Is Methodism inconsistent with intelligence and culture, that the better class of young people are forsaking it?' [10]

It is impossible to say to what extent the youth of Methodism were being lost at that time, but at least the danger of such loss was present. Methodism counted among its members a number of wealthy men—men whose wives, if not they themselves, had a certain amount of ambition concerning the education of their children. They were self-made men, like William McArthur, who had done so much to found the Methodist College, Belfast, or those Sheffield business men who had been responsible for the opening of Wesley College. Their very Methodist upbringing made them desirous of giving their children the chances they never had. But there were only four boys' schools available for laymen and not one of them could vie with the public schools.

[10] *The Watchman*, Vol. VII, p. 69.

The result was that the sons of these wealthy men were sent to non-Methodist schools and they received an education which finished at Oxford or Cambridge where the obtaining of a Degree was dependent upon their acceptance of the Articles of the Church of England. As a result of the environment in which they had been placed they had enlarged the circle of their friends and had gained in social prestige (which meant much in those days). In due course they inherited their fathers' wealth or by their own efforts carved a career for themselves. But by that time they were often no longer Methodists. They might, out of gratitude and a certain sense of loyalty to their parents, help Methodism by gifts of money, they might attend an occasional Methodist service, but they were not Methodists. Forced, while still at school, to attend the services of a denomination other than their own (usually the Church of England), it is not surprising that this was so. They began to feel that Methodism was 'inferior'. It had always thus been regarded by the Church of England, but then began a similar feeling from within Methodism itself, and Methodism began to suffer from it—at the very time when the social boundaries were being extended. As another writer said: 'Is it not a painful sign of the small effect of Methodism upon the higher classes of English society, that of the Members of Parliament, there are only three who profess allegiance to it, that we have not a single person belonging to aristocratic position among us,[11] and that large numbers of the wealthy and influential people of the country, especially in the manufacturing districts, have forsaken our Church?'[12]

Eight months after writing the first of the 'X. Y. Z.' letters, French brought forward further evidence of the great need for something to be done about Methodist secondary education.[13] Again, he pointed out the serious disadvantages under which Methodism laboured through its lack of higher education. Its members were excluded from the public schools and from the older universities, unless temporarily or permanently, the would-be undergraduate became a Churchman and acknowledged the Articles of the Church of England. John Wesley himself had been educated at Charterhouse and thence had continued his education at Oxford. He had received a higher education but his followers could not. A religious denomination must have

[11] Henry Hartley Fowler did not become the first Viscount Wolverhampton till 1908.
[12] *The Watchman*, Vol. VI, p. 417.
[13] ibid., Vol. VI, p. 412.

leaders. It was a serious matter if those leaders, however highly gifted, could not attain to the highest learning and wisdom simply because of the lack of proper training in their youth. It was true that ministers' sons had Kingswood and Woodhouse Grove, and that for laymen's sons there were the schools at Sheffield and Taunton, but these four, together with the Bible Christian School at Shebbear and the Primitive Methodist School at York, were quite inadequate to provide higher education for the entire body of Methodists.

The deficiencies in Methodist higher education were recognized, but nothing was done about it. The following Conference (1869) passed without any reference being made to the matter at all. It seemed as though the statement made by one minister was in fact the truth: 'The preachers have excellent schools of their own, and perhaps this is one reason why the want of our more respectable people has not been attended to.' [14] The problem was a pressing one, and the Conference proved itself singularly short-sighted in not realizing, apparently, either its presence or its nature.

But, though Henry French's proposed scheme was not taken up officially at that time, interest in higher education was at last reaching the point of action, and this action occurred during the last thirty years of the century. Matthew Arnold's slogan, 'Organize your secondary schools', had been the theme of the Schools Inquiry Commission's recommendations, and Methodism too was beginning to take it seriously. The action which this new interest inspired was shown in three main directions: in the founding of a Methodist Public School; in the reorganization of Kingswood and Woodhouse Grove Schools; and in the foundation of a number of schools for the middle classes. These three subjects form the topics of the next chapters.

[14] *The Watchman,* Vol. VI, p. 417. See also Vol. VII, pp. 6, 24, 86–7.

CHAPTER THIRTEEN

The First Methodist Public School

FROM TIME TO TIME in the foregoing pages reference has been made to the public schools. This chapter deals with the type of education given in such schools, its effect on Methodism, and Methodism's own contribution to it. It is necessary therefore to make clear what was meant by the term 'public school' during the period with which this chapter especially deals (1860–80). The Commission, appointed in 1861 under the Chairmanship of Lord Clarendon to inquire into public-school education, recognized only nine schools as coming under its review: Charterhouse, Eton, Harrow, Merchant Taylors', St. Paul's, Rugby, Shrewsbury, Westminster, and Winchester. But even when the Commission was making its inquiries the term 'public school' was being applied to a wider range of schools which included many of the proprietary schools founded to meet a demand for a certain type of education and in imitation of the best features of schools which had recently been 'reformed' by men of personality and vision. Many of the old-established grammar schools were gaining a national reputation owing largely to the work of their head masters. With the better transport facilities which enabled parents to send their children from one end of the country to the other with comparative ease, many of these schools began to establish boarding-houses—or to re-establish them. All such schools sent a number of their pupils at the end of their school career to the older universities; all emphasized character-building rather than the mere acquisition of knowledge. There was in fact little to differentiate the schools of this type from one another, though there was an increasingly clear line of demarcation between them and the schools catering for the lower middle classes. There was, indeed, a form of training known as 'public-school education' being given in many more schools than those listed for review by the Clarendon Commission, and this was due entirely to the reforms which had taken place in the nine schools to which that Commission directed its attention.

Until toward the close of the eighteenth century these nine schools had been the training-ground of no one social class. The poet William Collins, a pupil at Winchester, was the son of a local hatter; William Carey, pupil and later (1803–14) head master of Westminster School, was the son of a Worcester trades- man; John Foster, head master of Eton (1765–73) and his suc- cessor, Jonathan Davies (1773–91) were both Old-Etonians, the former the son of a Windsor tradesman, the latter the son of a barber. But, with the growing industrialization of the country from the end of that century onward, there was a sharper cleavage between the social classes, and the public schools came to cater exclusively for the education of the gentry and nobility. The evils of these schools were, however, notorious, and they were brought before the public eye by the rapidly developing influence of the Press, which between 1753 and 1792 had more than doubled its circulation, and by the growing interest in education, especially among the thinkers and reformers of the day. *The Edinburgh Review,* pursuing its anti-Tory policy, was particularly scathing about the education given in these schools and in the universities, with Sidney Smith and Henry Brougham prominent as writers in the campaign. The curriculum in these schools was predominantly classical, English and French litera- ture and history being read only in leisure hours. Teaching was of a very low standard, organized games were unknown, supervision out of school non-existent, and accommodation bad. In fact, there was scarcely any good to be associated with them. On the other hand, it is only fair to remember that although John Wesley went to such a school—Charterhouse—at the age of ten and a half years, and came under the prevailing practice of fagging and bullying which deprived him of his fair share of food,[1] he has nothing but good to say of his schooldays.[2] This is the case also of his brother Charles who was a pupil at West- minster.

However, evils did exist. Then appeared the reformers. The first, and one of the two most outstanding, was Samuel Butler, who became head master of Shrewsbury when that school had reached its lowest ebb in 1798. Butler, inspired by a new and enlightened outlook on boy life, brought that school into the forefront of English education, and the keynote of his success and of his principles is perhaps best expressed by himself in a letter which he wrote to a parent in 1827: 'I cannot force them

---

[1] L. Tyerman, *The Life and Times of John Wesley,* Vol. I, p. 19; John Telford, *The Life of John Wesley,* pp. 26–7.
[2] *Journal,* Vol. V, p. 373.

all [i.e. pupils] to be first-rate scholars, because all have not the same capacity; but if I train them to be honourable and virtuous men, I am conferring a greater benefit upon themselves and on society than by all the learning I can give them.' [3]

Some writers on educational history have decried Arnold as the chief reformer of public-school education, but, as far as Methodism is concerned, Arnold is the man who must be considered as the most influential, simply because his views on higher education were so close to those of Methodist educationists who saw education becoming more than ever a monopoly of the Church of England. They respected the man but feared the results of his teaching on their own denomination. In the successes of Thomas Arnold, who made religion the very centre of education, Methodists saw the practical working of the views which Wesley had held, and their denominational fears were not allayed by the fact that Arnold's churchmanship looked toward a union between the Church of England and Nonconformity. Arnold believed that education should turn the boy into the man as quickly as possible, since only thus could his soul be saved, and it was the business of the schoolmaster to save the souls of sinful boys, to make them Christian gentlemen. [4] These views were spread abroad by a number of Arnold's disciples, many of whom became themselves head masters of the new schools founded to meet the demand for the highly class-conscious type of education which wealth had produced.

The personality and the work of these disciples, too, was so attractive that keen Methodist denominationalists feared the more. Many of them were Church of England clergymen, and the schools of which they became head masters were closely connected with that Church. These reformers were activated by the evangelical spirit which had swept England. The same lofty ideals filled them as had filled Wilberforce and other members of the 'Clapham Sect'. They typified the resuscitated moral sense of the nation which had largely been roused by the Methodist revival.

'They were the sons, by natural and spiritual birth, of men who, in the earlier days of Methodism, had shaken off the lethargy in which, till then, the Church of England had been entranced—of men by whose agency the great evangelical doctrine of faith, emerging in its primeval splendour, had not only

[3] Samuel Butler, *Life and Letters of Dr. Samuel Butler*, Vol. I, p. 328.
[4] Edward C. Mack, *Public Schools and British Opinion, 1780–1860*, p. 256.

overpowered the contrary heresies, but had perhaps obscured some kindred truths.' [5]

The wealthy Methodist laymen on the whole were not keen denominationalists. In their own light they were loyal to Methodism, but, as was natural enough, they did not always consider Methodism when it came to providing the right type of education for their children, and, just because so many of the public schools [6] were in the hands of capable schoolmasters whose religious views were vital even though they were not Methodists, these wealthy Methodist laymen sent their sons to them without fear.

To a handful of thinking Methodists the dangers had become evident as soon as Thomas Arnold's success began to be discussed, and the foundation of Wesley College, Sheffield, supported by a group of wealthy business men, is an indication of the demand which grew greater as the century advanced. As we have seen, James Rigg had attended a meeting to consider a scheme for the foundation of a school for the sons of Methodist laymen as far back as 1847.[7] The type of school envisaged did not appear for thirty years, but the spark of the idea was there, and it began to be fanned in the 1860's largely owing to the missionary spirit and common-sense proposals of Henry French. Reference has already been made to the steps which he took to reveal the poverty of the Methodist contribution to higher education at that time, and to interest his fellows in setting up schools and educational institutions. With schools as attractive as the Woodard and the new proprietary schools he foresaw Methodist youth slipping away from the Connexion in even greater numbers.

One of the barriers to the establishment of an educational system in Methodism—one which led from the primary school upward—was the closed door of university education at Oxford and Cambridge. Until 1850 the door was fast closed—and this fact explains the importance of the founding of London University in 1828, where there were no religious tests. In 1850, however, as the result of considerable agitation largely in the older universities themselves, a Royal Commission was appointed to inquire into the state, discipline, and revenues of Oxford and Cambridge. Effect was given to many of this Commission's re-

[5] Abel Stevens, *History of Methodism*, Vol. II, p. 80.
[6] The term is henceforth used in the wider sense to include the new proprietary schools.
[7] James H. Rigg, *Reminiscences*, pp. 120–1.

commendations by legislation on the part of colleges and Parliament in the period 1854 to 1858, which led to an increased number of students at these universities being drawn from a wider range of social classes. The reforms which chiefly affected Methodism were the authorization of private halls and hostels, the recognition and admission of unattached, non-collegiate students, the wider recruitment of students from schools in all parts of the country, and the abolition of religious tests at matriculation and on graduation. The door was set ajar, but a Methodist was still debarred from proceeding to a Master's Degree, from taking a theological Degree, and from obtaining a Fellowship.

In 1868, the Liberal Government under Gladstone came into power and showed its opposition to privilege in any form. It abolished the purchase of army commissions, established Civil Service examinations open to free competition, passed the Education Act of 1870, and, in 1871, introduced the Universities Tests Act by which religious tests (with certain minor exceptions) were abolished at Oxford, Cambridge, and Durham. So much importance was attached to this reform that the Prime Minister himself opened the Debate. From that time onward, therefore, fellowships, degrees, and college and university offices (except those which by existing law were held by men in holy orders) were thrown open to Nonconformists.[8]

This was just the incentive that was needed. The Rev. William Arthur, not unnaturally in view of the position he then held as principal of the Methodist College, Belfast, had been especially interested in French's views, but he realized the difficulty of getting others to share those views sufficiently strongly to take action when the universities were closed to Methodists. After all, much of the usefulness and success of the type of school envisaged would be lost if it was not possible for pupils to pass on to the universities, free to take part in their whole life and privileges.

In the year in which the Universities Test Act was passed Conference debated the question: How could Methodism best make use of the privileges of the older universities and at the same time safeguard its youth against a slipping away from Methodism? A considerable body of opinion favoured the building of a Methodist hostel at Oxford or Cambridge, so that Methodist students would be able to live a corporate Methodist

[8] See Sir Charles E. Mallet, *History of the University of Oxford*, Vol. III.

life. Another favoured the building of a school which should be in close touch with one or other of the older universities. This was the project which Henry French advocated.

A committee was appointed, with Dr. W. F. Moulton, then a tutor at Richmond Theological College, as convenor, to make inquiries and to report to the next Conference. In the following March the President of the Conference visited Taunton and asked French to draw up a specific proposal. This was done, and it was based on the idea of a school in close touch with either Oxford or Cambridge, to which a large percentage of the school's pupils would pass, though it would cater also for boys leaving school before the age of eighteen. The proposal was adopted by the committee and inquiries began to be made for a site. The establishment of the school at Oxford was favoured by many since Methodism was more intimately connected with that university than with any other through its founder, but it was on Cambridge that attention was finally fixed. To what extent this was due to the superintendent minister there, the Rev. Thomas Adams, can only be a matter of conjecture, but certain facts are significant. Thomas Adams, while he was still a boy on his father's farm in Cornwall, had seen how his parents, and indeed the whole family, had had to pinch and scrape to enable his elder brother John to go to Cambridge where he eventually became senior wrangler and later the discoverer of the planet Neptune. Thomas must have realized then the importance and the existing difficulties of obtaining education. He must have realized still more these difficulties when he became a missionary in the Friendly Islands and acted as pastor, statesman, school-master, and numerous other providers of service to the inhabitants. Six weeks before he sailed for that work in the South Seas he married Maria French, sister of Henry French. It is difficult to believe that it was no more than coincidence that Thomas Adams should have been minister at Cambridge when negotiations for a school were being made and that it was in Cambridge that the school came to be founded. We do know that the aged minister walked miles in raising money for the school fund, and that it was he who in 1872 called the attention of the committee to an estate for sale in Cambridge which would be highly suitable for whatever educational project was finally agreed. This site could be obtained for £14,000 provided that it was used for education. A syndicate was formed which guaranteed the purchase price and arranged for the matter to be held over for final decision until the following Conference.

Meanwhile Dr. Moulton and the members of the committee amongst whom Mr. Percy Bunting was particularly active, having adopted French's plan, had been making inquiries into the methods and organization of public schools in various parts of the country, for it had by then been decided that the school should be one modelled on the best features of existing public schools.

In 1873 the Conference officially adopted the scheme in the following terms: 'The Conference, having considered the proposals to establish a High School in connexion with the Town of Cambridge, and to acquire The Leys Estate for that purpose, generally approves the design of establishing such a school, and gives to the Committee on Higher Education now appointed a discretionary power to acquire the estate in question, or other suitable property, provided they are satisfied of the expediency of such a step, and also that the means can be raised without undue pressure on the Connexion.'[9] At the same time the schemes which had been drawn up for the constitution of the Governing Body and for the general plan of the proposed school were approved.

Official sanction having been given, Dr. Moulton and Percy Bunting made still wider inquiries, visiting schools and educationists all over the country to discover the latest developments in higher education and scholastic methods. Marlborough College was finally selected as the chief model in this connexion.

The second head master of this school and the one who made it the great school it was to be was the 'Young master' of *Tom Brown's Schooldays*— G. E. L. Cotton, who had been a housemaster at Rugby under Thomas Arnold, and who had set out to organize Marlborough on lines similar to those used by Arnold. The curriculum was predominantly classical since a large percentage of the pupils went to Oxford or Cambridge, but a 'modern' side had been established. In the lower forms all boys followed the same course, based on Latin and Greek, but in the middle school there was a choice, and boys who so wished could take the 'modern' course which included French, German, English literature, experimental science, and chemistry. The fees were £72 per annum with a reduction for the sons of Church of England clergymen.

[9] *Minutes of Conference*, Vol. XIX, p. 184.

On this model, therefore, Methodism set out to establish a public school of its own which was to compare favourably with one of those already known throughout the country. There would inevitably be a danger of its becoming merely a poor imitation of one of these. Success depended largely upon the head master, and Methodism knew only too well its deficiencies in this respect. There was one man, however, who was suited to carry out such a task, and it speaks well for that man that he appears to have been the only one who did not realize the fact. The nomination of head master came before the Conference of 1874. William Arthur acted as spokesman for the committee, which knew better than anyone else the work that had already been done and still more the work that had yet to be done. He told the Conference: 'I must say for the Committee that after looking round and round for a man that could do the work, with the qualifications in view, first, that he must be a man in whom Methodists would have thorough Methodist confidence; and secondly, a scholar such as would command the respect of the University and the country, the feeling is on the part of everybody that we are shut up to one man: that without any of us knowing it Providence seems to have been taking that man quietly, step by step, out from the common level of Methodist preachers by one indication after another, just marking him out to us, so that when the time came you should say, This is the man.' [10]

That man was Dr. William F. Moulton. No other name was suggested, and it did seem as though Dr. Moulton was the only possible choice, but realization of this came as something of a shock to the Connexion who had come to regard him as one of the bulwarks of Methodist theological training. Nobody had any criticisms concerning the suitability of the choice, but there were many who raised objections to his leaving Richmond College, which would seem an impoverished place without him. However, the choice was made and Dr. Moulton was appointed the first head master of The Leys School.

One of the most brilliant scholars Methodism has produced, William Fiddian Moulton was educated at a small school in Worcester kept by an aunt of his, Miss Egan, and later at Woodhouse Grove School and Wesley College, Sheffield. The rigours of life at Woodhouse Grove appear to have 'made' him from the physical point of view, for when he was very young his

---

[10] W. Fiddian Moulton, *William F. Moulton*, pp. 116–17.

health was so delicate that he was not expected to reach manhood. Indeed his father was once summoned to his 'death-bed' at Woodhouse Grove, only to find him not only well, but playing in the playground! It was an assistant master there, Joseph Frankland, who first inspired in him a love of the Greek Testament. If Frankland is remembered for nothing else, Methodism and theology owe him a debt for that enthusiasm which he instilled in a boy destined to become one of the greatest Bible scholars of the country. Moulton was only fifteen when he left the Grove, having become head boy, and went for a further three years to Wesley College, Sheffield, where he was under Samuel Waddy, from whom he learnt many lessons which were to be useful to him later at The Leys, for if Moulton did consciously copy any educationist it was Waddy.

Leaving Wesley College he entered the teaching profession and followed what might appear a family profession. His grandfather had married Marie Egan, who came of a teaching family. His aunt kept the school for small boys at Worcester; an uncle taught at Kingswood School until he entered the Ministry; his father was a schoolmaster first at Dublin and later at Greenwich until he too entered the Ministry. An anecdote concerning him shows the remarkable powers of mind which came out in the son: 'One day, while he was Chairman of the Bedford and Northampton District, he was making up his schedules; at the same time he was reading a Latin author with Richard and a Greek author with John. Now he would be adding up a column, muttering, "I must write to that brother," and in the next breath, "Get on, John, what are you stopping for?"—"Can't find a nominative case, papa!"—"Look about three lines down, so and so."—"Oh yes." And John would construe. Then it was Richard's turn, and at every sign of hesitation his father would suggest the missing adjective or verb or whatever it might be. All the while the adding-up of columns was going on, and the muttered praises or objurgations on the brethren.' [11]

William Fiddian was the eldest son. The second, Dr. James Egan Moulton, entered the Ministry and eventually became President of the New South Wales Conference, but he too was a teacher, and it is as a teacher that he is chiefly remembered, for he founded and became principal of the Newington College, Sydney. The third son, John Fletcher, later Lord Moulton, the scientist and barrister, was for a time a schoolmaster, holding

[11] G. G. Findlay, *William F. Moulton*, pp. 15–16.

appointments first at Dr. Conquest's school at Biggleswade (where Dr. Rigg once taught) and later at Dr. Rusk's school at Northampton. During this teaching period of his life he was studying all the time and later when he sat for the mathematical tripos at Cambridge he passed out not only as senior wrangler but with the highest total of marks ever known, beating Darwin, son of the naturalist, who was second by an easy margin. Of such stock came the first head master of Methodism's first public school.

To return to William Fiddian Moulton—after leaving Wesley College at the age of eighteen he taught for a year at a private school at Devonport and then went as an assistant master to Queen's College, Taunton, where under Thomas Sibly he stayed for four years until he entered the Ministry. Later he was appointed an assistant tutor at Richmond College where he remained for sixteen years.

Dr. Moulton entered upon his duties at Cambridge with many misgivings. In fact, the only personal pleasure he could envisage at first was the fact that he would be able to meet more often those friends he had made on the committee which in 1870 was appointed to revise the Authorised Version of the Bible. No doubt he remembered words which he had spoken, unconscious of their possible later application to himself. When the original report of the committee on Methodist higher education was presented to Conference in 1872 he spoke of the nature of the head master's post in the school which was projected: 'The post must be made attractive enough to secure the services of a first-class man.' It was a task too which required the services of a courageous man, for the creation of a public school out of the traditions of a Nonconformist Church whose adherents had for long been debarred from taking a full share in the highest academic undertakings was a colossal task. 'I shall go as a matter of obedience,' wrote Dr. Moulton to Dr. Westcott, 'I don't think I am the man for such responsibilities, and no allurement would have induced me to undertake them. Now, however, I am pledged, not indeed to success, but to do my best.' [12]

The Conference of 1874 directed the Revs. William Arthur and George W. Olver to constitute a Governing Body. Their first meeting was held on 17th September of that year, and a scheme was finally drawn up and presented to the following Conference, by whom it was formally approved. In the same

[12] G. G. Findlay, *William F. Moulton*, p. 55.

year the Charity Commissioners gave it their blessing and in 1879 the school was incorporated by them as a charitable trust.

Previous to the Conference of 1875 the project for a students' hostel had again been brought forward in the form of an amendment to the school scheme, for it was felt that a hostel might be incorporated in the school, as had been done at the Methodist College, Belfast. The Committee did not favour the amendment, but made the tentative suggestion that the minister appointed as chaplain to the school might make his own house into a small hostel for undergraduates if there was a sufficient demand. This suggestion had been made at the instigation of the University authorities and it was felt that if such a scheme was tried and proved successful some such hostel might be started at Oxford also. In fact, no hostel ever materialized either at Oxford or Cambridge, though it seems probable that Dr. Moulton was thinking of it when he invited undergraduates to meet at his house. On many Sunday evenings an informal 'Wesley Society' met there, and the head master's house came to be regarded as the social centre for these young men who were entering the University in rapidly increasing numbers as prejudice against Nonconformity broke down and Methodist higher education developed. Thus was the Methodist life of the University drawn more closely together. The same thing happened at Oxford. When Hugh Price Hughes took up his duties as superintendent of the Oxford Circuit in 1881 he gathered together the Methodist undergraduates in the Wesley Guild and became, as he said, 'An undergraduate with undergraduates'.[13]

There were therefore in the foundation of this public school no divided aims as there had been in the establishment of all previous schools except Woodhouse Grove. There were no side projects for the training of potential ministers. The whole scheme centred round the school, and to avoid any possibility of divided aims there were to be no outlying houses whose masters made incomes from their pupils, as was the case in many of the other public schools. The idea had been considered and had been rejected. The school was to be a self-contained unit, its numbers limited for the time being to 240. Those responsible for drawing up the scheme had realized, however, that as the school developed changes would be necessary and they had

[13] D. P. Hughes, *The Life of Hugh Price Hughes*, pp. 137–42.

wisely made provision for the alteration of the school organization when necessary.

Two clauses of the scheme could not be altered, however:

1. That the religious teaching of the school should be in
accordance with that of the Methodist Conference.

2. That if the governors ever decided to give up the school
the property or its sale value must be given to educational purposes of The Methodist Church.

The first of these clauses might suggest a too-narrow sectarianism in the school. Any such tendency was carefully avoided.
It has never been forgotten that the school first came into being
to assist in the throwing-down of denominational barriers at the
older universities. From the first, therefore, there have been no
denominational distinctions, and the liberal tendencies of The
Methodist Church are clearly seen in this fact. All the Protestant
Churches have been represented among the boys, masters, and
Governing Body, whilst care has been taken to invite clergymen
of other denominations to preach in the school chapel. It is
worthy of note that today at other Methodist schools this is also
the case.

Inevitably the making of a school devolved largely upon the
head master, though he received loyal support from all members
of the Connexion, lay and clerical. Three principles governed
the minds of those who set about building this school on the best
traditions of a public school of its day:

1. Everything was to be of the best quality. Dr. Moulton
knew well the blighting influence of lack of adequate funds.
He had seen the working of that blight on other Methodist
schools and he determined to have none of it at The Leys. The
school was unendowed, but Dr. Moulton was not daunted and
his faith in the generosity of Methodists was not disappointed.

2. Religion was to be more than just an element of school
life. It was to be the underlying principle of all. In this connexion it is worth noting what were Dr. Arnold's views on the
same subject—the making a school a place of really Christian
education.

'The intellectual training was not for a moment underrated,
and the machinery of the school was left to have its own way.
But he looked upon the whole as bearing on the advancement of
the one end of all instruction and education; the boys were still
treated as schoolboys, but as schoolboys who must grow up to
be Christian men; whose age did not prevent their faults from

being sins, or their excellencies from being noble and Christian virtues; whose situation did not of itself make the application of Christian principles to their daily lives an impracticable vision. His education, in short, it was once observed amidst the vehement outcry by which he used to be assailed, was not (according to the popular phrase) based upon religion, but was itself religious.' [14]

It is evident that Dr. Moulton learned much from Dr. Arnold, and it must not be forgotten that The Leys was modelled chiefly upon what may be called an off-shoot of Rugby—Marlborough.

3. Although the school was Methodist it must be free from narrow sectarianism.

'Personal influence is needed in a school to take the place of parental influence at home. This personal influence is exercised both by the head master and his assistants. It was not till long after Arnold's time that the present friendly relations between boys and masters became common.'

So writes R. L. Archer in his *Secondary Education in the Nineteenth Century*.[15] Dr. Moulton had realized the truth of the first part of this statement and he knew how much personal influence could mean, so that in the early days of The Leys he gave his full attention to affairs in his new home to the exclusion of the many other interests his full life had brought him. He realized that organization was not enough—a fact which is all-too-often overlooked today in education as in other affairs. From the first he wanted to establish a close and friendly relationship between the boys and himself. He made it a rule that he was accessible at all times to any boy who wished to speak with him; like Arnold, he so arranged the time-table that he himself taught the youngest boys as well as the most senior; he regarded the dull boy not as a hindrance to the school's success but as an opportunity for the schoolmaster to put forth his best efforts. 'The triumph of teaching is won in the field of mediocrity', he once said during a Valedictory Address to the students of Westminster College in 1890.[16] He strongly objected to corporal punishment, though he did not hesitate to use it if he considered such punishment necessary. For the maintenance of discipline out of school hours he relied much upon his prefects.

The school opened in 1875 with sixteen boys whose ages ranged from ten to seventeen years, while Dr. Moulton had one

[14] A. P. Stanley, *The Life and Correspondence of Thomas Arnold*, Vol. I, p. 95.
[15] p. 63.
[16] *Wesleyan Education Report* (1890–91), p. 33.

assistant—Mr. Arthur Vinter, who later became head master of Woodhouse Grove, to help him. The school was notable at that time for the breadth of its curriculum. Church schools still tended to be conservative and sided with the old classics against the new science. Nonconformity, as was shown in the chapter on dissenting academies, tended to be more democratic and attuned to modern trends. The Leys, though it set out to model itself on the lines of the best in public schools, was no slave to those lines, and nothing was copied without good reason. It did not make the mistake of imposing a rigidly classical curriculum. Dr. Moulton, in his visits to other schools, had noted their defects as well as their good points, and he had learned from their omissions. The Leys therefore from the first attached considerable importance to modern languages and literature. As time went on, laboratories were built and equipped, and chemistry, physics, and biology entered the curriculum. In the early days there was an art school, and later were built workshops for metal- and woodwork. Dr. Moulton's desire to get to know each boy personally and to study his peculiarities and interests was at times carried to an extreme, as on the many occasions when he arranged for tutors from the university to visit the school and coach boys in such subjects as Hebrew, Sanskrit, and Spanish. These he called his 'special cases'. His wife remarked one day on his excessive expenditure on books. 'Yes,' was the reply, 'there were a number of special cases to be helped.' [17]

One of the most valuable contributions which a boarding-school can make to education is found in the organization of out-of-school activities—the various societies, clubs, and hobbies, in which a boy interests himself of his own free will. The secondary schools of Methodism have always been well provided in this respect, and the personal contact between master and boy has often been made more easily possible through such societies and hobbies, since in them masters and boys take an equal interest and equal responsibility.

In the very first term of The Leys' existence a Literary and Debating Society was started. It has since had a chequered career and several changes of name, but the interest has always existed. In 1878 the science master, A. H. S. Lucas (an Old Boy of Kingswood School who later became head master of Newington College, Sydney) founded the Natural History and Science

[17] G. G. Findlay, op. cit., p. 180.

Society. Dr. Moulton tried to develop leisure reading among the boys by providing a good library, though fiction in the early days does not appear to have been abundant. A Musical Society may be said to have had its origin in 1877 when a small orchestra attempted Haydn's First Symphony.

Another feature of the school was the Masters' Meeting. As the numbers in the school increased, so naturally did the teaching staff, the selection being almost entirely in the hands of the head master. When the staff had reached a certain number a weekly Masters' Meeting was inaugurated. In this the example of other schools was followed, but in one important respect this meeting differed from that of other schools, for Dr. Moulton made it a rule not to be present himself at these meetings. He felt that in his absence masters would feel more free to express their own opinions frankly and sincerely. Thus it frequently happened that he received suggestions from his staff which had already been threshed out, and the very fact that these suggestions had been made and discussed out of his presence made them, in his view, all the more valuable. He did not always adopt the suggestions, but he did always act upon them in shaping his own future actions. This innovation of a Masters' Meeting with the head master absent is one which must have done much to make the school what it is. There were occasions, of course, when it was only right and proper that the head master should be present at a meeting, and two or three times each term Dr. Moulton called one and took the chair himself. But at the routine weekly meeting when any subject connected with the school or its inmates might come up for discussion he was never present.

This same spirit of trust and loyalty to those who helped him to build up and administer the school he showed also in his attitude toward the boys themselves. The head master of one public school had told him that it took at least five years to produce a good and reliable prefect. Dr. Moulton disagreed with this view, and when any boy in the upper part of the school, however short a time he had been a pupil, showed himself worthy to be a prefect, he appointed him, and in judging worthiness Dr. Moulton did not merely take games and intellectual prowess into consideration. He gave these prefects privileges and freedom, and, as was stated above, he depended upon them very largely for discipline out of school hours. Like Arnold, whose pupils came to regard it as a shame to tell a lie, he relied implicitly upon a boy's word, and believed that the only method of making boys capable of trust was by trusting them. He regarded it as one of the school's chief duties to train boys to grow into men capable of exercising authority and commanding confidence, and that training, he believed, had to start from the very day a boy entered the school. He who was faithful in little things would be faithful in the great.

From the year in which the school was opened it developed steadily—in numbers, reputation, and premises. Although from the first the school set out to be a public school comparable with any other, and although money was generously subscribed, it was impossible to set up an architectural pile of imposing walls, label it a public school, and then set about developing a public-school tradition. The architectural beauties could only develop as the other aspects of the school developed. Had Matthew Arnold lived to see the school he might have been able to modify his views on the Philistines, for, unlike certain other Methodist foundations with Queen Anne fronts and 'Mary Anne behinds', as they have been facetiously described, The Leys was carefully planned throughout, and, as gymnasium, classrooms, dormitories, assembly hall, swimming-bath, and chapel were built, these were made to fit into one uniform design, as pleasing to the eye as was the developing tradition of the school to the mind.

The numbers in the school increased steadily and by the end of the second year there were sixty boys and five masters. By the end of ten years there were one hundred and fifty boys and the school was beginning to pay its way. The Twentieth-century Fund took a share in helping the school on its way: 'Recognizing the unique and important position of The Leys School as the only provision for a public-school education of its particular type and of a strictly Methodist character, and also the immense importance of bringing the school into closer relation with the education system of Methodism, by the establishment of scholarships to the school, the Central Committee resolves that a request for a moderate grant from this Fund for the providing of such scholarships shall be favourably considered.'[18]

The foundation of the school had been made possible by the spreading of Methodism into the moneyed classes with the redistribution of wealth during the nineteenth century. The constitution of the Governing Body on whom depended much of the direction of policy and finance exemplified this. The President,

[18] *Wesleyan Education Report* (1902–3), p. 77.

ex-President, and Secretary of the Wesleyan Methodist Conference; the President and ex-President of the Old Leysian Union (founded 1890) were *ex-officio* members, while the Methodist Education Committee appointed three members, the Ministerial Training Colleges, two, and the Masters one member. The remaining twenty governors were elected by the Life Donors Meeting which consisted of all persons who had subscribed £100 or more to the school. The school was largely controlled, therefore, by the moneyed classes of Methodism for whom the school was founded, and it can be objected that Methodism in this way kept alive class distinctions, but it is only fair to remember that today there are a number of scholarships offered annually to boys of ability whose parents could not otherwise afford to send them to such a school. There has been a danger of boys becoming snobs and lording it over their fellows who have been educated at local grammar schools or primary schools, and in the early days of the school this danger was realized. It was a danger which might easily be enhanced by rearing boys in a public-school atmosphere which perforce could not be representative of the average Methodist mode of life, and steps were early taken to minimize the danger and to show boys that privilege implied social responsibility. Just as Westminster College was originally planned and founded amid the slums of Westminster in order that future teachers might understand something of the problems and circumstances of those whom they would later serve in schools, so it was felt that much could be done by giving boys and staff of The Leys opportunity of coming into contact with those less fortunate than themselves. In 1882, largely at the instigation of Dr. Moulton himself, The Leys Christian Union was started amongst Old Boys, but it was not long before members felt that the mere meeting with one another was not enough: some active social service was required. This took practical shape as the result of a conversation between two members— J. H. S. McArthur and R. A. H. Bickford-Smith—when it was proposed that some form of mission work in the slum areas of London should be undertaken. The whole question was carefully sifted and leading Methodists were consulted, the Rev. Hugh Price Hughes being especially helpful and enthusiastic. So The Leysian Mission came into being in 1886, and The Leys School came to have its effect not only on the upper classes of Nonconformity but upon the poorest classes of no particular denomination, and took its share in what has been called 'The

Forward Movement' of Methodism which marked the close of the nineteenth century.

With the death of Dr. Moulton in 1898 fear was felt for the school, for he had become so much an integral part of it. The place had been built on a tradition of personality and personal intercourse. As an educational historian has written: 'The living force of education has always sprung from movements of the human mind and aspirations of the human heart; legislation and administration are mere tools which these movements and aspirations use.' [19] Dr. Moulton had realized this to the full and much of the school's success had been due to his wise following of the principle. His influence had spread far beyond the bounds of the school and had meant much to Methodist life in general and in particular to that which centred in the University. But Dr. Moulton had appreciated the dangers too. To outsiders he had become identified with the school, but when the time came it was found that his twenty-three years of administration had set the school on lines which were independent of individual personalities. The tone of the school was good, it had succeeded in its aim of fostering in its pupils high ideals based on sound Christian principles, and—what must appear incredible to those who belonged to the traditions of those other schools with which it set out to compete—it had made for itself a background which appeared more deeply rooted in time than in a mere twenty years or so. Some slight idea of what is meant can be judged from a work of fiction which is founded on a background of fact. *Goodbye, Mr. Chips* was written by an Old Boy of The Leys, James Hilton, son of a Methodist schoolmaster. He took as his background for this book his own memories of The Leys, and in the character of 'Mr. Chips' there is a hint of a man who was amongst the first pupils of the school, who later became acting head master, and who when he died was a governor of the school—the late J. C. Isard, by whom the present writer was given some sidelights on the school's early days. His estimate of the man who did so much to make the school should be recorded: 'Dr. Moulton was of paternal temper and in some measure infused the family spirit into the small initial community, not least in his own extreme tolerance of young monkeys and perhaps more in the large-mindedness which we older boys might discern, if not quite measure.' [20]

[19] R. L. Archer, *Secondary Education in the Nineteenth Century*, p. 147.
[20] From MS. letter.

Thus Methodism, following the general trend of higher education during the second half of the nineteenth century, came to possess its own public school in close connexion with the universities and comparable with Marlborough, Clifton, Haileybury, Lancing, and others.[21]   Today a public school is defined [22] as one represented on the Governing Bodies' Association or on the Head Masters' Conference, and today Methodism has eight such schools for boys—The Leys, Kingswood, Rydal, Culford, Truro, Woodhouse Grove, Ashville, and Wycliffe; and five for girls—Farringtons, Hunmanby Hall, Penrhos College, Queenswood, and Trinity Hall.

[21] For an estimate of public-school education as seen through the eyes of a head master of The Leys during the early years of this century, see W. T. A. Barber (Head Master 1898–1919): *The Unfolding of Life.*
[22] In the terms of reference given to the Fleming Committee of Inquiry appointed in 1942 to consider public-school education.

CHAPTER FOURTEEN

Development and Change at Kingswood and Woodhouse Grove

A T THE TIME when The Leys was being founded, much attention came also to be directed toward the two Wesleyan
Methodist Connexional schools. Allusion has already been made
to their foundation and there is no need here to retell the full
story of their growth,[1] but there are certain aspects of their
development to which reference must be made if a true picture
of the Methodist contribution to English secondary education is
to be obtained.

Kingswood School was intended by Wesley to be open to all
boys whose parents wished to send them there and who were
approved by the founder, and it was not until the early nineteenth century that it became a school for ministers' sons only.
Up to that time no other Methodist secondary school had been
founded, so that there was nowhere then for laymen's sons to be
educated within the Connexion. It was this lack, combined with
the reputation that Kingswood and, later, Woodhouse Grove had
won for themselves, that led to the foundation of Wesley College,
Sheffield, and Queen's College, Taunton.

By the end of the first half of the nineteenth century the village
of Kingswood had grown into a suburb, or more correctly a
slum, of Bristol, and it became increasingly obvious, even without a knowledge of Wesley's views on the siting of schools, that
it was no longer a desirable place in which to keep a boarding-
school. Accommodation, too, was insufficient for the number of
pupils, and the buildings in such a deplorable condition that
certain laymen who visited the school in 1846 felt 'humbled and
ashamed to have a school for the education of the sons of their
ministers in such a condition'. [2] In the same year an adverse
report on the school's water supply supplied the necessary spur
to action and Conference decided that the school must be moved.
A statement was circulated throughout the Connexion pointing

[1] The story is told in *The History of Kingswood School* by three Old Boys
of the School, and in *Woodhouse Grove School: Memorials and Reminiscences*
by J. T. Slugg, and *A Short History of Woodhouse Grove School* by H. W.
Starkey.
[2] *The History of Kingswood School*, p. 207.

out the necessity for this and appealing for funds. The statement included these pathetic words: 'A good education is all the legacy which the allowances of Wesleyan Ministers enable them to leave to their children.'

As has already been made clear in speaking of every single educational undertaking which Methodism has launched, the greatest problem which never was, and never has been, eased was that of finance. There must be many occasions when Methodism has looked enviously at the endowments to which Roman Catholicism and the Church of England have access, for Methodism, having appeared with the disappearance of feudalism and having found its growth originally amongst poor people who were often entirely destitute, was forced from the first to live a hand-to-mouth existence. Unlike the Church of England, it possessed no land from which to gain a steady income. Matters were eased slightly as members became more wealthy, but the generosity of the wealthy was directed to the meeting of present demands rather than future hopes, and such endowments as do exist today are comparatively insignificant. When one considers this lack of finance which has never been absent throughout the history of Methodism the contribution that Methodism has made to English education of all types becomes the more praiseworthy. It was not lack of idealism and foresight that caused the failure to do more than was done: it was plain lack of money. To pay for what was done, Methodist ministers and laymen made magnificent sacrifices.[3]

On the back of a copy[4] of the statement concerning the proposed removal of Kingswood School from Bristol appears a manuscript letter from the Rev. J. W. Cusworth, Governor from 1843 to 1857, who was largely responsible for making possible the removal of the school to Lansdown, Bath. This letter reads:

'My dear Brother, I hope when Mr. Stephenson visits Shetland you will be able with the rest of your brethren to do something for our New Kingswood School—an Institution in which we are all deeply interested. Do your best.'

This letter shows the spirit in which far-seeing men went about the British Isles to raise funds from already poor ministers for the rebuilding of the school for their sons. With it is another which contains on one side the names of eight ministers

[3] Some idea of the hand-to-mouth finances of the Connexional Schools can be gathered from reading the chapter on finance in *The History of Kingswood School*, pp. 239–50.
[4] Now in the Library of Kingswood School.

who have subscribed and on the other a letter from Mr. Stephenson:

'You will see what I have been able to do in Shetland. I wish I may be as successful elsewhere. I think you may reckon on seven or eight pounds in this instance as the result of my squeezing. I hope we shall be able to put things on a more satisfactory footing in this country. . . .'

At the end of the letter is an all-too-illuminating postscript: 'The toil has almost knocked me up.' It was by such means and by such men that Methodism catered for the education of its ministers' sons. And though Methodist laymen in the first half of the nineteenth century may have had reason for complaint that they had so little share in the government of Methodism and no Methodist schools for their own sons, they could not but admire the self-sacrificing spirit of their ministers.

The foundation stone of the new buildings on Lansdown was laid by James Heald, the first Methodist Member of Parliament, on 20th June 1850, and on 28th October 1852 the school was formally reopened on its new site, where it continued to build up a reputation which eventually earned for itself a place amongst the 'public schools'.

As has been shown in previous chapters, interest in, and understanding of, the various strata of education grew steadily during the nineteenth century, though a general action was not seen until the 1870's. In 1871, a university career had been made possible for Nonconformists generally, but it was still not possible for Methodist ministers' sons. There was a large gap in age between that at which the boy left Kingswood or Woodhouse Grove and that at which he could enter a university. These schools claimed, with justification, to give higher education, but their pupils left at the age of fourteen, just when they would normally be beginning to take an interest in learning for its own sake. The Schools Inquiry Commission spoke with regret of the early age at which boys left these schools. Dissatisfaction, however, had been felt in Methodism long before the appearance of that *Report*. True, a few boys went on from the Connexional schools to Sheffield or Taunton or to some private school, but this was only possible for the few.

From the foundation of Kingswood School the usual age for admission had been eight, though Wesley had stated in his *Short Account* that pupils were accepted between the ages of six and twelve. There were cases of boys who entered the school

242

at an earlier age than eight and yet stayed till fourteen. At the Conference of 1808 it was resolved that any boy who showed 'an outstanding genius' should be allowed to continue his education at the school beyond the age of fourteen, provided that his parents paid such sum as the committee thought proper. Apparently the committee was willing, on occasions, to charge no fee for that extra year, but this munificence was offset by the fact that the extra year was not granted every year—no doubt because no 'outstanding genius' appeared. The first of these extra years was granted at Kingswood in 1808 and at Woodhouse Grove in 1819. Between these years and 1861 thirty-six pupils were granted the extra year at Kingswood and twenty-three at Woodhouse Grove. In 1834 the Woodhouse Grove Committee of Management proposed that boys should enter the school at the age of ten and stay five years instead of six, but Conference rightly turned down the suggestion. Again in 1851 a further proposal was made that boys should enter at nine and leave at fifteen. Again the proposal was turned down, though previously in 1847 the Conference had made one slight alteration in the rigid leaving system—an amendment, as it were, to the step taken in 1808. They had decreed that an extra year should be granted free of charge annually to the boy in each school who in the opinion of head master, governor, and examiners, should be most suitable to receive it. This extra year was given not only for brilliance in study but also for general good conduct.

Nevertheless, these two schools were still merely third-grade schools according to the grading of secondary schools adopted by the Schools Inquiry Commission, and in 1871 the matter was taken up by an energetic layman, Sir Henry Fowler (later Lord Wolverhampton), the first Methodist to become a member of the Cabinet. The younger son of a Methodist minister, he was educated at Woodhouse Grove School (where he did not win the extra year!) and he was taught from the first, and came to hold as one of his guiding principles, that the only two things of importance in life were salvation and education. As Mayor of Wolverhampton in 1863 at the opening of the Wolverhampton Orphanage, he said: 'Education to be of any value must have Christianity for its basis. I should have very little sympathy with this institution as a benevolent means of feeding, clothing, and humanely training a large number of children, if the training imparted were dissociated from that sound Christian education which you know to be at the bottom, not only of all morality,

243

but of all real good in this world as well as of all happy prospects in the next. . . . Children thus educated will, in every sense of the word, do their duty in that state of life to which it shall please God to call them.'[5]

Although, as a schoolboy, Sir Henry had not made friends easily and had not spent a particularly happy time as a pupil at Woodhouse Grove School, yet he recalled with pleasure, toward the end of his life, that there was something about Kingswood and Woodhouse Grove Schools which made them different from the usual type of middle-class school, whose pupils all came from the same type of home and the same social sphere. He felt that these two schools lacked the priggishness and social snobbery and jealousy which Matthew Arnold so heartily detested and so vehemently criticized. In his legal and parliamentary career he had come to realize some of the disadvantages which confronted a Kingswood or Woodhouse Grove boy when he left his school so early. He himself had had to struggle to overcome the difficulties in gaining the education necessary for a high position in the State. He saw that primary schools were making progress whereas secondary schools stood still, and he deplored the fact. No doubt he realized the more clearly what this lack of higher education meant, since he lived in a town set in the heart of the growing industry and wealth of the latter half of the nineteenth century. Later still, the appointment of his son-in-law, Alfred Felkin, to an inspectorate of secondary schools no doubt gave him a source of official information which was to prove invaluable to Methodism through the Methodist committees of which he was a member.

At a meeting of the committee dealing with the Connexional schools in 1871, therefore, Sir Henry moved the appointment of a special committee—'something in the nature of a commission', as he called it. He pointed out that Wesleyan Methodism claimed to educate its ministers' sons, and yet turned them away from the Connexional secondary schools just at the age when they might be expected to be beginning to take an interest in learning for its own sake. Methodism ought to supply a complete education, so that a boy could compete for university scholarships on equal terms with boys from other secondary schools, or could pass straight into the higher grades of civil and commercial life.

But Sir Henry did more than ask for the appointment of a commission of inquiry: he suggested that this commission should

[5] E. H. Fowler, *The Life of Lord Wolverhampton*, p. 56.

consider the possibility of amalgamating Kingswood and Woodhouse Grove Schools into one school. The administration of such a school would cost no more, he thought, and the same number of pupils could be educated, but their education would no longer end at the age of fourteen. It would continue until the boys were old enough either to pass on to a university or to enter business with a solid educational background behind them.

The proposal was a revolutionary one, but coming at a time when Methodism was already embarking on the greatest step it had yet taken in regard to higher education—the foundation of The Leys—it was accepted as a proposal worth considering, and Conference approved the appointment of a committee to inquire closely into Connexional school affairs.

It consisted of twenty-one members, with the Revs. Robert N. Young and William F. Moulton as secretaries. Six of its members were to form a commission of inquiry: The Revs. Benjamin Gregory, W. F. Moulton, W. J. Tweddle, Sir Henry Fowler, and Messrs. P. W. Bunting and G. Lidgett.

The commission did its work most thoroughly, taking two years over it. It is interesting to note the type of witnesses from whom evidence was taken, for a wide and alert interest in contemporary education was shown, both as regards theory and as regards practice. The witnesses included Dr. C. J. Vaughan. head master of Harrow (1844–59), who had devised the 'English Form' at that school, which was nothing more than a separate school to cater for the education of local children; Mr. (later Sir) J. G. Fitch, one of the assistant commissioners under Lord Taunton who had reported on some of the Methodist secondary schools; the Rev. Dr. A. Barry, Principal of King's College, London, and later Bishop of Sydney; two former governors of Woodhouse Grove School; the governor and head master of each of the two Connexional schools; assistant masters from both; assistant masters from other non-Methodist schools such as Wolverhampton Grammar School; and a number of Old Boys of both schools. In addition to the verbal evidence of these and others, a questionnaire was circulated to ministers and leading Methodist laymen, asking two questions:

1. Should the Connexional schools be open to laymen?
2. Should the course of study at each school be bifurcated into classical and modern sides?

Opinion on the first favoured leaving matters as they were, though non-Methodist witnesses, such as Dr. Vaughan and J. G.

Fitch, were strongly in favour of opening the schools to laymen's sons. This particular matter came up again in 1874 and in 1880, and on each occasion Methodists voted against it, and it was not till the twentieth century that the step was taken.

The second question produced varying replies which resolved themselves into four heads:

(a) Bifurcation in each school.

(b) One school to act as preparatory to the other.

(c) One school to give a classical, the other a modern, course.

(d) The leaving of matters as they were.

The commission decided to concentrate their attention on (b). The proposal was as revolutionary as had been Sir Henry's proposal for combining the two schools, for the schools were separated by two hundred miles. On the other hand, the proposal proved that Methodists were alive to what was going on around them. From 1860 onward there had been a growing interest in preparatory schools, largely due to the raising of the entrance age at the large boarding-schools. Preparatory schools were being established in considerable numbers, for they were regarded as the nurseries of the public schools, and the plan which has become common today was just being started—the public school administering its own preparatory school. This system of a continuous 'ladder' from entrance to the preparatory school to the close of school days had first been seen in certain large Roman Catholic schools over one hundred years previously.[6] It seems probable that Christ's Hospital had its own preparatory school early in the nineteenth century, and in 1862 a scheme was drawn up at Clifton College for the establishment of its own preparatory school. But these are the only examples of such schemes prior to 1870, and it is a tribute to the foresight of certain Methodists that they envisaged such a scheme. It obviously had considerable advantages, especially for Methodist ministers, the routine of whose family life is sufficiently upset by circuit changes without having the frequent changes of schools necessitated if the minister made use of local educational facilities. Under the proposed scheme, a minister who entered his son at the preparatory school would know that the boy's life was settled for the whole period of his education, that the whole of

[6] See article on 'Preparatory Schools of England' in the *Year Book of Education* (1939) by the present writer, which is a summary of part of a thesis which can be consulted in the Library of the University of London.

that education would be set in one mould, under masters of similar principles if not of similar views, and that when the boy reached the end of his school career he would have reached an age and should have reached a standard which would enable him to enter a university.

The commission also made detailed inquiries into the routine life of each school—into the vexed question of governor and head master, curriculum, accommodation, food, and staffing. Their *Report* was passed to the General Schools Committee and thence to Conference in 1873, and a large committee was appointed to consider the recommendations.

Most of them were agreed, but there was a reversion to Sir Henry Fowler's original proposal, and the recommendation was made that Woodhouse Grove School should be sold and Kingswood enlarged to house three hundred pupils. Conference, without a murmur of protest or dissent, passed this recommendation as part of the original Commission's *Report,* the whole being reported in the *Minutes* as follows:

'1. That while regarding with considerable favour the abstract principle, that it is desirable to admit the sons of laymen into our Connexional schools, the Conference, in view of many practical difficulties, is not prepared to adopt this change in our arrangements.

'2. That the system of dual government must, for the present, be maintained, but that its evils ought to be guarded against to the utmost by an exact definition of the several provinces of the governor and head master.

'3. That the local committees be directed to secure, by means of higher salaries or otherwise, a more efficient class of assistant tutors.

'4. That the whole system of education in our two schools shall be concentrated, and the schools themselves be concentrated in one locality.

'5. That the Woodhouse Grove estate be sold, and the proceeds of the sale devoted to the erection on the New Kingswood estate of additional buildings, for the use either of the higher or of the lower school, as may be hereafter determined.

'6. That a special committee be appointed to make such arrangements as are necessary for carrying out the concentration of the schools in one locality, powers being given to this special committee to act as occasion may require.

'7. That while approving of the general principles of the new scheme for the management of the schools, the Conference confides the details to the special committee.

'8. That the question of the financial relations of the Schools' Fund to the Children's Fund, with a view, in particular, to secure an effective regulation, from year to year, of the amount to be drawn from the Children's Fund in augmentation of the revenues of the Schools' Fund, and to the due apportionment of the Schools' Fund among the different schools, both for boys and girls, be remitted to the careful consideration of the special committee, in conjunction with the Committees of Management of the schools for girls.

'9. To this special committee the Conference refers all matters relating to the general management of the schools, whether for boys or girls.'[7]

When Conference had passed this it awoke to what it had done —or was awakened by the protests which came from all parts of Methodism, but especially from the north of England, which had come to regard Woodhouse Grove as its own special school. The Woodhouse Grove Committee of Management, upon whom the proposal to sell their school had come as a complete surprise, appealed to Conference. Pamphlets on the subject appeared. There was considerable newspaper correspondence. The President of Conference was urged and even begged to use his prerogative and hold up the implementation of any part of the proposals until Conference could once more have a chance of discussing them. He agreed to do this, and the matter came up before the Conference of 1874, but this time there was no inclination to sleep during discussions. The resolutions of the previous year were suspended, and the original report approved, the idea of either school being sold and the other enlarged being allowed to lapse for the time being.[8] Conference felt, however, that in concentration lay the only solution of the financial problem and there were many who believed that it would be advantageous also from an educational point of view. Meanwhile, however, the system of one school being preparatory to the other was to be put into effect as soon as possible. It was agreed that from July 1875 Woodhouse Grove School should act as the preparatory school, taking boys up to the age of approximately thirteen; Kingswood receiving the boys when they reached that age. A new Scheme of Management was drawn up,

[7] *Minutes of the Wesleyan Methodist Conference*, Vol. XIX, pp. 151–2.
[8] ibid., Vol. XIX, p. 509.

the chief points being that the management of both schools should henceforth be in the hands of one Governing Body, that the direction of education at both schools should be by one head master, and that the upper school should have its course of studies divided into 'classical' and 'modern' sides.[9]

One obvious difficulty was that of transport. Hitherto, on the whole, boys whose fathers were stationed in the south had gone to Kingswood and boys whose fathers were stationed in the north had gone to Woodhouse Grove. Railway travel by that time was moderately good, but there was likely to be great hardship caused by the cost of travel. It was agreed therefore that all ministers should contribute to a common fund, the amount of the contribution being reviewed from time to time by the Governing Body. Payment toward the cost of boys' travel would be made from this fund, so that no minister would have to pay more than another just because he happened to be stationed far from the school.

Dr. J. M. Raby resigned from the headmastership of Woodhouse Grove School and was appointed head master of the Primitive Methodist Connexional secondary school at York— Elmfield College. Thomas G. Osborn was appointed head master of the new joint school. Mr. Osborn lived at Kingswood School, and naturally could not be continually travelling the two hundred odd miles to the north, so that much of the success of the junior department depended on the senior master there, James Deaville, who later became head master of Kent College, Canterbury. It was largely due to these two men that the scheme worked for eight years with remarkable success. Its object was the provision of a better education and this object was achieved. Of the forty-seven boys who entered the school in 1871 and who spent the last years of their school life in the senior part of the school, eleven passed on to Oxford or Cambridge.

The head master purposely copied some of the best of the current public-school practice at Kingswood, as many of those who had supported the scheme had hoped he would. The curriculum was revised, being divided, as has been stated above, into two sides, as was done at The Leys and other public schools.

[9] Subjects of instruction were to be as follows: *At both schools*—A thorough English education, including Biblical knowledge, history, geography, singing, and drawing. *In the lower school*—Writing, Latin, French, arithmetic, elementary mathematics, object lessons in science. *In the upper school*—(classical side) Latin, Greek, French, German, mathematics, physical science; (modern side) Latin, French, German, mathematics, book-keeping, land-surveying, physical and political science.

The success of this experiment was helped by the greater specialization made possible amongst the respective staffs of the two departments. A prefect system was modelled on the arrangements made in other public schools, and this was coupled with a curious system of monitors who were paid a small weekly or monthly sum for the carrying out of routine duties.[10] This gave masters more time for that leisure which is so necessary if a secondary-school teacher is to give of his best in the classroom. There is no doubt that this revolutionary scheme resulted in a raising of the academic standard, but more important than that, it resulted also in a sound attitude toward the academic work. The head master made the most of the opportunity that was his to concentrate at the senior part of the school the pick of the masters of both schools, but the new attitude toward work was due in no small measure to the consciousness on the part of the boys that a future career depended upon themselves. There were no wealthy patrons to assist them, no endowments to send them to Oxford or Cambridge. A career at one of these universities depended upon the winning of an Open Scholarship or Exhibition, and many were won then and have been won since.

The working of the scheme, however, did not prove as economical as had been expected. It proved indeed to be more costly than the maintenance of the two schools separately, and it was this financial difficulty that dictated the end of the experiment which in all other respects had proved outstandingly successful.[11] There were, too, a number of Methodists who began vociferously to object to the education of ministers' sons 'beyond their station'. For such an attitude there can be no excuse and those who expressed such views can never have appreciated the meaning of education, still less the educational work of Methodism. The error of their ways was pointed out by a writer in the *Kingswood and Grovian Quarterly*: [12]

'Two things strike us forcibly in examining in detail the course of study laid down: first, that it is far more comprehensive and

[10] For example: Bun monitors, responsible for distribution of the supper buns each evening; a post monitor responsible for stamping and posting letters; a sickroom monitor, responsible for doing certain tasks to help the nursing staff.
[11] Today all the largest of the Methodist secondary schools have their own preparatory schools or departments. For example—St. Faith's for The Leys; Prior's Court for Kingswood; Oakwood Park for Rydal; Brontë House for Woodhouse Grove; Treliske for Truro; Cotlake House for Queen's College, Taunton; Cadogan House for Culford; Vernon Holme for Kent College, Canterbury.
[12] No. 4 (June 1880), pp. 109–10.

thorough than that of any grammar school for some hundred years; secondly, that it supplies a curious comment on the recommendations of certain brethren to reduce our present standard of education, recommendations which some have actually not been ashamed to urge in Conference! The fact is, that the standard set up by Wesley one hundred and thirty years ago was, in some respects, considerably higher than that to which we now aspire, notwithstanding the great strides made of late years in education everywhere, and the fact that Kingswood still stands in the front rank of the schools of our land. In those days Wesley thought six years barely sufficient for the ordinary school course, adding four years more for "a course of academic learning"; now, when the range of subjects taught everywhere is greatly increased, when the career in life open to a well-educated youth is immeasurably better than in Wesley's day, there is talk of reducing the time to five years.'

Nevertheless, the view that overmuch attention was being paid to the education of ministers' sons was widespread and insistent, and the period of education was reduced from six to five years.

It was a tragic move, all the more tragic when considered beside the clear-sighted and successful efforts then being made to provide better education for laymen's sons at The Leys. The true educationists, those most closely associated with the actual administration of the Connexional schools, found ways and means of avoiding the five-year rule, but it was not till 1896 that Wesley's term of education (six years) was officially restored. With the best will in the world the lack of endowments and pressure of economic needs could not be avoided, and the proposal to concentrate all the education of ministers' sons at either Kingswood or Woodhouse Grove began to be heard again, especially after 1878 when the Thanksgiving Fund voted a capital sum to the Connexional schools which would, it was thought, be sufficient to meet the expenses involved in transferring all educational activities to one school.

In 1880 the General (Schools) Committee proposed to Conference that concentration should take place at one or other of the schools, with the period of schooling being continued at five years. This again roused great opposition and the matter was referred to District Synods for further consideration. It appeared on their agenda for March and at that time a pamphlet entitled *Suggestions respecting the Connexional Schools for Preachers' Children* was circulated.

In due course the Synods debated the matter and the results suggested that few of their members really understood the problems which had necessitated the proposal in the first place. Only five Synods were in favour of concentration at Kingswood; all agreed that the period of schooling should remain reduced; some were in favour of concentration at Woodhouse Grove rather than at Kingswood; some felt that a return to the old plan of two separate schools would be the best solution. There was, however, a majority in opposition to concentration at Kingswood.

The two schools had many friends outside the District Synods and to the 1881 Conference was addressed a petition signed by a large number of Old Boys of both schools, strongly urging the policy of concentration. This petition puts the facts so clearly that it is quoted in full:

'As the question of the maintenance or destruction of the Connexional boys' schools as they stand at present is now approaching a crisis, we, the undersigned, feeling ourselves to be in the best position to speak of the advantages obtained under a system which has been tried for the last six years, have been sorry no opportunity has been given us of publicly expressing our opinion on its merits or demerits. Constrained by the threatened extinction of the present system, we venture at the last moment to address you on the subject, and to request that your final vote may not be given in aid of a policy which we believe will be disastrous, not only to preachers' sons, for many generations, but to the education and well-being of Methodism at large. And for the following reasons:

'1. As regards expense, the plan of concentration at Kingswood (rejected by so many District Meetings) is now distinctly found to be the cheapest in the long run.

'2. As regards the character of the education now given at Kingswood, stigmatized by some as "too good for their station in life" (a) the standard is no higher than in past days, even those of John Wesley: the difference consists in the larger number of boys who now attain it, in other words, in the thoroughness of the "average boy's" work.

'(b) In nearly every case a preacher's son has no help toward his start in life but his education, which has been hitherto valued as a priceless privilege. The education of their children has always been in Methodism part of the preacher's allowance; how much prized it is needless to say.

'(c) An inferior education would be injurious to the further prospects, both of our Ministry and of Methodist culture, for a glance at the list of candidates this year will show what a large proportion is drawn from Kingswood and Grove boys alone, while the large number of these now engaged in education is a sufficient proof of the work of the school in this department.[13]

'(d) In this age of universal education, we believe that the proposed step is a retrograde movement, and that our spiritual life and power for good will be injured by our falling behind the times in this matter; and we are convinced that if the decision against which we complain is ratified by Conference, results will soon be apparent to the world which will make Methodism a laughing-stock in every educational circle in the land.

'3 (a) By this step you will throw away the whole of the money, the labour and time of preachers, and the talents of other distinguished men in our Connexion, all sunk in an experiment which has, confessedly on all hands, produced the most brilliant results, results steadily improving every year, and results, be it observed, obtained not from a few picked and clever lads, but from the average boys of the school as a whole, for anyone who knows Kingswood and Grove systems, and the character of Mr. Osborn's management, will resent an imputation to the contrary as a libel upon our School.

'(b) Might we also refer to the fact that Conference has appointed a committee which investigated all the details of the case, and considered every possible way of escape from debt, with a deliberate care that leaves nothing to be desired. That committee, with its full knowledge of the circumstances of our schools, proposed a plan as the result of their joint wisdom. It will seem very strange if, after all this, the Conference should decide to overthrow by one vote the decisions of its wisest leaders, upon the recommendation of a majority of its District Meetings, whose investigations and discussions may fairly be said to be crude and partial compared with those of the committee appointed by Conference.

'In conclusion we would express our deep concern for the name of the schools. Every minister is proud of them now, but would they be if next year our school were beaten by many that have been hopelessly behind it for years? If, to take a particular instance, the number of successes in the Oxford Local Examinations fall off by twenty, as might well be the case, for the united schools during the last six years have passed twenty more boys

[13] See *The Kingswood and Grove Quarterly*, No. 4, pp. 132–3.

per annum than did the two separate ones; also the number of successful Oxford candidates from the united schools during the last six years is very nearly as large as the number passed during the previous eighteen years since the system of Oxford Middle Class Examinations commenced. Such facts speak for themselves, and loudly call upon you not to legalize these fatal measures.'

This was the first occasion on which the Old Boys as a body had spoken and their opinion carried considerable weight, for there was no gainsaying the fact that the Connexional schools had produced fine results. After much discussion and some bitterness it was decided to concentrate the education of ministers' sons at Kingswood, where the period of education would continue to be five years only.

On 13th June 1883 the combined Kingswood and Woodhouse Grove School broke up for the last time, but Woodhouse Grove was not dead. Conference, in making its decision, had stated that the estate should be retained and appropriated to some Methodist educational purpose, and a company—the Woodhouse Grove School Company Limited—similar to those which were being formed in various parts of England at that time, was formed to lease the premises from the Conference and to establish a secondary school, for it was felt by north-countrymen that there was ample scope for more than the one Wesleyan school (Wesley College, Sheffield) which already existed there. In October 1883 the school reopened therefore with sixty-four boys, mainly drawn from Lancashire and Yorkshire, and still more vacancies booked for the following year. Woodhouse Grove had become one of the 'Company' schools then being founded in various parts of the country to cater for the higher education of middle-class families, and the education of ministers' sons was concentrated at Kingswood. The memory of the past is perpetuated in the name of the Association of Old Boys: 'The Kingswood and Old Grove Union,' and it is peculiarly fitting that the two names should be thus linked, for a study of the development of secondary education in Methodism reveals these two schools forming, as it were, the trunk of a tree, and branching off from it as the century developed were numerous off-shoots which in turn added their contribution. There are few Methodist schools or colleges in the world which do not owe their origin to some former pupil of the two first Connexional schools of Methodism. Methodism has always been a growth expanding from within and Methodist education shows the same trait, which explains at the same time the triumphs and the deficiencies of its secondary education—the former due to the spirit of fellowship shown in whole-hearted social service, the latter due to the financial difficulties with which Methodism has had always to contend. It was, for example, an Old Boy of the Grove who was mainly responsible for the founding of Wesley College, Sheffield, while an Old Boy of Kingswood was the second master there when it opened; an Old Boy of the Grove was the first head master of The Leys, while his successor had been a pupil at Kingswood. The first head master of Queen's College, Taunton, had been a master at that school, and his two successors had been pupils there. It was a former head master of Kingswood who founded Rydal School, while several of the first head masters of the 'Company' schools were former pupils or masters at one of the Connexional schools.

These examples, which could be considerably extended, possibly suggest a too-narrow field of search on the part of those responsible for appointing head masters, but Old Boys of these schools were not concerned only with Methodist schools. Over fifty secondary schools of this country during the nineteenth century had at one time or another head masters who had been pupils at Kingswood or Woodhouse Grove, and amongst these were Tonbridge, Brighton College, the Liverpool Institute, the Stationers' Hall, London, and Grammar Schools at Huddersfield, Burnley, Tavistock, Penrith, and Helston.

Nor were they concerned only with English schools. Missionary interest is naturally closely connected with evangelicalism, and the saying of Wesley's that 'the world is my parish' had a practical meaning for pupils of all the Methodist secondary schools, and many former pupils founded schools and colleges in all parts of the world. The following are amongst the best-known of those which were founded by former pupils of Kingswood and Woodhouse Grove: The York Castle School, Jamaica; Kingswood College, Grahamstown, South Africa; Doveton College, Madras; Wesley College, Colombo, Ceylon; Newington College, Sydney; Wesley College, Melbourne; Prince Albert College, Auckland, New Zealand; and Wesley College, Haiti.

CHAPTER FIFTEEN

The Forward Movement in Education

WESLEY PREACHED the necessity of changing men's hearts, but he never meant, as some of his followers in the nineteenth century appeared to believe, that individual salvation automatically implied the salvation of the whole world. Co-operation, the active fellowship between man and man, of all classes, all abilities, and all races, was necessary if results were to be achieved. That was what came once again to be realized in Methodism toward the end of the nineteenth century, and during the 1870's Methodism began to express the principle in practical fashion. It became more active in its evangelism than it had been since the death of Wesley, and this revival of activity which had been the hall-mark of early Methodism has been labelled 'the Forward Movement'. It was directed primarily toward the lower classes from whom Methodism with its middle-class bias was tending to drift, but it affected Methodism as a whole, particularly through its youth, and showed itself in many different ways, though all were connected with social service.

The Rev. Dr. T. B. Stephenson founded the National Children's Home in 1869, and it is typical of the spirit of Methodism that this minister from the first insisted on the word 'Home' and saw to it that his centres of work for destitute and orphaned children were homes in more than mere name. Central halls were founded in great cities, through which Methodism went to the people as Wesley had gone one hundred and fifty years earlier, for these halls were more than mere preaching centres: they were the centres for social services of health, advice, and companionship which today are commonplace, but which in the nineteenth century were rare. Sparsely populated rural circuits were organized into rural 'missions', and partly to staff them Cliff College was opened as a training centre for evangelists; the importance of women in this social work was recognized by the establishment of the Wesley Deaconess Order (1890).

Methodism, in fact, began to look beyond the narrow world of the chapel and to realize afresh its responsibility in social life outside itself. The Christian contribution of Methodism to that life in the eighteenth and early nineteenth centuries had been the humanizing of society, but during the early nineteenth century Methodism had tended to draw aloof from the mob. Total abstinence was still not one of the features of Methodism, but the fight against drunkenness was beginning, and Methodism was taking upon itself the championship of virtue against the vice of immorality, gambling, crime, and what remained of the slave trade. The evils of slum conditions and the degradation of destitution, the non-observance of the Sabbath—these and kindred evils were no longer accepted as part of the normal conditions of life upon earth, the pill of their acceptance being coated with the sugary promise of eternal life thereafter.

Speaking at City Road Chapel at the centenary anniversary of Wesley's death, and answering the oft-levelled criticism that Methodism was 'other worldly,' the Rev. Hugh Price Hughes—the recognized leader and orator of the Forward Movement—said:

'We believe that the vision which John Wesley had was a vision not of heaven, but of earth changed and purified and blessed by the power of Jesus Christ. . . . For my own part, I know very little about heaven. It is down here on earth that our sympathy ought to go forth, down here where there is a public-house at the corner of every street, where the pavements are crowded with scoundrels and their victims, and where it is so difficult to do right. We believe that love to our neighbour requires that we should vote at the election of Poor Law Guardians, and of School Boards, and of Town and County Councils. We believe, also, that we are bound, when qualified, as part of our religious duties, to stand as candidates for civic offices. . . . We recognize our social duties, and fully appreciate the incalculable and imperishable services rendered to Christianity by the pioneer of our social work, Dr. Stephenson.'[1]

Those words were spoken in 1891, and it had taken twenty years by then to convince Methodism as a whole of the truths expressed. Although a start was made in the 1870's, Wesleyan Methodism was slow to shed its traditional conservatism, and it was largely because of this slowness that in 1880 the Salvation Army opened its campaign against middle-class respectability and the aloofness of puritanism. The Quakers were in turn awakened by the militant spirit of the Salvation Army, and wealthy members like Cadbury and Rowntree started a methodical philanthropy and dropped their previous exclusive-

[1] *Wesley: the Man, his Teaching, and his Work*, pp. 356-7.

ness. Gradually Wesleyan Methodism began to lose its strong denominationalism and to make advances to the other branches of Methodism, sowing the seeds which flowered in the union of the Methodist Churches in 1932.

Hugh Price Hughes used to claim that Robert Browning was the poet of the Forward Movement, but he pointed out too that though God was in His heaven all was not right with the world, and that it was in the power of youth to improve matters. For this reason he was a strong supporter of education. Through the newspaper that he founded in 1885—*The Methodist Times*— he voiced the central theme of his life: the existence of a great common element in Christianity. He tried to broadcast his belief that only by educating children to realize the existence of this common element could it become a practical principle.

The Forward Movement was then closely connected with education, and the year 1871 may be taken as the year in which Methodism began its Forward Movement in secondary education. In that year the Universities Tests Act was passed. Today, the casual reader considers it merely as one of the many educational Acts passed during the latter part of the nineteenth century, but to contemporary Nonconformists it meant momentous social change. One direct result had been the foundation of The Leys school.

One school, however, was not enough. During the century commercial life had developed. New methods of manufacture, of farming, of communication, and of publicity had compelled a change in the economic and social system. Increased wealth required increased expenditure; keener competition meant the squeezing out of the small man; and the one-man business, though much in evidence until well into the twentieth century, began to give way to company business. With it all the attitude toward education changed. Where a living had to be earned and a trade to be learned, previously the practical education provided by apprenticeship had been more sought after than theoretical education, but, with the new methods of commerce and the development of science, theory became necessary before practice could be begun and the public began to turn to the schools for their theory. The middle classes, who were by then the wealthy classes, were those chiefly affected, but feudal traditions died slowly and the new-rich middle classes hankered after the things that previously had been the privilege of the upper classes alone. One of these was the form of education labelled

'Public School'. There were only nine public schools recognized by the Clarendon Commission in 1864, but enterprising men, many years before that date, had begun to found schools modelled on the older schools. The financial difficulties of those undertakings were too great, however, for most individuals to bear and so education came to make use of commercial practice and shareholding companies were formed to build, equip, and maintain schools of the type required. The fact that these schools were founded on such lines did not cheapen them. They set out to copy the best traditions of the public schools and on the whole they succeeded, largely owing to the fact that many of their first head masters were pupils or assistants of the 'great' reforming head masters of the nineteenth century who had retained the best and driven out the worst. But sometimes there was a too-slavish imitation of the mere framework without a true understanding of the principles involved. A case in point was Dunheved College, founded by Methodists in Launceston in 1873, in which the chief feature was the provision of studies for pupils!

It happened that when the Universities Tests Act was passed Hugh Price Hughes was stationed at Oxford and it was there and at that time that he began his practical work as an apostle of the Forward Movement. He founded the Wesley Guild, whose members were mainly undergraduates. E. E. Kellett writes as one who knew him at that time:

'There were no outbursts, no "purple patches"; everything was plain and unadorned. . . . No subject was mentioned, but spontaneously and unconsciously he began to *work* upon it. Usually of course his mind took a practical rather than a spectacular turn; he always seemed to be devising, rejecting, renewing a scheme of action. For example, the conversation turned upon Kingswood School. His whole line was, "Can something be done there?" "Don't you think something might be effected here?" He had to the full the statesman's power of assimilating ideas; but those ideas nearly always took a practical shape.' [2]

Like Wesley, he directed the energies of undergraduates toward the needs of the poor, and in the ragged school mission which he started at Oxford he gave a practical example of the working of his views. That same tendency was seen in his interest in the foundation of the Congregational Mansfield College and later in the foundation of the Leysian Mission.

[2] Quoted by D. P. Hughes, *Life of Hugh Price Hughes*, p. 138.

That was the background that was beginning to be formed in Methodism from about 1870 onward, and in which was set the greatest step forward in Methodist higher education. It is no coincidence that this took place at a time when the outlook of Methodism was changing from one of individualism to one of collectivism, with what had been a Liberal minority becoming the dominant voice of official Methodism.

The first proposal for the establishment of a system of Methodist secondary education had been put forward in 1868, but whatever interest that and the ensuing correspondence in *The Watchman* had evoked, no action had started, and it was not until 1874 that a proposal obviously based on the former one was put forward in Conference. It was an appropriate occasion for the opening of the question of Methodist secondary education. After the silent, undisputed passing of the resolution to sell Woodhouse Grove School at the previous Conference and the subsequent outcry, it was well known that the Conference of 1874 would be especially wide-awake to matters of education. At that time, too, the scheme for the foundation of The Leys was in the forefront of Methodist minds. That, then, was the occasion which the Rev. William Arthur chose to push home the work already done through the Press and private conversations. Supported by the layman largely responsible for the foundation of the Methodist College, Belfast, he moved:

'That this Meeting hears with much satisfaction of the continued prosperity and extension of the Methodist Day- and Sunday-schools and of the Children's Home. While the Meeting highly values the services, both general and specific, which are rendered by the foregoing Institutions, and by the Sheffield and Taunton Colleges, it is of opinion that, in order to meet existing wants and duly to complete the educational arrangements of Methodism, it is not only desirable to provide such Higher Education as is contemplated by the Cambridge Scheme, in harmony with the Resolutions of the last Conference, but also to promote the establishment, in various parts of the country, of Methodist Middle-class Schools, so organized as to furnish suitable instruction by the best methods and on moderate terms.' [3]

The Resolution was passed and the General Committee instructed to inquire into the matter and report to the next Conference, for it was manifest that a great deal of preliminary

[3] *Minutes of Conference,* Vol. XIX, p. 524.

survey was necessary before a system of middle-class schools could be realized.

The Committee's report, embodying a scheme, was duly presented to the 1875 Conference.[4] It was obvious from the first that the chief difficulty would be the usual one of finance, and the unadorned plainness of the proposals suggest that money-saving was in the forefront of the minds of men who, however much they might wish to copy the example set by Canon Woodard, were prevented by lack of money. Each school, once it had been established, was expected to be self-supporting, since no aid could be expected from Government or Connexional funds. The schools were to be day-schools, though accommodation for boarders could be provided, subject to the managers' approval, in the house of the head or second master (or mistress). It was, in fact, the scheme, already being successfully administered for primary schools, raised to the higher curriculum standard of secondary schools.

There for three years the matter rested. A few further details were worked out and there was a considerable amount of discussion, but no practical results. Apart from the inevitable financial difficulties there was no excuse for further delay. In the mid-century one of the greatest drawbacks in secondary education was the lack of a recognized standard and this had resulted in a confusion of apprenticeship with education in its wider sense. But that drawback had been largely removed, especially when the Oxford Local Examinations had been started in 1858 and the scope of the matriculation examination widened. Something had to be done for the middle classes of Methodism, however. They were the most powerful in the Connexion, and there was a real danger lest for lack of schools for laymen's sons and daughters future generations should drift away from Methodism.

A special committee was appointed to make further inquiries into education other than primary, and in 1878 it made its report. In general, it merely reiterated arguments which had been used repeatedly during the previous ten years, but it did emphasize for the first time the need for boarding-schools rather than day-schools—a fact which suggests better acquaintance with the scheme evolved by Canon Woodard in 1847 in which was stressed the importance of boarding-schools.

The matter was referred back to another committee for still

[4] See Appendix D, p. 332, *infra*.

further inquiry and consideration and this committee supported the lack of initiative being shown by Conference by finding that the whole matter was one of extreme difficulty, needing 'further interchange of thought and opinion'. The need for boarding-schools seems to have frightened many, and no doubt it was this, together with the need for economy, which prevented speedier action. The committee did, however, draw up a Memorandum which was widely distributed amongst members of the Connexion in order to acquaint them with the urgency of the problem. It pointed out that the subject must be approached from a national as well as from a Methodist point of view, and it dealt with the subject under two main headings:

1. The provision of secondary day-schools, which would be administered by the existing General Education Committee and which would supply the type of education which had been given for many years in some of the Methodist primary schools to the children of artisans, farmers, and others—an education which was more advanced than that which primary schools were expected to give.

2. The provision of secondary boarding-schools similar to the schools already existing except that they would be under Connexional supervision.

The Memorandum clearly indicated the anxiety which the success of the Woodard schools had engendered in the minds of Methodists.[5] The fees in these Woodard schools were so graded that people of all income levels could find a school to suit them, and there was a real danger lest Methodists, desiring a boarding-school education for their sons, should make use of the advantages offered in these Church of England schools, one of whose objects was the winning back of dissenters to the Church.

It proposed, therefore, that the Education Committee should foster and supplement, by loan or gift, local efforts to establish schools (there were a number of private schools, many of them founded by Old Boys of Kingswood and Woodhouse Grove Schools, and it was felt that some of these might be brought more directly under the control of the Connexion); establish an experimental model school on the pattern of the Woodard schools; found an association for carrying on, with local assistance, schools in places where they would be likely to succeed; promote

[5] The following Woodard schools had by that time either been opened or were about to be opened: Lancing, Hurstpierpoint, Ardingly, Denstone, and King's College, Taunton.

the establishment of cheaper schools as branches of some of the existing Connexional schools; establish boarding-houses in large towns so that children from country districts might, under good influence, take advantage of grammar- or other day-schools in towns; employ an agent to investigate the circumstances of different districts of the country and watch for openings for successful efforts.

It was a most useful Memorandum, but it was only a Memorandum. After ten years of 'interchange of thought and opinion' it was time for something more practical than a mere scrap of paper to be produced. Although during this period much practical success was being attained in Methodist education, it was largely due, as it always had been, to individual enterprise. Conference, as the representative body of the whole Connexion, did not do all it might have done to assist such enterprise, for no longer was the Connexional organization needing to be nursed. It had already been weaned, and there was opportunity to enlarge and revivify the Connexion by expanding its organization for the training of youth. Yet, in spite of the warnings and the encouragement of individuals, Conference did nothing but agree that the problem was one of 'extreme difficulty' and advise that 'opportunity should be given for further interchange of thought and opinion'! Even the concluding words of the Memorandum appeared to have little effect:

'The future of our Church lies with the youth; and if the more intelligent and better educated of these should be gradually drafted off into other communities, the usefulness, if not the existence, of Methodism would be seriously imperilled.'

It was fortunate that a step was taken at that time which undoubtedly played a large part in implementing proposals concerning secondary education. For many years the position of laymen in the organization of the Wesleyan Methodist Connexion had been a vexed one. There is no need here to show how laymen came gradually to take a leading place in that organization.[6] Suffice it that in 1878 Districts were empowered to send not only ministers but elected laymen to the annual Conference, and it was arranged that henceforth Conference should meet in two sessions: A ministerial session which would meet first and deal with purely ministerial affairs, and a representative session in which there would be as many laymen as there were ministers. It was this session which henceforth dealt with administrative

[6] See Maldwyn Edwards, *Methodism and England*, pp. 228–40.

and financial matters. It was a momentous change and one which had taken long in coming, and to mark the occasion a Thanksgiving Fund was started which soon reached a total of £297,518. Much of this was spent in settling old debts, but some of it was set aside for schemes of extension such as education, and this fact added weight to the Memorandum which was being circulated and discussed. In May 1878 it came before the various District Synods, some of which took the initiative and approved of the establishment of a school or schools in their own area. The chief credit in this respect goes to the Cornwall District, which not only approved the general recommendations of the Memorandum, but took steps to implement them. A Committee was appointed and it was decided to found a secondary school for boarders and day-boys at Truro. This school, opened in January 1880 and moved in 1882 to its present position dominating the town, was the first of a number of similar schools founded in all parts of the country—two others before the Conference of 1880.

This action by the Cornwall District impressed Conference, and in 1879 it authorized the allocation of £10,000 from the Thanksgiving Fund for the assistance of such local action, and appointed trustees to make appropriate grants. It forbade the Education Committee to assume responsibility for starting schools, however, and so missed the opportunity of founding a Connexional system of secondary schools which had been for long advocated by a minority. In 1880 Conference expressed its satisfaction at the local efforts being made and empowered the Education Committee (1) to consider schemes for the further establishment of such schools and to give advice as required; (2) to report to Conference on such schemes; (3) to act on behalf of the Conference in such cases in the interval between one Conference and the next; (4) to present to the Conference annually any suggestions for the promotion of the interests of Methodist middle-class education.

A list of secondary schools which became in any sense connected with official Methodism and which were founded before the close of the nineteenth century is appended.[7] Two of them were private schools and three more were founded by the Primitive Methodists, the United Methodists, and the Bible Christians respectively, but most of them were 'Company' schools, started by means of share capital under Articles of Association which

[7] See Appendix E, p. 334, *infra*.

provided for the payment of dividend limited to five per cent. Each school had its own Board of Directors and when a grant was made from the Thanksgiving Fund, Conference was represented on this Board. There were no endowments and Conference could not undertake to make further grants, so that each school had to rely for its income on pupils' fees.

Thus was started a system of Methodist secondary schools, but at that time there was no attempt to Connexionalize the schools. The Conference merely assumed a paternal attitude of interest without assuming any paternal responsibilities.

It is unnecessary here to deal in detail with the foundation of each school. They were all open to day- and boarding-pupils, and though the administration was Methodist, there were no religious tests, the schools being open to all-comers, as was Wesley's own school in its earliest days.

The expansion of Methodist secondary education was both a sign and a cause of the broadening of Methodist cultural life. Shakespeare was no longer regarded as one whose works were only fit for the fire,[8] novelists began to be referred to in the pulpit and were no longer regarded as immoral wasters of time, the theatre was still suspect, but it was not long before the plays of Galsworthy and Shaw linked it with Methodism's own efforts toward social reform. There were enlightened views on science too. At the Ecumenical Conference of 1891 Percy Bunting gave an address on the influence of modern scientific progress on religious thought, in which he accepted Darwin's theory of evolution and tried to relate it to religion. It is only right, however, to remember that this broader cultural life was only beginning. Methodist writers have shown how drab and hide-bound much of Methodism still was.[9] Nevertheless there was enlightenment and a growing sense of culture, and it was largely education that was responsible. In all the Methodist secondary schools English had been part of the curriculum since their foundation; libraries were provided and pupils encouraged to make full use of them, often through customs which appear eccentric but were none the less effective—the silence-at-meals rule at Kingswood, the read-

[8] The Rev. John Pawson, President of the Wesleyan Methodist Conference in 1793 and 1801, burnt Wesley's annotated edition of Shakespeare's works as 'useless lumber'. (See G. Eayrs, *Wesley: Christian Philosopher and Church Founder*, p. 81.)

[9] See Herbert E. Palmer, *The Mistletoe Child* (1935); Edward Thompson, *Introducing the Arnisons* (1935), *John Arnison* (1939). The first-named of these authors was an Old Boy of Woodhouse Grove School; the second, of Kingswood.

ing aloud during sewing at Laleham. Many of the staff at the schools, by their own enthusiasm, inspired boys with a genuine interest in science and, in fact, in intellectual matters not for their examination value, but for their own sake. It is significant that it was during the closing years of the nineteenth century that out-of-school activities were being organized—debating societies, scientific societies, musical societies. A Shakespeare play was first performed at Laleham in 1875, and became an annual feature of the school's activities.

With all this expansion of interest, Methodism lost nothing of its spiritual life, and at a time when in many of the boarding-schools the cult of athleticism was beginning to overshadow all other aspects of school life, Methodism continued to instil a 'Nonconformist conscience' and to centre the life of its schools in religion. Speaking of these secondary schools in 1891, a Cornishman said: 'I want to see a stream of this young Christian influence flowing forth from us, helping to purify the Press, public life, country life, municipal life, political life of the land.' [10] This again was the voice of the Forward Movement.

[10] George J. Smith in *Wesley: the Man, his Teaching, and his Work*, p. 350.

CHAPTER SIXTEEN

The Education of Girls

LITTLE HAS BEEN SAID about the education of girls, though the activity connected with the foundation of Methodist 'Company' schools was directed equally toward the foundation of schools for boys and for girls. The history of Methodist girls' education is parallel to the history of girls' education generally, showing the same deficiencies, but showing also a fair contribution to it once a start had been made.

Particularly praiseworthy were the efforts made for the primary education of poor children, in which there was little differentiation between boys and girls. The work of providing teachers for these schools caused a demand for secondary schools in which a broad cultural background could be given. In higher education, private enterprise established schools which, like all the private schools of the eighteenth and nineteenth centuries, were of all degrees of efficiency and inefficiency, and whose educational standards and age-ranges varied considerably.

Wesley's views on girls' schools were no different from his views on boys' schools. In his schools for primary education at the Foundery, Newcastle, and Kingswood (Old House), boys and girls were educated together and followed the same curriculum. In his view they were all children, all subject to the same shortcomings, all requiring the same treatment to fit them for the life to come. In considering higher education, just as he warned parents not to send their sons to the big boarding-schools unless they wished to send them straight to hell, so elsewhere he warned them against the large boarding-schools for girls, in which pupils taught each other 'pride, vanity, affectation, intrigue, artifice, and, in short, everything which a Christian woman ought not to learn'. In fact, he continued: 'I never yet knew a pious, sensible woman that had been bred at a large boarding-school, who did not aver, one might as well send a young maid to be bred in Drury Lane.' [1] He himself was shocked one day (in 1772) when he was being entertained by a Methodist gentleman who had become well-to-do and who had sent his daughters to a fashionable school. Wesley, recording the visit, wrote: 'The children

[1] *Works*, Vol. VII, p. 84.

that used to cling about me, and drink in every word, had been at a boarding-school. There they had unlearned all religion, and even seriousness, and had learned pride, vanity, affectation, and whatever could guard them against the knowledge and love of God.' [2]

But he gave credit where it was due. Some years afterwards he visited a Quaker boarding-school for girls and was 'much pleased' with the pupils. [3]

It was the large boarding-school that Wesley did not like. As has already been emphasized, the keynote of Wesley's educational theory was its family aspect. He would like to see girls taught at home by their mothers, just as his seven sisters had been taught at home by Susanna Wesley, but he uttered an amusing warning against letting their grandmothers have any hand in the education! [4] He was essentially a practical man, however, and he realized that home education was not always possible. In such circumstances he recommended that the girls should be sent 'to some mistress that truly fears God; one whose life is a pattern to her scholars, and who has only so many that she can watch over each as one that must give account to God.' [5]

During his lifetime Wesley came to know a number of girls' schools in various parts of the country. One of his early favourites was at Publow, near Bristol, which was kept by a Mrs. Owen and her daughters, and which owed its existence in some measure to Wesley's encouragement. [6] There the number of pupils was never allowed to rise much above twenty, since the principals felt they could not deal efficiently with more—a sentiment with which Wesley was in entire agreement. At first he was so impressed by the conduct of this school that he wrote: 'Here is a family indeed. Such mistresses, and such a company of children, as, I believe, all England cannot parallel!' [7]

At one time Wesley was so enthusiastic about the pupils there that he called them a 'lovely family', [8] but the school did not continue to be what it was when he first knew it, and Wesley related how imperceptibly it fell from its original simplicity, [9] and was eventually taken over by another friend of his, a Miss Bishop, when the Misses Owen moved to London about 1780.

Under Miss Bishop the school found new life. It was, said

[2] *Journal,* Vol. V, p. 452. [3] ibid., Vol. VII, p. 59.
[4] *Works,* Vol. VII, p. 96. [5] ibid., Vol. VII, p. 84.
[6] *Journal,* Vol. V, p. 484 n. [7] ibid., p. 484.
[8] ibid., Vol. VI, p. 78. And see also p. 210.
[9] *Letters,* Vol. VII, pp. 62–3, 74.

268

Wesley, 'worthy to be called a Christian school. It is what the school at Publow was!' [10] Proof that Wesley did not underestimate the teacher's task is provided in a letter which he wrote to Miss Bishop:

'Mr. Baxter well observes (or, indeed, Archbishop Usher, to whom he refers, had done before him) "that whoever attempt to profit children will find need of all the understanding God has given them". But, indeed, natural understanding will go but a little way. It is a peculiar gift of God. I believe He has given you a measure of it already, and you may ask and expect an increase of it. . . .' [11]

This school, too, was a boarding-school small enough to ensure that each pupil was recognized as an individual and for the group to be in fact a family. Wesley only mentioned one large school, and he did so with some surprise at the manner in which the head mistress, a Mrs. Edwards, 'a person of no extraordinary natural abilities, teaches near a hundred children, and keeps them in as good, if not better, order than most schoolmistresses in the kingdom!' [12] This was a boarding-school at Lambeth.

Another school which greatly interested him was one for girl orphans at Leytonstone, under the charge of Mary Bosanquet. A daughter of a well-to-do family with an income of her own, she was early converted to a more active form of Christianity than was usually practised at that time among folk of her standing, and, because of her decision, she was driven from her father's house. Amongst her close friends was Sarah Ryan, who for a time was matron at Kingswood School. In 1763 these two ladies opened a school for girl orphans at Leytonstone which continued until the death of Sarah Ryan five years later. Miss Bosanquet then moved the school to a farm at Cross Hall, Yorkshire, where it continued until her marriage to the Rev. John Fletcher of Madeley in 1781. There were approximately forty pupils, but in spite of what he considered high numbers Wesley gave it his highest praise when he called it 'one truly Christian family',[13] and remarked: 'How willingly could I spend the residue of a busy life in this delightful retirement.' [14]

From what has been said above concerning girls' schools specifically mentioned by Wesley, it is impossible to draw any fine distinction between primary and secondary education. Nor

---

[10] *Journal*, Vol. VI, p. 336.   [11] *Letters*, Vol. V, p. 335.
[12] *Journal*, Vol. VII, p. 344.   [13] ibid., Vol. V, p. 152. See also p. 195.
[14] ibid., Vol. VI, p. 72.

is there any need to do so. The movement toward the modern conception of higher education for girls was only beginning, and any practical measures for their education tended to have a good influence on the movement as a whole once those measures ceased to consist of merely superficial 'accomplishments'.

Although, therefore, Wesley had some interest in the education of girls it was not a direct interest, and he never attempted to do for the daughters what he did for the sons of Methodism. This is not surprising since most girls in Wesley's day who received any form of higher education received it at home at the hands of private tutors. If Wesley gave any thought to the question of his preachers' daughters he probably hoped that the majority would be educated at home as his own sisters had been. He was content, like most of his contemporaries, to let private schools meet the demand, small as it was, for girls' education. Probably he gave the matter little attention. All he was interested in was their spiritual capacity and in this respect he regarded men and women as equals. But in thus regarding them he did make an important indirect contribution to women's education in the nineteenth century, for in Wesley's day women of all classes except the very lowest were regarded as counterparts of Rousseau's Sophie—mere dolls of inferior intellect planted on earth as playthings for men and as a means of propagating the race. Girls were advised to 'be ever cautious in displaying your good sense. It will be thought you assume a superiority over the rest of the company. But if you happen to have any learning, keep it a profound secret, especially from the men, who generally look with a jealous and malignant eye on a woman of great parts and a cultural understanding.' [15] It was against such a conception of education and women's place in society that a number of clever women, many of whom came from the parsonages of England, rebelled and worked to raise their mental and social status. They owed their reforming zeal and self-realization in no small measure to the awakening caused by Methodism. Wesley died in 1791, but it was largely because of the manner of his life during the previous sixty years that the 'blue-stockings', as they were nicknamed, were at that very time fighting, not for the political emancipation of women, but for an acknowledgement of women's rights as human and reasoning beings. Their chief means of making known their

[15] Dr. Gregory, *A Father's Legacy to his Daughter* (1774).

270

effort was that of books and pamphlets,[16] and, as would be expected if this reform movement did in face owe something to the Methodist revival, religion featured in their works and beliefs. They fought against the 'pitiful worldly shifts and sleight-of-hand tricks',[17] the mode of so-called education which concentrated on superficialities calculated to attract the unmarried male, but they fought also to raise 'the depressed tone of public morals and awake the drowsy spirit of religious principle'.[18] The author of these last words was Hannah More, a lady who did not begin her educational writings until middle age when, as a result of her conversion to Methodism, she started a campaign of practical philanthropy and women's educational reform.

It is difficult to gauge the exact extent of Methodism's contribution to the improved status of women which became more pronounced as the nineteenth century advanced, but that Methodism was one of the contributory factors cannot be denied. Miss Sara Burstall, one of the pioneers of women's education in the nineteenth century, certainly attributed to Wesley and the Evangelical leaders at least something of the enlightenment which led later to the improvement in the status of women.[19] Methodism's emphasis on the importance of the individual and on the equality of male and female in its Class Meetings did tend to alter current views. The direct contribution of Methodism to women's higher education was negligible until late in the nineteenth century, but the indirect influence, through the recognition of women's place in society, was considerable.

The 'blue-stockings' of the eighteenth century were voices crying in the wilderness as far as immediate results were concerned, and during the following century the social etiquette of the Victorians tended to glorify 'accomplishments'—'drawing-room tricks', as a Methodist lady described them toward the end of the century. The emergence of wealthy middle-class families

[16] The most important of these works were: Mary Wollstonecraft, *Thoughts on the Education of Daughters*, with *Reflections on Female Conduct in the most important Duties of Life* (1789), *Vindication of the Rights of Women* (1792). Mrs. Catharine Macaulay, *Letters on Education with Observations on Religious and Metaphysical Subjects* (1790). Maria Edgeworth, *Practical Education* (1798), *Letters for Literary Ladies* (1795). Hannah More, *Strictures on the Modern System of Female Education* (1799), *View of the Principles and Conduct prevalent among Women of Rank and Fortune* (1799).

[17] Mary Wollstonecraft, *Vindication of the Rights of Women*, Prefatory Note, p. xx.

[18] Hannah More, *Strictures on the Modern System of Female Education*, p. 313.

[19] In her *Public Schools for Girls*, p. 15.

with no cultural background only increased the demand for the superficial and showy education provided in most of the private schools. The Queen herself strongly objected to anything approaching a masculine type of woman, and there was a widespread belief that a learned woman was a masculine woman. Private schools, therefore, which advertised a wide range of accomplishments such as singing, reading aloud, fancy penmanship, embroidery, and the playing of the piano, guitar, or harpsichord, flourished exceedingly and were able to command absurdly high fees. The Methodist newspaper, *The Watchman*, contained numerous advertisements for private schools giving such an education. Such a school probably was that administered in the middle of the nineteenth century by the youngest daughter of Samuel Tooth, who built City Road Chapel. It was a select school for daughters of Evangelicals in the Church of England and for Methodists who could afford the high fees. Its pretentious nature can be judged by the fact that its head mistress never referred to her pupils as 'girls' but as 'young ladies'.[20] Miss Cobbe in her autobiography published in 1904 recalled how in the mid-nineteenth century girls' education had become 'more pretentious than it had ever been before and infinitely more costly; and it was likewise more shallow and senseless than can easily be imagined'.[21] With fees ranging up to £500 per annum, a daily round of work on useless subjects, one hour's walk during which French, German, or Italian verbs were recited, and similar punishments inflicted for lying and stooping, girls became even more starved intellectually than they were when, educated largely at home, they did at least learn something of practical value in their sheltered lives. So matters might have continued, but a number of factors were at work to awake people to the foolishness of this conception of education. Amongst these factors were the increasing provision of popular education, the work of the evangelical party in the Church of England with its strong humanitarian and philanthropic interests, the growing necessity for women to earn their own living, and the spread of Methodism from the very poor upward to the increasingly wealthy middle classes.

At the close of the eighteenth century, Maria Edgeworth, supported by her father, had tried to make people realize the importance of the teacher's task, but little practical good had been

[20] J. H. Rigg, *Reminiscences*, pp. 130, 132.
[21] See *Public Schools for Girls*, p. 58.

achieved, and in the middle of the nineteenth century women teachers not in the primary schools were mere governesses, underpaid and overworked, whose social position was little above that of domestic servants. F. D. Maurice realized this all too clearly since his sister was such a teacher, and it was largely through his influence that the Governess Benevolent Institution was founded in 1843 in an attempt to alleviate real distress. A group of men who called themselves 'Christian Socialists', of whom Maurice was one, realized that if teachers were to gain the social prestige of other professional classes, some standardized form of testing and grading qualifications was essential, and Maurice persuaded some of his fellow-lecturers at King's College, London, to form a committee with a view to doing this for women teachers. Meanwhile, Miss A. M. Murray had been working along similar lines of thought in her attempt to found a college for women, and in 1848 these reformers united and Queen's College, London, was opened with Queen Victoria's blessing. From that beginning the work of producing a system of higher education for women spread fanwise, for amongst the College's first students were a number of women of vision and practical organizing ability who made education their life's work. By such means the responsibilities and previous hardships of women teachers began to be recognized. Mere 'accomplishments' began to be seen in their true perspective with the establishment of examinations for women, and when state education was still regarded with suspicion Oxford and Cambridge opened their local examinations to students, including women, who were not members of the universities. Girls' schools, especially those founded by students of Queen's College, eagerly seized the opportunities thus provided for testing mental capacities by common standards, while the University Extension lectures started by Miss Clough added momentum to the spread of a sound cultural background for girls as well as for men.

Methodism's contribution to the raising of status for women teachers was a small one, but a real one. The actual question of status was not considered at all, and whereas F. D. Maurice had started his reforms from the top, Methodism started from the bottom. The whole interest of Methodist education has always centred on the pupil, but one cannot teach pupils without having well-taught teachers, and recognition of this fact caused Methodism to make a small contribution to women's education —at first by means of its training college at Westminster which took students of both sexes. This arrangement was soon recognized as being far from ideal, and when, in 1871, the number of would-be students had increased beyond the available accommodation, Conference sanctioned the purchase of an estate in Battersea as a Women's Training College, concentrating at Westminster on men students only. At a cost of £14,783 'Southlands' College, a principal's house, and two practising schools were built and within three years over a hundred women teachers were being trained there.[22]

Once it is established that a teacher must have a wider and deeper background of knowledge than that covering merely the instruction which he or she intends to give to pupils, there appears an obvious connexion between primary and secondary education, and normally it will be necessary for an intending primary-school teacher to be educated in a secondary school, and for an intending secondary-school teacher to pass through a university—quite apart from any specialized training that may be given in a teachers' training college. This principle was not realized in the early nineteenth century, and that is one reason why the monitorial systems of Bell and Lancaster could only achieve limited results, and why the early training colleges found themselves in difficulties.

As we have seen in Chapter Eight, as soon as Methodism started establishing primary schools the same problem arose which had confronted Sir James Kay Shuttleworth and the Committee of Council on Education when national schools started to be established—that of the training of teachers. What was done to meet the problem has been traced in outline above, but for purposes of this chapter it should be noted that among the seven students who were first sent to train as teachers at David Stow's Normal Seminary, Glasgow, was a woman; and that when, on 6th October 1851, the first ten students assembled at the Methodist Normal Training Institution, Westminster, there were two women among them, a number which within a year was increased to twenty-one (and forty-seven men). The curriculum, in so far as actual subjects were concerned (for great importance was attached to character training which could be given only in part by formal lectures and instruction in set subjects) consisted of reading, writing, English grammar, history and etymology of the English language, English and general history, arithmetic, book-keeping, algebra, geometry, mensuration, geography,

---

[22] Southlands College was transferred to Wimbledon in June 1930.

mechanics, elementary physics, Latin, drawing, music, school management, and, for the women, sewing and 'instruction in all kinds of knowledge suitable and likely to be useful to females'.

Such a range of subjects might come easily to students today who have completed a secondary-school education up to school-certificate standard, but in the middle of the nineteenth century scarcely one of them had received any comparable education. It is true that a number, especially in the Methodist primary schools, stayed on at the primary school beyond the average leaving-age. Girls in particular did this, since legislation was making it illegal in an increasing number of trades to employ young girls, so that the money-making incentive to leave school early was eliminated. Most would-be teachers, however, were forced to depend on self-help and the uncertain aid they could get during their preliminary training as pupil teachers. They were thus deprived, with few exceptions, of the stimulus of any tutorial system. Yet when they went to a training institution their main task was 'not to acquire general knowledge but to acquire right methods of making it available to the moral and religious, as well as intellectual, improvement of young persons'.[23] It was manifestly impossible to learn how to teach when the basic knowledge of what to teach was lacking. It was realization of this fact that led to the gradual increase of the period of training in Normal Institutions. That was the best that could be done under existing circumstances, but the needs gave rise to an increased interest in primary schools which could give instruction beyond the usual standard, and proposals for establishing more of such schools specially to receive pupils from the ordinary primary schools were made.[24] Unfortunately, for many years nothing came of the proposals.

It was realized, too, that in an age of strongly marked social strata the attraction of potential teachers from classes other than the very lowest would help matters. That was in the mind of Miss A. G. Burdett-Coutts when in 1858 with the approval of the President of the Council, she circularized Training Colleges in an attempt to recruit middle-class girls to the teaching profession. She set forth the advantages of the pupil-teacher system and the teaching profession—but found it necessary to bolster up the 'advantages' with an appeal to their charitable instincts.[25]

[23] *Report of the Committee of Council on Education* (1844), p. 11.
[24] *Report of the Hadow Committee* (1926), pp. 7–8.
[25] *Wesleyan Education Report* (1857), pp. 47–51.

As far as Methodism was concerned, her appeal met with little response, for there were no girls' schools other than private ones to which the appeal could be addressed. But Miss Burdett-Coutts's hopes of attracting middle-class girls to the profession were realized in some small measure, and as the years passed the measure was increased as Methodist secondary schools for girls came to be established and steps taken to show middle-class girls that there was a certain social responsibility attached to wealth and position. Perhaps the appeal to charitable instincts was not such a hopeless appeal after all, for amongst the fashionable girls' schools of the day there were inevitably some which, however imposing the list of useless subjects on the time-table, yet gave real education—a tradition and a spirit which is caught rather than taught. Such a school would appear to have been one at Stourbridge owned by three sisters, the Misses Stinson, which existed for a short period in the mid-century. Being purely a private venture, it came to an end when the sisters married, but Dr. Rigg, who was no flatterer, says of it: 'For common sense, good, plain teaching, suitable to well-to-do middle-class Methodist girls, moral tone and influence, without affection or overdoing, I never knew, within its numerical limits, a more useful or valuable school'.[26]

As in the case of boys' schools, it was largely private enterprise that paved the way, and one Methodist girls' school in particular was a pioneer in making girls of the more wealthy Methodist families realize their social responsibilities and so further the cause of education and social progress in this country.

In 1847 Dr. William B. Hodgson became Principal of Chorlton High School for boys. He had always advocated the need for schools for girls similar to those being founded at that time for boys, and as secretary of the Liverpool Mechanics' Institute he had persuaded his committee to open a girls' school and a class for women teachers. When he went to Chorlton he continued this work and started classes for girls. Amongst his first pupils was Hannah Pipe, in whom he saw a potential teacher of unusual ability. When, owing to financial difficulties caused by the death of her father, she was compelled to earn her own living as a growing number of women were by then being forced to do, Dr. Hodgson encouraged the girl to start a school of her own.

It began as a day-school in the house in Wright Street, Manchester, where Miss Pipe lived with her mother. It was at once

[26] J. H. Rigg, op. cit., p. 158.

a success, and in 1852 she moved to a larger house and began taking boarders. Like her educational predecessors, she objected to the flamboyances of such titles as 'Academies for Young Ladies' and on her own door-plate were inscribed simply the words 'Mrs. and Miss Pipe's School'. A pupil of that period has written: 'Very soon the schoolmistress was merged in the school-mother, and the school became another home.' [27]—Words which recall the words of Wesley, who believed that every school should be a family. For Hannah Pipe, imbued as she was with a pioneer spirit, had deeply enrooted in her personality the precepts of Methodism. Her own home relationship with her widowed mother showed the reality of the Methodist teaching of Christianity as an essentially family affair. Her father had been a Methodist Local Preacher, and his family had been one in which the spirit of service and communion with God as Father of the family was at the heart of all their activities. At this time two influences started to work in the young lady. She read Stanley's *Life of Dr. Arnold* and was henceforth a disciple of his educational views, and she became closely acquainted with the Rev. Alfred Barrett and his family, who was the local Methodist minister. This minister, who later became the principal of Richmond Theological College, was one of a growing number of Methodists who believed that more should be done for the education of Methodist middle-class parents, folk who had made fortunes, who were themselves whole-hearted Methodists, but whose children were likely to be lost to Methodism unless Methodist schools could be found for them. When he moved to London in 1852 he urged Hannah Pipe to transport her school thither, where, he felt, the need was greater. Miss Pipe disagreed, feeling that her service was needed amongst the industrial families of the North—good Methodist families, but families in which the cultural background was pitifully meagre.

Nevertheless, in 1855, she decided to take her school to London, though she determined to make it a boarding-school so that families from the North could continue, if they wished, to send their daughters to her.

So Laleham Lodge in King's Road, Clapham Park, was opened as a boarding-school. The name of the school is some indication of the influence Dr. Arnold had had upon her. He was, she wrote, 'A man, a true man; one who realized the dignity and excellence of complete manhood, "valiant for the truth upon

[27] A. M. Stoddart, *Life and Letters of Hannah E. Pipe*, p. 47.

the earth", speaking the truth in love. No feebleness or idleness of head or heart marred the power and symmetry of his character. He lived in earnest. He lived to purpose. . . . Moral beauty is more gladdening than physical.' [28] Hannah Pipe was essentially a modest woman, and like Arnold she believed that only those should teach who were themselves learners. For this reason she chose the name 'Laleham' to indicate that she recognized the experimental nature of her work, just as Arnold's principles had been threshed out by his early work before he went to Rugby. The success of women like Miss Clough, Miss Beale, and Miss Pipe at that time may perhaps partly be attributed to the more modest manner in which they carried on their pioneer work for women's education. Whereas the earlier reformers like Maria Edgeworth and Mary Wollstonecraft had furiously and vociferously attacked, these later reformers quietly acted.

The work and personality of Hannah Pipe had been noticed by other Methodists beside the Barretts, and many supported her venture in London, and hoped that she would make her school a denominational one, but in this matter she was no narrow sectarian, and her views are best expressed in her own words in a letter to a friend:

'We are, as you have understood, Wesleyans. Most of my pupils are Wesleyans likewise, but some belong to the Church. They have all alike gone with us to chapel, however, although we have, close by, in the Park, a very excellent and able evangelical clergyman. We have attended occasional services at his church, and he is kindly willing to prepare for confirmation any of my girls who may desire it. As Wesleyans we are in full sympathy with the Church of England, differing, as you are no doubt aware, not in doctrine, but in immaterial points of Church government. I should therefore be most happy to send part of my girls to church were it not that I prefer to keep them all on Sunday under my own personal care, which would be impracticable if we attended two places of worship.' [29]

It was Methodism primarily that held her interest, for she saw clearly what so many in Methodism had not at that time seen— the cultural poverty of Methodist families.

'My ambition was to get hold of those girls with money and without refinement from their earlier years, and to open their

[28] A. M. Stoddart, *Life and Letters of Hannah E. Pipe*, pp. 50–1.
[29] ibid., pp. 104–5.

eyes to all that is best in this life and in that which is to come. The inrush of wealth without the discipline of generations behind it was apt to vulgarize their minds, and I desired to place before them, and to awake within them, their responsibility, their duties, their relation to the Giver of all things, their kinship with the poor, the worth of all things "lovely and of good report"; the worthlessness of an existence which buys but does not create its life. I knew how important it was to train a generation of wives and mothers.' [30]

Starting with sixteen pupils, the school, like its predecessor, was an immediate success, and four years later a larger house was taken and called 'Laleham'. This in turn had later to be enlarged, and during the years when Dorothea Beale was developing the great institution for women's higher education at Cheltenham, this Methodist lady was developing the boarding-school for girls which was the earlier counterpart of The Leys and whose place is now supplied by Queenswood and Farringtons.

Hannah Pipe was no revolutionary, but her watchword was: 'I must not teach as I have been taught.' She believed in the necessity for individual contact with each one of her pupils, and although to many of them at first she seemed remote and august, her personality gradually reached each one, so that she came to be regarded as a 'mother' rather than as a schoolmistress. The work of her school she centred around the daily Bible lessons and a Saturday afternoon talk. She did not agree with many of her contemporaries on the wholesale sweeping away of what were known as 'accomplishments'. In a letter to a parent, too long to quote in full, she thus described her object in carrying on the school:

'To the accomplishments, as they are commonly called, I give due honour and assiduous attention, believing them to be of real and great value, and in their proper place a measure of most healthful influence. And I hold that it is possible to combine a serious and thorough education with the fullest attention to whatever things are externally graceful. But while these things are duly cared for, my energies and efforts are mainly concentrated on the training of those powers of mind and heart that fit a woman for the thoughtful and intelligent performance of her duties in life; the cultivation of judgement and imagination, the implanting of sound tastes and the formation of sound habits. The lessons of each day are preceded by a morning Bible class.

---

[30] A. M. Stoddart, *Life and Letters of Hannah E. Pipe,* pp. 62–3.

Through this instrumentality chiefly my school has been governed.

'Education in its widest sense I take to be a process by which all the faculties of our human nature are carried to full harmonious development—a process conducted by manifold agencies human and divine, and continuing through this life into that which is to come.

'This work of teaching I love and honour. It is to me no dreary necessity, no mere mechanical routine.' [31]

Miss Pipe had a gift of friendship and this meant that she never lacked helpers in her work, and just as the other pioneers of women's education gathered round them a number of distinguished and broad-minded scholars, so did she. In addition to her resident staff at Laleham there was a group of visiting teachers who were teachers and not mere lecturers. Miss Pipe knew the uselessness of occasional lectures and she ensured the educational value of the lectures she arranged by a system of note-taking and correction of those notes by the staff—a system not unlike that normally carried on in the universities of today. Amongst these visiting lecturers over a period of years were Sir W. Sterndale Bennett (Music), George Macdonald (Literature), Professors Sheldon Amos (Law), W. K. Parker (Science), Henry Morley (Literature), S. R. Gardiner (History), Meiklejohn (Literature and Ethics), who before gaining his professorship at St. Andrews University carried on a girls' school near Laleham, Hodgson (Economics, Ethics, and Hygiene), Ord (science), Sir William Huggins (Astronomy), and Mr. Adolf Sonnenschein (Mathematics).

The subjects which these gentlemen taught are illuminating, and show Miss Pipe's independence as an educationist. At a time when science teaching was only in its infancy in boys' schools, Laleham had its own laboratory and science was a regular part of the curriculum. Her very breadth of vision, however, involved her in difficulties, for either the distinguished names of her visiting staff, or, more likely, the subjects which they taught, caused some concern to conservative Methodists, and the orthodoxy of her conduct of the school was questioned. As a result three pupils were removed by their parents, but Miss Pipe carried steadily on. Only to her friend, the Rev. Alfred Barrett, did she feel it necessary to make a defence of her views, and that was not so much a defence as a confession of her faith, revealing her as a true educationist: 'Perhaps I listened even more

[31] A. M. Stoddart, *Life and Letters of Hannah E. Pipe*, pp. 60-1.

carefully to strange doctors and doctrines than to those of my own circle, knowing that I must be naturally prejudiced in favour of these and against those. This prejudice I dreaded lest it should defraud me of any truth. But, thank God, I do not scorn the wisdom of my fathers. I receive it with reverent thankfulness and joy. Only because I hold it to be most precious do I sift it.' [32]

Meanwhile the struggle for women's education in the country generally was being won, and if one had to choose a definite turning-point one would cite the publication of the *Report of the Schools Inquiry Commission* in 1868. When the Commission was appointed in 1864 supporters of women's education saw their opportunity. The terms of reference on which the Commission was to act did not include girls' schools, but neither did it exclude them. Amongst the commissioners were one or two men who were sympathetic toward the movement, and the Commission was persuaded, largely through the instrumentality of Miss Emily Davies, to include inquiries concerning girls' education, these inquiries being placed under the supervision of one of the assistant commissioners, James Bryce, a staunch supporter of the movement. Accordingly in 1865 the Misses Buss and Emily Davies were called to give evidence before the Commission, and in the following year Miss Beale also. The unmasculine nature and personality of these three witnesses appear to have impressed the commissioners even more than the evidence they gave.

The publication of the *Report* stirred interest in the country as little else had done, and not the least of the interest was centred in that part which dealt with girls' education. Attention was called to the shortcomings which Miss Pipe herself had experienced and vowed not to fall into—want of thoroughness, slovenliness and showy superficiality, inattention to the elements of education, undue attention to accomplishments which in any case were badly taught, and want of organization. At the same time evidence showed that the capacity for learning was nearly the same for girls as it was for boys. As regards the teaching, there were two main defects: the poor quality of the teaching which teachers themselves had experienced, and the complete ignorance concerning methods of teaching. All these defects would, said the *Report*, best be eliminated by more and better schools for girls. That was as far as the Commission could go.

[32] A. M. Stoddart, *Life and Letters of Hannah E. Pipe*, p. 77.

Its inquiries had been made public, the defects and the needs had been made known. But the Government would go no farther. Development had to continue through private enterprise.

That was a point which a leading article in *The Watchman* [33] carefully avoided when reviewing appreciatively those parts of the *Report* which dealt with girls' schools. It expressed the attitude of an onlooker all too clearly when it mentioned the possibility of founding girls' grammar schools as a matter which 'others must settle'. It implied that the only thing Methodism could do was to adopt an air of benevolent interest and 'devoutly rejoice in the steady progress of a higher style of female education'.

Not all Methodists, however, adopted this attitude. Just as, at that time, there was a sharp increase in the realization of a need for boys' secondary schools, so there was a demand for girls' schools, and here it was the ministers' voices which were heard loudest, and with reason. Laymen of means could send their daughters to Laleham or one of the other private schools such as Avonbrook at Tewkesbury or Flook House, Taunton, but most ministers could not afford the fees demanded, and the allowance which the Connexion paid for the education of ministers' children was a mere £12 per annum.

Wesley himself made no proposals for the education of preachers' daughters, though the 1770 Conference had decided that Circuits must at least help to educate all preachers' children, and one or two of their daughters had been sent to Mrs. Owen's school at Publow in the eighteenth century. In the eighteenth century, however, there were no special schools for ministers' daughters such as were provided in Kingswood and Woodhouse Grove for their sons, and the publication of the Schools Inquiry Commission's *Report* appears to have spurred some of the ministers to action, for a letter in *The Watchman* at that time called attention to the fact that though there were schools for boys no provision was made for girls apart from a sum 'so small that it can suffice only for a second-rate education at a day-school'.[34] Unfortunately, there were not even second-rate day-schools in many parts of the country, while the frequent change of circuit made a boarding-school education desirable, to say the least.

A proposal was put forward, therefore, that a house should be

[33] Vol. VI, p. 369.   [34] ibid., p. 108.

bought near Westminster (why that locality was chosen is not made clear), and that a school for ministers' daughters should be established there. Nothing came of the proposal, but by the following year the demand for a school had reached such proportions that Conference was forced to act, and recorded:

'In accordance with a suggestion of the General Committee, the Conference appoints the following persons to be a Committee to inquire and report to the General Committee, at its meeting prior to the Conference of 1870, whether any, and what steps, can be taken to make better provision for the education of the daughters of our Ministers.' [35]

Private enterprise, as on many other occasions, worked more quickly than official Methodism, however, and though this was a matter which directly affected ministers only, it was laymen who made possible the quick action. On 30th September 1869 a girls' school was opened at 'Five Elms', Clapton, with Miss Henley, herself the daughter of a minister, as head mistress. At the following Conference, faced with a *fait accompli*, the Connexion took over the school, and in the following year a neighbouring house, 'Beechholme', was also rented, the two houses providing accommodation for seventy pupils. It was in that same year that the property which is the site of the existing school for ministers' daughters was presented to the Connexion by John Fernley of Southport. It was presented on the understanding that it was used as a school for ministers' daughters, and John Fernley, then an old man, spent the last months of his life in preparing it for that purpose.[36] At Trinity Hall, as the school was called, came to be centred the main endeavours for the education of ministers' daughters, and the Clapton schools were eventually closed. Unfortunately, however, Trinity Hall, like the Connexional schools for boys, suffered from financial difficulties and these reacted badly on the education given there in the early days, for the period of a girl's residence had to be fixed at four years.[37] Since girls entered the school at the age of twelve they had to leave before reaching the age required for admission to the universities, and it was not until 1906 that the gap between school and university was bridged by allowing girls to remain for a fifth year.

The period round about 1870, as has been made clear in the

[35] *Minutes of Conference*, Vol. XVII, p. 593.
[36] See the *Wesleyan Methodist Magazine*, Vol. CXXX, pp. 644-51.
[37] *Minutes of Conference*, Vol. XIX, p. 415.

foregoing pages, was one of considerable educational activitiy in Methodism which was at last beginning to make a real contribution to the drive toward an organized system of secondary and higher education. In 1871 the 'National Union for improving the education of women of all classes' was founded by a group of ladies and this led to the foundation of the Girls' Public Day-school Company which opened the first of its schools (at Chelsea) in 1873, and which, by the end of the century had opened thirty-three in various parts of England. An association for 'Promoting the Application of Endowments to the Education of Women' further exemplified the growing organization of the movement. This association had as its object the drawing-up of schemes for translating the rather nebulous reference to girls' education in the Endowed Schools Act into effect: 'In framing schemes under this Act, provision shall be made as far as conveniently may be for extending to girls the benefits of endowments.' The first school founded under such a scheme appeared as a result of the surplus moneys of the King Edward School for Boys, Birmingham, and others followed at Bedford, Dulwich, Monmouth, and Tonbridge. By 1898 eighty such schools had been founded, estimated Alice Zimmern in her *Renaissance of Girls' Education in England*.

The foundation of these schools did much to help the education of Methodist girls, though official Methodism always had a watchful eye on the denominational nature of the teaching. Old Girls did much to spread the essentially sensible ideas underlying this spread of girls' education. There was recognized a close relationship between school and home—a recognition that did not appear in the case of boys' schools. 'It is interesting to note that the pioneers who brought these schools did not forget that dogging the footsteps of these girls were certain home duties, which would always tend to linger with girls.' [38] Discipline was strict, but in comparison with that in boys' schools it was secured by personal influence rather than by fear. Since the mistresses were not bound by any historical traditions or conventions, they tended to be less conservative than their brothers. 'Literature, art, and other cultural subjects are taught with more genuine enthusiasm and welcomed with less regard to their examination value.' [39] In other words 'accomplishments' had not died out

[38] Miss E. Strudwick, High Mistress of St. Paul's School for Girls, in a chapter on 'Secondary Schools for Girls' in *Education Today and Tomorrow* (1945), p. 69.
[39] R. L. Archer, *Secondary Education in the Nineteenth Century*, p. 248.

entirely. The best features had been retained and incorporated in the new curriculum.

Just as the names of the Misses Beale, Buss, Clough, and Davies are recalled when women's education in the nineteenth century is considered, so Methodism should recall the name of Hannah Pipe. She was not the national figure that the others became, and criticism might be levelled because she did not, in spite of opportunity, take a more active part in the struggle for women's education generally. She undoubtedly had the ability to take a full share in the work, but, like many other true educationists, she felt that her work lay in direct and constant touch with children—with the small group amongst which circumstances had placed her, and here she concentrated all her efforts in making her contribution to education as perfect as possible. Nevertheless, she was not blind to what was going on around her, outside her particular sphere, and she took a lively interest in the vexed question of girls' higher education.[40]

In many ways Miss Pipe may be compared with Miss Buss, who had also started her career as a teacher while still only a girl herself. Both these ladies have been described as 'motherly', the personality of both reduced punishment to a minimum, a talk with a refractory pupil being normally all that was required. Both took a life-long interest in former pupils and were never too busy to attend to the interests and maternal problems of former pupils. Both were keen to absorb, sift, and practise new ideas, both believed (like Thring of Uppingham) in the power of environment, both attached considerable importance to science, and especially that part of science which closely affected a school—hygiene. (It was Dr. Hodgson who had first called Miss Pipe's attention to this.) Both were truly pioneers, for they were developing and practising their ideas before the *Report of the Schools Inquiry Commission* had drawn attention to the imperfections of girls' education.

Mere personality will not make a head mistress 'great', and amongst the additional qualities necessary is organizing ability. It is well to recall some of the routine machinery of her school, for it is that which in many ways made it a pioneer in English boarding-school education for girls.

Miss Pipe had an eye for detail and was a good organizer, but she was no dictator, and there was a weekly staff meeting in which new plans were discussed, the work of individual pupils

[40] A. M. Stoddart, *Life and Letters of Hannah E. Pipe*, p. 175.

considered, and the curriculum reviewed, and changed as required, for from 1860 onward the content of girls'-school curricula changed rapidly. This same capacity for working with people is seen, too, in her relations with pupils, each of whom she met privately for half an hour each week. This made for a close and sympathetic relationship between pupil and teacher, though faults were never condoned. As one might expect in view of her admiration for Dr. Arnold, Miss Pipe made use of the older girls in the maintenance of discipline. A small committee of the girls was entrusted with duties of supervision which would otherwise have had to be undertaken by the staff. They were given authority and were allowed certain privileges. The experiment (one of the earliest in a girls' school) worked well.

As regards school work, reference has already been made to the use of lectures and note-taking. The reading aloud of English prose and verse was a subject to which importance was attached, and this was combined once a week with an evening's sewing, books of fiction being read aloud by pupils in turn while the remainder listened, and gained useful, and at that time unusual, instruction in English literature. A good library was a central feature of the school's equipment. So carefully planned was every hour of the day that there was a danger of 'staleness,' and this Miss Pipe tried to overcome by imposing on each girl a 'daily half-hour's solitude' to be spent either in the gardens or in the dormitory; in reading, needlework, or pure rest.

These matters illustrate the painstaking organization of the school, and in fact, there was a danger lest the school should become too much bound up in itself, as did many of the boys' public schools which drew their pupils from similar social classes. This danger was, one imagines, enhanced, at least in the early years of the school's history, by the absence of external examinations, for Miss Pipe did not believe in any system of examinations except that arranged within each school. Her views on examinations formed the subject of an interesting letter which she sent to Miss Emily Davies when the latter was drawing up her scheme for what was later to become Girton College.[41] While she believed that some form of common examination as a qualification for women teachers would be useful, she could not feel 'equally hopeful of its beneficial operation upon young ladies in general'. She regarded examinations as a necessary evil in some schools and colleges, but not in hers. Whether one agrees with her views

---

[41] A. M. Stoddart, *Life and Letters of Hannah E. Pipe*, pp. 175–81.

or not, one cannot but be impressed by the eminently sensible views she expressed in her letter to Miss Davies, and the fact that her views had no bad influence on her pupils is proved by the large number of Laleham girls who were among the first to take advantage of those higher studies at the universities for which Miss Davies worked. This was due, believes an old pupil (Miss Alice Gardner who in 1879 was placed in the First Class of the History Tripos at Cambridge), to girls being led to regard knowledge as something to be sought simply for its own sake.

A scheme for counteracting any tendency for the school to regard its life as the only life and to teach girls in practical fashion something of their social responsibilities outside school, family, and home was brought into effect in 1875 after many years of consideration. An Orphanage was opened in connexion with the school. Situated at Streatham, it was near enough for pupils from Laleham to go to it and express as part-time teachers some of the knowledge and principles that had been impressed upon them in the school. Thus was inculcated those lessons in social service which the boys of The Leys learnt later in their Mission in the East End of London, and which is a characteristic of Methodist education. The Orphanage was maintained largely by donations from the Laleham pupils and their parents, but its chief importance lay in the fact that the girls themselves helped to give instruction there, and therefore to learn something of the lives of girls not so fortunate as themselves. In 1878 the Orphanage was moved to larger accommodation in Balham, where it was eventually taken over by the National Children's Home as a hostel for girls receiving secondary education.

The importance of Laleham lies in the fact that it filled a dangerous gap in Methodism. Compared with schools such as those of the Girls' Public Day-school Company, which were being founded in all parts of the country at that time, the number of pupils influenced was small, but the influence was great and it was an influence which was passed on. The assistant mistresses too, like the masters who served under Dr. Arnold and became themselves head masters, were influenced by the personality and methods of Miss Pipe. A number of schools were founded which Miss Pipe called affectionately her 'colonies'. A preparatory school for boys was founded by Miss Edwards (English and Latin mistress at Laleham 1876–81), girls' schools by Miss Oldfield (English and Latin mistress in the 1860's) at

Clapham Park, by the Misses Barrett at Highgate, and by Miss Levick at Sydenham.

Laleham brought to many homes that 'sweetness and light' whose lack Matthew Arnold so deplored in Nonconformity. It showed them that there was a world beyond the confines of chapels, prayer-meetings, and the narrow fellowship of a Methodist circuit and chapel—a world of beauty and squalor, which needed the service of those well supplied with this world's goods. It showed the girls of the wealthier Methodist families that they had duties outside those already provided for them in their own small circles.

Laleham was the forerunner of the present Farringtons School, for when Laleham, never anything but a private school dependent on the life first of Miss Pipe and later of the Misses Swindells, who took over when she retired, closed, it was realized that there was a gap in Methodism which needed to be filled. 'After the closing of Laleham the necessity of a school for girls of an educational standard similar to that provided by Leys for boys, was increasingly recognized.' [42] Laymen closely connected with The Leys formed a committee of Methodist ministers and laymen; a company was formed and set about the task of founding a school which would give 'a high-class education for girls of the same standard and as complete as that given to boys in public schools'. It was to be a Methodist school and its religious teaching was to be evangelical. Since it was modelled on the pattern of boys' public schools, the House system was adopted, and in 1911 the school opened at Chistlehurst on land formerly occupied by General Farrington, one of the Duke of Marlborough's officers, after whom the school was named. Financial matters were no problem at this school which from the first catered for wealthy families, and when one reads that at the opening of the school some forms contained only one girl, that the number of pupils was fourteen, and that there were five resident mistresses besides visiting teachers and the head mistress, one cannot but criticize the circumstances which made it possible for so much money to be lavished on so few people while other Methodist schools were struggling against financial difficulties which ultimately proved too much for some of them. However, the money was there, and the school achieved its object of obtaining a place amongst the girls' schools of this country comparable to that of The Leys amongst the boys' schools.

[42] *The Farringtonian* (Commemoration Number, 1911), p. 6.

Another well-known Methodist school of today owes much to the work of Miss Pipe, and caters for a similar type of pupil —a school, incidentally, which was also first sited in Clapham Park, though today it occupies extensive grounds at Hatfield. Queenswood in 1893 was a small school for the education of Methodist ministers' daughters, but in that year when the grave financial difficulties of the Ministers' Children's Fund were made known, Conference decided to close the school. As in the case of the proposed closing of Woodhouse Grove School ten years earlier, there was considerable opposition and the Middle-class Education Committee was asked to consider the possibility of continuing the school as one for girls other than ministers' daughters—one which would be similar to those at St. Heliers, Penzance, Folkestone, and elsewhere.[43]

This opportunity for reorganization was welcomed, a limited liability company was formed with a capital of £6,000, and in September 1893 Queenswood reopened as a middle-class school for girls, a number of places being reserved for ministers' daughters at reduced fees. Starting with twenty pupils the school was an immediate success, growing steadily under its first head mistress, Miss Waller, who had been head mistress of West Cornwall School, and later of Miss Ethel Trew, another lady worthy to be remembered as a 'great' head mistress and educationist.

In 1881 Miss Buss was able to write with a sense of achievement though not of complacency: 'There is now no such thing as a women's education question apart from that of education generally; and the real question which has still to be fought for many a long year, I fear, is one as old as education itself: how far is the child of either sex to be trained to the measure of the stature of a perfect human being?' [44] That is a question which subsequent Education Acts and, still more, the lives of individual educationists have tried in vain to answer, and, humanity being what it is, there is as yet no answer.

Miss Buss had cause for satisfaction. In that year (1881) Cambridge University, after several years of experiment and battle against prejudice, gave formal permission for girls to make use of its examination papers; in 1878 the University of London had opened its degree examinations to women on the same terms

---

[43] *Wesleyan Education Reports* (1893–4), p. 95, (1894–5), p. 61.
[44] Quoted by R. L. Archer in his *Secondary Schools in the Nineteenth Century*, p. 254.

as men; the new Victoria University, Manchester, had just provided degrees for women in its Charter; Girton College had firmly established itself at Cambridge; Newnham College had opened; Somerville and Lady Margaret Hall were beginning to take up similar positions at Oxford; the Girls' Public Day-school Company was busily engaged in founding high schools in various parts of the country, to which parents of moderate means could afford to send their daughters. The education of girls no longer aimed at the superficialities thought to attract husbands. There was now definite training of girls for the professions. As Alice Zimmern, writing in 1898, had pointed out: 'The educational movement has been parallel with many social changes. The fluctuations of business, the lowering of interest, and the complex causes which made saving difficult to men engaged in business or professions, have added greatly to the number of women who must now earn their living. Thirty years ago it was the custom to wait till the father's death closed the parental door, when daughters, untrained to work, unaccustomed to privation, were sent out into the world, to seek their bread as best they could.'[45] Methodist daughters needed to earn their living no less than others. They could find their training in one of the schools being established if they were fortunate enough to live in one of the larger towns which were being chosen as sites for such schools, but there were many who did not live in big towns. A fortunate few were wealthy enough to be sent to private boarding-schools, but most had to choose between what education could be picked up in the local primary school reinforced by home training, or being sent to a denominational school which was not Methodist. This was the position that was voiced in Methodism when Connexional Schools for girls were started, but the problem had been realized before that. Lord Wolverhampton in 1863, then Mayor of Wolverhampton, called attention to the education of girls in general. He believed that the boys of that day were receiving a much better education than their fathers had received, but he doubted whether the girls were receiving anything as good as their mothers had. There was an excess of what was useless and ornamental, and what they wanted was a robustness and accuracy and judgement which, combined with the acquisition of the ordinary branches of knowledge, would be an incalculable advantage. Girls' schools needed to be stripped of mawkish sentimentality and the teaching reduced

[45] Alice Zimmern, op. cit., p. 245.

to a science as it was in the national schools.[46] This opinion was shared by others, and when, in 1874, Conference ordered the Education Committee to inquire into the possibility of founding Methodist secondary schools, schools for girls as well as for boys were mentioned.

This was the beginning of the period of 'Company' schools to which reference was made in the previous chapter. It was not till six years later, however, that the first of them was established for girls, and by that time it was recognized throughout Methodism that there was little difference between the educational needs of boys and girls, and the schools founded from then onward show that the provision of boys' schools was paralleled by the provision of similar schools for girls. These schools were to supply education at reasonable fees (normally £30–£50 per annum) so that parents who could not afford to send their daughters to the more expensive private schools would be provided with the chance of sending them to Methodist schools. By that time Methodism was fully conscious of the organized efforts being made by others interested in girls' education, denominational and otherwise.[47] It was realized that Methodist schools could be established only in certain centres, and partly for this reason the majority of the schools founded were both boarding-and day-schools, so that parents who wished could make use of the boarding facilities in order to avoid sending them to schools of other denominations which might mean their loss to Methodism. At the end of the nineteenth century such a fear was real. There was, too, a growing habit amongst the middle classes of sending girls as well as boys to boarding-schools, the better rail facilities being a contributory factor to this changed attitude.

It was a group of Cornish Methodists who opened the first 'Company' school for boys, but it was a group of Methodists in the Channel Islands who took the lead in respect of girls' education, opening the Jersey Ladies' College at St. Heliers in 1880, and preparing pupils for London University examinations. The North Wales Wesleyan School Association followed later in the same year and founded Penrhos College for boarders only. In 1883 the 'Day- and Boarding-school for Girls to be called the West Cornwall College for Ladies' opened in the middle of Penzance—the first secondary school for girls in the Duchy.

[46] E. H. Fowler, *The Life of Lord Wolverhampton*, p. 58.
[47] 1872, the Girls' Public Day-school Trust; 1879, the Girls' School Company Limited; 1883, the Church Schools Company Limited; 1900, the Church Education Corporation. All these provided girls' schools only.

The West Country was responsible for another early girls' school—Edgehill College, Bideford. The boys' school at Shebbear had gained for itself a deservedly high reputation, and in 1882 at the Bible Christian Conference it was proposed that a sister school should be established. Although interest in such a project was not unanimous, it was sufficiently strong to cause the appointment of a small committee to inquire into possibilities. Meanwhile, the proposal once having been made, interest in it increased, for Devon at that time, largely owing to the work of Sir Thomas Dyke Acland, was something of a pioneer in higher education. It was felt that what had been done for boys could and should be done for girls, and once the Bible Christian Conference had approved the project arrangements for the establishment of the school were made whole-heartedly. Proof of the importance attached to its educational work was provided in the fact that the Bible Christians appointed one of their ablest ministers, the Rev. W. B. Reed, to be the resident governor, while the daughter of another minister, Miss Wooldridge, was appointed head mistress. In January 1884 Edgehill College was opened just outside Bideford with fourteen pupils. As the school grew in numbers, expansion of buildings and land took place. Today there are nearly three hundred pupils, half of them boarders.[48]

In 1886 Kent College, Folkestone, was opened by the Kent School Association 'under Methodist auspices with the object of providing training for home and business life, and for further study at a university based on broad religious principles'.[49] The Cornwall School Association founded a second school in the following year—Redbrooke College, Camborne, the first head mistress being one of the early students of Newnham College, Miss Kay.

Provision of education for the daughters of Methodist families was therefore increasing, but it did not satisfy, and one of the chief criticisms of Methodist educationists was voiced by T. G. Osborn during the proceedings which marked the centenary anniversary of John Wesley's death.

'There is one great gap in our educational system that I trust to see filled up before long. The last five and twenty years have seen more advance in the higher education of girls than in any other department. We have not as a Connexion held aloof from

---

[48] See Richard Pyke, *Edgehill College, 1884–1932*.
[49] *Girls' Public School Year Book* (1945), p. 150.

this movement: our preachers' daughters have noble schools, and there are flourishing middle-class schools at Jersey and Folkestone, and Penzance and Penrhos, and elsewhere. Moreover, Methodism is rich in private schools for girls, inferior to none, giving just the special training of a cultured home that we most covet for our daughters. But for those who pass on to higher educational work we have no place. There is no college as distinguished from high school. We cannot afford to lose our most cultured women; they have been the life and strength of Methodism. No other Church has recognized them so fully, and been so much indebted to them, as the Methodist churches, and we have greater work yet for them to do. And yet at present we are losing them in great numbers, by obliging them, just when most impressionable, to live and work under hardly neutral, probably antagonistic, influences. Our brethren in America do not do that; even the young churches in Australia are wiser than that. And I trust the time shall soon come when we shall have a Ladies' College for Methodists.' [50]

That hope has never been realized. At the same time, even when those words were being spoken, conditions at the universities were changing and religious tests were being imposed less and less, until in the twentieth century it has become doubtful whether a Methodist Ladies' College is necessary or even desirable. Women can go direct from a number of Methodist schools to the universities in which today is always found a nucleus of a Methodist society composed of young men and women centring around the home and the church of one or more of the Methodist ministers stationed in the town, those ministers often being specially placed there owing to their interest in, and appeal to, the undergraduates.

The established reputation of the Methodist secondary schools for girls today is based on the pioneer work of the last century. Financial difficulties have been met, no less serious than those in the boys' schools, but the very difficulties have often helped to forge the organization that exists today and which includes schools like Queenswood, Farringtons, Trinity Hall, Penrhos, Hunmanby Hall, Edgehill, West Cornwall School, Kent College (Pembury), and the East Anglian School.

[50] *Wesley: the Man, his Teaching, and his Work*, p. 260.

CHAPTER SEVENTEEN

A System of Methodist Secondary Education

T HE YEAR 1891 saw the centenary of John Wesley's death. It was a time of stock-taking, and both in public (as in the meetings held at City Road Chapel) and in private every aspect of Methodist work came under review.[1] It can be regarded as marking the time when the Forward Movement was fully active, when Methodism was taking a more sensitive and sensible part in affairs outside itself. Education was not the least of the matters which came under review, and the result showed that, although the contribution which Methodism had made to primary education was already large, that which had been made to secondary education, however excellent in quality, was not great in quantity. During the official opening proceedings of Woodhouse Grove as a 'Company' school, one speaker had stated that he had been making careful calculation and had discovered that there were at least 7,000 boys from middle-class homes whose higher education was unprovided for by public or private Methodist efforts. More schools were needed. Even fifty, he said, would not be too many.[2] Between the time when those words were spoken and 1891 a number of new Methodist secondary schools for boys and girls had been opened, but the total of fifty has never been reached. The chief difficulty has always been that of finance, for most of these schools had to rely on pupils' fees alone for their income.

Methodism was convinced that it had to make its own contribution to secondary education if Methodism was to survive, but it was growing seriously perturbed as to whether it would be allowed to control its schools if it did provide them, for there was a growing tendency toward secularization and State control. By 1891 all the university professors were laymen, and although the tradition of head masters in holy orders still survived largely in the public schools, there were few grammar schools which still had clergymen as head masters.[3] The number of assistant

---

[1] See *Wesley: the Man, his Teaching, and his Work*, which is a collection of the sermons and addresses delivered at the City Road Chapel at the Centenary Commemoration of John Wesley's death.

[2] *The Grovian*, No. 1, p. 5.

[3] *Secondary Education Report* (1895), p. 15.

masters who were clergymen was also decreasing. While there was much to be praised in this interest of the laity in secondary education, and many in Methodism welcomed it, yet there was also a growing anxiety about the root principle of Methodist educational policy: the place of religion as the main factor.

It was, however, becoming clear that the State would have to take drastic action to relieve the chaotic state of English higher education. There were a number of private schools which were controlled and inspected by no one but their proprietors, whose main object, all too often, was not education but the amassing of as large a fortune as possible; there were a number of denominational schools each centring round the particular beliefs of their respective denominations; since 1874 the Charity Commissioners had administered the Endowed Schools Act, but they had no connexion with any other Government department; the Department of Science and Art was officially under the Lord President of the Privy Council and Committee of the Council of Education, but, without reference to this Council, it made grants to technical schools established by the County Councils and to School Boards who were directly under the Education Department; the Board of Agriculture, since 1889, had made grants toward agricultural education; the Schools Boards allowed education in their schools above the normal standard of primary education; the Education Department itself which ought to control higher as well as primary education had little to do with secondary schools at all. There was confusion on all sides and it was evident that drastic reorganization could not be far off. Methodism realized that, and was no longer content to adopt a *laissez-faire* attitude over any branch of education.[4]

State action began in 1894 when a Royal Commission was appointed under the chairmanship of James Bryce (later Lord Bryce) 'to consider what are the best methods of establishing a well-organized system of secondary education in England, taking into account existing deficiencies, and having regard to such local sources of revenue from endowments or otherwise as are available or may be made available for this purpose, and to make recommendations accordingly'.

The Methodist Education Committee was asked to supply information concerning its proprietary and endowed schools. A statement was prepared which at least proved that Methodism

[4] For a study of this chaotic state, see Elie Halévy: *A History of the English People*, 'Epilogue, 1895–1905', Book II, pp. 1–95.

was beginning to take the provision of secondary schools as seriously as it had undertaken the provision of primary schools. Its schools were listed in six categories:

1. *Connexional Boarding-schools*
(a) Kingswood School, Bath, with accommodation for 290 boys.
(b) Trinity Hall, Southport, with accommodation for 58 girls.

2. *Middle-class schools for boys*
(a) Woodhouse Grove School, Apperley Bridge, with accommodation for 134 boarders and 30 day-boys.
(b) East Anglian School, Bury St. Edmunds, with accommodation for 72 boarders and 25 day-boys.
(c) Victoria College, Congleton, with accommodation for 60 boarders and 40 day-boys.
(d) Kent College, Canterbury, with accommodation for 100 boarders.
(e) Trowbridge High School, with accommodation for 70 boarders.
(f) Truro College, with accommodation for 130 boarders and 40 day-boys.

3. *Middle-class schools for girls*
(a) West Cornwall College, Penzance, with accommodation for 26 boarders and 74 day-girls.
(b) Redbrooke College, Camborne, with accommodation for 25 boarders and 50 day-girls.
(c) Kent College, Folkestone, with accommodation for 70 boarders and 70 day-girls.
(d) Jersey Ladies' College, with accommodation for 70 boarders and 140 day-girls.
(e) Queenswood School, with accommodation for 55 boarders and 50 day-girls.

4. *Proprietary schools*
(a) Wesley College, Sheffield, with accommodation for 100 boarders and 150 day-boys.
(b) Queen's College, Taunton, with accommodation for 270 boarders and day-boys.
(c) Harrogate College, with accommodation for 76 boarders and 17 day-boys. (Increased accommodation was then being provided.)
(d) Dunheved College, Launceston, with accommodation for 50 boys (boarders).
(e) Penrhos College, Colwyn Bay, with accommodation for 70 girls (boarders).

5. *Public schools*

The Leys School, Cambridge, with accommodation for 210 boarders.

6. *Private schools,* of which, as the Rev. D. J. Waller, Secretary of the Wesleyan Methodist Education Committee, pointed out, there were a considerable number conducted by Methodists for boys and girls in various parts of the country.

The fees in these schools varied considerably, those in the middle-class schools varying between £30 and £50; those in the proprietary schools between £36 and £55; and those at The Leys School being £90 to £100.[5]

Methodism was beginning to make fair provision for the secondary education of children from middle-class families of moderate means, but no specific provision was made for the lower middle classes—those for whom Canon Woodard had founded Ardingly with fees of only £13 per annum. On the other hand much had been done for those classes through the primary schools. As Dr. Rigg pointed out in his *Essays for the Times*:[6] 'It is certain that the Wesleyan schools are, for the most part, better attended, and that they retain their children at school more steadily and to a later period than any other schools.' This was due in some measure to the wider curriculum provided to meet the demand for education.

In addition to the Wesleyan Methodist schools listed above there were the Irish schools, the Primitive Methodist Elmfield College at York, the Bible Christian Shebbear College for boys and Edgehill College for girls, and the United Methodist Ashville College at Harrogate.

The Bryce Commission recognized the value of such contributions as Methodism was making and was careful to make clear in its *Report*[7] that such enterprise should not be thwarted by overmuch State interference:

'The interference of the State should be confined within narrow limits and virtually restricted to the ordering and advising the local authorities, the prevention of needless competition or conflict between them, and the protection of private and proprietary schools from any disposition on the part of those authorities, should such a disposition appear, to force competitors out of the field. Such a code of regulations and such a system of examinations and inspection as the Education Department has applied to

[5] Fees in the two Connexional Schools for ministers' children were met mainly by grants from the Ministers' Children's Fund.
[6] p. 512.   [7] Vol. I, p. 266.

elementary schools would in our view be not only unfitted but positively harmful to secondary education.'

On the other hand, though this warning was given, something had to be done to produce order out of the chaos that existed, and the Commission recommended the creation of a Ministry of Education, with all Government departments dealing with secondary education centralized under one Minister; the formation of an advisory body—the Education Council; and the decentralization of actual organization under local authorities who would cater for local needs, though in this connexion the warning was given again: 'We have sketched out a plan whereby private and proprietary schools may be turned to good account, and have discountenanced any idea of driving them out of the field and thereby making secondary education purely a matter of State concern.' [8]

As long as private enterprise, therefore, worked for the public good and not for mere personal profit, the State would act as little more than a benevolent adviser, but it was the State's duty to guarantee that private enterprise was thus working and therefore all schools should be open to sanitary inspection; and if they wished to be recognized as part of the secondary-school system of the country they should also satisfy the proposed Ministry of Education as to the adequacy of their buildings, equipment, teaching-staffs, curricula, and fees. They would, in fact, have to submit to inspection and examination.

Herein the Methodist authorities were not confident of themselves. Finances were shaky, and this meant that there were potential shortcomings in respect of other matters mentioned in the *Report*. But above all, Methodism felt that it should and could expand its secondary-schools' organization still more, and in 1898 a joint committee was appointed, consisting of the Middle-class Education Committee and the Special Committee on secondary education, to inquire into the constitution and equipment of the Connexional secondary schools and the possibility of establishing some satisfactory relationship between middle-class schools which were Methodist in character and management, but which were not included in the existing arrangements of the Middle-class Schools Committee.[9]

The most pressing and all-too-obvious problem of the schools was that of finance, as the committee quickly reported, and one of the most disturbing features of the problem was the fact that

[8] Bryce Commission *Report*, Vol. I, p. 324.
[9] See *Minutes of Conference* (1898), pp. 321–2.

debts were being incurred not only on capital expenditure but in the normal routine running of the schools. To put matters on a better footing the committee took a step which twenty years earlier would have caused a storm of protest, but one which in 1898 was regarded as eminently practicable: they proposed adapting the curricula of the schools so that they would become eligible to receive grants from the Science and Art Department and from the County Councils for technical instruction.

'Technical instruction' was widely interpreted, and included the whole field of mathematics and science, modern languages, and geography. Many secondary schools had benefited from grants which were made by County Councils,[10] especially when the tax collected from customs duties on spirits ('Whisky money') had been allocated to them for this purpose. It was, however, a significant move when Methodism decided to make its schools eligible for such grants.

The *Report* appeared at an opportune time, too, in that in 1898 the 'Twentieth-century Fund' was started, which aimed at raising one million guineas for the carrying out of various schemes of extension in the Connexion.[11] £200,000 was allocated to education. The committee was therefore in the unusual position of knowing that such recommendations as it might make would not be pigeon-holed through lack of funds to implement them.

In the following year Conference directed a special inquiry to be made into the state of Wesleyan Methodist secondary education with a view to its adaptation to existing and future needs of the Methodist people, consideration being given to the possibility of forming an 'Association of Secondary Schools' in order that fees might be graded, the profits from schools charging higher fees being used to compensate the losses incurred in the maintenance of schools charging lower fees. This was one step toward the establishment of a system of secondary schools.

Although the Bryce Commission had so far appeared to have done little as far as practical results went, in the last year of the century there were indications that some at least of its recommendations were to be put into effect. A Board of Education was established which took over the functions of the Science and Art Department, the educational duties of the Charity Commissioners, and the Education Department. It was given authority

[10] As a result of the Technical Instruction Act (1889) and the Local Taxation (Customs and Excise) Act (1890).
[11] Started in 1898, the fund was closed in 1908, by which time £1,073,782 had been raised at a cost of less than £30,000.

to inspect secondary schools, and working with it was a Consultative Committee of eighteen men and women. These indications of official action caused Methodism to focus its attention the more carefully on its provision of secondary education, for though a valuable beginning had been made, no one could claim that anything in the nature of a Methodist system of secondary education existed. There was no grade of schools directly connected with the nine hundred primary schools which it had provided. Conference directed, therefore, that inquiries should also be made into the practicability of promoting the most promising of the primary-school pupils into secondary schools.

It was obvious, however, that whatever the results of the inquiries such measures could only be achieved if some form of Methodist educational system was established which would include both primary and secondary schools.

In February 1900 a number of questions were circulated to the directors and proprietors of the middle-class schools, concerning finance, premises, health and sanitation, number of pupils, fees, curriculum, and staff. The detailed information obtained was the basis on which the distribution of the educational share of the Twentieth-century Fund was made.

Amid so much educational activity on the part of the State, the question of religious instruction in schools had inevitably come to the fore and in 1900, 'In view of the proposed legislation in reference to secondary education, the Conference declares itself opposed to grants of public money being made to denominational secondary schools without the protection of a conscience clause, and also records its strong opinion that in cases where public education authorities establish secondary schools no formularies distinctive of any particular denomination shall be permitted to be taught therein, and no dogmatic or ecclesiastical tests should be introduced'.[12]

Fear of undue interference by the State in their schools only strengthened the Methodist desire to bring more of them directly under Connexional control, for it was felt that, whereas a single school under a Board of Directors might be compelled to give way to such interference, the Connexion itself was sufficiently powerful to check interference in schools under its control.[13] This desire was strengthened by the difficulties in which some of

[12] *Minutes of Conference* (1900), p. 304.
[13] It is only right to recall that in fact no such interference occurred, the spirit of the Bryce Commission's *Report* being observed.

the 'Company' schools were finding themselves. The demand for the type of education provided had continued to increase; schools had been enlarged to meet the demand, but the increased expenditure was not balanced by increase in the amount of school fees. All too often there was confusion between capital expenditure and normal maintenance costs. The difficulties were further complicated by uncertainty over State aid. Grants had been made available to denominational schools under certain conditions, one being that the schools were not maintained for private profit. In defining 'private profit' it was at first ruled that schools managed by a public company (as were most of the Methodist middle-class schools) in which no dividend exceeding five per cent. was paid annually were eligible for grants, but in 1902 this concession was withdrawn, and it was ruled that no 'Company' school was eligible.

It had therefore become still more imperative for the companies to be wound up and for the schools to be acquired by the Connexion so that grants could be obtained. With this end in view a scheme was drawn up for the connexionalization of schools and for their settlement on such a Trust as would entitle them to gain Government grants and become recognized secondary schools.

Meanwhile, though the setting-up of the Board of Education had resulted in a slight simplification of the administrative muddle, secondary education in England was far from being organized and changes were obviously imminent. Realizing this, the Conference of 1901 had tried to straighten out its own somewhat muddled educational administration and had made the Secondary Education Committee responsible, as its name implied, for all secondary education, which hitherto had been dealt with by the General Education Committee, the Secondary Education Committee, and the Middle-class Schools Committee. The same Conference set up a special committee to consider any Education Bill which might be introduced by the Government in the next session of Parliament—a committee consisting of the Secondary Education Committee, the Committee of Privileges, and one minister and one layman from each District.

The Education Bill of 1902 had a stormy passage, and though it was introduced by the Prime Minister himself in March, it did not become law until the following December. It affected the whole of English education, but it affected most of all denominational education.

By that time Methodist educational policy had become based on three main principles which were in no sense narrowly sectarian: First, that a Christian undenominational school should be available for every family and that the control of such schools should be in the hands of representative bodies in the localities in which the schools were situated. Second, that grants of public money should only be made to denominational schools if they were managed by responsible persons representing the public as a whole (and not representing any one denomination.) Third, that religious instruction should be given in all schools.

Methodism would, in fact, welcome a genuine national system of education, as was made evident when it had supported the establishment of School Boards. But the 1902 Act abolished these, and for this main reason the Act caused more than disappointment to Nonconformists in general. The Wesleyan Methodist Conference reiterated its desire for a system of Christian unsectarian schools:

'This Conference once more declares that the primary object of Methodist policy in the matter of Elementary Education is the establishment of School Boards everywhere acting in districts of sufficient area, and the placing of a Christian Unsectarian School within reasonable distance of every family.

'The Conference, therefore, deeply regrets that the present Education Bill is intended to destroy the School Board system, and to make no adequate provision for the just claims of those parents who do not wish their children to be driven into Denominational Schools.

'The Conference has no wish to abolish the Denominational Schools or to prevent them from being used with equitable restrictions for the purpose of giving Denominational Education to those children whose parents desire it. But the Conference expresses once more its deep conviction that no increased Grant from public funds should be made to Denominational Schools, unless the increased Grant is accompanied by adequate and representative public management. If, however, Denominational Schools are to be almost wholly maintained from imperial taxes and local rates, the "irreducible minimum" of the rights of conscience and of public justice demands that at least a majority of the Local Education Authority, and of the Governing Committee of every school, shall consist of publicly elected persons.' [14]

True, this statement referred mainly to primary schools, but

[14] *Minutes of Conference* (1902), p. 112.

302

the principles involved affected the whole of education. A fierce battle started which did not confine itself to words. Numbers of Nonconformists refused to pay rates since it was from them that payment was to be made for Sectarian Schools. A wave of 'passive resistance' (which was not entirely passive) swept Nonconformity. The official Wesleyan Methodist view should be quoted:

'Without expressing an opinion on what is known as "Passive resistance", the Conference expresses its profound sympathy with many men and women who have deemed it to be their duty as Christian citizens to resist by lawful means the payment of compulsory education rates. The Conference would earnestly call the attention of His Majesty's advisers to the great and growing gravity of this movement, and, as loyal subjects of the British Crown, would represent to them that, in the interests of civil order and domestic peace, it is essential that heed should be paid to the conscientious convictions of millions of the King's loyal subjects.' [15]

As far as higher education was concerned, rating powers were limited; the very term 'higher education' was vaguely used and was found to include much that had previously been labelled 'elementary' education; in fact, in the Wesleyan Methodist view, the provisions for secondary education were permissive when they should have been compulsive. Methodism did, however, come to realize that primary and secondary education—and all the other divisions of education—were not independent of each other. Barriers between them did exist, but they were artificial and for the first time there were signs that this was being realized both by the State and by the Churches. One obvious aid to the breaking down of this undesirable state of affairs was seen in the recruitment of teachers, and educationists began more realistically to look to the secondary schools for the recruitment of primary-school teachers.[16] The primary schools needed new blood; the secondary schools were capable of supplying it.

In 1903, with the completion of the Twentieth-century Fund within sight, £70,000 was allocated to the connexionalization of secondary schools, and in that same year four schools were purchased—the East Anglian School, Trowbridge High School, Truro College, and Wesley College, Sheffield. To control and manage these and other schools to be acquired later, a Board of

[15] *Wesleyan Methodist Education Report* (1903–4), p. 19.
[16] See *Regulations for the Instruction and Training of Pupil Teachers* (1904).

Management was appointed, consisting of ministers and laymen, which was empowered to appoint sub-committees to report on questions of staffing, curriculum, co-ordination of education, grading, and the general administration and efficiency of Methodist schools.[17]

A Trust Deed had also been drawn up upon which all Connexional schools were to be administered, but this occasioned a battle of terminology with the Board of Education. In the original draft of the Deed all schools acquired were to be controlled by Conference. Conference, however, though legally weighty, had a fluid membership, and the Board refused to sanction the contribution of its grants to any schools controlled by so large and changing a body as the Methodist Conference. Throughout these and later negotiations the Board of Education considered that each school ought to be considered as a separate entity, but, as the Methodist authorities pointed out, unless the various schools were considerably helped by a central body which could give general oversight and financial assistance, some would cease to exist. At length, therefore, the Board agreed to accept for all purposes a central authority with whom to deal on matters relating to Methodist education, viz. the Board of Management for Methodist Residential Schools, provided that this Board should delegate to a local Committee of Management the control of purely local matters affecting each individual school.[18]

Although on paper this all sounds cumbersome, in practice the arrangements have worked well, since the local Governing Body of each school has full freedom of action, with the moral support —and active support in matters of finance—of the central Board of Management in any matters of difficulty.

Thus was founded in the early years of this century a system of Methodist secondary education which today controls eight residential schools for boys and five for girls. In addition there are other schools which are essentially Methodist though they are not directly controlled by the Board of Management—The Leys, Kingswood, Queenswood, Trinity Hall, Penrhos, Farringtons, and the two Irish schools.

[17] See Appendix F, p. 336, *infra*.
[18] *Minutes of Conference* (1903), pp. 516–17.

CHAPTER EIGHTEEN

Twentieth-century Development

FOLLOWING THE 1902 Education Act there was naturally considerable activity in the development of secondary education, especially in the north of England where, during the previous century, cities had sprung up mushroom-like to supply industry with workers. Sheffield decided it was time for investigation into its educational affairs. From the resultant inquiry it became evident that the weakest spot in the educational arrangements of the city was secondary education. The existing schools for boys were doing their best, but it was not enough. The Grammar School and Wesley College were performing a useful work,[1] but the latter was essentially a boarding-school and consequently the difficulties with which it had to cope were wellnigh insuperable, for the premises were not far from the centre of the city, with all its smoke and noise. By 1902 only one-sixth of its pupils were boarders, yet it was on boarders that it relied financially. Michael Sadler was one of the principals in the city's inquiry into its education and in his recommendations he proposed that there should be one first-class secondary school upon which no expense should be spared. Not only should the premises be good, but the staff also should be large and thoroughly efficient. With help from the city authorities, he said, either the Grammar School or Wesley College could be raised to the necessary standard, but it would be better to give substantial help to one than to give small assistance to both. At the very time when this *Report* appeared, Wesley College was being taken over by the Methodist Board of Management, and Sadler knew that a conscience clause was included in the Deed on which the school would be administered. This might cause difficulties. Amalgamation between the two schools was proposed therefore, the title of 'Grammar School' being retained, and the premises of Wesley College housing both schools. Such a plan, if carried out, would do for Sheffield what had been done for Bradford, Manchester, and Birmingham.

Methodism had to decide whether it should continue to administer a denominational school at a loss or whether it should

---

[1] *Report on Secondary and Higher Education in Sheffield* (1903), p. 18.

hand over a school to the Sheffield authorities to be administered as an undenominational school. The decision was not a difficult one, and in the same year in which the Methodist Board of Management had acquired it, the school was sold to the Sheffield authorities to be fused with the Grammar School and to form the present King Edward the Seventh School.

Although one school was thus lost to Methodism, another was gained shortly afterwards—the only private school to be acquired by the Connexion—Rydal School.

Rydal Mount, as it was first known, was founded in 1885 by T. G. Osborn, who gave up the head mastership of Kingswood School to become proprietor and first head master. Osborn was educated at Wesley College, Sheffield, and Trinity College, Cambridge. In 1866 he became temporary head master of Kingswood in the place of William Elton. This temporary post became a permanent one and at Kingswood he spent twenty years. They were momentous years, for it was during that time that the experiment of administering Woodhouse Grove as the preparatory school for Kingswood took place (starting 1875), so that Osborn became head master of both schools. Then in 1883 came the concentration of the two schools at Kingswood, and again Osborn guided the school through what might have been failure to the success that the school has maintained ever since. Yet, in spite of the success that Osborn achieved during those twenty years of difficult variety he was never able to become used to the 'dual system' of government. As he said, 'My greatest difficulty has been that I am only a visiting master'.[2] It was this feeling that was chiefly responsible for his resignation in 1885 in order to found the school at Colwyn Bay. Already by that time a 'public-school tradition' was recognized, but Osborn aimed at nothing pretentious. He wanted to make his school one in which there should be a domesticity which he believed to be incompatible with the life of a large 'public school'—a family spirit, education of the highest possible order, and religious culture. During the last fifteen years of the nineteenth century the school made for itself a name in Methodism such as no private school for boys had ever before achieved. But no one could forget that it was a private school, and when, in the early years of this century, it seemed that the school must close there were many prepared to fight against such a loss. Here was a worthy object for which

[2] For an outline of Osborn's head mastership of Kingswood School, see *History of Kingswood School*, pp. 296–300.

the Twentieth-century Fund could be used, and in 1905 the Conference gave its approval to the purchase of the school and appointed a Governing Board to draw up, with the concurrence of the Committee of the Education Section of the Fund, a Scheme for the constitution and management of the school.[3] It differed, however, from other schools acquired by the Connexion in that it was not controlled by the Board of Management. It was saved for Methodism, but there were many who wished to see it more fully under the control of the Connexion. Numbers in the school again declined and it was found that the school was losing £1,000 per year. In 1915 the head master, G. F. A. Osborn, son of the founder, resigned and Conference decided to place the school under the Board of Management and to appoint one of its ministers, the Rev. Alfred J. Costain, as head master.[4]

At that time the school taught only twenty-six boarders and ten day-boys, but at once these numbers began to increase until by 1920 there were 220 boys, all boarders.[5] The foresight of the Conference on this occasion was amply rewarded, and today Rydal (as the school became known in 1919) is one of the well-known boarding-schools of the country—and that not only because of its prowess on the Rugby football field!

During this same period (1905), negotiations were also carried on between the Twentieth-century Fund trustees and the Directors of the Woodhouse Grove School Company, for here was another school which by tradition and results was peculiarly Methodist. The property belonged to the Maintenance and Education of Ministers' Children's Fund, and it was decided to transfer the estate and the school to the Board of Management for Wesleyan secondary schools. The Board of Education was consulted and a scheme drawn up whereby the property was to be vested in the Trustees of the Wesleyan Secondary Schools Trust Deed of 1903, with the Board of Management as the Governing Body. Conference adopted the scheme in these words:

'That whereas the Woodhouse Grove School has been discontinued as a school for the sons of Ministers and is not required for that purpose: And whereas considerable sums of money have been and are proposed to be expended in equipping the

---

[3] See *Minutes of Conference* (1905), pp. 77-8, and for the Scheme of the school's constitution see *Wesleyan Education Report* (1905-6), pp. 92-8.
[4] *Minutes of Conference* (1915), pp. 59-60.
[5] The Scheme of Management and Constitution was revised in 1922. See *Wesleyan Education Report* (1922-3), Supplement.

premises as a Public Secondary School: The Conference directs that the property be transferred to a governing body to be formed under a scheme to be sanctioned by the Board of Education with the approval of the Wesleyan Board of Management of Secondary Schools: Provided always that if the Conference shall declare by resolution that the premises are no longer required for the purposes of such Secondary School or that some other premises are more suitable therefor, the same shall be sold and the purchase money shall be paid and applied either in the purchase of other premises to be settled for the purpose of such Secondary School or in such other manner as the Conference shall direct.' [6]

Thus did one of Methodism's oldest secondary schools return to the direct supervision of the Connexion through its Board of Management to help lay the foundations of a Methodist secondary-school system which has steadily developed throughout this twentieth century, increasing importance being attached to higher education as control of primary schools was handed over to the State. It is largely due to the lack of State initiative shown in secondary education (until 1944) that Methodism has concentrated on providing and developing secondary schools.

'The Methodist Church believes in the widest possible extension of education, from Nursery Schools to the University, for all sections of the community.

'It would also put in the forefront of its educational activities maintenance in the highest efficiency of its Methodist Training Colleges, and the continuance and development of Methodist Residential Schools in which, in addition to the high academic attainment, every stress shall be laid upon the development of true character and sound religious teaching.' [7]

These words were recorded by Conference in 1939, but they were being formulated in the years following the passing of the 1902 Act, when Methodism was coming to realize that an educational system which is efficient at the top will help to ensure an efficient educational system throughout—a fact which the pioneers of women's education had realized during their struggle in the second half of the nineteenth century.

On the other hand, Methodism was, and is, a practical educator, unwilling to carry dead weight merely for the sake of

---

[6] *Minutes of Conference* (1905), p. 74. For legal Deed relating to this transfer, see *Wesleyan Education Report* (1905–6), pp. 103 ff.
[7] *Methodist Education Report* (1939–40), p. 7.

showing an accumulation of possessions. It is quality that Methodism has fostered. Several of the schools founded in the last years of the nineteenth century had insufficient financial backing to enable them to expand with the growing requirements of twentieth-century education, while the functions of others tended, after 1902, to overlap with the functions of the local education authorities. The Victoria College, Congleton; Bromyard High School; and Redbrooke College, Camborne, were closed. The Ladies' College, St. Heliers, Jersey, which drew many of its girls from this country, was seriously affected by the wreck of the *Stella*, which frightened parents from sending their daughters overseas, and the College was sold. Dunheved College, Launceston; Trowbridge High School; and Bourne College were acquired by the Cornwall, Wiltshire, and Birmingham Education Authorities respectively. These apparent losses to Methodism were, however, offset by foundations and developments later in the century.

At the beginning of the war of 1914–18 a move was made to close the ranks of Nonconformist education, and in 1915 the Board of Management appointed five of its members to represent Methodist interests on the Nonconformist Council for Secondary Education—a Council representing Baptist, Congregational, Presbyterian, Wesleyan, Primitive, and United Methodist Churches, which sought to bring good Nonconformist secondary schools to the notice of Free Church parents.

In Methodism itself it was perhaps the 1920's which showed the greatest advance in secondary education, and an administrative step which helped was the reconstitution of the Wesleyan Education Committee so that the whole of education was brought under constant review, by the appointment of three executive sub-committees of experts in higher, secondary, and primary education, each of which was to present a Report on its own sphere of interest to the meeting of the full Education Committee every six months. This co-ordination of activities has done much to eliminate administrative muddle and to make possible certain financial economies. In that same year two more schools became Connexional property—Kent College, Canterbury (a boys' school) and the West Cornwall College (a girls' school—the oldest secondary school for girls in the Duchy).

During this period one fact was becoming increasingly obvious —that the potential usefulness of Methodism as a provider of day (primary) schools was fast decreasing. At the close of the nineteenth century there had been 743 schools.[8] By the 1920's there were less than 200. This is due to no fault, no treachery to principles or past traditions: it is due entirely to two healthy facts—the increasing interest of civic and county authorities in education, and the broader view of education which was being taken by Nonconformists. Methodism during this present century has supported the policy of a national system of Christian non-sectarian education, the policy which successive Governments during their terms of office have attempted to put into effect. The attention of Methodism therefore tended to become focused on that section of education which continued largely to be supported on the voluntary principle.

Two teacher-training colleges existed—at Westminster and Southlands, and now even more reliance began to be placed on a matter whose importance had been realized ever since 1845— the value of the teacher of character and personality. Henceforth, Methodism would rely more and more on training teachers in the educational principles of Methodism with its insistence on the indivisibility of religion and education, and less and less on the provision of mere bricks and mortar, at least as far as primary schools were concerned. The importance of the teacher has become even greater, one would suggest, since the 1944 Act came into operation. With a dangerous tendency toward mere utilitarian intellectualism the teacher of human views and high ideals based on a solid foundation of Christian faith has become all-important.

The other section of education on which Methodism began more and more to focus its attention was, as we have seen, secondary education. It was felt that the day secondary schools under Local Education Authorities could not develop character by religious teaching, personal example, and individual influence as could boarding-schools provided by a religious denomination. As this book has tried to show, the great advances in, and the vital character of, education have been provided by living Christians, men and women of ideas and ideals. Parliamentary Acts and State pronouncements have merely been the rivets in our educational structure.

These two operational centres of Methodist educational thought and endeavour may be said to have fused together in 1930. Even before the close of the nineteenth century students at

[8] The highest number of schools provided by Methodism was in 1889, when there were 847.

Westminster College had begun to read for external degrees. Some, having obtained their degrees, began to infiltrate into the secondary schools of the country. Thus began a new Methodist contribution to education—the contribution of trained teachers genuinely and broadmindedly Christian in their life and teaching to the secondary grammar schools of the country. The movement was considerably fostered when in 1930 the course at Westminster became one of four years, the first three being spent in reading for an internal degree of the University of London, the last being spent in working for a Teacher's Diploma and Certificate at Westminster College itself. This meant that from then onward the majority of schoolmasters trained at Westminster would be graduates, eligible for posts in secondary grammar schools. Of those who left the College in the summer of 1947, 21 out of 47 went to such schools (or Independent or Direct Grant 'public schools'), and 16 to secondary modern schools.

But, though it is right to call attention to what is an interesting and suggestive fact, one must not imagine that Westminster College—nor Methodism in general—is turning its back on the poor who received its first attention. One just cannot speak in such terms today. Inadequate as it still is, education in this country today is universal and it is free. The conclusions drawn in 1849 and the resultant action taken cannot be imposed on 1949. Methodism, like the State, is alive to the needs of all the educational stages—university, secondary grammar, secondary technical, secondary modern, primary, and nursery schools—and it is alive, too, to the fact that there are many children who through no fault of their own are alone in the world. Any survey of Methodist education would be incomplete without reference to a humanitarian undertaking which has spread far beyond the bounds of denominationalism. Tempting as the story is, space does not allow for telling of Dr. Stephenson and his National Children's Home and Orphanage.[9] It is necessary to point out, however, that Stephenson and those who have followed him in caring for unfortunate children interpreted the word 'home' in the fullest possible sense, and the needs of education dictated much that they have done and are doing. Children received into their homes have represented a fair cross-section of humanity so far as mental powers are concerned and there have always therefore been a number of children in the

[9] See Maldwyn Edwards, *Methodism and England*, Chapter 8, and *The Seven Lamps*—Year Book of the N.C.H. & O. (1934).

N.C.H. & O. who ought to be given secondary education. This fact was realized from the beginning and gradually means were evolved for ensuring that a secondary-school education was made available. Laleham, for example—the house in which Miss Hannah Pipe had built up her school for girls—was for a time used as a home for N.C.H. & O. girls who were receiving secondary-school education. Long before the 1944 Act was passed arrangements were made by the N.C.H. & O. to bridge the gap between primary school-leaving age and the start of wage earning. Some children were sent to secondary grammar schools, some to technical schools and colleges, some passed on to training colleges and universities. In no cases have capable children been denied the chance of developing their capabilities. In fact, a feature of the N.C.H. & O. has been the way in which it has kept abreast of the times, always on the alert to meet changing circumstances. In 1938, for example, the Methodist Temperance and Social Welfare Department, the Christian Council for Refugees from Central Europe, and the N.C.H. & O. combined to rescue seventy boys from the Nazi-dominated Germany and Austria, special arrangements being made at the Riversmead home to start a bilingual school since none of these boys knew any English when they arrived. A large percentage of these refugees (the original number was later increased) showed themselves to be of 'academic' secondary-school capacity, and they were sent to schools and colleges to meet their needs.

It is this broadminded view of education and of life that Methodism is today developing; largely through its secondary schools in which ideals can be geared to practice, often through a direct connexion between the schools and children not so fortunate. As was pointed out earlier in this work, the connexion between Methodist training of teachers and its secondary schools is an increasingly close one. Westminster and Southlands would not have progressed academically as they have done had it not been for the Connexional secondary schools and those other schools closely connected with Methodism. Nor, it is suggested, would the Connexional schools have flourished as they have done without the close connexion which many of them have had with the training colleges.

Until 1928 there was no school in the north of England which could provide for girls what Woodhouse Grove and Ashville did for boys. Trinity Hall was reserved for ministers' daughters and Penrhos was far removed from the industrial areas of Yorkshire and north-east England, where lived a number of middle-class Methodist families. In the 1920's the demand for a girls' school nearer to these areas began to be voiced by District Synods. The Connexion at that time only possessed one girls' school (West Cornwall School) and it was decided to take action. The late C. J. F. Atkinson, then chairman of the governors of Woodhouse Grove School of which he was an Old Boy, showed his Yorkshire upbringing by speedy and sound initiative. Hunmanby Hall, near Filey, and its estate of fifty-six acres, a former home of Lord Chetwode, was bought for £10,000 in April 1928 and in September of the same year the school was opened with seventy-six pupils under Miss F. A. Hargreaves, B.A., as head mistress. Applications for places in the school were received in such numbers that it was evident that extensions would have to start forthwith, and that there would be no difficulty in maintaining the school at its full capacity. Today there are approximately three hundred pupils.

Another important room in the Methodist educational structure was added in 1935. Since its foundation the East Anglian School at Bury St. Edmunds had served its locality and Methodism well, but in the 1920's the sphere of its influence developed under the head mastership of Dr. J. W. Skinner, M.A. In 1925 there were 76 boarders and 52 day-boys. Thenceforward the numbers increased steadily and to accommodate them a number of residential buildings surrounding the main school were bought, but by 1934 it had become evident that this accommodation was not sufficient both for the numbers in the school and for the development demanded by modern education. Further extension would cost at least £15,000. A neighbouring house and estate came into the market. It was one of those tangible records of a great past which have been disappearing so rapidly during this century with rising demands for housing estates and decreasing endowments wherewith to maintain great houses. Culford Hall was once a Benedictine priory, but at the dissolution of the monasteries Henry the Eighth granted it first to Christopher Coote and then to Sir Nicholas Bacon, father of Francis Bacon. The present Hall was built by the first Marquess Cornwallis, Viceroy of India, in 1804 to designs drawn by William Wyatt. Twenty years later the Hall was bought by Richard Benyon de Beauvais for £200,000 and a large sum was spent on improvements. In 1889 the fifth Earl Cadogan was the owner, and in December 1904 King Edward the Seventh and

Queen Alexandra spent several days there as guests of Lord and Lady Cadogan.

This was the estate, rich in tradition and story, which was bought in 1935 by the Methodist Connexion.[10] The decision was no quixotic one. Methodism has always been true to its name and no step has ever been taken which has not been most carefully considered and planned. In this instance the problem was not an easy one. £15,000 at least would have to be spent on the existing East Anglian School to bring it up to date; £21,000 was asked for the Culford estate, and a further £25,000 at least would be required for adaptation. Eight months were spent in making full inquiry into the various factors involved before the decision to buy was taken.

On 3rd October 1935 Culford School was opened by the Rt. Hon. Walter Runciman, M.P. (then President of the Board of Trade and Treasurer of the Methodist Education Fund). Today it is full with 280 boarders and 118 day-boys, and its opening has made it possible to use the buildings of the old East Anglian School for boys as a new East Anglian School for girls which today has 114 boarders and 115 day-girls.

Further developments took place in Yorkshire. During the early years of this century, Ashville College, under the head mastership of the Rev. Alfred Soothill, had been making steady progress, and in 1927 when J. T. Lancaster became head master, bringing to that post a considerable experience of public-school education at The Leys, it had become imperative that a preparatory school or department should be opened. Plans were drawn up for the necessary buildings, but before they could be put into operation an old property was newly acquired—the eighty-year-old rival known as New College. In that year, therefore (1930), Ashville College acquired a preparatory department (the buildings of New College being used for that purpose) and a new interest, for the joining together of two schools, both with traditions fostered during a period of nearly one hundred years, though it must inevitably produce a host of problems, should also enhance the richness of education. The problems were further complicated, however, and by their solution Ashville College was made greater both materially and spiritually when, two years later, amalgamation took place with Elmfield College, York.[11] Within three years, therefore, three schools successfully became

[10] See *Methodist Education Report* (1935-6), pp. 17-20.
[11] Commemorated in 1938 by the opening of Elmfield House.

one, and it is a tribute to all three that union did in fact produce strength. Today there is a joint Old Boys' Association which is all the stronger for the union implicit in it.

Changes occurred, too, in the West Country. Truro School was honoured by the then Prince of Wales, Duke of Cornwall, when His Highness laid the foundation-stone of a School Chapel and Assembly Hall in 1927. Two years later a large house standing in its own grounds overlooking Mount's Bay from the hill above Penzance was bought for West Cornwall School. At first this house was used as a boarding-house, and teaching continued to be carried on at the cramped Chapel Street premises in the centre of the town. In 1939, however, York House on the hill was enlarged and the Chapel Street buildings given up, the whole school being centred in an ideal setting on the outskirts of the town.

It was in 1939 that the decision was taken to move another girls' school. Kent College, Folkestone, had been founded as a sister school to the one for boys at Canterbury in 1885 by the Kent Wesleyan Methodist Schools Association. With the increasing difficulties of carrying on a boarding-school within a town (difficulties, it will be remembered, recognized by John Wesley nearly two hundred years before), and the facilities for buying country estates from old families who could no longer afford their upkeep, it was decided to move the Folkestone school to Hawkwell Place, a house and well-wooded estate of eighty acres near Pembury. This move took place just before the outbreak of war, and there was an immediate increase in the number of pupils. When war broke out, there was naturally a still more immediate decrease, but the school carried on, confidence was gradually restored, and in 1942 the school was acquired by the Connexion.

Such have been the most important structural alterations and additions to the Methodist secondary-school system during this century, but they are by no means the only ones. There is, in fact, no single school which has not been enlarged and beautified and the value of its contribution to general education proportionately increased. At the close of the war of 1914–18 it was realized that no school could hope to survive which was not adequately housed and whose equipment was not capable of maintenance in accord with the rapid development of modern life and education, particularly on the scientific side. As we have seen, Methodism had been something of a pioneer in the teaching of science during the nineteenth century, and since then it has never ceased to extend its scientific studies and teaching. Amongst the new buildings of the last thirty years, science laboratories and classrooms equipped with modern aids to education have been prominent. There have been great advances too in the amenities provided for the social life of the schools. Preparatory schools have been founded in direct connexion with each of the leading secondary schools; most schools have their own chapels; enlightened masters and mistresses have seen to it that education has been given a broad scope by providing visual beauty and well-stocked libraries; all have good sports fields; some have their own swimming-baths. There is no aspect of modern education which has not been considered and, where possible, provided. But this has not been done by the wave of some magician's wand. The satisfaction of wants has been an arduous business; there has been a continuous struggle, sometimes for existence, always for betterment of environment and culture, combined with a deep sense of spiritual values. Much of what has been done has only been possible through the generosity of Methodist laymen who owe much to the Church of their fathers and who, partly because of what Methodism has done for higher education, have remained loyal to Methodism and at the same time have achieved greatness—for few Methodists have had, nor have desired to have, greatness thrust upon them. These men have acquired wealth and position and they have given generously of that wealth to the schools which had done so much for them and their families. To such benefactors are due many of the improvements and additions to which attention has been called. There is, too, another source from which the schools draw considerable help. Each of them has its Old Pupils' Association which is never merely an excuse for social gathering. Such gatherings occur, and through the opportunity they provide for reminiscence and the re-living of a more carefree life (as it inevitably seems with passing years!), no doubt the spirit of Methodist education is rejuvenated, but they are activated by two main considerations—gratitude and service. The former, as long as it does not end in mere sentiment, is good, for it leads directly to the latter, and the schools of today are helped by the foundation of scholarships, by material gifts which enrich the life of the schools, and by the help which is often given to boys leaving who need a helping hand as they set out on the life beyond the school.

We are too close to the event to assess the results of the upheaval of war on the Methodist secondary schools—an upheaval which was still affecting them when the State took its greatest step forward in secondary education by the passing of the Education Bill of 1944. As far as immediate events were concerned, it is probably true to say that Kingswood was the chief sufferer, largely because of its tradition as the oldest Nonconformist school in the country. To cut a long and, for those involved in the making of the decisions, a tangled story short,[12] Kingswood was evacuated to Uppingham and perhaps it is not without significance that a school such as Kingswood should have been partnered during those war years by a school made great through the vision and the practical enterprise of a man like Edward Thring (1821–87), who not only built his own school materially and spiritually but was largely responsible for forming the Head Masters' Conference, which, Thring wrote a few years after its first meeting, had 'utterly broken up the exclusiveness of the old schools and created a feeling of friendliness and union among all schoolmasters'.[13]

The preparatory school for Kingswood, which in 1939 was Westwood (opened in the summer of 1933), was evacuated to Prior's Court, near Newbury. In striking contrast to the negotiations for the evacuation of the main school, arrangements for the younger boys were made in a single hour's interview with the owner of Prior's Court. Today, Kingswood is back in its old quarters on Lansdown, with Westwood as one of its Houses, Prior's Court having been bought in 1946 as a permanent preparatory school for Kingswood.

The Leys was required by the Ministry of Health as an Emergency Hospital, and so this school also suffered the upheaval of sudden removal. Unlike Kingswood, however, The Leys evacuation was not complicated by the arranging for two schools to live together in harmony: in this instance the Atholl Palace Hotel, Pitlochry, was taken over as a school, and, thanks to local hospitality, the West Pitlochry Kirk was used as a chapel. From the strictly utilitarian academic standpoint, this move was as upsetting as it could be, but from a broad educational standpoint one wonders whether the enforced uprooting and readjustment of outlook on the part of staff and pupils was not an advantage rather than a disadvantage. At Cambridge the school

[12] See *Kingswood: The Bursar Remembers,* E. P. Aust, pp. 70 ff.
[13] G. P. Parkin, *Edward Thring,* p. 178.

had firmly established itself as a public school in the centre of the university atmosphere and influence. At Pitlochry, the school was largely dependent upon itself: for individuals, living as they were in a lovely and comparatively wild countryside, life became an adventure—a more practical adventure than it could normally be at Cambridge; the school, too, realized its entity as a school, for the house system had to be modified so much that the unit for all practical purposes was no longer the house but the school.

Similar upheavals were being suffered by other Methodist schools—and similar blessings were there for those with eyes to see. But obviously the blessings were not too obvious to men and women harassed by care and thought for their charges, worried also on more personal counts as 1940 grew suddenly ominous. Rydal School was partially commandeered, and the main school took up temporary quarters at Oakwood Park, Conway. As in the case of Kingswood, this estate was later bought and became the preparatory school when Rydal moved back to its old home at Colwyn Bay. Culford saw the other side of the picture of evacuation, for instead of being itself uprooted, it received the East Anglian School for girls at Cadogan House on the estate. Here the chief problem was one of accommodation. Truro and West Cornwall School were in supposedly safe areas and were unmolested by governmental demands, but the former received Kent College, Canterbury, part of this school joining with Truro School, and part finding additional accommodation in a neighbouring house and hotel. Hunmanby had to find quarters farther west—the main school at Ilkley, and the junior school by the side of Lake Bassenthwaite. To the Lake District also went Ashville College—to Windermere. Woodhouse Grove, Kent College (Pembury), Queen's College, Taunton, Shebbear, and Edgehill were unaffected by evacuation.

It is a matter for rightful pride that not one of the Methodist schools or colleges suffered vitally during those years of danger and uncertainty. Plans had been prepared, as far as that was possible, before the enemy began its attempt to destroy the life of this country, and the spirit of service which is inherent in the Methodist educational system was tested as never before, for it must be remembered that each school lost some of its potential vitality by the loss to the Forces of younger members of staff, men and women. The test was passed triumphantly. Because of foresight and hard work there was no major break in the continuity of Methodist higher education. There is one office in the Methodist Connexion about which one reads little, but which should be placed high in any estimate of those to whom credit is due for successful guidance in times of crisis. The post of Secretary of the Methodist Education Committee is, all too literally at times, a thankless one. The holder has always been a minister, but he needs to be a minister of a special type. Beside possessing such academic qualifications as will gain for him the confidence of educationists inside and outside Methodism, he needs the humility and the capacity for menial routine work of an office boy, the organizing ability of an administrator, and the greatness and nobility of a diplomat. Methodism owes a great deal to those men who have held this office since it was instituted over a hundred years ago, for upon them has fallen the brunt of the work of co-ordinating the educational efforts of Methodism.

It will be remarked that whereas in foregoing pages dealing with the eighteenth and nineteenth centuries personalities have figured largely, in this sketch (for it does not attempt to be more than that) of the twentieth century personalities are notably absent and more material matters only are considered. This omission is no accident. It is unfair, if not impossible, truly to estimate personality until that personality can be set, as it were, in a picture which has breadth and depth of background which only time can paint. In thinking of the education of this century, names of people at once crowd to the mind, but, simply because they do crowd, they have been ruthlessly excluded from these pages and the life and vitality of the story has accordingly been sacrificed. But life is there. The schools would not be doing the work they are doing if it were not so.

CHAPTER NINETEEN

Conclusion

IN THE FOREGOING PAGES facts have been pre ented to illustrate the contribution that Methodism has m de to secondary education. The number of schools provided, the reason for their foundation, the class of boy or girl they educated, the subjects taught, some of the men and women who taught them: these have been cited as evidence that Methodism's contribution has been a not unimportant one. But her main contribution is something which cannot be expressed in hard fact and statistics. It may be summed up in the word 'fellow hip', which was developed during a pupil's school life and revealed itself fully and proved its vitality in social service and self-discipline after schooldays had ended.

This fellowship is as much a characteristic of Methodism today as it was in the nineteenth century and in the days of Wesley himself. Its outward form has varied with the passing years, but throughout it has linked together in a spiritual bond the various strata of society which, in the nineteenth century, were widely separated from each other by station in life and by wealth, so that it did much to avert social revolution in this country.[1]

It is not possible to express in exact terms either the nature of this fellowship or its origin. One can point to the origin of Methodism itself and the self-sacrificing lives of John Wesley and his travelling preachers, to the emotional but often deeply spiritual songs of Charles Wesley, to the original appeal of emotionalism linked with reason, to the detail, gradually evolved, of Methodism's organization, centred in the class meeting and the societies in which men and women of all types and classes met together to share experiences and work. All this contributed, and it was in the secondary schools which Methodism founded that leaders were trained to use the practical results of such fellowship in service to God and the community. It is acknowledged today by many that the influence of Methodism for social

[1] For a full understanding of what England owes to Methodism see W. E. H. Lecky, *A History of England in the Eighteenth Century*; J. R. Green, *History of the English People*; Elie Halévy, *A History of the English People in 1815*, Vol. I.

good on the life of the nation in the nineteenth century was great. It would be wrong to claim that the secondary schools alone were responsible for this, but the fact remains that the majority of the Methodist leaders of the second half of the nineteenth century were educated in those schools.

In 1875 the President of the Wesleyan Methodist Conference, in his address to the societies, spoke of the 'happy homes' which had become a feature of Methodism, and pleaded for their continuation by a conscientious cultivation of family religion.[2] The word 'family' has occurred many times in these pages, for it defines a characteristic of Methodist secondary schools and explains something of the nature of Methodist fellowship. The difficulties of schools organized under dual control have been dealt with, but, whatever the difficulties, the governor was the visible sign of a father in the school family who guaranteed, as it were, the place of religion as the focal point of education. He was supported by men on the staff of varying personalities and gifts, all of whom believed implicitly in the reality of God the Father and the necessity for life to be inspired and maintained by spiritual force. In 1866 Dr. Rigg wrote in his *Essays for the Times*:[3]

'Education neither begins nor ends at school. It begins in the mother's lap, is carried forward with all but decisive power, for good or evil, by the earliest influences of the home circle, and is finally completed by those examples, incentives, and associations which, after school years are past, assert their sway over the character of youth in the scenes and occupations of opening life.'

The associations provided for boarders particularly in the Methodist secondary schools were just the type of associations which could and did show the youth of Methodism the reality of that indefinable spirit called fellowship. Religion occupied a central position in them, but it was a form of religion which did not confine itself to attendance at church, the observance of certain rites like prayers, or the inclusion of religious instruction in the curriculum. Great importance was naturally attached to these matters, but there was something deeper and more decisive. Religious instruction was never considered a mere subject as in so many undenominational schools of the nineteenth century. It was always an essential part of the curriculum and one which was correlated to other subjects; it was given by men and women

[2] *Minutes of Conference*, Vol. XIX, p. 730.　　　　[3] p. 469.

who were neither sceptical, indifferent, nor ignorant, but by men and women who were themselves religious. Their example proved a better method of teaching than that which found expression in mere words. Religious instruction was given by them, but, more important, the other subjects of the curriculum were also taught by these same men and women, so that pupils came to see that the whole mental world of culture was bound up with religion.

Lest this should suggest that other subjects suffered, it should be recalled that once religious tests had been abolished at Oxford and Cambridge a new era dawned for Methodism, and it was possible for E. E. Kellett, recalling his schooldays at Kingswood from 1877 to 1882, to claim that 'among the twenty or thirty with whom I was brought into more or less close association, one who could foretell the future would have seen two Fellows of the Royal Society, three Fellows of Trinity, Cambridge, four or five Fellows of other colleges, five or six professors of various subjects, some eminent head masters, and several distinguished doctors, lawyers, and educationists.' [4]

The Methodist secondary schools number among former pupils many men who became outstanding in various walks of life. There is nothing remarkable about this, for all schools have their distinguished Old Boys, but it should be remembered that no boy who went to a Methodist school had a ready-made social position awaiting him: he had to make his way in society without the assistance of money or influence. It is relevant to state, therefore, that former pupils, recalling their schooldays, have never done so without gratitude and a tribute to the influence of their school's traditions and to the interest, work, and example of those who taught them.

The influence of personal example cannot be over-estimated, and for this reason considerable attention has been paid in these pages to individual men and women. It was they who made the schools 'families' and made possible the peculiar contribution of Methodism to higher education. In her work for secondary education Methodism built slowly, sometimes too slowly, but she built well, because there were always men and women who realized the importance of education, not merely to their own denomination but to Christianity as a whole. They were imbued with an evangelical spirit which found its expression in education, through which they were enabled to share the life they could

[4] *As I remember*, p. 263.

not live alone. They came to realize that the mere training of teachers was not enough, that a personal example was more important than a knowledge of a subject. In all true family life there must be reciprocity, and this principle they applied to matters of the school—to matters of mind and spirit which were never divided. Such an education could best find its expression in boarding-schools and realization of that has led modern Methodism to attach great importance to the residential school, where, more than in any day-school or primary school (where children are not old enough to be firmly and finally convinced of a religious philosophy of life), the education of personal example and practical fellowship can be given.

In all their endeavours the service of God came first, but a true understanding of the implications of that service produced a sense of service to the community. When the State began to take an interest in secondary education, Methodism put aside exclusively denominational considerations and supported the State. But she never put aside her insistence on the place of religion in education, and her contribution to secondary education has been therefore not merely a spirit of fellowship, but a spirit of Christian fellowship. They were apt words which John Wesley had engraved on the front wall of his school at Kingswood:

IN GLORIAM

DEI OPTIMI MAXIMI;

IN USUM

ECCLESIAE ET REIPUBLICAE

They express that spirit of Christian fellowship which has remained a characteristic feature of Methodist secondary education, and which has done so much to bring more sweetness and light into the dark places of this and other countries.

A Short Account of
the School in Kingswood, near Bristol

(Published in the year 1768)

1. Our design is, with God's assistance, to train up children in every branch of useful learning.

2. We teach none but boarders. These are taken in, being between the years of six and twelve, in order to be taught reading, writing, arithmetic, English, French, Latin, Greek, Hebrew, history, geography, chronology, rhetoric, logic, ethics, geometry, algebra, physics, music.

3. The school contains eight classes.

In the first class the children read *Instructions for Children*, and *Lessons for Children*; and begin learning to write.

In the second class they read *The Manners of the Ancient Christians*; go on in writing; learn the *Short English Grammar*, the *Short Latin Grammar*; read *Prælectiones Pueriles*; translate them into English, and *The Instructions for Children* into Latin; part of which they transcribe and repeat.

In the third class they read Dr. Cave's *Primitive Christianity*; go on in writing; perfect themselves in the English and Latin Grammar; read *Corderii Colloquia Selecta*, and *Historiæ Selectæ*; translate *Historiæ Selectæ* into English, and *Lessons for Children* into Latin; part of which they transcribe and repeat.

In the fourth class they read *The Pilgrim's Progress*; perfect themselves in writing; learn Dilworth's *Arithmetic*; read Castellio's *Kempis*, and Cornelius Nepos; translate Castellio into English, and *Manners of the Ancient Christians* into Latin; transcribe and repeat select portions of *Moral and Sacred Poems*.

In the fifth class they read *The Life of Mr. Haliburton*; perfect themselves in arithmetic; read Select Dialogues of Erasmus, Phædrus, and Sallust; translate Erasmus into English, and *Primitive Christianity* into Latin; transcribe and repeat select portions of *Moral and Sacred Poems*.

In the sixth class they read *The Life of Mr. De Renty*, and Kennet's *Roman Antiquities*; they learn Randal's *Geography*; read Cæsar, select parts of Terence and Velleius Paterculus; translate Erasmus into English, and *The Life of Mr. Haliburton* into Latin; transcribe and repeat select portions of *Sacred Hymns and Poems*.

In the seventh class they read Mr. Law's *Christian Perfection*, and Archbishop Potter's *Greek Antiquities*; they learn *Bengelii Introductio*

[1] Reprinted from *Works*, Vol. XIII, pp. 249–55.

ad Chronologiam, with Marshall's *Chronological Tables*; read Tully's *Offices,* and Virgil's *Æneid*; translate Bengelius into English, and Mr. Law into Latin; learn (those who have a turn for it) to make verses, and the *Short Greek Grammar*; read the Epistles of St. John; transcribe and repeat select portions of Milton.

In the eighth class they read Mr. Law's *Serious Call,* and Lewis's *Hebrew Antiquities*; they learn to make themes, and to declaim; learn Vossius's *Rhetoric*; read Tully's *Tusculan Questions,* and *Selecta ex Ovidio, Virgilio, Horatio, Juvenale, Persio, Martiale*; perfect themselves in the Greek Grammar; read the Gospels, and six books of Homer's *Iliad*; translate Tully into English, and Mr. Law into Latin; learn the *Short Hebrew Grammar,* and read Genesis; transcribe and repeat *Selecta ex Virgilio, Horatio, Juvenale.*

4. It is our particular desire, that all who are educated here may be brought up in the fear of God; and at the utmost distance, as from vice in general, so in particular from idleness and effeminacy. The children, therefore, of tender parents, so called (who are indeed offering up their sons and daughters unto devils), have no business here; for the rules will not be broken in favour of any person whatsoever. Nor is any child received unless his parents agree, (1) That he shall observe all the rules of the house; and (2) That they will not take him from school, no, not a day, till they take him for good and all.

5. The general rules of the house are these:

First. The children rise at four, winter and summer, and spend the time till five in private; partly in reading, partly in singing, partly in self-examination or meditation (if capable of it), and partly in prayer. They at first use a short form (which is varied continually), and then pray in their own words.

Secondly. At five they all meet together. From six they work till breakfast; for as we have no play-days (the school being taught every day in the year but Sunday), so neither do we allow any time for play on any day: He that plays when he is a child, will play when he is a man.

On fair days they work, according to their strength, in the garden; on rainy days, in the house. Some of them also learn music; and some of the larger will be employed in philosophical experiments. But particular care is taken that they never work alone, but always in the presence of a Master.

We have three Masters: One for teaching reading, and two for the languages.

Thirdly. The school begins at seven, in which languages are taught till nine; and then writing, etc., till eleven. At eleven the children walk or work. At twelve they dine, and then work or sing till one. They diet nearly thus:

Breakfast.—Milk-porridge and water-gruel, by turns.
Supper.—Bread and butter or cheese, and milk, by turns.
Dinner.—Sunday.—Cold roast beef.
        Monday.—Hashed meat and apple-dumplings.
        Tuesday.—Boiled mutton.
        Wednesday.—Vegetables and dumplings.
        Thursday.—Boiled mutton or beef.
        Friday.—Vegetables and dumplings. And so in Lent.
        Saturday.—Bacon and greens, apple-dumplings.

They drink water at meals: nothing between meals. On Friday, if they choose it, they fast till three in the afternoon. Experience shows, this is so far from impairing health, that it greatly conduces to it.

Fourthly. From one to four, languages are taught; and then writing, etc., till five. At five begins the hour of private prayer; from six they walk or work till supper; a little before seven the public service begins; at eight they go to bed, the youngest first.

Fifthly. They lodge all in one room (now in two), in which a lamp burns all night. Every child lies by himself. A Master lies at each end of the room. All their beds have mattresses on them, not feather-beds.

Sixthly. On Sunday, at six, they dress and breakfast; at seven, learn hymns or poems; at nine, attend the public service; and twelve, dine and sing; at two, attend the public service; and at four, are privately instructed.

6. The method observed in the school is this:

The First Class

Morning, 7. Read. 10. Write till eleven.
Afternoon, 1. Read. 4. Write till five.

The Second Class

Morning, 7. Read *The Manners of Ancient Christians*. 8. Learn the *English Grammar*; when that is ended, the *Latin Grammar*. 10. Learn to write.

Afternoon, 1. Learn to construe and parse *Prælectiones Pueriles*. 4. Translate into English and Latin alternately.

The Third Class

Morning, 7. Read *Primitive Christianity*. 8. Repeat *English* and *Latin Grammar* alternately. 9. Learn Corderius; and when that is ended, *Historiæ Selectæ*. 10. Write.

Afternoon, 1. Learn Corderius, and *Historiæ Selectæ*. 4. Translate.

The Fourth Class

Morning, 7. Read *The Pilgrim's Progress*. 8. Repeat the *Gram-*

mar. 9. Learn Castellio's *Kempis*; and when that is ended, Cornelius Nepos. 10. Write; and learn arithmetic.

Afternoon, 1. Learn *Kempis*, and Cornelius Nepos. 4. Translate.

The Fifth Class

Morning, 7. Read *Mr. Haliburton's Life*. 8. Repeat the *Grammars*. 9. Learn Erasmus; afterward Phaedrus; then Sallust. 10. Learn arithmetic.

Afternoon. 1. Learn Erasmus, Phaedrus, Sallust. 4. Translate.

The Sixth Class

Morning, 7. Read *Mr. De Renty's Life*. 8. Repeat the *Grammars*. 9. Learn Cæsar; afterwards Terence; then Velleius Paterculus. 10. Learn geography.

Afternoon, 1. Learn Cæsar, Terence, Paterculus. 3. Read *Roman Antiquities*. 4. Translate.

The Seventh Class

Morning, 7. Read Mr. Law's *Christian Perfection*. 8. Mon., Wed., Fri.—Learn the *Greek Grammar*; and read the *Greek Testament*. Tues., Thurs., Sat.—Learn Tully; afterwards Virgil. 10. Learn chronology.

Afternoon, 1. Learn Latin and Greek alternately, as in the morning. 3. Read *Grecian Antiquities*. 4. Translate and make verses alternately.

The Eighth Class

Morning, 7. Read Mr. Law's *Serious Call*. 8. Mon., Thurs.— Latin. Tues., Fri.—Greek. Wed., Sat.—Hebrew; and so at one in the afternoons. 10. Learn Rhetoric.

Afternoon, 3. Read *Hebrew Antiquities*. 4. Mon., Thurs.— Translate. Tues., Fri.—Make verses. Wed.—Make a theme. Sat.— Write a declamation.

All the other classes spend Saturday afternoon in arithmetic, and in transcribing what they learn on Sunday, and repeat on Monday morning.

The price for the board and teaching of a child, including his books, pens, ink, and paper, is fourteen pounds a year, while he is in the school: After he has gone through the school, twenty; and he is then to find his own books.

N.B.—The following method may be observed by those who design to go through a course of academical learning:

First Year

Read Lowth's *English Grammar*; Latin, Greek, Hebrew, French *Grammars*; Cornelius Nepos; Sallust, Cæsar; Tully's *Offices*; Terence, Phaedrus; Æneid; Dilworth; Randal; Bengel; Vossius; Aldrich and Wallis's *Logic*; Langbaine's *Ethics*; Hutchinson on the Passions;

Spanheim's *Introduction to Ecclesiastical History*; Puffendorf's *Introduction to the History of Europe*; *Moral and Sacred Poems*; Hebrew Pentateuch, with the Notes; Greek Testament—Matthew to the Acts, with the Notes; Xenophon's *Cyrus*; Homer's *Iliad*; Bishop Pearson on the Creed; ten volumes of the *Christian Library*; *Telemaque*.

Second Year

Look over the *Grammars*; read Velleius Paterculus; *Tusculan Questions*; *Excerpta*; *Vidæ Opera*; *Lusus Westmonasterienses*; *Chronological Tables*; Euclid's *Elements*; Wells' Tracts; Newton's *Principia*; Mosheim's *Introduction to Church History*; Usher's *Annals*; Burnet's *History of the Reformation*; Spenser's *Faerie Queene*; Historical Books of the Hebrew Bible; Greek Testament, *ad finem*; Kurou Anabasis; Homer's *Odyssey*; twelve volumes of the *Christian Library*; Ramsay's *Cyrus*; Racine.

Third Year

Look over the *Grammars*; Livy; Suetonius; Tully *De Finibus*; *Musæ Anglicanæ*; Dr. Burton's *Poemata*; Lord Forbes's Tracts; *Abridgement of Hutchinson's Works*; *Survey of the Wisdom of God in the Creation*; Rollin's *Ancient History*; Hume's *History of England*; Neal's *History of the Puritans*; *Milton's Poetical Works;* Hebrew Bible—Job to the Canticles; Greek Testament; Plato's *Dialogues*; Greek Epigrams; twelve volumes of the *Christian Library*; Pascal; Corneille.

Fourth Year

Look over the *Grammars*; Tacitus; *Grotii Historia Belgica*; Tully *De Naturâ Deorum*; *Prædium Rusticum*; *Carmina Quadragesimalia*; *Philosophical Transactions abridged*; Watts's *Astronomy*, etc.; *Compendium Metaphysicæ*; Watts's *Ontology*; Locke's *Essay*; Malebranche; Clarendon's *History*; Neal's *History of New-England*; Antonio Solis's *History of Mexico*; Shakespeare; rest of the Hebrew Bible; Greek Testament; Epictetus; Marcus Antoninus; *Poetæ Minores*; end the *Christian Library*; *La Fausseté de les Vertues Humaines*; *Quesnell sur les Evangiles*.

Whoever carefully goes through this course will be a better scholar than nine in ten of the graduates at Oxford or Cambridge.

Remarks on the State of Kingswood School (1783)

My design in building the house at Kingswood was to have therein a Christian family; every member whereof, children excepted, should be alive to God, and a pattern of all holiness.

Here it was that I proposed to educate a few children according to the accuracy of the Christian model. And almost as soon as we began, God gave us a token for good; four of the children receiving a clear sense of pardon.

But at present the school does not in anywise answer the design of the institution, either with regard to religion or learning.

The children are not religious. They have not the power, and hardly the form, of religion. Neither do they improve in learning better than at other schools: No, nor yet so well.

Insomuch that some of our friends have been obliged to remove their children to other schools.

And no wonder that they improve so little either in religion or learning; for the rules of the school are not observed at all.

All in the house ought to rise, take their three meals, and go to bed, at a fixed hour. But they do not.

The children ought never to be alone, but always in the presence of a Master. This is totally neglected; in consequence of which they run up and down the wood, and mix, yea, fight, with the colliers' children.

They ought never to play. But they do, every day; yea, in the school.

Three maids are sufficient. Now there are four; and but one, at most, truly pious.

How may these evils be remedied, and the school reduced to its original plan? It must be mended, or ended; for no school is better than the present school.

Can any be a Master that does not rise at five, observe all the rules, and see that others observe them?

There should be three Masters, and an Usher, chiefly to be with the children out of school.

The Head Master should have nothing to do with temporal things.

[1] *Works*, Vol. XIII, pp. 268–9.

	6	6.30	7	8	9
Mon.	Get up, Wash	Public Prayer Meeting	Reading and Exercises	Family Prayers. Breakfast	Latin
Tues.	,,	,,	,,	,,	,,
Wed.	,,	,,	,,	,,	,,
Thurs.	,,	,,	,,	,,	,,
Fri.	,,	,,	,,	,,	,,
Sat.	,,	,,	,,	,,	All
Sun.	,,	,,	,,	9–10.30 Reading	10.30–12 Preaching

It is evident that the school time-table was not as rigid as the above would

various English and

10–12	12.30	1.30	4.30–6	6–8	
School ccounts	Dinner and Exercise	Writing and Geography	Public Prayer Meeting	Supper, Family Prayers, Bed	Mon.
,,	,,	Writing, Spelling, French	As for Monday, followed by private bands	,,	Tues.
,,	,,	Writing, Accounts, History	As for Monday	,,	Wed.
,,	,,	Writing and Accounts	As for Tuesday	,,	Thurs.
,,	,,	French Translation. Lecture	As for Monday	,,	Fri.
e classes Oral work	recite	HALF HOLIDAY			Sat.
12–1.30 Private bands, Dinner	1.30–2 Memorizing Scripture	2–4 Preaching and Reading	4.30–6 Public Prayer Meeting	,,	Sun.

ggest, the time set aside for reading exercises and accounts being given to athematical subjects.

SCHEME for the foundation of Secondary Schools placed before Conference in 1875

Believing that there are many places in England in which it is practicable to establish, with great advantage to the Connexion, self-supporting Middle-class Schools, of a superior order, and conducted on Methodist principles—the Conference approves and adopts the following General Regulations for the establishment and working of such schools, it being understood that the Education Committee will afford advice, from time to time, respecting the establishment, organization, and management of such Schools:

1. Each School shall be under the direction of a Board of Managers, three-fourths of whom shall at the time of the constitution of the said Board be members of the Wesleyan-Methodist Society; and any vacancies in the Board shall be so filled up that the proportion of members of Society upon it shall not fall below two-thirds.

2. The Board of Managers shall have power to fill up any vacancy which may be created by the death of a Manager, or by the retirement of a Manager with the consent of the Board.

3. The Superintendent Minister, for the time being, of the Circuit with which the School is connected (or, in his absence, one of his colleagues, whom he shall depute), shall be, *ex officio,* entitled to a place and vote at all meetings of the said Board of Managers and to act as its Chairman.

4. Proper accounts of each School shall be kept, and duly audited once in every year; and a statement of the general and financial condition of the School shall be annually presented to the March Quarterly Meeting of the Circuit with which the School is connected.

5. As these Schools cannot receive aid from the Government grants they shall be established and maintained on the principle of self-support.

6. Any profits which may accrue after payment of the cost of the outfit and maintenance of any School, shall be applied to the improvement or extension of the School in which they have been gained, or toward the creation or assistance of similar Schools; or, if this be not considered expedient by the Board of Managers, the said profits shall be devoted to the purposes of the Wesleyan Education Committee, or to such other purposes as that Committee, with the Board of Managers, may approve.

7. Any property, real or personal, given to or purchased by the

---

[1] *Minutes of Conference,* Vol. XIX, pp. 693–5.

Managers for School purposes, shall be held by them upon trust for the School; and any moneys given for such purposes, and not required for immediate expenditure, shall be suitably invested by the Managers, who shall dispose of the annual proceeds thereof in harmony with the foregoing Regulations.

8. These Schools shall be open to the children of parents of any religious community, but the truths and duties of Christianity, as held by the Wesleyan-Methodist Connexion, shall be taught in the Schools; and they shall be visited by the Ministers of the Circuit with which they are connected.

9. Except in special cases, the Schools shall be in the charge of trained and certificated Teachers.

10. Provision shall be made for the Annual Examination of the Schools by competent and independent Examiners.

11. The principal Teachers of the Schools shall be Members of the Wesleyan-Methodist Society.

12. If the Board of Managers of any School shall at any time be of opinion, after consultation with the Wesleyan Education Committee, that it is undesirable any longer to carry on the School, it may be closed by the Managers, who may dispose of the School effects, and of any moneys held by them for the School, in such manner, consistently with the terms of their trust, as they, with the concurrence of the Wesleyan Education Committee, shall determine.

Methodist Secondary Schools

(This list contains only the names of schools founded before 1900 which have had some official connexion with Methodism or which are well known today as owing their origin to Methodist secondary education in the nineteenth century.)

Founded	School	Founded by
1748	Kingswood School, Bristol	John Wesley
1812	Woodhouse Grove School, Apperley Bridge, Yorkshire	Wesleyan Methodist Connexion
1834	Shebbear College, Devon	Samuel Thorne; later acquired by the Bible Christian Connexion
1838	Wesley College, Sheffield	The Wesleyan Proprietary Grammar School Company Limited
1843	West of England Proprietary Grammar School (Queen's College), Taunton	West of England Wesleyan Proprietary Grammar School Company Limited
1845	Wesleyan Commercial and Classical School (Wesley Colledge), Dublin	Irish Wesleyan Methodist Connexion
1852	Kingswood School reopened at Lansdown, Bath	Wesleyan Methodist Connexion
1856	*Laleham Lodge, Clapham Park* [1]	Miss Hannah E. Pipe
1864	Elmfield College, York	Primitive Methodist Connexion
1868	Methodist College, Belfast	Irish Methodist Connexion
1869	*Five Elms, Clapton*	Wesleyan Methodist Connexion
1870	*Beechholme, Clapton*	Wesleyan Methodist Connexion
1872	*Trinity Hall, Southport*	Wesleyan Methodist Connexion
1873	Dunheved College, Launceston	Methodist Company
1876	Bourne College, Quinton, Birmingham	Primitive Methodist Connexion
1877	Ashville College, Harrogate	United Methodist Connexion

[1] Italic type denotes girls' school.

1880	Truro College	The Cornwall Wesleyan Methodist School Association Limited.
1880	*The Ladies College, St. Heliers, Jersey*	Jersey Ladies' College Company Limited
1880	*Penrhos College, Colwyn Bay*	North Wales Wesleyan School Association Limited
1881	East Anglian School, Bury St. Edmunds	The East Anglian Wesleyan School Association Limited
1882	Wycliffe College, Stonehouse	G. W. Sibly, Esq.
1883	Woodhouse Grove School reopened as a Company School	Woodhouse Grove School Company Limited
1883	*West Cornwall College, Penzance*	The Cornwall Wesleyan Methodist Girls' School Association Limited
1883	Trowbridge High School, Wiltshire	The Western Counties Wesleyan Methodist Schools Association Limited
1883	Victoria College, Congleton	Cheshire and North Staffordshire Wesleyan Middle - class School Association Limited
1884	*Edgehill College, Bideford*	Bible Christian Connexion
1885	Rydal (Mount), Colwyn Bay	T. G. Osborn, Esq.
1886	Kent College, Canterbury	Kent Wesleyan Methodist School Association Limited
1886	*Kent College, Folkestone* (now *Pembury*)	Kent Wesleyan Methodist School Association Limited
1887	*Redbrooke College, Camborne*	Cornwall Wesleyan Methodist Girls' School Association Limited
1894	*Queenswood, Clapham Park* (now at Hatfield)	Queenswood School Company Limited
1898	*Bromyard High School, Herefordshire*	Bromyard Wesleyan Methodist High School for Girls Company Limited.

Board of Management for Secondary Schools

1. The Conference shall annually appoint a Board of Management for Wesleyan Secondary Schools, which shall consist of the following:

(a) *Ex-officio* members: the President of the Conference, the Secretary of the Conference, the Officers of the Board.

(b) Twelve ministers.

(c) Twelve laymen.

2. The Secondary Education Board shall be empowered to deal with all matters affecting Wesleyan Secondary Education and Secondary Schools.

3. The Board shall have control as to the Education and the management of such Wesleyan Secondary Schools as may be established on a Connexional basis and settled on a Connexional Trust Deed.

4. The Board, in carrying out the duties devolved upon it by the Conference, shall have the authority to appoint Sub-Committees for special work, including the following:

(a) An Education Sub-Committee, which shall be specially charged to consider and report to the Board as to all questions concerning the Staff, the Curricula, and Co-ordination of Education, and grading of the several Schools, and as to their Educational administration and efficiency.

(b) A Finance Sub-Committee which shall examine and supervise the entire expenditure of each School, and report periodically to the Board. No new or extraordinary expenditure shall be incurred without its being submitted to the Finance Committee and sanctioned by the Board.

5. The Board shall appoint a Local Committee of Management for each School or group of Schools, consisting of persons who are interested in the Schools and who are willing to undertake the duties of Management. Arrangements shall be made for joint meetings of the Local Management Committees and the Sub-Committees of the Board.

6. Two Treasurers—a minister and a layman—and two Secretaries —a minister and a laymen—shall be appointed.

---

[1] *Wesleyan Education Report* (1903–4), pp. 89–90.

7. A layman, qualified to assist in the Co-ordination of the several Schools and in advising generally as to the Educational administration of the Schools, may be employed by the Board when it is thought to be desirable.

8. The expenses of administration should be borne by the Schools according to a scheme to be framed by the Board.

Bibliography

BOOKS CONCERNING INDIVIDUAL SCHOOLS

Aust, E. P., *Kingswood: The Bursar Remembers* (1947)

Balgarnie, W. H., *Handbook and Directory of Leys School* (1934)

Brash, W. Bardsley, *The Story of our Colleges, 1835–1935* (1935)

Henderson, J. W., *Methodist College, Belfast* (1939)

Pyke, Richard, *Edgehill College, 1884–1934* (1934)

Slugg, J. T., *Woodhouse Grove School: Memorials and Reminiscences* (1885)

Starkey, H. W., *A Short History of Woodhouse Grove School* (1912)

Woolmer, T., *How it was done at Stow School* (1888)

Anonymous, *The Establishment, Principles, Discipline, and Educational Course of the Wesleyan Proprietary Grammar School, Sheffield* (1839); *Queen's College, Taunton: Old Boys' Directory* (1932); *The Jubilee of Woodhouse Grove School* (1865); *Rydal School* (1935); *History of Kingswood School* (by Three Old Boys) (1898); *G. W. Sibly* (privately printed, Gloucester) (1930)

SCHOOL MAGAZINES

The Kingswood and Grove Quarterly
The Kingswood Magazine
The Grovian
The Leysian
The Farringtonian
The Queenswoodian
West Cornwall Magazine
The Magazine (King Edward VII School, Sheffield)

NEWSPAPERS, PERIODICALS, PRINTED SPEECHES, AND REPORTS

Aldersgate Magazine
Arminian Magazine (1778–97)
Edinburgh Review
Methodist Magazine (1798 onward)
Methodist Recorder
Methodist Times
Minutes of the Bible Christian Conference
Minutes of the Primitive Methodist Conference
Minutes of the United Methodist Conference
Minutes of the Wesleyan Methodist Conference
Proceedings of the Wesley Historical Society (from 1896)
Public and Preparatory Schools Year Book
The Watchman

Wesley: the Man, his Teaching and his Work (1891)

Wesleyan Education Reports (from 1839)

Year Book of Education

Year Book of the National Children's Home and Orphanage

Reports of the Sheffield Wesleyan Proprietary Grammar School (1841 and 1854)

Report of the Newcastle Commission on Popular Education (1861)

Report of the Clarendon Commission on Public Schools (1864)

Report of the Schools Inquiry Commission on Schools other than those falling within the scope of the preceding two Commissions (1868)

Report of the Bryce Commission on Secondary Education (1895)

Special Reports on Educational Subjects (Vol. VI: *Preparatory Schools*) (1900)

Report on Secondary and Higher Education in the City of Sheffield (1903)

Report of the Hadow Commission on the Education of the Adolescent (1926)

Report of the Departmental Committee on Private Schools (1932)

Report of the Spens Commission on Secondary Education (1938)

Report of the Norwood Commission on Curriculum and Examinations in Secondary Schools (1941)

Report of the Fleming Commission on Public Schools (1944)

GENERAL WORKS

Acland, A. H. D., and Smith, H. L., *Studies in Secondary Education* (1892)

Acland, T. D., *Some Account of the Origin and Objects of the new Oxford Examinations* (1858)

Adams, J., *Modern Developments in Educational Practice* (1922); *Educational Theories* (1927)

Adamson, J. W., *A Short History of Education* (1919); *English Education 1789–1902* (1930)

Almond, C., *History of Ampleforth Abbey* (1936)

Archer, R. L., *Secondary Education in the Nineteenth Century* (1921)

Arnold, Matthew, *Culture and Anarchy* (1869); *Reports on Elementary Schools, 1852–82* (1889); *A French Eton* (1892)

Balleine, G. R., *History of the Evangelical Party in the Church of England* (1908)

Barber, Aquila, *Memories of the late Rev. William Barber* (1930)

Barber, W. T. A., *The Unfolding of Life* (1917)

Barnes, A. S., *The Catholic Schools of England* (1926)

Binns, H. Bryan, *A Century of Education, 1808–1908* (1908)

Birchenough, C., *History of Elementary Education in England and Wales from 1800* (1914)

Birt, H. N., *Downside* (1902)

339

Body, A. H., *John Wesley and Education* (1936)

Bogue (David) and Bennett (James), *History of Dissenters* (4 volumes) (1808)

Bourne, F. W., *The Bible Christians: Their Origin and History* (1905); *The Centenary Life of James Thorne of Shebbear* (1895)

Bready, J. W., *England: Before and After Wesley* (1938)

Bunting, Thomas P., *The Life of Jabez Bunting, D.D.* (1859)

Burstall, Sara A. and Douglas, M.A., *Public Schools for Girls* (1911)

Butler, Samuel, *The Life and Letters of Dr. Samuel Butler* (1896)

Clarke, Adam, *Memoirs of the Wesley Family* (1823)

Clarke, J. B. B., *An Account of the Infancy, Religious and Literary Life of Adam Clarke* (1833)

Clarke, Henry W., *History of English Nonconformity* (1911)

Cloke, H., *Wesleyan Methodism's Contribution to National Education, 1739–1902* (A Thesis for the Degree of M.A. at the University of London, 1936)

Cobbe, Frances P., *Life* (1904)

Court, Lewis H., *The Romance of a Country Circuit* (1921)

Crowther, Jonathan, *History of the Wesleyan Methodists* (1815)

Dobbs, A. E., *Education and Social Movements, 1700–1850* (1919)

Dymond, G. P., *Thomas Ruddle of Shebbear* (N.D.)

Eayrs, G., *Wesley: Christian Philosopher and Church Founder* (1926)

Edgeworth, M., *Letters for Literary Ladies* (1795); *Practical Education* (1798)

Edwards, Maldwyn, *John Wesley and the Eighteenth Century* (1933); *After Wesley* (1935); *This Methodism* (1939); *Methodism and England* (1943)

Evennett, H. O., *The Catholic Schools of England and Wales* (1944)

Fay, C. R., *Life and Labour in the Nineteenth Century* (1933)

Findlay, G. G., *William F. Moulton* (1910)

Findlay, J. J., *The Children of England* (1923)

Fitch, J. G., *Thomas and Matthew Arnold* (1897)

Fowler, E. H., *The Life of Lord Wolverhampton* (1912)

Fowler, H. H., *Institutions of Wesleyan Methodism* (1858)

Freemantle, A. F., *England in the Nineteenth Century* (1930)

Gardiner, D., *English Girlhood at School* (1929)

Gerard, John, *Stonyhurst College* (1894)

Graves, John, *Policy and Progress in Secondary Education, 1902–42* (1943)

Green, J. R., *A Short History of the English People* (1874)

Gregory, Benjamin, *Sidelights on the Conflicts of Methodism* (1898); *Autobiographical Recollections* (1903)

Gregory, Dr., *A Father's Legacy to His Daughter* (1774)

Guilday, P., *English Catholic Refugees* (1914); *English Catholic Colleges on the Continent* (1915)

Halévy, Elie (trans. by Watkin and Barker), *A History of the English People* (London, 1924)

Hammond, J. L. and Barbara, *Lord Shaftesbury* (1923)

Hans, Nicholas, *Educational Traditions in the English-Speaking Countries* (1936)

Harrison, A. W., Barber, B. Aquila, Hornby, G. G., and Davies, E. Pegia, *The Methodist Church: Its Origins, Divisions, and Reunions* (1932)

Hayman, J. C., *A History of the Methodist Revival in its Relations to North Devon* (1871)

Healing, C. A., *Thomas Healing* (1908)

Healing, E., *Arnold Healing* (1927)

Henderson, Archibald, *Bernard Shaw* (New York, 1932)

Holmes, Edmund, *What Is and What Might Be* (1911)

Hughes, Donald, *The Public Schools and the Future* (1942); *Some Educational Foundations* (1945)

Hughes, Dorothea P., *The Life of Hugh Price Hughes* (1904)

Huxley, Leonard (ed.), *Thoughts on Education from Matthew Arnold* (1912)

Jackson, Holbrook, *The Eighteen Nineties* (1913)

Jackson, Thomas, *Recollections of My Own Life and Times* (1874)

Jones, M. G., *The Charity School Movement in the Eighteenth Century* (1938)

Kandel, I. L., *A History of Secondary Education* (1938)

Kellett, E. E., *As I remember* (1936); *Religion and Life in the Early Victorian Age* (1938)

Kendall, H. B., *The Origin and History of the Primitive Methodist Church* (N.D.)

Kirk, K. E., *The Story of the Woodard Schools* (1937)

Leach, A. F., *Educational Charters and Documents* (1911); *The Schools of Medieval England* (1915)

Lecky, W. E. H., *A History of England in the Eighteenth Century* (1892)

Leclerc, Max, *L'Education des classes moyennes et dirigeantes en Angleterre* (Paris, 1898)

Livingstone, R., *Education for a World Adrift* (1943); *The Future in Education* (1944)

Loury, H. F., *The Letters of Matthew Arnold to Arthur Hugh Clough* (1932)

Lucas, A. H. S., *A. H. S. Lucas, Scientist: His Own Story* (Sydney, 1937)

Macaulay, Catharine, *Letters on Education* (1790)

McCullagh, Thomas, *Sir William McArthur* (1891)

Macdonald, F. W., *As a tale that is told* (1923)

Mack, Edward C., *Public Schools and British Opinion, 1780–1860* (1938)

McLachlan, H., *English Education under the Test Acts* (1931)

Mallet, Sir Charles E., *History of the University of Oxford* (1924)

Maurice, Frederick, *The Life of Frederick Denison Maurice* (1884)

Milton, John, *Tractate on Education* (1673)

Moore, R. W. (ed.), *Education: Today and Tomorrow* (1945)

More, Hannah, *Strictures on the Modern System of Female Education* (1799); *View of the Principles and Conduct prevalent among Women of Rank and Fortune* (1799)

Moulton, H. Fletcher, *Life of Lord Moulton* (1922); *James Hope Moulton* (1919)

Moulton, J. Egan, *Moulton of Tonga* (1921)

Moulton, W. Fiddian, *William F. Moulton* (1899)

Murray, Victor A., *The School and the Church* (1944)

Myles, W., *Chronological History of Methodism* (1803)

Newton, A. W., *The English Elementary School* (1919)

Norwood, C., and Hope, A. H., *The Higher Education of Boys in England* (1909)

O'Leary, Margaret O., *Education with a Tradition* (1936); *The Catholic Church and Education* (1943)

Otter, Sir John, *Nathaniel Woodard* (1925)

Palmer, Herbert E., *The Mistletoe Child* (1935)

Parker, Irene, *Dissenting Academies in England* (1914)

Parkin, G. R., *Edward Thring* (1900)

Patterson, W. M., *Northern Primitive Methodism* (1909)

Peake, A. S., *The Life of Sir William Hartley* (1926)

Percival, A. C., *The English Miss Today and Yesterday* (1929)

Pyke, Richard, *The Golden Chain* (1940)

Rattenbury, J. E., *Wesley's Legacy to the World* (1928)

Richmond, W. K., *Education in England* (1945)

Rigg, James H., *Essays for the Times on Ecclesiastical and Social Subjects* (1866); *The Living Wesley* (1891); *Reminiscences* (1904)

Sandford, E. G. (ed.), *Memoirs of Frederick Temple* (1906)

Schwickerath, R., *Jesuit Education* (1905)

Sharpless, Isaac, *English Education in the Elementary and Secondary Schools* (New York, 1892)

Sharpley, A. E., *Life of David James Waller, D.D.* (1913)

Shepherd, T. B., *Methodism and the Literature of the Eighteenth Century* (1940)

Simon, J. S., *John Wesley and the Religious Societies* (1921); *John Wesley and the Methodist Societies* (1923); *John Wesley and the Advance of Methodism* (1925); *John Wesley the Master Builder* (1927); *John Wesley, the Last Phase* (1934)

Smith, Frank, *A History of English Elementary Education, 1760–1902* (1931)

Smith, George, *History of Wesleyan Methodism* (1866)

Smith, Swalloe, and Treffry (ed.), *The Story of the United Methodist Church* (1932)

Smith, W. O. Lester, *To Whom do Schools belong?* (1943)

Somerville, D. C., *English Thought in the Nineteenth Century* (1929)

Southey, Robert, *The Life of John Wesley* (1820)

Stanley, A. P., *The Life and Correspondence of Thomas Arnold* (1844)

Stephen, Sir Leslie, *English Thought in the Eighteenth Century* (1881)

Stevens, Abel, *The History of the Religious Movement of the Eighteenth Century called Methodism* (1858); *History of Methodism* (1878)

Stoddart, A. S., *Life and Letters of Hannah E. Pipe* (1908)

Strachey, Lytton, *Eminent Victorians* (1918)

Symons, W., *Early Methodism in West Somerset* (N.D.)

Telford, John, *A Sect that Moved the World* (1907); *The Life of James Harrison Rigg, D.D.* (1909)

Thompson, Edward, *Introducing the Arnisons* (1935); *John Arnison* (1939)

Thorne, James, *James Thorne of Shebbear* (1873)

Thorne, S. L., *Samuel Thorne, Printer* (1875); *William O'Bryan* (1888)

Torr, W. G., *John Thorne* (Adelaide, 1925)

Toulmin, Joshua, *Historical View of the State of Dissenters in England* (1814)

Townsend, W. J.; Workman, H. B.; Eayrs, G. (ed.), *A New History of Methodism* (1909)

Tyerman, L., *The Life and Times of the Rev. John Wesley* (1890); *The Life of George Whitefield* (1890)

Waddy, A., *The Life of the Rev. Samuel D. Waddy, D.D.* (1878)

Warner, Rex, *English Public Schools* (1945)

Watson, Foster, *The Old Grammar Schools* (1916)

Wesley, John, *The Works of the Rev. John Wesley, A.M.* (14 volumes, 1872); *Sermons on Several Occasions* (3 volumes, 1876); *The Letters of the Rev. John Wesley, A.M.* (Standard Edition, 8 volumes, ed. John Telford, 1931); *The Journal of the Rev. John Wesley, A.M.* (Standard Edition, 8 volumes, ed. Nehemiah Curnock, 1909)

Whitehead, John, *The Life of the Rev. John Wesley, M.A.* (1796)

Whiteley, J. H., *Wesley's England* (1938)

Wilson, J. D. (ed.), *The Schools of England* (1928)

Wollstonecraft, Mary, *Vindication of the Rights of Women* (1792)

Woodward, E. L., *The Age of Reform* (1938)

Zimmern, A., *The Renaissance of Girls' Education in England* (1898)

Index